*The
Story of
Wivenhoe*

Mrs. Liz Humphrey, Mr. Jeremy Reid and his son, Thomas, in the belfry of the parish church of St. Mary the Virgin December, 1988.

Photograph by Sue Murray, L.R.P.S.

*For Reg and Jean
with Every Good Wish*

The Story of Wivenhoe

NICHOLAS BUTLER

Nicholas Butler

21.ɪɪ.89

Quentin Press Limited
Wivenhoe 1989

First published in 1989 by
Quentin Press Limited
10 Brook Street, Wivenhoe,
Essex CO7 9DS

Design and Layout by
Vince Rayner, Wivenhoe, Essex

Type Conversion by S.B. Datagraphics
Wyncolls Road, Colchester, Essex

**Printed in Great Britain by
BPCC Wheatons Ltd, Exeter**

ISBN 0-947614-01-X

© Nicholas Butler 1989

For
Seley Little

H.R.H. The Duke of York at the premises of James W. Cook & Co. (Wivenhoe) Ltd. 6th January, 1986.

Essex County Newspapers

Contents

	Preface	ix
1	Saxon, Mediaeval, Tudor	1
2	Seventeenth Century	
	1 Religion and Politics	15
	2 Admiralty Contracts	18
	3 The Corsellis Family and the Town	27
3	The Rebows and Wivenhoe Park	31
4	Eighteenth Century	
	1 The Grandees and the Clergy	41
	2 Dr. Flack, Dr. Tunmer and the Baths	43
	3 John Hall	44
	4 Commerce, Fishing and Boatbuilding	46
	5 The Inspector and the Comet	48
	6 Smuggling	51
	7 Education	53
	8 Sporting and Social	54
5	Francis Slater and John Gurdon	61
6	The Big Yachts 1801–1881	
	1 The Dawn of an Era: Philip Sainty and Pearl	83
	2 Grandees and Tradesmen	89
	3 Education and Religion	95
	4 Thomas and John Harvey	104
	5 Sporting and Social	113
	6 The Railway	117
	7 Mid-Victorian Expansion	123
	8 The End of an Era: John Harvey and Chloris	126
7	Late Victorian and Edwardian 1881–1914	
	1 The Earthquake	129
	2 Wivenhoe Park: Hector Gurdon-Rebow and Charles Gooch	133
	3 Wivenhoe Hall: James Jackson, Claude Egerton-Green and Alexander Barlow	137
	4 John Sinclair Carolin	141

7	5	Edwin Wilkins and Forrestt's	144
	6	The River or the Shipyard?	156
	7	The Social Scene	163
	8	Bayard Brown and the Sporting Scene	169
	9	Education	178
	10	Politics and Amenities	186
	11	The Wivenhoe Flier	197
	12	Spoiling for a Fight	202
8	Into the Slump and Out of It 1914–1965		
	1	1914–1918	211
	2	Unemployment	218
	3	The Changing Scene	227
	4	Charles Gooch the Younger	249
	5	1939–1945	252
	6	Brave New World	264
9	The University of Essex		
	1	The Making of a Troublespot	273
	2	The Troubles Begin	287
	3	The Angry Brigade	294
	4	1973-1974	299
	5	The Survival Game	307
	6	Interim Report	311
10	Who Are These People?		
	1	Expansion	321
	2	Big Lorries into Small Roads	325
	3	Making the Party Go	331
	4	The End of An Aeon	342

Appendix A	Witchcraft	351
Appendix B	The Australian Connection	353
Appendix C	The Place-Names of Wivenhoe	355
Footnotes		359
General Index		379
Index of Boats and Ships		399

Preface

Some years ago I wrote the *Week in Wivenhoe* column for the *Essex County Standard* and whenever I included an historical piece was likely to receive a letter from one or other of three Old Wivenhovians: Mr. Daniel Chapman, Mr. Richard Doubleday and Mr. William G. Harlow.

Mr. Chapman lived at Barking, Mr. Doubleday at Brighton and Mr. Harlow at Truro, yet their interest in the town was lively and vital. Every detail of its history was of interest: the price of a bath, the site of a public house, the date of an auction. I felt that the material they had given me, unique and perishable, ought to be preserved. It was they who first inspired me to write this book.

These men were interested in the town because they had grown up here in the days when it was socially self-sufficient, when everybody knew everybody else, when every family married into every other family, when every Wivenhovian was defined in terms of every other Wivenhovian.

The contemporary citizen draws on a worldwide culture and knowledge from a television receiver; by the same token his immediate surroundings count for far less. In some ways this is a change for the better, but not for the historian because the oral tradition has disappeared.

For example, during my researches I talked to Mr. Albert Scales, who told me about men hiding in the woods near St. Osyth to avoid the press gang, and of watching girls in crinolines climbing up into railway carriages in the hope of catching a glimpse of ankle. He did not remember these things personally, of course; they had been handed down as verbal heirlooms.

How I wish I had begun to write this history when I first came to Wivenhoe, thirty years ago! For the Old Wivenhovians then alive and vocal would have added much more colour to my later chapters. Alas, by the time I started work they were mostly gone and the oral tradition with them.

Happily, many of the older generation can still identify closely with Wivenhoe. I am particularly grateful to Mr. Don Mason who supplied me with several tapes of information, assuring me that I had only scratched the surface. I believe him. I am very sorry that, like my three first correspondents, he cannot read what I have written.

The University of Essex interviewed several now-deceased Wivenhovians and I must thank the Department of Sociology there for lending me four extended essays, by Gavin Douglas, Jonathan Hodgkinson, Mavis Peters and a fourth anonymous student, which record conversations with former crewmen, fishermen and others. I must also thank the University of Essex for enrolling me as an outside reader and showing me its press cuttings albums from which much of Chapter 9 is drawn.

Another Old Wivenhovian to whom I am extremely grateful is Mr. E. H. C. Squire, whom I visited several times at his Ipswich home. Despite a failing memory and hearing he was anxious to help me in every way, and provided me with copious notes and illustrations before he died.

It was not easy to shape the vast mass of material at my disposal, but the form of this book owes much to a short manuscript history of Wivenhoe by Mr. C. M. J. Dunn, which the author very generously put at my disposal. He also lent me other notes, answered my queries and produced material from the archives of The Nottage Institute.

I had hoped that The Nottage would let me reproduce some of its photographs, but this was not to be. I gathered, directly and indirectly, that this was *either* because of security, *or* because the Institute had been let down in the past, *or* because if it acceded to my request it would have to cope with large numbers of similar requests. The last reason is, I fancy, the correct one. With respect, I must urge the trustees of The Nottage to be amenable to authors, subject of course to a suitable fee and acknowledgement.

Another scholar who encouraged me was Mr. A. F. J. Brown, the local historian, who lent me his personal notes and answered many queries. A third was Mr. John Leather, who identified many of the vessels listed in my index.

I have certainly not lacked illustrations, largely thanks to Mr. David Clarke of the Castle Museum, who invited me to bring him the photographs I borrowed from Wivenhovians which he then copied free of charge. Thus he – and Wivenhoe – gained an archive. Besides this, I must thank Mr. Clarke for reading my manuscript and making some suggestions, also Miss Shirley Dow. It has also been read twice by Mr. Seley Little who has supported and forwarded the work.

It is odd that with so many cameras about how few good photographs are taken. So I asked Mrs. Sue Murray to take some for me, which she did, and at a nominal charge. Mr. Doug White has also taken photographs; I am sorry that space precludes my printing more than one of them.

The best visual chroniclers of the local scene are usually the staff

Preface

photographers at Essex County Newspapers. I was dismayed to discover that after a few years the negatives of their invaluable work are thrown away, albeit for the very good reason that there is not enough space in which to store them. Surely the best of these pictures ought to be saved? Here, for the asking of the Essex Record Office is a priceless archive. However, I am most grateful to Essex County Newspapers for allowing me to reproduce photographs in its current files.

As I was making my final revisions, Mr. John Stewart, who had contemplated writing his own history of the town, very kindly placed his notes and photographs at my disposal. They corroborated several facts and gave me new and valuable information.

For the kindness, enthusiasm and encouragement of the individuals already named I am most grateful. Without their help this history would have been far shorter. As it is, I have had to prune my original text drastically to produce a book that the average reader can afford.

On the whole, this has improved it, though I regret the elimination of much social detail. For instance, on page 167 I refer to the Wyvenhoe Minstrels, (in 1884). In fact, I discovered four other minstrel references. The Wivenhoe Star Minstrels gave concerts in December, 1888, March, 1889, and January, 1891, and The Wivenhoe Black and White Minstrels in April, 1895. (See the *Essex County Standard* 15:xii:1888, 9:iii:1889, 24:i:1889 and 13:iv:1895). Evidently, minstrelsy as a social phenomenon flourished in the late eighties and early nineties, and from the dates given the men who blacked up were probably sailors who crewed the big yachts.

If you would like to know more about any subject in this book, contact me and I will give you references if I can. In turn, if you find any mistakes tell me and I will correct them.

One subject which cries out for more detailed treatment is the University of Essex. The darkest hours of the Second World War provoked the brightest rays of hope and idealism. Twenty years later two men walked round Wivenhoe Park in an atmosphere of the brightest hope and idealism, but turned their backs firmly upon ideals to produce something that had the name and the addition of a University but the substance of an institution and which has been to a large extent an essay in human misery. And the time is ripe. For Essex has achieved twenty-five years and while we are far enough from the troubles to see them in perspective we are near enough to interview the people involved. At this moment, it seems to be drifting into the arms of industry. A full-length book might rekindle the spirit of the early days when the staff and pupils genuinely believed that what they belonged to *was* a university. Moreover, it is important to understand what happened in order to avoid the same mistakes.

I must thank the B.B.C. for permission to quote from *The Making of a*

University, by Albert Sloman, *(1964)*, on pages 285, 312 and 315, and from *Yes, Minister*, by Jonathan Lynn and Anthony Jay, *(1983)*, on page 310, also the *Daily Express* for allowing me to reproduce the cartoon on page 290, and *The East Anglian Daily Times*, The Essex County Council, The Essex Record Office, The National Maritime Museum, The National Portrait Gallery and The Victoria and Albert Museum for permission to use photographs from their collections.

I also have to thank, for interviews, information, advice, the loan of photographs and general encouragement the following individuals and, I dare say, a few others whose names I have inadvertently omitted from this list:

Mr. John Adams, Mr. V. E. Annis, Mr. D. M. Archer, Mr. E. G. Barnes, Mrs. Penny Bell, Mr. D. Benson, Mr. Des Blake, Mrs. P. Bokenham, Mrs. Evelyn Boosey, Mr. James Boutwood, Mrs. Margaret Britton, Mr. Paul Brown, Father Michael Butler, Mr. John Button, Pastor V. L. Cameron, Mrs. Peggy Carrington, Mr. Will Carver, Mrs. D. Chaney, Mr. Daniel Chapman, Mrs. Marjorie Chester, Mr. Richard Chopping, Mrs. Marguerite Cole, Mr. Thomas Colleran, Mr. David Collins, Mrs. Winifred Cooper, Mr. Roger Cordery, Mr. David Corsellis, Mr. and Mrs. E. Cowlin, Mr. David Craze, Mrs. Gail Cross, Mrs. T. H. Cullen, Mrs. Pamela Dan, Mr. Philip Dan, Dr. William Dean, Mrs. Dorothy Demuth, Mr. Michael Dew, Mrs. Ann Dowden, Mrs. E. G. Edwards, Mr. P. J. Edwards, Mr. C. G. Ellis, Mrs. Winifred Ellis, Mrs. K. G. Everitt, Mrs. P. J. Excell, Mr. Anthony Faulkner, Mr. John Fieldgate, Rev. D. B. Gaye, Mr. Ted Gilders, Mr. Mick Glozier, (who has lent me photographs in the name of his father, Mr. Tilf Glozier), Mr. and Mrs. Charles Gooch, Miss A. C. Gould, Mr. Malcolm Goodwin, Mr. C. J. Grant, Mr. John Graveson, Professor R. H. Graveson, C.B.E., Q.C., Miss Angela Green, Mrs. L. Grimsdell, Rev. and Mrs. Stephen Hardie, Mr. Guy Harding, Mr. James Harvey, Miss M. L. Harvey, Mr. and Mrs. Ernest Hatch, Mr. and Mrs. Peter Hill, Mr. Frank Hodgson, Mr. Ian Hunter, Captain R. J. Husk, R.N., Mr. Glendower Jackson, Mr. Richard Jacobs, Mr. L. R. James, Mrs. E. M. Jennings, Mr. L. W. Kemble, Mr. Anthony Kemp, Mr. Geoffrey King, Mr. and Mrs. E. J. Knappett, Mrs. Hilda Knowles, Mr. Gordon Kuphal, Mr. Michael Lane, Mr. John Leather, Mr. and Mrs. P. L. J. Le Poer Power, Miss Annabel Llewellyn-Cooper, Mr. Harry C. Lott, Mr. Patrick McEune, Mr. and Mrs. R. J. McEune, Mrs. M. Marshall, Mr. Graham Martin, Mr. G. W. Martin, Mr. L. H. Martin, Sir Oliver Millar, Mr. T. B. Millatt, Mr. James Moore, Mr. Glyn Morgan, Mrs. Joyce Moulton, Mrs. Ruth Munson, Mr. Brian Oakley, Mr. Peter Overton, Mrs. Violet Page, Mr. George H. Pattinson, Mr. George Paul, M.F.H., Mr. and Mrs. H. L. Payne, Mrs. Patricia Pearce, Dr. J. B. Penfold, Mrs. Maud Prior, Dr. and Mrs. Walter Radcliffe, Mr. Ted Ramsdale, Mr. F. P. Reed, Mr. John Revell, Mr. Ernest Revett, Mrs. Frances Richards, Mr. R. O. Richardson, Mr. Cecil E. Riches,

Preface

Mr. Michael Ripley, Rev. J. W. R. Robinson, Lt.-Col. J. G. Round, Mr. Bob Russell, Mrs. Muriel Ryder, Mr. Albert Scales, Mrs. C. G. Scofield, Miss Dorothy Skilton, Mr. and Mrs. Robert Skilton, Sir Albert Sloman, Mr. Don Smith, Dr. M. J. Sommerlad, Miss J. A. Stark, Mr. Walter Trickett, Mrs. Ivy Turner, Mrs. Janet Turner, Mr. Alan Tyne, Mr. C. Vinson, Mr. Alfred Wakeling, Mr. E. Warrington Smyth, Mrs. F. E. Watsham, Mrs. Claire Weston, Mr. David Weston, Mrs. Olive Whaley, Mr. Doug White, Mr. Denis Wirth-Miller, Mr. Walter Wix, Mr. John Worsp, Mr. Lewis Worsp, Mr. Derek Wright and Mr. Jeremy Wyatt.

I also have to thank officials of the following organisations who found books for me, answered my letters, sent me material and advised me:

The Brisbane City Council, The British Library, The Canadian High Commission, The Colchester Borough Council, The East Anglian Film Archive, The English Place-Name Society, The Essex Record Office, both at Chelmsford and Colchester, Eton College, The Gilbert and Sullivan Society, The Institute of Historical Research, The John Oxley Library at Brisbane, The Merthen Trust Ltd., The National Army Museum, The National Maritime Museum, The Naval Historical Library, The Nomenclature Board of Tasmania, The Pepys Library at Magdalene College, Cambridge, The Public Records Office at Kew, The State Library of Tasmania, The Suffolk Record Office, The Swedenborg Society, The Universal Press of St. Kilda, The University of Bristol Theatre Collection, The Windermere Iron Steamboat Company, The Windermere Nautical Trust and The Wivenhoe Town Council.

Finally, I must thank Mr. Vince Rayner for the design and layout of this book, also for his faith in it. And a special palm to the staff of the Local Studies Department at the Colchester Public Library, not only for routine assistance over a long period, but for valuable suggestions and encouragement.

Nicholas Butler
2, Rose Lane,
Wivenhoe, Essex

September, 1989

CHAPTER 1

Saxon, Mediaeval, Tudor

The lady who lived up at the big house had everything to make her existence a happy one. She adored, indeed idolised, her husband, a rich Member of Parliament called Isaac Martin Rebow, (the accent is on the second syllable); she had two lively small daughters, her neighbours were congenial and the house itself, a handsome, stone-faced mansion, was surrounded by two hundred acres of parkland, itself the centre of an estate comprising numerous small farms.

However, in the summer of 1778 Mr. Rebow went away for two or three months with the Essex Militia of which he was a deputy-general. Mrs. Rebow hated to be parted from him, but consoled herself by writing frequently. She was also kept busy looking after young Mary and Sarah, and there were visits from local grandees.

One summer afternoon, Mrs. Corsellis from the Hall, and a Miss Dyer, who was staying with her, came to tea. Miss Dyer urged her hostess to use the seawater baths at the little riverside town down the road. Mrs. Rebow consulted her husband and her doctor, who both favoured the idea, bought herself a petticoat, "for decency sake" and on 21st August wrote to her husband:

We are all vastly well, & I have the Pleasure to tell you I tumbled into the Wivenhoe Bath both Yesterday, & this Morning with the greatest Success imaginable, find it has every good Effect upon me, & like it prodigiously. The Bath I think is very much improv'd since I saw it last . . . for it is very light; there is a pretty little room to dress in, the Water is perfectly clear, & very salt, & the People are Civil, & Obliging to a degree . . . [1]

The big house where Mrs. Rebow and her family lived has known several different masters since those days and, quite recently, a remarkable change in its status and fortunes, all of which I must relate in some detail, but only because it lies within the parish of the riverside town which is the subject of this history.

Let me start at the beginning.

Two thousand years ago the River Colne was probably the same shape as it is today, its indeterminate mouth littered with sandbanks, its seven miles of gentle curves winding up to the British settlement which the Romans conquered in A.D. 50 and renamed Camulodunum.

What of the surrounding countryside? Was the Colne at that time bounded only by endless forests of oak and elm? Or were there other settlements, albeit nominal, on either side? In particular, what of the spur of sand and gravel on the northern bank some two miles below Camulodunum, such an obvious place for landing boats and building houses? Were there only trees above the level of the highest spring tides? Or was there already a clearing, a cluster of wooden huts with smoke rising from them and human faces gazing, curiously or incuriously, at the Roman galleys, with pigs and children roaming about and coracles drawn up on the shore?

When was Wivenhoe founded? Archaeology can help us only in a negative way. Though Essex is rich in Iron Age and Roman remains, none have so far been found here, save for a Roman glass water bottle discovered intact when The Quay was excavated in 1932, and some Middle Bronze Age pottery.[2]

Yet the Romans were never far away. It was they who marked out the northern boundary of what is now Wivenhoe Park with their big road called Stane Street, which ran due west from Hamford Water on the coast. At Alresford Creek was a villa, tiled and tesselated; it is assumed there were many more in the area. There are Roman bricks in the foundations of the parish church, very likely taken from the deserted Camulodunum, after the legions had left.[3]

If there was no settlement by Roman times, then one was certainly made between the fifth and and eleventh centuries, for it was during this period that it received its Saxon name, first recorded in *Domesday Book*.

"Hoh" is Anglo-Saxon for a ridge. The first two syllables are not so easy, but the English Place-Name Society thinks they belong to an individual. Somewhere within those six dark Saxon centuries a man called Wifa may have owned or farmed this parish, which is why it is called Wifa's Ridge to this day, the "f" having softened down into a "v" and "en" being an old inflexional form.[4]

During this period the settlement discovered local government, based on a land unit known as the hundred. Wivenhoe is in the extreme eastern tip of the Lexden Hundred and since modern government has inherited the geographical boundaries of the old it belongs to Colchester, except the small area to the

Saxon, Mediaeval, Tudor

north of Anglesea Road with the Dene Park Estate, which is in Tendring.

Each parish contained one or more manors; each manor had its own manorial court, which dealt with petty crime, weights and measures, fences, rights of way, the rotation of crops and the ownership and conveyance of copyhold land. The parish of Wivenhoe comprised a single manor, though at times the small manors of Cockaynes and Keelars, which lay out towards Alresford, were owned by the same family.

Each manor had its own customs. Wivenhoe's included the rather unusual system of inheritance known as borough English, whereby if an owner of copyhold land died intestate the property passed, not to his eldest, but to his youngest son.

Practically all we know of Wivenhoe during the early Middle Ages is that it was a chattel, initially unimportant, that passed from one family of local grandees to another. However, *Domesday Book* (1086), gives us a comprehensive glimpse. It tells us the town contained twelve acres of meadow, pasture for sixty sheep, enough woodland for a hundred pigs, and a mill. The adult inhabitants comprised five villeins, (the higher class of serf), twenty bordars, (the lower class), and two slaves. We can be sure that these Wivenhovians were not only farmers, but fishermen, particularly of shellfish, that their houses, timber-framed with wattle-and-daub between, were grouped round a small church made of brick and stone, and that the largest and most imposing house belonged to the lord of the manor.[5]

Genealogists think that William I's followers included a man called Robert Gernon. *Domesday Book* records that he was one of the biggest landowners in the county. Wivenhoe, which before the Conquest had belonged to someone called Aluric and two freemen, was now held of Gernon by a subtenant called Nigel.

Either before or during the reign of Henry I, Gernon's fief passed to the Batayle family. In 1246, Henry III granted the right of free warren to Simon de Batayle. His successor, Sir Richard Batayle, had two daughters, one of whom, Margery, married Sir William de Sutton and brought him the manor, which became the Suttons' principal seat.[6]

Sir William had a son and grandson both called John. It was almost certainly the elder Sir John who appeared before a commission with two other Suttons, the Prior of Mersea and numerous other defendants, including four Wivenhovians, to answer charges of theft and cattle rustling.[7]

At the end of May, 1381, the long-standing grievances of the villeins exploded into open revolt all over Essex. They wanted to abolish villeinage, so they destroyed the only tangible proofs of it, the manorial court rolls. Those of Wivenhoe were burnt. Yet as regards records the town is well served. Numerous court rolls from 1307 to 1815 exist, as do bailiffs' accounts from 1302 to 1534, though with gaps in both series.

At the manorial court of 8th January, 1382, the first after the burning of the rolls, it was decided to reinstate seventy-two tenants, doubtless because labour was in short supply. The rector, Sir John Cobbe, appeared before this court in 1389, charged with hunting in the lord's warren. On two other occasions he was charged with poaching, once with some of his parishioners.[8]

The manor was inherited by the younger Sir John de Sutton's sister, Margery, who married John de Walton, and it descended to the Waltons' grand-daughter, Joane. On 14th January, 1414, a chantry was established at the parish church; two chaplains were to pray for the souls of Joane's brother, Richard, and his wife, Isabel, in the chapel of St. John the Baptist, which suggests a link with St. John's Priory in Colchester and is perhaps the origin of St. John's Road off Brook Street.[9]

1. *Thomas Westeley, chaplain to the Countess of Oxford (d. 1535). He is seen in his mass vestments, with a chalice and wafer. This brass is in St. Mary's Church.*

From an original brass rubbing by Patrick McEune

Joane de Walton married Sir John Howard; their daughter, Elizabeth, married John de Vere, twelfth earl of Oxford, at some time prior to June, 1429. The earl had a vineyard at Wivenhoe and a barge was built for him at Colchester. Morant tells us that he persuaded Henry VI to give him the fishery in the Colne, which belonged to Colchester, but that after three civil actions Colchester corporation won it back. A staunch Lancastrian, he and his eldest son, Aubrey, were beheaded in 1462, during the Wars of the Roses.[10]

The earl's second son, John, no less zealous for the red rose, fled to France after the battle of Barnet. In 1473, he and a companion in arms, William Viscount Beaumont, seized St. Michael's Mount in Cornwall, where they were besieged for two months before surrendering to the Yorkists. They were imprisoned in France, but by 1484 the earl escaped. Richard III was now king and had given Wivenhoe to Sir Thomas Montgomery.

The thirteenth earl landed in Wales with Henry Richmond in the summer of 1485, commanded his right wing at Bosworth, took a leading part in his coronation and received back all his lands. Morant tells us that the manor house at this time was "a large and elegant seat", which had "a noble gatehouse with towers of great height, that served for a seamark". The earliest parts of the house pulled down in 1927 dated from about 1530, so it may have been rebuilt at this time.

2. and 3.   *Elizabeth, Countess of Oxford (d. 1537), and her first husband, William, Viscount Beaumont (d.1507).*

From original brass rubbings by Patrick McEune

When Viscount Beaumont returned to England his vast estates were likewise restored to him and in 1486 he married his second wife, Elizabeth, the daughter of Richard Scrope. However, in the following year the earl was entrusted with Beaumont's lands and in 1495 with his person, which suggests that the viscount had gone mad, perhaps as a result of his privations in France. He lived with his viscountess at Wivenhoe Hall. There he died, on 19th December, 1507, and was buried in the chancel of St. Mary's, his grave marked by a handsome, full-length brass. By April, 1509, his widow had become the earl's second wife. For the best part of a dozen years she had tended an invalid; she was now one of the most important noblewomen in the country. When the earl died in 1513, aged seventy, she continued to attend state functions; she was with Katherine of Aragon at the Field of the Cloth of Gold and Cardinal Wolsey suggested she should be a governess to Princess Mary, an honour she declined because of ill-health.

In 1530 an official called Richard Dolphine wrote to Wolsey from Wivenhoe commending Lady Oxford's hospitality. Wolsey had earlier called her "old". Her date of birth is unknown but if, when she married Viscount Beaumont, she was only sixteen, (and her groom, incidentally, three times as old), she was now sixty at the very least and would live to be sixty-seven, a considerable age in those days.[11]

The earl was buried at Earls Colne, in a tomb made for himself and his first wife; his countess chose to be buried beside her first husband in the parish church. So she was, in 1537. The title and estates then passed to the earl's nephew, a young profligate who died in 1526. The fourteenth earl's second cousin, John, became the fifteenth and served Henry VIII very well, in particular by promoting the downfalls of Cardinal Wolsey, Katherine of Aragon and Anne Boleyn. He stayed at Wivenhoe for at least part of 1538, in order to escape the plague at Earls Colne. In the same year the manor house was visited by Sir Richard Rich, one of the adroit men of that reign, and, probably also in 1538, by Thomas Lord Audley.[12]

At the Dissolution, the earl received the priory of Earls Colne; in 1539 he appropriated the chantry at Wivenhoe and gave it to one of his servants, Robert Rochester. A commission set up in 1545 to investigate chantry chapels and in particular to assess their value, had no difficulty in snuffing this one out, for it was obviously now a racket.[13]

The sixteenth earl, son of the fifteenth, lived grandly and was known as a sportsman and good landlord. His son, the seventeenth earl and the last to concern us, was Edward de Vere, temperamental, eccentric and recklessly extravagant. In 1585 he sold Wivenhoe, which there is no reason to suppose he ever visited, to a courtier from Norfolk, Roger Townshend.

Morant tells us that one of the de Veres made the road now called The Avenue. Prior to this the only route into the town was the present Belle Vue Road. It is probable that The Cross was so named simply because it marked the junction of three roads.

Elizabethan Wivenhoe must have looked attractive and cohesive. Some of the sturdy, timber-framed houses between the church and river were now two storeys high, but the church itself rose far above them, for in about 1500 it acquired a tower in which bells rang and a clock chimed. The Colchester court rolls for 1509 record "Brokestrete", the road which crosses what is now an almost invisible trickle into the Colne, but which once carried ships up to a quay where sand and gravel were loaded as ballast in lieu of the heavy, stabilising cargoes they discharged at the Colne ports. It is likely that the population of the town already numbered three hundred.[14]

They included people of substance. Let us look at the will of Henry Foote, a yeoman farmer with a wife and small daughter, dated 29th March, 1595.[15]

The testator bequeathed his house and lands to his daughter. Most of his sheep, horses, mares, geldings, lambs and bullocks were to be sold and this money, together with the sum of £40, invested for his daughter and given to her either when she was eighteen or married; but if she died before her majority and without issue then the £40 was to be divided into smaller bequests: St John's College, Cambridge, would receive £10 for its poor scholars, particularly the rising talent from the Colchester Grammar School, the poor of Wivenhoe would receive £5 and various relations would be remembered. In any event the testator gave the poor of Wivenhoe 3s 4d on the day of his burial and a like sum the following Christmas.

The will refers to a hall, parlour and solar. This last was an upstairs room. Between 1570 and 1640 there was a general move to build brick hearths and chimneys, which transformed domestic life and enabled upper storeys to be built on. The fireplace at 21, High Street, almost certainly dates from this time.

Other buildings that are probably either sixteenth century or earlier include *The Falcon*, for centuries a focal point of social life, which has arches of a distinctively Tudor pattern, Nonsuch House and the three houses adjoining on the south side of East Street, evidently once all part of the same building, 31, West Street, (probably built from ships' timbers), *The Black Buoy* and 1 to 13, High Street. If a contemporary Wivenhovian were transported to Tudor times he would soon find his bearings, for the church stood where the Saxons first built one, the layout of the few streets was the same and the properties I have mentioned, though thatched, would, by their shape and position, quickly make themselves known.[16]

Apart from the manor house, the most important building was the church. Its account books, covering the late Elizabethan and early Stuart periods, have survived and much social history may be gleaned from their pages. The first entry, in 1562, records the passing of the old order. A silver massing chalice was sold to a London goldsmith for £8 5s 0d. At about the same time the church sold a coverlet, "wch was old and mothe eten", certain "old gere", most likely the newly discarded vestments, and a hearsecloth, the pall used to cover the wooden frame set over a corpse when it was brought into church. Windows were mended and the whole of the interior covered with "whyting", followed by "blackying the nether p'tes", presumably to produce a skirting that would disguise bootmarks. Stools were made, as stools were continually made and repaired throughout this period. 13d was paid "for p'rettyng the belhowse", which I think means pargetting the exterior of the church tower. The altar was replaced by a communion table built for the purpose; the Ten Commandments were prominently displayed and the church invested in a book of homilies, an official document appointed to be read in lieu of sermons if there was no licensed preacher.[17]

All these things happened between 1562 and 1565. In 1566, "a new Shopp in the Chirche yarde" was built and fitted up, at a total cost of £3 8s 7d, evidently to bring in a regular income, which indeed it did. Very likely the three or four shops which exist to this day in a corner of the churchyard are based on, and may contain elements of, this original Elizabethan shop.

Between 1566 and 1568 a gallery was built, which confirms one's impression of a large and thriving community. Presumably it was on the north side of the nave, as west end galleries were not general until the following century and later the church had both north and west galleries. The cost, including more stools and refreshments for the carpenters, was £4 13s 6d.[18]

So now the church was a plain stone room with an upper storey, which every Wivenhovian of fourteen years upwards was obliged by law to enter on Sunday and other holy days, occupy a stool according to his place in the social pecking order and take part in a curious experiment — The Elizabethan Settlement, religion prescribed by secular authority.

The administration of the church and the morals of its parishioners were in the hands of two churchwardens, chosen from the richer and more important members of the community. Their principal duty, to compel universal church attendance, was almost impossible. Some people declined to attend on religious grounds: the Catholic Recusants had begun their long war of attrition and on the other flank, well represented in Essex, were those who thought the Settlement had not gone far enough. Then, as now, some people were naturally agnostic, unable to sit still on a wooden stool for an hour or so, or simply disliked being coerced.

The churchwardens presented a list of miscreants to the Archdeacon of Colchester and these people subsequently appeared before his archidiaconal court at St. Peter's Church, Colchester. For instance, in 1572, John and Peter Gray, "being reproved for not coming to church, reviled the churchwardens, calling them knaves and churls", as indeed churchwardens at this time were constantly reviled, usually in stronger language than this.[19]

Here, the justice was generally lenient. In the case just cited the charge was proved and the culprits commanded "to confess before the congregation and to reconcile themselves with the churchwardens". This meant that the two Grays would have appeared before their fellow parishioners the following Sunday

Saxon, Mediaeval, Tudor

in the white sheets of penitence and with long white wands in their hands.

If the accused failed to appear or comply with the court's verdict, he was excommunicated. As time went on more people were willing to accept a stigma which, ironically, was often administered by a layman acting as the archdeacon's surrogate.

It was not easy to keep order in church. In 1599, John Langley and William Fordham were presented to the archdeacon for brawling with their stools,[20] and there were many cases of bad language and behaviour in churches and churchyards.

Charges of immorality were presented at this court, as in 1582 when William Sparke had committed fornication with Frances Smyth. Unwanted babies were a heavy burden on the rates and for this reason, if no other, the authorities took a firm line about such matters. The defendants were excommunicated, but later absolved.[21]

Excessive drinking, especially if allied to gambling, was obviously anti-social. The churchwardens reported that William Rich, "dyd . . . suffer in his house drinking, tippling and playing at dice for mony upon Sabothe daye". It was reported of a man called King and his wife, "that they kepe vitling upon sabothe and holy days in sermon and service tyme and the Churchwardens Coming to their house ther gesse (guests?) scorned them as they had bene obstinat rebelles, asking them yf they had penn and ynck to wrigt ther names . . . This ys ordinarly every Sabothe daye so that hir Majestys officers dares not goe in the streetes by them". Does this mean one constable or more? Without effective authority to back them up, the churchwardens were powerless.[22]

The court took care of the rates. In 1596, Henry Foote was accused, "that he, being a wealthy man", as indeed his will indicates, "doth refuse contributions to the relief of the poor, and that his example is a great and main hindrance to the rest". Foot sturdily contended that he had paid the twopence a week at which he had been assessed for this purpose.[23]

The churchwardens were assisted by sidesmen, by the parish clerk whose duties included writing up the accounts and vestry minutes, also leading the singing in church, and a sexton who dug graves and rang a bell whenever anybody died.

Thus the rector was free, apart from his family and glebe, to attend to his job. Unfortunately, the quality of the Elizabethan clergy was initially extremely poor. Some were barely literate, most unable to preach a sermon.

In 1586, the rector of Wivenhoe, Edmund Burgess, appeared at the Assizes for publicly varying the words of the Prayer Book, as follows: "Lett us also comend in our prayers my Right Reverend syster Elizabeth . . . ", and being afterwards demaunded what his meaning was to saye the Queenes Majestie was his syster ... (he said) that he was King Henryes sunne and that the Queene was his syster both by father and mother". It sounds as if he was dotty, but the authorities were chary of anything remotely treasonable and he was charged with sedition. The verdict is unknown, but he kept the living of Wivenhoe, and also that of Fingringhoe, until he died, in 1589.[24]

He was succeeded by Brian Atkinson, whose brief and stormy incumbency was marked by two or three appearances in the archdeacon's court. His own churchwardens presented him as a man "of evil and scandalous behaviour, to the offence of the parishioners and elsewhere", for he was suspected of adultery with a woman at Brightlingsea and was evidently extremely quarrelsome. It was probably with some justification that Thomas Beckes, "a common droncard in our parish ... most shamefully rayled upon Mr. Atkinson our parson and upon his Curat and called them knaves", and that one of his female parishioners called him "a whoremasterly knave".[25]

It would seem that the churchwardens were the most important men in the parish. They were certainly conscious of their position, *vide* their presentation of a man who "most shamefully hath used us in speeches not decent for men in our place, viz. knaves, slaves, busy slaves; and pickthankly knaves". However, they themselves could be presented, as they were in 1595 because one of them, William Abell, could not tell "who hath the harlott in John Browne's howse with child neyther from when she came nor wither she is gone", and again in 1598 because the lead roof of the church was ruinous and "they suffered morris dancing upon the Sabaoth daye".[26]

Atkinson was rector from 1589 to 1591. His successor, John Martelmore, had an even briefer reign and was followed in 1592 by William Woodruffe. An entry in the churchwardens' accounts in 1602 accuses Woodruffe of appropriating the town shop for his own profit. Taken all round, the last thirty years of Elizabeth's reign were extremely unsatisfactory as regards matters spiritual in Wivenhoe.[27]

The money collected during the Sunday service, a fair sum, was used to buy clothes, food, medical treatment and pay burial fees, also to pay for the care and upbringing of bastards and, in particular, for boys to be apprentices. There was a poor house, or "Charity house" as one testator called it, while another gave money specifically for "two hospitals or two almshouses".[28]

Doctors and teachers were licensed by the bishop. In 1593, the wife of William Giles was presented for "using Surgery" without a licence. Miles Gurnell, accused of being a drunkard, brawler and railer was also said to be living in sin with a woman who was an unlicensed schoolteacher.[29]

Though some, perhaps most, Wivenhovians might never see the lord of the manor, his court, over which his deputy presided, was still extremely active. It supervised the building and repair of the tenants' houses, appointed

Saxon, Mediaeval, Tudor

breadtasters, aletasters and parish constables, discountenanced sharp and dishonest practice, cleaned the streets, looked after Wivenhoe Common, (the large area to the north of the town where everybody might graze cattle), and, above all, controlled the tenure of land.[30]

Between them, the local ecclesiastical and secular courts dealt with minor offences. We have seen that the archidiaconal court took cognizance of gambling on Sundays. However, the case of the licensed victualler who was charged at the Lexden Petty Sessions with maintaining "unlawful games, to wit (bowling) alleys, cards and slidethrift", (shoveha'penny), probably originated in the manorial court. Most games, including football, were unlawful at this time. Trespass was sternly discouraged. It was always difficult to find enough fuel for heating and cooking, but anyone who carried away "the lord's park pales" was fined 20d and put in the stocks for three hours or so. The stocks, whipping-post and cage, (a small lock-up), were almost certainly sited on Anchor Hill, because the cage was there in the eighteenth and nineteenth centuries.[31]

I assume that from the time it was founded Wivenhoe built boats. The first reference to a shipyard is in 1575, when we are told that it was being worked by John Quixle. However, there is an even earlier reference to what may well be a shipyard. For in 1507 it is recorded that "Richard Quykesley took, for 6d a year rent, half a rood, (1/8 of an acre), of vacant land lying next to a 'dokke' of the lord, on the south, abutting west on land of John Cuttelee called le Werkyng yerd and East on a way leading to le Wherfe". It would seem that the Quixley family ran the Wivenhoe shipyard, probably upstream of the town, throughout the sixteenth century. Towards the end of the century we learn that there were four "lading places" at the town: those belonging to the Earl of Oxford, Richard Cock, William Giles and John Maior. Two of these men describe themselves as sailors; very likely merchandise as well as fish was landed on The Quay.[32]

I assume that from the time it was founded Wivenhoe had a fishing fleet. Towards the end of the period covered by this chapter an occasional document confirms this. Thus, a list of vessels for 1528 records that Colchester, Wivenhoe and Brightlingsea together owned twenty-two of the 222 crayers plying the North Sea. A crayer was a small trading ship. A return for 1564-5 tells us that Wivenhoe had twelve ships. Six years later a customs officer in London made a register of coasting traders. He credited Brightlingsea with eleven and Wivenhoe with three, none of Wivenhoe's being over twenty tons.[33] Very likely the number of ships at Wivenhoe had not altered much between these two dates, so we may guess that the town owned about a dozen ships at this time, of which a quarter were merchantmen and the rest fishing boats. In 1582, it seems that Wivenhoe had nine ships. Such lists, before the days of official

11

The Story of Wivenhoe

4. *Sir Roger Townshend (1543?-1590).*

National Portrait Gallery

registration, were probably inaccurate; Wivenhoe would not have wanted the government to know how many ships it had because they might have been commandeered in time of war.[34]

The county as a whole provided ships, men and money for the great naval centrepiece of 1588, albeit reluctantly. Wivenhoe supplied at least one man, the lord of the manor, Roger Townshend. Townshend hailed from Rainham in Norfolk; his estates in Essex were but a fraction of his possessions. Although his name occurs in a list of sea captains drawn up in 1587, he was not a sailor nor did he command a ship in the Armada campaign. Since he nevertheless took part it seems likely that he commanded soldiers aboard one of the bigger ships.[35]

On 28th May, 1588, a fleet of 130 ships, large and small, sailed from Lisbon with instructions to proceed up the English Channel, contact the Duke of Parma, who was leading an army in the Netherlands, and assist him to invade England. Slowly running before the wind, in the shape of a huge crescent, came the Armada. A small English fleet engaged it three times. Our ships proved faster and handier, our gunnery more expert. On 26th July, the Lord High Admiral, Lord Howard of Effingham, knighted five of his commanders, including Townshend, aboard his flagship. There followed the decisive action off Gravelines, after which the Armada fled back to Spain, a prey to unseasonable weather, a lack of provisions and consequent disease.

The English fleet also suffered horribly. On 10th August, Lord Howard wrote to Burghley:

> *Sickness and mortality begins wonderfully to grow amongst us; and it is a most pitiful sight to see, here at Margate, how the men, having no place to receive them ... die in the streets ... The Elizabeth Jonas, which hath done as well as ever any ship did in any service, hath a great infection in her ... Sir Roger Townshend, of all the men he brought out with him, hath but one left alive ...* [36]

So it would seem that the *Elizabeth Jonas* was Townshend's ship.

Two years later, Sir Roger died and his eldest son, John, knighted by the Earl of Essex at Cadiz, became lord of the manor. A few months after the death of Queen Elizabeth, Sir John died too, mortally wounded in a duel. His son, Roger, succeeded him.[37]

CHAPTER 2

Seventeenth Century

1 Religion and Politics.

References to Wivenhoe in the archidiaconal court indicate that as the seventeenth century wore on life became, apparently, more settled, with a general decline in fighting, swearing, working on Sundays and shove ha'pennying in alehouses; though drunkenness, the begetting of bastards and failure to attend church or receive holy communion remained hardy perennials, and some people, such as John Langley, were incorrigible.

Langley, he who had brawled with his stool in the previous chapter, was presented in 1612 for being drunk and absent from church, in 1617 for being excommunicate, and later in the same year simply as one who "commonly doeth disturbe diverse of the Churche". There was the affair of the servant girl, Abigail Howell. She became pregnant and her master, Jeremiah Bigges, was presented for quietly packing her off to Ardleigh without telling the authorities, presumably because the guilty party was his son, for it was later alleged that Jeremy Bigges junior and John Brown had defamed her. Brown denied the charge. In 1606 the rector himself, Henry Wace or Wast, was presented three times for being absent from his benefice.[1]

However, he was succeeded in the following year by John Cornwall whose thirty year reign gave great satisfaction to at least twenty-four of his leading parishioners. In 1619, they petitioned Sir Roger Townshend to save them from certain "pernitious contentions". They had every faith in their rector, but the puritanical element, which before the century was out would have a church of its own, was evidently making itself objectionable. It may be that the petition was ultimately heeded, for Cornwall was succeeded by an extremely strong-minded protegée of Sir Roger's who arrived in Wivenhoe at least three or four years before he received the living from Cornwall.[2]

Thomas Cawton was born at Rainham, Norfolk, in 1605. He decided to become a clergyman at an early age. His parents were not rich, so Sir Roger's

5. *Thomas Cawton (1605-1659).*

patronage was invoked and Cawton went to Queen's College, Cambridge, at his expense. Here, he studied languages and gained such a reputation for strait-laced piety that he and his companions were known as Cawtonists.³

Most of what we know about him is contained in a panegyrical biography written by his son, who tells us that in 1637 Cawton found the town "notorious for all manner of vice and wickedness". In particular, the new rector disapproved of fish being sold on Sundays. So he argued with the fishermen and preached against them, "with hard and cutting rebukes", until they capitulated. He also preached against the "sectaries", or Dissenters as they were eventually known, so that the parish was almost free of them. Such fanaticism might well have turned the town against him. On the contrary, "No man was ever more beloved of his people than he was . . . " Evidently, the Elizabethan Settlement was working at last. The clergyman had arrived, the man who, in the literal meaning of his title was not a man of God, but a man of learning, dominating his flock by his intellectual superiority.

Cawton was practical. Concerned that the parish might go downhill after his departure, he used the profits from his first three years to rebuild the rectory, which was falling to pieces, and at the same time added fishponds and orchards. Here was a place which would attract the right sort of man. It also made a pleasant home for Cawton and his family, for after it was completed he married the daughter of a Sudbury preacher, Elizabeth Jenkin, and three children were born to them here.

No doubt the Cawtons might have stayed at Wivenhoe until the end of the Civil War when the rector, temperamentally a puritan fanatic, but politically an ardent and vocal Royalist, would have been deprived of his living. Unfortunately, his health was poor and twice a year he succumbed to an ague which his son thought was promoted by the local climate. Then, as now, the low-lying marshes of the Essex coast had a general reputation for unhealthiness. Daniel Defoe, writing in the following century, tells us that gentlemen who came to this part of the world for wildfowling often returned "with an Essex ague on their backs".⁴ At the end of his seventh year in the parish the rector very nearly died and his doctors told him that for the sake of his health he must leave, as indeed other Wivenhovians have left the town at various times. So he obtained the valuable living of St. Bartholomew, Exchange, in London.

The history books tell us that East Anglia sided with Parliament in the Civil War. Very likely the locals disliked the war to the extent that it disrupted their lives, but took whatever advantages were offering, as did Giles Wiggoner, a sailor and boat-owner, who in 1644 carried arms and provisions in his vessel the *Sunflower* to the Royalist garrison at Scarborough.⁵

In the summer of 1648 the Civil War was drawing to a close. The Roundheads had precluded siege warfare by knocking substantial holes in the fortifications of towns which still had walls, but for some reason Colchester remained unbreached. On 12th June a Royalist force led by Lord Goring was reluctantly admitted to the town; the next day Lord Fairfax appeared with 5,000 Roundheads and the Royalists were besieged until they surrendered on 27th August.

At first the garrison was able to obtain supplies. James Round, M.P., one of the defenders, tells us that on 17th June two ships brought provisions and men from Kent and that corn was unloaded into hoys which took it up to The Hythe. Presumably the corn changed boats at Wivenhoe, for above the town the Colne is much shallower. Later, cannon were brought to Colchester by Wivenhoe ships.[6]

During the ensuing eleven weeks, anyone who climbed the church tower and looked towards Colchester would have observed a thunder and lightning effect, flashes in the sky followed by loud reports, from those guns and many others, and the town would have buzzed with rumours of what was happening three miles away.

The next year, Thomas Cawton joined the declaration of ministers against the execution of King Charles and having delivered a royalist harangue was eventually put in prison. Then he became involved in the plot to restore Charles II instigated by Christopher Love, and fled to Rotterdam where he became pastor of the English church. There he died, in 1659.[7]

2 Admiralty Contracts.

Before the century was out two packet boats were making regular journeys from Wivenhoe to London with bays, says and perpetuanas, returning thence with wool for Colchester, but the threat to the livelihood of the town from the pirates and privateers who swarmed in the North Sea was considerable. So in October, 1650, the Council of State commissioned two of Giles Wiggoner's ketches to guard the Essex and Kentish coasts.[8]

One of them may have been the *Nonsuch*, for in 1650 a ketch of that name was almost certainly built at Wivenhoe. In turn, that ketch was probably the naval man-of-war referred to in official documents from 1654 to 1667 and the vessel which inaugurated the Hudson's Bay Company in 1668. It would be pleasant to be certain about this; instead, we must be content to be almost certain.

The evidence that the *Nonsuch* was built at Wivenhoe is contained in a *register of naval ships* from 1660 to 1668 compiled by Samuel Pepys. The Navy is credited with a ketch called *Nonsuch* built by Mr. Page in 1650 and sold in November, 1667. Some of the ships have no yards against their names. It seems that if Pepys did not know where a ship had been built he did not guess. Is the rest of the entry accurate? Since the ship came into service four years after 1650, it would have been logical to enter her as "Bought 1654". If the entry is incorrect, then it is not the only error on this page, for the *Roe* is entered as built in 1665 and the *Roe Kitchin* in 1655. These two dates should be transposed. On the other hand, there is nothing to indicate that the *Nonsuch* was not built at Wivenhoe in 1650, and indeed we know that vessels of this size and character were habitually built here.[9]

A ketch at this time was a ship of up to one hundred tons, with a mainmast stepped pretty well in the middle and a substantial mizzen, but no foremast. Both mainmast and mizzen set square sails. She had a large foresail, and a jib attached to a long, protruding boom. Though small for a man-of-war, the *Nonsuch*, at forty-three tons, was not small for a ketch. For the first four years of her life she was evidently a merchantman, and for the first four years of her naval life escorted merchant vessels.

In the mid-seventeenth century the well-dressed Parisian invariably wore a fur hat. The fur was that of beavers, caught by Red Indians in the forests of northern Canada. In the 1650's, two enterprising Frenchmen, Medard Chouart and Pierre Radisson, realised it would be far cheaper to ship the furs direct from Hudson Bay to Europe during the warm weather when the bay was free from ice. Their idea was badly received, both in Quebec and France, because it would take the fur trade out of French hands. However, they went to England and after various delays and reverses a small group of courtiers and financiers, headed by Prince Rupert, backed their scheme. On 30th March, 1668, this consortium bought a ketch called *Nonsuch* from a merchant, Sir William Warren, for £290.[10]

Was this the ketch allegedly sold by the Royal Navy in 1667? In the absence of documentary evidence the matter can be neither proved nor disproved. However, we do know that Sir William dealt regularly with the Navy Board. So why should these ketches not have been one and the same? The king was sympathetic and lent the consortium another, slightly larger, ketch from the Royal Navy, the *Eaglet*. Aboard the *Eaglet*, commanded by Captain William Stannard, was Pierre Radisson; aboard the *Nonsuch*, commanded by Captain Zachariah Guillam, was Medard Chouart. Early in June, 1668, the voyage was begun.

The *Eaglet* returned to Plymouth, having sustained storm damage, but by 19th August the *Nonsuch* had crossed the Hudson Straits and reached a harbour at the entrance of Hudson Bay. She crossed the bay and on 1st October anchored in a river which was christened Rupert. The crew built a log cabin on the shore, which they called Fort Charles.

With the spring came the Indians and trading began; then, as the weather grew warmer, Captain Guillam prepared for the return voyage. By early October the *Nonsuch* had reached England. Though the cost of the voyage had not been recovered it had been a great success. On 2nd May, 1670, the king granted a charter to "the Governors and Company of Adventurers trading into Hudson's Bay", and the Hudson's Bay Company was founded. In the same year the *Nonsuch* was sold to an unknown buyer for £152 10s 0d. It is the last we hear of her.

Over two hundred men-of-war were built during the Commonwealth, in marked contrast to the desultory activity of the previous reign. The First Dutch War, (1651-4), in particular, kept the naval dockyards so busy that some of the smaller commissions were farmed out to private builders. It was at this time that the first two men-of-war were built in Essex, the *Jersey* at Maldon and the *Fagons* at Wivenhoe.

In the seventeenth and eighteenth centuries men-of-war were divided, according to size, into six classes or "rates" which, from about 1655, were roughly related to armament. An official document drawn up in that year tells us that a first rate ship, such as the *Naseby*, had 91 guns, a second rate 64, a third rate 60, a fourth rate 38, a fifth rate 22 and a sixth rate 8. The *Fagons* had 22 guns. She was a frigate and probably the largest vessel built in Wivenhoe until the following century. No designs for her have survived, indeed there almost certainly were none. Her name was evidently derived from St. Fagans, a Parliamentary victory in 1647.

During the Commonwealth the Navy was mainly run by the Admiralty Committee of the Council of State, known as the Admiralty Commissioners, which had overall control, and the Navy Commissioners, a body of five, and later seven, men who shouldered most of the responsibility. The Navy Commissioners were able and conscientious, none more so than the indefatigable Major Nehemiah Bourne who supervised the building of the *Fagons* from Harwich where he was stationed.

We first hear of the *Fagons* early in 1654. A letter from an official surveyor to the Navy, one Humphrey White, dated 24th March, tells the Commissioners how the new frigate being built by Robert Page at Wivenhoe is coming along and asks for instructions. The next day the Admiralty sends the Commissioners a letter from the ship's first commander, Captain Thomas Elliott, a bailiff of Aldeburgh, Suffolk, complaining of the delay and asking them to expedite matters. On 9th May, the Admiralty had to consider a complaint from Mr. White about Captain Elliott, who had allegedly drunk the king's health and ordered three guns to be fired. However, this was stoutly contradicted by Giles Wiggoner who wrote to the Admiralty on 28th May enclosing a deposition signed by himself, Robert Page and seven other Wivenhovians that Mr. White, when he went aboard the *Fagons*, had called the captain knave, rogue and malignant dog, and offered to fight him.[11]

By 22nd May, the *Fagons* was in the water at Wivenhoe and Captain Elliott was ordered to rig and fit her, then take her round to Harwich where she would

Seventeenth Century

6. *The twentieth century reconstruction of the Nonsuch: the vessel in frame.*

Photograph by A. C. Littlejohns, A.M.P.A.

7. *Reconstruction of the Nonsuch: carving the stern panel.*

Photograph by R. Warington Smyth

be put on shore, washed and tallowed. On 5th June, Mr. White sent another letter to the Commissioners, asking them to galvanise Mr. Page, as "he is very slow and indifferent, although the masts are all in". However, by 3rd July the *Fagons* was at Harwich and by 24th August had sailed for Hosely Bay where Captain Elliott hoped to complete his crew by bringing the numbers on board up to a hundred or more.[12]

In January, 1656, Captain Elliott captured a small, eight gun man-of-war from Biscay and brought her into Plymouth. In March he was ordered to the French coast, "where the pirates lie, much among our trade", but before he went be brought another prize into Plymouth, the *Cornelius* of Ostend, which he won after a six hour chase which cost him his yards and rigging.[13]

Such was the routine work of a small man-of-war at this time; convoying, moving men and supplies, general patrol duties and from time to time the excitement of a fight at sea with perhaps a prize to show for it. At the Restoration the *Fagons* was renamed the *Milford*. She continued to convoy merchantmen, fight pirates and take prizes, and between whiles was patched, peeled and remasted.

She took part in the Second Dutch War, (1665-7). Samuel Pepys refers, in his diary, to an engagement between eight British men-of-war and a fleet of thirty Dutch merchantmen and three Dutch warships, in December, 1664:

> *Captain Seale of the Milford hath done his part very well, in boarding the King Salamon – which held out half an hour after she was boarded – and his men kept her an hour after they maister her; and then she sunk and drowned about 17 of her men.*[14]

In 1669, the *Milford* joined Sir Thomas Allen's Mediterranean fleet; at Leghorn, on 7th July, 1671, she perished. There was gunpowder on board, but the quarteers, the men who fired the guns, nevertheless aired the breadroom, which involved filling it with smoke from coals in an open kettle. Fire broke out and with gunpowder on board there was no hope of saving the ship. Three of her guns were literally blown ashore; practically everything else was lost.[15]

Robert Page built four other warships at Wivenhoe.

We first hear of the *Roe* and the *Hind* on 8th November, 1655. Page is building two ketches and asks for more money; later, he describes them as advice boats. By 11th February, both ketches are launched and their captains have appeared at Wivenhoe: Jeremy Country for the *Roe*, Richard Country for the *Hind*. They write simultaneous, and almost identical, letters to the Admiralty, to say that their ships are launched, they have each nine weeks' supplies on board and men are difficult to obtain. On 15th February, they tell the Admiralty they have been busy pressing men and taking on provisions. The *Roe*, incidentally, was a good deal bigger and heavier than her sister ship, and by the same token had a larger complement.[16]

Seventeenth Century

8. To celebrate the tercentenary of the Hudson's Bay Company a replica of the ketch Nonsuch was built at Appledore in 1965, to the designs of R. Warington Smyth.

Photograph by R. Warington Smyth

The Story of Wivenhoe

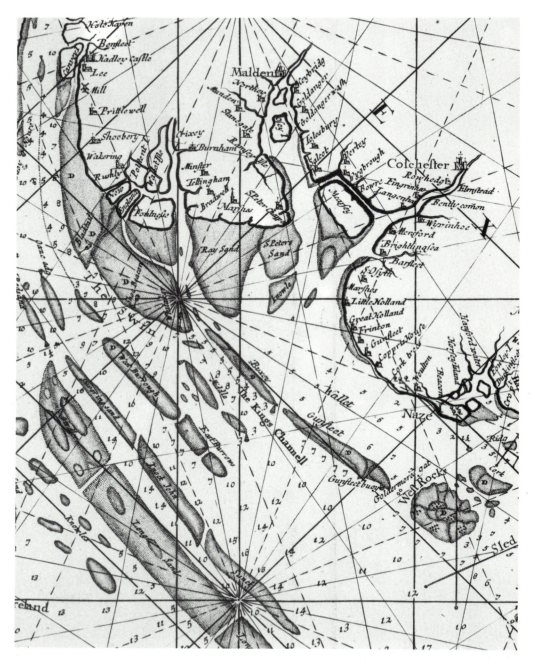

9. *Detail from a map of the Thames Estuary made c. 1693-1698 by Greenvile Collins.*

National Maritime Museum

Seventeenth Century

The two ketches, commanded by the two Countrys – who must surely have been brothers, if not twins – move down the Colne in late February to take up the tasks allotted to them by the Commonwealth: Jeremy to patrol the Norfolk and Suffolk coast, Richard the mouth of the Thames between Orford Ness and the North Foreland. They keep a sharp lookout for the Dunkerkers and Ostenders which are feared by everyone, protect merchant shipping, forward their muster books to the Admiralty when required and keep the authorities regularly informed. From time to time they put into port, to clean and repair their ships, and take on more provisions.[17]

Life aboard these patrol vessels is packed with adventure. On 4th August, 1656, Jeremy Country reports from the *Roe*, which is near Kings Lynn, that he has been plying on his station and after a long chase captured a Dunkirk frigate with four guns and a crew of thirty-five. The prize is now in Yarmouth. On the same day, Richard Country writes from the *Hind* at Harwich, to say that he has been to the Ness, but at first failed to see or hear any of the enemy's men-of-war. Then he heard guns to the north, went in that direction and came across two Ostenders which had fallen in with a fleet of colliers. The colliers told him that the Ostenders had between twelve and fourteen guns apiece, so rather than engage them he went to Harwich for assistance. He had only eight guns himself and this was an age of commonsense, not heroics. "Plying on one's station" is a standard phrase in this correspondence, equivalent to "patrolling one's beat".[18]

The menace of the small ships from the Continent was unceasing, though it diminished considerably during the Commonwealth. At about this time twenty citizens of Colchester complained to the Admiralty of the havoc done to their trade by the Ostenders:

We beg you to employ two nimble ketches to ply betwixt Harwich and the brest of Kent. As these private vessels are small and well piloted, the employing of Wivenhoe vessels will be an effectual means to keep this coast clear, for they know the passage amongst the sands.[19]

No doubt it was in response to this that the Navy Commissioners ordered a new ketch from Giles Wiggoner.

The villainy was not all on one side. In the autumn of 1659, the Council of State considered an incident in which Captain Robert Walker of Wivenhoe had allegedly plundered a hoy of Dunkirk, pretending that he and the crew of his ketch were all Swedes. The Council ordered Walker's ketch to be detained and he brought before them to answer this charge.[20]

After the Restoration, reports from the *Roe* and the *Hind* are intermittent; presumably there were others which have not survived.

On 11th December, 1667, the *Hind* was wrecked on the Scilly Isles. In March, 1670, the *Roe* also was wrecked, near Tenerife.[21]

On 16th January, 1664, Robert Page agreed to build a ketch at £6 a ton, which I assume was the *Wivenhoe*. Work had evidently started before the end of the year, for in January, 1665, a certificate was issued to say that the second instalment of money was now due to the builder. In November, Sir William Batten, Surveyor to the Navy, wrote to Samuel Pepys to say that if money came into the Navy Office he begged payment of timber and plank bills to the poor men at Wivenhoe. In 1670, Page himself petitioned the King and Council for the £405 he should have received for the *Wivenhoe*, together with £497 for other work and supplies, which may have included a ketch apparently ordered in 1667. He was probably paid in the end because in 1671 he submitted a tender for the construction of third and fourth rate ships.[22]

After the success of the first voyage to Hudson Bay, the adventurers soon embarked on another. The *Eaglet* was returned to the Navy; in its stead they borrowed the *Wivenhoe*. In company with the *Prince Rupert* she made two voyages to Hudson Bay. Many years later, the Canadian National Railway named a station after her. In April, 1672, the Hudson's Bay Company returned her to the Navy. She was turned into a fireship, took part in the Third Dutch War, (1672-3), did some convoy work and was sold as useless in 1685.[23]

The Record of Naval Vessels lists a small ketch called the *Roe Kitchin* which Robert Page built in 1655. It seems odd that he should have launched two ships with the same name in the same year. She evidently received her second name in 1661 when she was converted into a galley, in which food was prepared for the nobility who ate it aboard a far grander one moored alongside. Little is known about her, for little would have been recorded, but in 1667, she was promised "to the gentleman who takes care of the Queen-Mother's goods". She was evidently also used for general duties; in the following years she is said to be at, or likely to sail to, the coast of Norfolk, Harwich, The Downs and Deptford. According to *The Record*, she was given to a certain Captain Straughan in 1669, who I suppose must be "Honest John" Straughan, a navy agent from Leith mentioned by Pepys.[24]

I assume that throughout the seventeenth century Wivenhoe built itself fishing boats and small merchant ships, and that its economy was largely based on the sea. This, of course, included smuggling, of which the following incident may be an example. It occurred in 1683. Francis King, a Wivenhovian who was master of a pink called *Success*, was charged by the Privy Council with evading customs duty. He had, so he said, taken his ship over to Bourdeaux earlier in the year, where he had picked up wines and spirits for Rotterdam. At Rotterdam he met a Scotsman who gave him what were alleged to be ten parcels of clear paper, which he agreed to take to London, but turned out to be books on which duty should have been paid. King pleaded ignorance, but the Privy Council handed him over to the Customs and he had to give sureties to appear before the King's Bench.²⁵

3 The Corsellis Family and the Town.

Sir Roger Townshend, (1588-1637), had two sons, Roger and Horatio. Roger died in 1648 and Horatio succeeded to the family baronetcy and estates. A royalist, he was one of the deputation which formally invited Charles II to return; he was made a viscount. Shortly before the Restoration, however, the manor changed hands.

Zegar Corsellis was a London merchant and elder of the Dutch church, who came to England from Flanders in about 1576. He produced a large family. His second surviving son, Nicholas, also a merchant and elder of the church, bought the manor and advowson of Wivenhoe in 1657 for £15,700. He died in 1665.²⁶

The year of his death was also, of course, that of the Great Plague which by the autumn had reached Colchester and its environs. Plague, a natural hazard in those days, had already killed 149 Wivenhovians in 1603-4, including the rector, William Woodruffe, and thirty-nine in 1625, and though all steps were taken to keep infection away, exceptions were made. A Wivenhovian, Hewers, brought his packet boat up to The Quay filled with Londoners fleeing the City. He was intercepted by another man, John Branch, who had a commission to prevent people landing without certificates to prove they came from plague-free areas. Nevertheless, the passengers swarmed ashore. Branch ordered two bystanders, Thomas Collin and Thomas Clarke, to help him. Instead, they helped Hewers. Was this compassion? How much had Hewers charged his passengers for risking his life to save their's?²⁷

The Christian name Nicholas is used so often in the Corsellis family that those bearing it have to be numbered. The man who bought the manor was Nicholas Corsellis I. His younger son, Nicholas Corsellis II, had a house in London, but evidently worked mostly in Colchester, trading in a wide variety of goods, including the famous Colchester bays made by his fellow ex-patriots. He collected money to help the Dutch community after the siege and in 1660 was made an elder of the Colchester community.²⁸

Nicholas Corsellis II died in 1674. On his monument it was inscribed that, "the printer's art was taught to Englishmen by Corsellis, a Fleming prayed and paid for by Henry VI", a myth that needs a word of explanation.²⁹

It is accepted that in 1477 William Caxton printed the first book in this country. Nevertheless, at the end of the sixteenth century a Latin commentary was discovered at Oxford which described itself as printed in 1468. It was eventually decided that the typeset was too advanced, so it was concluded that the date had been misprinted, 1468 for 1478.

This was not the end of the matter. Richard Atkyns, a cavalier who had impoverished himself in the Civil War, expected to be rewarded by Charles II, but to make quite sure wrote a tract to prove that the king might lawfully have the monopoly, and the revenue, of printing. The tract describes how printing was brought to this country by Henry VI, who smuggled Frederick Corsellis out of Holland and set him up at Oxford. What had been introduced to this country by the king ought therefore to remain under his aegis. At the time Henry VI was supposed to be organising this invention he was a prisoner in the Tower of London. The legend was appropriated by the Corsellis family.

We have seen that the building of the *Wivenhoe* ketch coincided with the Second Dutch War, (1665-7). These wars must have also seriously affected local trade and even prompted a fear of invasion. A bulletin to the Admiralty from Harwich, dated 29th June, 1667, tells us that at Wivenhoe's request a company of foot had been sent to Mersea Island. Next month the sound of gunfire was heard at Harwich, and on 25th July, "at noon one from Wivenhoe arrived, (presumably a fishing boat), who heard hot shooting yesterday, from six to nine at night".[30]

After Thomas Cawton left Wivenhoe in 1644 it is most likely that the town had no rector, for a parochial inquisition discovered there was none in 1650, but in 1656 two Puritan ministers, both with Cambridge degrees, were appointed in rapid succession, William Blagrave in June and Thomas Tarrey in October. Tarrey moved to Thrapson two years later. These men were put in by Cromwell's commissioners, the "Triers" as they were known, and by that token may well have been competent. Tarrey was succeeded by William Cunyham, who was presumably ejected at the Restoration, for in 1661 the name Marcus de Power first appears in the parish register. Although Robert Page and three other men were summoned to appear before the Bishop of London, in 1666, to "make out their respective informations against Mr. Depower their minister", he evidently stayed until he was succeeded by Samuel Bridge, described as a "black nonconformist", in 1676.[31]

The authorities soon discovered it was impossible to stamp out nonconformity, so in 1672 the Declaration of Indulgence granted licences for such places of worship. Sixty-nine were issued in Essex, including one for the houses of John Tyler and William Giles in Wivenhoe. This was the town's first nonconformist church.[32]

The first Essex minister to take advantage of the act was John Argor, another Cambridge man, who came from Layer Breton. In 1672 he became a minister at Copford and it was there he died, in 1679, aged seventy-seven. In the last years of his life he also had a congregation at Wivenhoe. He was described as "a very serious and lovely Christian, who . . . in his advanced years often had raptures of joy".[33]

Seventeenth Century

The Third Dutch War, (1672-4), was generally disliked. All we know of the town's part in it is that fourteen impressed Wivenhovians served aboard the *Warspitt, King, Industry, Victory, Prince* and *Gloucester*.[34]

It was probably in the seventeenth century that the three adjoining houses on The Quay called Maple Cottage, Trinity House and Quayside Cottage, were built, also the nearby Anchor House and the present British Legion Hall, West House in West Street, 8 and 9, East Street, and 41, The Cross, later the home of the schoolmistress and town councillor, Betsy Grasby. *The Falcon*, which may have been a public house in Tudor times, was certainly one in the seventeenth century because token coinage has been found with the date 1636 and the word "falcon" on it. There are title deeds to prove that The Storehouse, a private house on The Quay, was in this century also a public house. Originally, *The Maiden's Head*, and then *The Maidenhead*, it was later *The Swan* and at one time *The White Swan*. It is possible that the name was changed because the churchwardens, who dined there annually, thought it indelicate.[35]

Timber frames with thatched roofs; we should know many of our existing buildings if we saw them in their Stuart habiliments and are lucky that so many have survived, for timber, thatch and indoor fires are a perennial hazard. In 1641, some Wivenhovians petitioned the Quarter Sessions about one, Edward Mayer, whom they described as an "obstenate and refractorie fellowe who will not live in Ranke and order amongst his neygbours". His home was a boat drawn up on the foreshore whose chimney, close to other thatched roofs, might have started a wholesale fire.[36]

We may assume that the mill, mentioned for the first time in a bill of 1641, was already, if not in that form, centuries old. It was a watermill, which stood near the corner of the present Belle Vue Road and Rectory Road, using the brook which runs in a cleft of land there. Another bill for the same year indicates there were already mud walls to keep the tide from the saltings. It was in 1641 also, that the town was presented at the Quarter Sessions for failing to keep the causeway to Fingringhoe in good repair; it was presented again in 1656 for allowing it to be blocked by boats. Evidently, this route, used by horse-driven vehicles at low tide up to the present century, was important.[37]

One building in seventeenth century Wivenhoe has hardly changed from that day to this: Garrison House, whose northern wall contains one of the finest pargettings in the county.

Pargetting, a form of raised plasterwork, may, apart from its ornamental value, have been intended to save exterior walls by breaking up the fall of rain. Garrison House, obviously important because of its position, is thought to have been built as an official meeting place of local worthies. Recent restoration, (1987-8), has brought to light wall paintings in an upstairs room which, like the pargetting, probably date from the early seventeenth century, though a

10. *Garrison House. This photograph was taken during the alterations of 1987-1988.*

Essex County Council

drainpipe displays the date 1678. There is another piece of pargetting, a vine trellis motif, under the eaves of 11-13, High Street, and in an upstairs bedroom of the same house there are also wall paintings. We have already noticed the pargetting on the church which has not survived.[38]

This splendidly crude art was created instinctively by anonymous men who would never have called themselves artists, indeed were probably unable to draw, let alone write. Nor would they have called themselves sculptors, yet it was they who carved the naked girls on the sterns of the ketches described in this chapter, by whose magical powers the boats would weather every storm and their crews return safely. The Elizabethan Settlement proscribed idols, the Commonwealth frowned on undue ornament, yet in the middle of an officially ordered Christianity this pagan decoration throve. The beauty these men created as an essential part of a seaworthy vessel is totally lost to us; happily, some fragments of their work survive as pargetting.

CHAPTER 3

The Rebows and Wivenhoe Park

In the late sixteenth and early seventeenth centuries Colchester received a stream of refugees from the religious persecutions in the Netherlands. They settled, built that part of the town which is still called the Dutch Quarter and became famous for their weaving. Among the earliest refugees was a family called Rebow which, it is thought, came from Ypres.[1] Rebow, incidentally, is pronounced with the accent on the second, not the first syllable.

The Rebows prospered. John Rebow, (1603-79), was one of Colchester's leading citizens. His grandson, Sir Isaac Rebow, (1655-1726), inherited a small fortune which he made into a large one, in particular by investing in the South Sea Bubble and contracting three lucrative, and socially advantageous, marriages. A staunch Whig, he was elected M.P. for Colchester ten times. Sir Isaac's grandson, Isaac Lemyng Rebow, (1705-35), was returned to Parliament unopposed in 1754, as one of the two members for the borough. His fellow M.P. was his father-in-law, Captain Matthew Martin, of Wivenhoe and Alresford.

Captain Martin made his name when, in the service of the East India Company, he commanded the *Marlborough*, a ship of thirty-two guns. As he was sailing from India with a rich cargo, he was, so the story goes, beset and pursued by three French men-of-war. On the third day of the chase he devised a scheme to shake them off. As night fell only a single light appeared on his ship. An impromptu raft was constructed upon which was mounted a mast with a lantern at its peak, so that when it floated this light would show at exactly the same height as the one aboard the *Marlborough*. As the cask was set adrift, the light on the ship was extinguished. The enemy approached the cask mistaking it for the British ship and prepared to fight. Then the cask sank, the French were nonplussed and by this time Captain Martin was far away.[2]

Matthew Martin lived at Wivenhoe House, an imposing mansion which he built near the manor hall, and later at Alresford Hall, which he bought in 1720, two years before the above incident. He died in 1749. His daughter, Mary,

11. *Captain Matthew Martin (?-1749).*

Essex Record Office at Colchester

married Isaac Lemyng Rebow, who in 1734 bought an estate of 140 acres from a rich local family, the Beriffes of Brightlingsea. It is now called Wivenhoe Park.

When their only son, Isaac Martin Rebow, (1731-81), inherited the Park he was about three years old. He went to Eton, then Trinity College, Cambridge, and grew up into an extravert, convivial young man who attended race meetings and owned a yacht.

In 1754, aged twenty-two, he stood for Parliament. His platform was the restoration of Colchester's charter, which had been taken away because of corruption, but as he paid his agent the colossal sum of £1,879 17s 3d it seems that he himself bribed the electorate. When the charter was restored he became an alderman and recorder of the town. John Olnius and Charles Gray were, in fact, elected members for the borough, but Rebow challenged the result and, after the eighteenth century equivalent of a recount, took Gray's seat. He topped the poll in 1761, came second in 1768, was returned unopposed in 1774 and was top again in 1780.

Rebow's political views, if any, are unknown. There is no record of his ever having spoken in the House and he only voted on two or three occasions. George III described him as "a bad attender" and "doubtful in his conduct".[3]

When he was twenty-six he built himself a mansion in Wivenhoe Park. Thomas Reynolds, a London architect, designed him a substantial house of four storeys which was described as "after the style of Chelsea Hospital".[4] It was apparently completed by 1762.

The government, concerned at the poor showing of the military in the rising of 1745, passed the Militia Act of 1757 which required men aged eighteen to forty to serve for three years in any part of the United Kingdom. There were sufficient alarums to keep the Essex Militia in being until the end of the Napoleonic War. The regiment was divided into two battalions. Lieutenant-Colonel Rebow, aged twenty-seven, was put in charge of the East Essex, 528 men disposed in twelve companies, all in primary-coloured uniforms. Established in 1759, it was disbanded on a full-time basis two years later, but continued to meet for training in the summer months. Whether or not Rebow was a good soldier, he was evidently conscientious, for he did not absent himself and took an interest in his troops' appearance.[5]

When he returned to Wivenhoe Park, the new mansion must have been almost ready for its young lord and master. Between 1777 and 1780, Rebow's foreman, Thomas Lupton, employed six men in damming up the stream which flowed through the grounds, to make a couple of lakes, side by side; originally a third was envisaged. Numerous trees were planted. In 1780 alone, the parkland which now surrounded the house was enriched with two hundred spruce firs, and as many larches, together with large numbers of pines, cypresses, cedars and laurels. Rebow's gardeners cultivated apples, plums, cherries, melons, cantaloups, grapes, mulberries and even nectarines and pineapples. In the farmland beyond, wheat, corn, rye, barley and oats were grown on a rotation basis, together with a wide variety of vegetables, including peas, cabbages, turnips, and some, such as broccoli and cauliflowers, which were then almost unknown.[6]

Thus this rich young man dispensed his greatgrandfather's fortune, boldly, but enterprisingly and intelligently, as he explored the world about him. He created Wivenhoe Park as we know it today and in the sublime self-confidence of that sublimely self-confident age became a politician, soldier, judge and farmer without training for any of these professions. He enjoyed every good

12. *Isaac Martin Rebow (1731-1781).*

Essex Record Office at Colchester

thing life had to offer, lived happily ever after and the only thing to ruffle his contentment, so far as we know, was a touch of gout.

He may have thought that his greatest blessing was his wife, Mary, whose high spirits, lively wit, practical ability and deep, unswerving love are revealed in a collection of 116 letters which she wrote to him before and after their marriage.[7]

She was the daughter of Captain Martin's son, Thomas, and by that token Rebow's first cousin. She was reasonably well-educated for those days. She read the newspapers and a few books at least, had a harpsichord and a guitar, was adept with her needle and practical in the kitchen. Though she and her sister, Sarah, were the co-heiresses of Alresford Hall, the Martins were not rich.

The Rebows and Wivenhoe Park

13. *Wivenhoe Park, the engraving made in 1835 by T. Barber.*

Photographed for this book by Bill Collins

The pre-marital letters, written between 1767 and 1772, are full of love for Rebow. Marriage, never mentioned, is everywhere implied, indeed it seems as if the cousins are already engaged:

> *Ye utmost Wish my Heart ever formed, was to be approv'd by You, & if every Thought, Word, or Action of my Life being devoted to You, & You only, can Merit a Continuance of your Regard, I may venture to flatter myself it will last for life, & "That our Loves & Comforts will increase, even as our Days do grow".*[8]

Her date of birth is unknown, but circumstantial evidence suggests that she was a good deal younger than her prospective husband. He died aged forty-nine, so we could expect her to outlive him, which she did – and by a quarter of a century. The first letter is indicative. Rebow, aged thirty-five, is "Dear Sir". The one quoted above is revealing; she casts herself as Desdemona, the dutiful, submissive child bride of the middle-aged Othello, whose attitude towards his wife is largely paternal. I guess that Mary Martin was fifteen to twenty years younger than Isaac Martin Rebow.

35

Yet this hardly accounts for the sometimes almost desperate tone in which she pleads for his love. She seems to be looking for a protector, which is not surprising, since her mother is dead and her father, seen through her eyes, cuts a very poor figure.

Did Rebow return her love? We can assume he was at least fond of her from three simple facts. First, he kept her letters. Second, she was completely candid with him, which means that she knew her confidences would be sympathetically received. Third, she wrote about his mother, who indeed was also her aunt, in a way which shows she had an equal claim on his affections.

Mrs. Rebow evidently saw Mary continually, was on good terms with her and both knew and approved of her love for her son. Family relationships have their ups and downs, as did this one, but we can see Mary's affection for her aunt in the practical assistance she always gave her.

At the end of August, 1770, Mrs. Rebow wanted to move into the "Wivenhoe house", as Mary calls it, which I assume was the former home of Captain Matthew Martin, now owned by her brother and occupied by Mrs. Rebow's gardener, John Groves, and his wife. It seems that her brother had promised her the house, but she did not trust him and insisted on a seven year lease and a rent of £20 per annum to complete the contract. The house itself needed attention, so Mr. Martin's servants set to work that autumn, while Mary was asked to send patterns of material, as new curtains were needed for the "chintz" bed and the windows of her aunt's bedroom.

In the new year Mrs. Rebow was reported as "prodigiously pleas'd" with the alterations and in early March "mightily pleas'd" with the lease. However, the months passed and she did not move. Servants were a perennial problem. One maid disliked the country and could not stand a house with bugs in it; another drank and was likely to set herself alight if she retired to bed with a candle; John and Mary Groves were "ye greatest of all Liars", so a new gardener had to be found; and her butler, who had not gone to church recently, was "a Roman Catholic toad". Mrs. Rebow's complaints about her retainers were endless. However, move she finally did and was soon at work on her new garden, which made her arms and shoulders stiff. In June, 1772, she invited Mary and Sarah to visit her.

Rebow and Mary were married between 18th August, 1772, when the correspondence breaks off, and 3rd July, 1778, when she next writes to him, from Wivenhoe Park, as his wife. All the evidence suggests that the wedding took place almost immediately after the final 1772 letter.

For Rebow was now forty and had been wooed for over five years, and it is likely that his mother also prodded him in the direction of the altar. Why, therefore, should he have waited longer? When he reviewed his troops in 1775 there was a ball for the officers' ladies. Would a ball have been held if the colonel himself had no lady? The letters of 1778 refer to the Rebows' two eldest children, Mary Hester and Sarah Emma, in terms which make it plain they are no longer toddlers. Above all, if Isaac and Mary were not married why are there no more letters?

On 9th April, 1778, the East Essex assembled at Colchester and in early June marched to join twenty or so other battalions at Coxheath, an area of open ground south of Maidstone, where over a thousand men lived under canvas and trained to defend this country from a French invasion. By the end of June, Colonel Rebow had left Wivenhoe to join his battalion and share its somewhat primitive life.[9]

During his absence that summer, Mary Rebow wrote him at least twenty-two letters. The lively young girl who worshipped her cousin was now a lively young wife and mother; but her feelings were unaltered. Before she died, in 1776, Mrs. Rebow must have been pleased with the way things had turned out.

The agony of being parted from him is just as acute. Her first letter mentions a minor complaint, but "... my Spirits are better ... which I chiefly attribute to ye having been with You all Night in imagination..."[10] She tells him everything: of their children and retainers, of their neighbours, of trips to Alresford Hall and Wivenhoe Church, of the work on the park and the estate. To read these letters is to look out from the new, finely-proportioned Georgian windows, on a hot summer's day – "smoking Hot" is how she describes the July weather[11] – and see the deer cropping the parkland established scarcely two decades earlier, the freshly-dug lakes and the kitchen garden beyond, and workmen laying out the carriageways to complete the formal, yet not too formal, pattern of a moderate-sized, eighteenth century, country house and garden. Over to the west, small trading vessels can be seen passing slowly up and down the Colne, which has been artificially straightened to receive them; in other directions lie the farms which support the estate, fields of wheat, barley and rye fringed with trees, and the tiny figures of men with horses and carts, scythes and pitchforks; the placid, perennial English countryside, as it always had been, as it surely always would be.

She confers regularly with an individual called, simply, "the Farmer", and passes on information about the crops, the pigs, the deer, a colt which needs to be exercised and the small beer brewed on the estate. This passage is typical:

Best part of ye Peas were got in o' Friday (viz.) two good Jaggs & a small one, of such Peas, as ye Farmer is sure will not be match'd in this County, this Year; There is one more Jagg, which were not enough to carry before tomorrow, but as we have had no Rain yet, I hope that will be in good time. The Corn all comes on apace, & looks very fine, ye Farmer intends to Cart ye Rye Thursday, or Friday next, if ye Weather permits... [12]

"Jagg" is a dialectal word for a cartload; at this point she discreetly reproduces the farmer's way of speaking. Three days later there is rain, gentle but with an occasional thunderstorm. The harvesting continues throughout July and August. The peas are gathered in, and oats, rye, wheat, barley and turnips.

Every letter mentions the children. At first, Mary, who appears to be at least a year older than Emma, has a swelling in her neck and a "loss of flesh" which needs the attention of the family doctor, Mr. Sterling. She soon recovers. The letter of 7th August opens with a timeless nursery scene:

> *I wish my Dearest Love you cou'd but hear ye <u>ratchet</u> our Girls are making at this Instant; for to be sure it is pretty much in ye stile of Bedlam broke loose; thank God, they are in Charming Health & Spirits . . .* [13]

They have a nurse, and Miss Roberts, evidently a governess, is also in attendance. Bevan, the butler, who in his master's absence has little to do, spends a lot of time taking them for walks, playing to them on his flute and generally keeping them amused. The same letter records a sweetly pretty incident at Wivenhoe on Sunday:

> *. . . I have never told you how our sweet Mary behav'd at Church; You never saw any thing equal to her Joy and astonishment all through; & she was as good as it was pofsible for a Child of that Age to be. She desir'd to have a Book as well as we, out of which she pretended to read, & to Sing Psalms as regularly as pofsible, & when we knelt down brought ye Book to me & desir'd to know if God Almighty was in her book. I told her Yes, upon which she went & knelt on her Hafsock, & says in a low Voice, pray God Blefs my Papa, pray God Blefs my Mama, & pray God blefs Mifs Obberts. I took Nurse with me in Case she shou'd have been a little refractory, that she might have gone with her out of ye Church, but there was not ye least occasion for her, for she did every thing as she was bid . . .*

The Rebows were evidently on good terms with their neighbours. They often exchanged visits with the Corsellises, the Harveys and other notables. Mary Rebow used to go over to Alresford in the whisky, a two-wheeled vehicle rather like a governess cart, which she drove herself, sometimes taking the children with her.

She was obviously fond of tea, cards and conversation. On 14th August, she describes an "all girls together" party:

> *. . . as I was desirous to get Mrs. B. to Alresford o' Tuesday, for reasons before mention'd, I prevail'd on her & Mifs D. to meet us there, & a very <u>Laughable Day</u> we*

had, for Mrs. B. is no Changling, & You know how wicked Mrs. C. can be when she is in ye humor for it, & she chose among many odd things to draw Mrs. B. into an history of ye Courtship & her Wedding Day, & Night, which was so truly ridiculous, & extraordinary, that I thought I shou'd have drop'd with Laughing, but for fear of Accidents, will leave ye particulars till we meet . . . [14]

National and international affairs are referred to when they are felt locally. Thus, on 5th August, she tells her husband that when Mr. Corsellis learned from Lord Rochford that Admiral Keppel had beaten the French navy he paid a guinea to have the church bells rung, while a certain lieutenant chipped in with a hogshead of beer, "& there was nothing but illuminations, Bonfires, firing of Cannon, & all kind of rejoicing . . . " Then, alas, she reads in the newspaper that the rejoicing was premature. However, there is another brace of buck to be killed, the rye is coming in and the wheat promises well . . . [15]

Nor does she concern herself with her husband's military exercises, save to worry whether the privations of life under canvas and the ardour of manoeuvres may not affect his health. She keeps him supplied with toothpicks, sends him medicine, which she entreats him to take, begs him to write oftener and on one occasion discreetly remonstrates:

. . . I am very well pleas'd there is not time for ye Bottle, for as you know my opinion of some of your Party, it relieves some of my fears . . . [16]

Well she might; Rebow's mess, its table primed with partridges and venison from his estate, was famous for its hospitality.

One topic becomes paramount: her overwhelming desire to be with him. The children, too, appear anxious to see Papa again. She begs him to return by 27th August, and since the last pre-marital letter is dated 18th August, 1772, I suspect this is their sixth wedding anniversary. If he cannot be back then she will go to Maidstone where lodgings can be obtained. The last letter, of 19th August, tells us that the Corsellises are off to Coxheath.[17] I assume that Mary Rebow and the children followed almost immediately.

No picture of Mary Rebow survives, but her words, and indeed her omissions, give a vivid impression of her personality. For instance, she hardly ever writes about her clothes, nor personal possessions such as jewellery, nor grand public occasions. Her concern is with other individuals who are close to her, and the scene described is essentially domestic. I find it pleasantly remarkable that the most important lady in the parish displays not a trace of arrogance or condescension.

In the early summer of 1779 the East Essex went to Norfolk and by September was probably at Yarmouth.[17] Rebow evidently spent about three weeks with his troops because he received five more letters from Mary, written between the end of July and the middle of August. They cover familiar ground. The crops, the children, the neighbours, local excursions and the French menace all make a final appearance. The last letter, dated 17th August, says that in the event of a French landing the women, "and all such useless lumber", are to leave Colchester, as indeed some people did flee the town, while Mary and Emma are still romping around, Emma "ten times more wild than ever".[18]

So the correspondence ends and I suppose it was then that Isaac Rebow resigned the command he had held for over twenty yars, probably because of failing health, for by July, 1780, he was very ill, though he was re-elected to Parliament that year. He died on 22nd September, 1781.

Mary Rebow probably enjoyed nine years of married life at Wivenhoe Park. She lived there until she died, in 1804. On 29th March, 1796, her daughter Mary married Francis Slater, of 60th Foot, at St. Margaret's, Westminster. They and their children inherited the estate.

CHAPTER 4

Eighteenth Century

1 The Grandees and The Clergy.

Nicholas Corsellis III succeeded his father to the manor of Layer Marney and his uncle James to the manor of Wivenhoe. He married Elizabeth Taylor, the youngest daughter of a London vintner who kept *The Devil Tavern* at Temple Bar; she was known to later generations of the family as "The Barmaid". Their eldest child, Nicholas Corsellis IV, was born and christened at Wivenhoe.[1]

It is a family tradition that when the South Sea Bubble collapsed, in 1720, one of its victims, Sir Caesar Child, Bart., of Woodbridge, Essex, fled from his creditors to Wivenhoe Hall, where he lived for some time. At any rate, his daughter, Frances, married Nicholas Corsellis IV and in consequence several Corsellises were christened Caesar over the next two or three generations.[2]

Nicholas Corsellis V was born at Wivenhoe and educated at Lincoln College, as were his father and grandfather. He became a justice of the peace, a steward of Felsted School and, doubtless to acquire the livings of Wivenhoe and Layer Marney, which he did in 1771 and 1773 respectively, a clergyman.[3]

He was never rector of Wivenhoe, but he lived at the Hall and the few glimpses we catch of him suggest that he enjoyed the vigorous, outdoor life of an eighteenth century squire. In the eighties he became the secretary of the Colchester Association Against Horse Stealers, and we find him presiding at *The Falcon* over a similar organisation based on Wivenhoe and the adjoining parishes, "for apprehending, prosecuting, and more speedily bringing to justice, Housebreakers, Horse-Stealers, &c. &c".[4]

He appears to have been a domestic tyrant. Mary Rebow records that one evening, in a fit of rage, he turned his butler out of doors and gave half the other servants notice, which threw the Hall into confusion and considerably alarmed his wife. The next day Mrs. Corsellis was to have given Mary Rebow dinner, but since her husband had taken the only servant who could wait at table to the Chelmsford races, she was obliged to walk over to the Park and beg to be excused.[5]

14. and 15.   *Nicholas Corsellis III (c.1661-1728) and Elizabeth Corsellis III, neé Taylor (d. 1734).*

Pencil drawings loaned by Mr. E. H. C. Squire

In the summer of 1789 he fought a duel on Lexden Heath with C. A. Crickitt, the M.P. for Ipswich, the cause of their quarrel being "some severe language" addressed by the clergyman to the politician. Both parties survived: "Mr. Corsellis, after receiving his adversary's shot, fired his pistol in the air;" – magnanimity or contempt? – "on which Mr. Crickitt expressed himself satisfied, and the affair here terminated".[6]

Nicholas Corsellis V kept both his benefices, together worth £320 a year, until he died, aged eighty-two. He was buried in the chancel of St. Mary's.[7]

The Corsellises were the most important family in the parish, but from the 1780s the Rebows reigned at the Park and near the Hall stood Wivenhoe House which, according to a map made in 1734 by a schoolmaster, Hayward Rush, was equally imposing. Three storeys high, it possessed, according to oral tradition, fifty-two windows, and its wrought-iron gates stood where Chapel Street does now, above the present railway cutting. The east elevation of the town which Rush drew on his map suggests it was actually on the west side of the High Street, where the railway bridge is now, commanding an easterly view of the Colne. If this were so it would explain why there was a gap in the High Street at this point up to the time the land was used for the railway line. I assume this is where Mrs. Rebow lived. Very likely it was pulled down soon after she died, or we should know more about it.[8]

Eighteenth Century

We know little of the eighteenth century rectors, but the Rev. Charles Lind shines with the reflected glory of his son, John, (1737-81), who graduated at Balliol College, Oxford, went as a chaplain with an embassy to Constantinople, then left the church and wrote political pamphlets.[9]

Nonconformity struggled on. At times the Presbyterians attracted congregations of 150 or more, a healthy proportion of a population that in 1700 numbered between 650 and 700. At the beginning of the century there were two meeting houses, one for Presbyterians, the other for Baptists; by the end of it both had apparently closed.[10]

2 Dr. Flack, Dr. Tunmer and the Baths.

As the century progressed, so the health of the parish became increasingly organised, and the social standing of the Wivenhoe doctor improved dramatically when Horace Flack opened a public bath in about 1750.[11]

Flack was in Wivenhoe by 1722, for in that year he married Mary King, and had begun to practise medicine by 1729, for in that year he treated some soldiers aboard Captain Robert Martin's smack, *Wivenhoe*, who had been wounded in a fight with smugglers. At his death he owned a shipyard and graving bridge, a house on The Quay with a shop "fit for a surgeon or apothecary", together with adjoining granaries and stable, and part of The Quay itself.[12]

He was not the only available doctor. Samuel Fillto, who had arrived in Wivenhoe by 1722, rented a stable in a storehouse from Nicholas Corsellis IV for £3 a year; in turn, his landlord paid him £1 for shaving his father on a regular basis. However, there was evidently no full-time doctor, for in 1790 the parish sent a young woman called Mary Whitley to a Colchester surgeon to be cured of a "large rotten ulcer" on her left leg.[13]

Horace Flack died in 1756. His assistant, Thomas Tunmer, took over the bath, which flourished under his management. The local tradition, which places it at the foot of Bath Street, is amply confirmed by an indenture which refers to "a tenement used as a public house formerly called the Woolpack and now known by the name of the Ship at Launch, together with the Storehouses, Granary and Warehouse theretofore converted into a Stable and Bath . . . "[14]

In 1757, Tunmer married Anna Flacke, very likely the daughter of his former employer; she died four years later. He then fathered an illegitimate child on Mary Lee, whom he christened Thomas Tunmer Lee. Later, he married a young spinster from Sudbury, Hannah Cole.[15]

By 1755 the Bath was enlarged and an advertisement tells us that it was "furnished in a Genteel Manner, for the Reception of Company", and that a guide and dresses were now provided. The prices charged at Wivenhoe this year, one guinea for a season's bathing or two shillings for an individual dip, (reduced to one shilling the following year), indicate as much.[16]

Dr. Tunmer had several local competitors, including Harwich, where there were at least two baths. So he added a warm bath and two smaller baths for children, distributed handbills and in 1771 produced a pamphlet of forty pages: *A Treatise on Sea-Bathing in General, and Its Effects, both Hot and Cold; particularly of the Nature and Qualities of the Sea-Water at Wivenhoe, near Colchester, in Essex.*[17]

The pamphlet describes the baths. The Great Bath was twelve feet long, eight feet wide and five feet deep, with steps into it on one of the longer sides. It contained nearly 3,590 gallons and was emptied every day. Before the water, pumped out of the Colne, was "let in" either to the Great Bath or the smaller, warm one, it stood for a few hours in a reservoir to let the mud settle.

Wivenhoe never became a full-blown spa, but the town had reason to thank Dr. Tunmer, for it was he who eliminated smallpox. He started to give inoculations in 1762. So while an epidemic of 1726 claimed forty-nine lives, or roughly every fourteenth Wivenhovian, one of 1762-3 killed only thirty-eight, and a third, in 1766-7, twenty-three. After the second epidemic, the parish advertised that it had been free from smallpox for six months, in other words told the public, and in particular tradesmen and sailors, that it was safe to go there. Before long the poor were inoculated free of charge, which incidentally saved the parish the considerable expense of nursing and burying them.[18]

Nor was this the end of Dr. Tunmer's activities, for in 1763 he told the public that he was taking a course in midwifery and for the first year he practised this skill would deliver all the poor women who came to him free of charge.[19]

In 1761 he was joined by John Andrew Robins, a surgeon and apothecary from the Bristol Infirmary, and in 1787 Newton Tills arrived, armed with two years' experience at St. Thomas's Hospital, London. Dr. Robins joined the Colchester Medical Society in 1778, the first Wivenhoe doctor to do so. He was succeeded, in 1797, by Benjamin Smith.[20]

In 1777 Dr. Tunmer retired to Mendlesham and Thomas Munnings, the landlord of *The Anchor*, became Master of the Baths, but we hear little more of them, though as late as 1798 the town was much resorted to for sea bathing", and, as we have seen, Munnings was patronised by the first lady of the parish.[21]

3 John Hall.

William Hall was a master mariner who owned his boat; his wife was Mary Feedham; her uncle Jonathan was a notable benefactor. At about the time of their son, John's, birth, in 1739, the Halls bought a property on Wivenhoe Heath called Sayer's Grove, adjoining the Colchester to Elmstead Road.

Eighteenth Century

16. *John Hall (1738-1797), attributed to Lawrans. c. 1777.*

National Portrait Gallery

William Hall died in 1751, but one of his friends urged that John should be sent to study engraving in London, so at the age of fourteen he was apprenticed to an accomplished craftsman there, Simon Francois Ravenet. The second half of the eighteenth century was a golden age for English engraving and John Hall was among the finest practitioners in the country. He is particularly well known for his versions of pictures by the Anglo-American artist, Benjamin West, among them *Penn's Treaty with the Indians, Cromwell Dissolving the Long Parliament* and *The Battle of the Boyne*. The last-named pleased George III so much that he made Hall his official Historical-Engraver. Hall also produced portraits of such notables as Sheridan, Gibbon, John Gay, Matthew Prior and Dr. Johnson. He married Mary Gilles, who is said to have been a next-door-neighbour of his in Soho, and they had a family of eleven or more. Their third son, George William, became Master of Pembroke College, Oxford, and later Vice-Chancellor of Cambridge University. John Hall died aged fifty-seven and was buried at Paddington.[22]

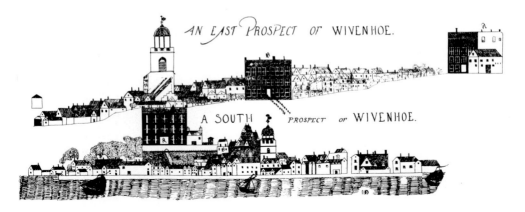

17. *An East Prospect and A South Prospect of Wivenhoe*, two views of the town taken from the map made by Hayward Rush in 1734.

From the drawing made by Harry William Hook in 1929

4 Commerce, Fishing and Boatbuilding.

The economic life of the town was largely bound up with the river because not only was Wivenhoe a centre for fishing and boatbuilding but also a port for Colchester. Throughout this century and the next goods were offloaded into lighters and carried up to the Hythe which Daniel Defoe tells us could be reached only by hoys and small barks.[23]

As the century wore on the river trade grew. The town sent the farm produce of the neighbourhood to London and in turn supplied the neighbourhood with imported fish and coal. It had several coalyards and by the end of the century seven granaries. The enterprising Wivenhovian spread his net widely. In 1790 a warehouse was advertised for sale, "suitable for a corn and coal merchant".[24]

Fishing was very important. Wivenhoe was particularly noted for the fine quality of the soles landed there, and for sprats which, consumed by the Colchester artisans, were known as "weavers' beef". The oysters, which Defoe thought the nicest in England, were of prime importance. They were taken from the mouth of the Colne and then kept in special pits on The Quay before being barrelled and sent, via Colchester, to London and elsewhere. In the eighties, a Wivenhovian, Frederick Nicholson, sold them at his stall in the Colchester High Street. In 1789, he and two fellow citizens, William and Benjamin Sandford, founded an Oyster Protection Society.

This burgeoning industry employed several coopers, also boatbuilders, one of whom launched a hundred oyster smacks in two decades at the turn of the century. Three of Nicholas Corsellis IV's tenants had oyster pits, two near the shipyard, the other below Anchor Hill; they paid their rents in oysters.[25]

Eighteenth Century

One trade, however, perished. In 1713, two hoys brought wool to the town every week from London, returning thence with woven cloth; eventually Wivenhoe succumbed to the demise of the clothmaking industry as, soon after, did Colchester.[26]

The land beyond the town, save for the heath, was, of course, farmland, mainly arable, and besides the trades I have already mentioned, Wivenhovians served each other as blacksmiths, farriers, wheelwrights, carpenters, bricklayers, plumbers, gardeners, butchers, bakers, shoemakers, grocers, millers and brewers. Malting House and Yard mark the site where Clarkson Cardinal pursued this last-named trade until he joined the Army in 1759; he was succeeded by Samuel Winch. In that same year a brewer from Elmstead, John Bawtree, married a Wivenhoe girl. Very likely he acquired The Maltings, because when this property was sold in the year of his death, 1772, it was described as brick-fronted and sashed, which suggests that he had prospered, which indeed he had.[27]

The Hayward Rush map shows a large, boat-shaped indentation in the river bank immediately upstream of The Quay, obviously a dock. It is marked as the home of a shipbuilder called Austin Stanley, (probably the Austin Staples who was a churchwarden in 1739), and Rush tells us that this yard, "has sent many large Vessels to Sea of 30-40 Tuns each". There are other shipyards on the map, which suggests that it was Wivenhoe's only one. Indeed, it was the obvious place, a piece of marshland next to the water and The Quay, but out of everybody's way. Very likely it was where the ships referred to in Chapter 2 were built and it must have been the yard owned by Horace Flack, just a stone's throw away from the baths.

In 1750, this yard was leased to a shipwright called John Iffe. He was succeeded by George Wyatt, who bought and sold ships besides building them. It appears he was kept busy. He built medium-sized cargo vessels, and sloops, (small, general purpose coasters), such as the 62 ton *Mayflower*, in 1757, and the 89 ton *Providence*, in 1772.[28] He doubtless also built smacks.

Boatbuilding fostered two subsidiary trades, ropemaking and sailmaking. Until he died, in 1760, one Michael Harrison pursued both. His apprentice, Joseph Durrell, succeeded him as sailmaker and bequeathed this business to his descendants. Two years later William Popps announced that he had taken over Harrison's rope walk. He died in 1789 and his house, factory and stock were all bought by William Browne who, it seems, had brought his rope-making business over from Nacton, near the River Orwell, in 1770. These premises were at The Cross; almost certainly they included the building called Ropery House. Like Durrell, Browne kept the trade in his family.[29]

Towards the end of the century Wivenhovians began to own cargo boats, other than those they themselves sailed, as a form of investment, albeit a

47

precarious one. In the decade 1786 to 1795 there were thirteen such investors; from 1796 to 1805 there were twenty-eight and the gross tonnage of the vessels owned had almost trebled.[30] The town possessed, as it were, its own floating stock exchange.

5 The Inspector and The Comet.

Wyatt died in 1776; his tomb is close to the south side of the church tower. For a while his widow carried on, but in 1779 decided to lease the yard; it was taken by Moses Game, who built two ships for the Navy, the *Inspector* and the *Comet*.[31]

The *Inspector*, a 97 foot sloop of 311 tons with an armament of sixteen guns, was launched on 29th April, 1782. Sans masts and rigging, she was towed round to Sheerness for fitting out. Her principal task was to convoy merchant ships between London and Scotland, but she spent her first winter shored up in the River Elbe and later ranged as far afield as Belfast Lough.[32] In 1793, she sailed for the Leeward Islands and took part in the capture of St. Lucia and Guadeloupe the following year.

The *Comet*, launched on 11th November, 1783, was heavier, 424 tons, but had only fourteen guns because she was a fireship, destined, when opportunity arose, to be set alight and sent among enemy ships. We know nothing of her first ten years, which means that she was engaged in civilian work, for the Navy often built ships to be commissioned if and when needed.

In 1793 she joined the Navy and Admiral Howe's Mediterranean fleet; in the early summer of 1794 she took a minor part in the first of several victories over the post-revolutionary French navy, known as The Glorious First of June. This boost to public morale was reinforced by another, at Cape St. Vincent; but then came mutiny.

The grievances of the lower deck, particularly as regards poor pay and harsh conditions, all totally justified, had been simmering for years, yet the rising at Spithead, in the spring of 1797, was a remarkably civilised affair and when the Admiralty realised it was not the beginning of a national revolution, made peace. However, on 12th May a more serious mutiny erupted at The Nore, a Naval anchorage to the north west of Sheerness. At first only a few ships were involved, but on 30th May, Admiral Adam Duncan, who was about to fight the Dutch, was deserted by nearly all his North Sea Fleet, including the *Inspector* and the *Comet*.

A glance at the captains' logs of these two vessels is instructive.[33]

Charles Locke, commanding the *Inspector*, seems to have been a literal-minded, unimaginative captain. He records floggings and sending the jolly boat to impress men. Well might the crew of such a man rebel. We can sniff insurrection on 22nd May, when the sailors refused their wine, which they

Eighteenth Century

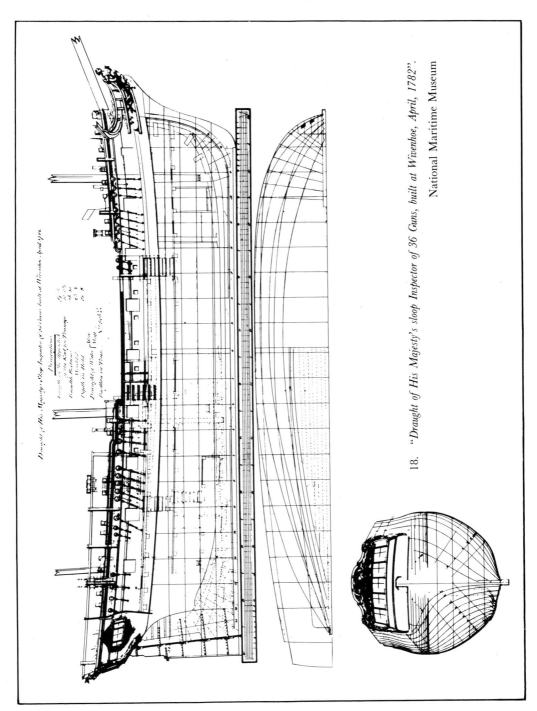

18. "*Draught of His Majesty's sloop Inspector of 36 Guns, built at Wivenhoe, April, 1782*". National Maritime Museum

declared was bad. The next day Captain Locke awarded one, William Ramsay, two dozen lashes for mutinous conduct. When he was informed that the crew as a whole intended to mutiny he put four of the ringleaders aboard another ship. Six days later came the explosion:

> ... at 2 (our) people Mutinied & hoisted Red Flag at T.F.G. (top fore gallant) mast Head & took command of the Ship from Captain & Officers when two Delegates came on board...

and the next day the *Inspector* was at The Nore. Delegates were what we now call trade union leaders. Captain Locke records impersonally that the captain, himself, was confined to his cabin where he presumably remained throughout the mutiny.

The captain of the *Comet*, Henry Duncan, appears to have been altogether more intelligent and humane. His log, innocent of floggings, is written in a flowing hand quite unlike the stiff copperplates of his brother captains. This is what he had to say about the afternoon of 29th May:

> Light Airs and Fair at one Fired a Salute of 17 Guns in Commemoration of King Charles's restoration to the Crown ... at 4 (p.m.) a Gang of Ruffians came on Board and in authoritative manner ordered the Ships Company to take Charge of the Ship and to carry her round to the Nore – as they meant to take their own Ships viz H M Ships Nassau, Standard, Lion & Bellingueux they termed themselves Delegates and behaved with great Insolence to the Officers threatening to hang Mr. Williams, (the pilot), if he hesitated in getting the Ship under weigh – consequence and for the Safety of the Ships Company to comply with their unreasonable demands – the Ships Company conforming in every Respect to mine and the rest of the officers Commands at 7 weighed and Sailed in a Company with the above mentioned Mutinous Ships...

Though Captain Duncan realised immediately that he must yield to the delegates, he was nevertheless able to take the initiative. The mutineers kept their own log for the *Comet*, from which we learn that when she sailed, Captain Duncan called the hands aft, talked to them and said that if they so wished he and his officers would take the ship round to The Nore. The ship's company, in turn, hoped that the officers were not under the impression they were to be given orders by the crew. On these amicable terms the *Comet* sailed with the other ships to join those already at The Nore.

Captain Duncan describes The Nore anchorage, thick with vessels, as looking like a wood. It was so crowded, indeed, that the two Wivenhoe vessels touched each other; the *Inspector* ran across the *Comet* and carried away a topsail yard arm. For a few days the Thames was blockaded and no merchant ships allowed to pass up and down, an attempt to deprive London of goods. The *Comet* was one of the ships used to make the blocking line and the *Inspector* one of those used to patrol it.

By 11th June it seemed as if the mutiny was coming to an end, for the Admiralty had imposed a blockade of its own, to starve the fleet into submission, and the ships seemed uncertain whether to fly the red flag of insurrection or the white ensign of obedience. Two days later it was all over. The *Inspector* served in the English Channel, the West Indies and the North Sea. In 1800 she went to the Baltic and in 1810 was sold.[34]

On 7th July, 1800, a small British fleet sailed into Dunkirk Road, intending to capture or destroy four French frigates. It caught one and in the action expended four fireships, including the *Comet*.

6 Smuggling.

Moses Game's civil commissions included the 70 ton sloop *Edward*, launched in 1783, and doubtless many others, for he had another yard at East Donyland. However, either he overreached himself or the Navy was tardy in paying him, for in March, 1784, he was bankrupt. Again, the shipyard was to let. We know that three smacks, of fifteen, seven and six tons, were built there, but from 1789 to 1800 the record is bare. However, in September, 1787, the 6 ton smack *Liberty*, built at East Donyland and owned by Moses Game, now described as a shipbuilder of Rowhedge, was seized by the Customs at Harwich and "cut in pieces".[35]

In other words, the *Liberty* had been caught with contraband aboard her. Smuggling, rife from the mid-seventeenth century, grew to an open scandal in the eighteenth. The high tariff rates were generally and fiercely resented. Since Parliament itself was corrupt the public felt no obligation to be honest and many people were too poor to mind the risk of death or transportation. Most of the contraband came from France to the South Coast, but large quantities of hollands, (gin made in the Low Countries), and other spirits, tobacco, tea, silk and soap, were brought to Essex. The goods were generally landed on open beaches, at such places as Clacton, Frinton and Great Holland, so the Wivenhovians who participated must, for the most part, have contributed boats, manpower and an expert knowledge of the coast.

Yet smuggling was firmly established at Wivenhoe. A case in the Quarter Sessions for 1713 puts this beyond doubt. Information was received by the excisemen that smuggled brandy was hidden in a certain house, but when they took a constable to help them find it, he bawled out, "Take care of the pigs in your cherry gardens", evidently a code signal to the occupiers and he swore that if his hands were not tied, i.e., if he were not a constable, he would knock one of the excisemen's brains out.[36]

At first the public and even public officers sided with the smugglers, while the authorities, badly equipped and informed, were practically impotent. As the century wore on the excisemen grew in number, and their vessels were larger and better armed, while ashore they could count on military support. Nevertheless, they were frequently outfought and constantly outwitted by the smugglers who were also well armed and organised, both on land and sea.

By 1720, Wivenhoe had become the station for the local revenue cutter and remained such until revenue cutters were discontinued in the following century. Until 1730 there was only one to patrol the entire Essex coast. She was commanded by Captain Robert Martin of East Donyland, already noticed in Section 2 of this chapter, who operated under a contract with the local authorities.[37]

He was not unsuccessful, *vide* this report in the *Ipswich Journal* of 31st March, 1739:

> *London, Mar. 24. Yesterday nine Smugglers were brought under a strong Guard to the Custom-House that were taken in a Cutter with Tea, hovering off the Coast by Capt. Martin, Commander of the Custom-house Sloop belonging to Wivenhoe in Essex, after a desperate Engagement wherein the Capt. and several of his Men were knock'd down and wounded.*

Smuggled goods were auctioned, as in 1743 when 5,900 gallons of neat old Bourdeaux and Nantes brandy were sold by inch of candle to the highest bidder.[38] The captured vessels were either burnt or sawn in pieces.

When he died, in 1763, Captain Martin was succeeded by the commander of his 73 ton *Princess Mary*, Captain Daniel Harvey of Wivenhoe. In the latter part of the century six cutters, all named *Repulse*, and all, it is believed, owned by Captain Harvey, were employed in succession on the Colchester station. The first, built in 1774, had a crew of eleven, the second twenty-four and the third forty-two. On 1st August, 1778, Mary Rebow took tea with Captain Harvey. She reported to her husband that, "He seems very well in Health, but very low & dejected, & I don't find has the least Prospect of getting either his Men or his Vessel . . . " He was presumably dejected at losing his third *Repulse*, which had run aground off the French coast in May, and his men, who were in a Calais gaol, the British and French being at war. However, the crew was returned to Brightlingsea and the ship, having been retaken by an English vessel, was repurchased by her former owner.[39]

The fourth *Repulse*, built either in 1778 or 1779, was the largest of all the forty-four cutters employed on the Colchester station. She had a tonnage of 210, a crew of fifty men and a boy, and her armament comprised sixteen carriage and twelve swivel guns. In October, 1780, Captain Harvey advertised for seamen or landsmen, guaranteeing them immunity from impressment.[40]

The last two revenue cutters were smaller. The fifth, built in 1783, was 143 tons and the sixth 123. In 1789, Harvey was succeeded by Captain George Munnings, who recaptured an English brig from French privateers in 1793.

With the Napoleonic Wars smuggling passed through a watershed. While they lasted it virtually ceased. Thereafter, when the laws were tightened up, excisemen better organised and the tariffs eventually lowered, it became increasingly sporadic and clandestine. Ingenious hiding places were devised on ships and ashore, and there were skirmishes with officials, but what had been a way of life was now more of a game.

7 Education.

Male Wivenhovians were generally brought up to their fathers' professions and that was all the learning many of them received. However, there was also, though tenuously, some formal education. A charity school was opened in 1718; six years later it had ten boys and five girls. It was still open in 1774. Very likely it was here that Hayward Rush, the schoolmaster who drew the 1734 map, taught, and William Powell, who died in 1787. In 1773, Richard Wenham publicly thanked "those gentlemen and others" who had supported him and announced that he taught boys "Writing, in all its Hands, Arithmetic Vulgar and Decimal, Algebra, Geometry, Mensuration, Surveying, Gauging, Dialling, and other useful Branches of Mathematics, and Merchant-Accompts, or the true Italian Method of Book-Keeping", a fair way of introducing the more intelligent young to shopkeeping and shipbuilding.[41]

There were also private girls' schools in the town. In 1763, Mrs. Tunmer, the doctor's wife, announced that she taught young ladies needlework, and took the greatest care of their behaviour and morals. In the following year Mrs. Alefounder came from Colchester to start a boarding school whose curriculum included needlework, music, dancing and writing. In 1768, Mrs. Field arrived to take up the same task and in 1782 Powell's boarding school for young ladies was advertised, the latter charging £14 4s 0d per annum, including washing. It is not known how well, or for how long, these establishments survived. They evidently depended on clients from outside Wivenhoe and presumably were connected with Dr. Tunmer's efforts to turn the town into a spa and raise its social status.[42]

8 Sporting and Social.

We know that as this century opened, Wivenhoe had two ale-houses. It probably had several, places differing little from private houses, save that hanging signs proclaimed that their owners sold beer, generally home-brewed, to their neighbours. As time goes on, so we can fill in the picture and colour it a little.

Our first source is a ledger recording the contributions made by Wivenhovians, through its overseers, to the poor.[43]

In 1722, when the ledger opens, it records that one, Lamb, paid money in respect of "Kings New House", and three years later this is amended to "Thomas Lamb for Kings Arms". *The King's Arms* comes and goes until 1756 when Lamb is paying for "land at Kings Arms" as do his successors in title, which suggests that the inn closed but the name remained.

In 1726, the ledger mentions one, Scrambler, who was at *The Swan*, and 1729 tells us that Chris Harvey was at *The Anchor*. There was a sale of wood from a stranded ship at *The Blue Anchor* in 1758 and another sale eight years later at *The Anchor*, surely the building which to this day fronts Anchor Hill and The Quay.[44] In 1732 John Howes kept *The Black Boy*. Charles II was given this nickname because of his swarthy appearance and inns with this title tend to date from the mid-seventeenth century. So may this one.

In 1735 and 1736, Edward Dowser or Douser is at *The Lamb*; I can find no other reference to this ale-house. In 1741 Henry Everitt is at *The Falcon* which, of course, was now well over a century old. In 1752 we see that Mrs. Howse kept *The Sun*, which was situated near *The Black Boy* off Brook Street. In 1767, Jonathan Barker was at *The Grapes*, the only reference to such an inn: commonsense suggests a connection between the name and the pargetting under the eaves of H. A. Dennis, the bakery in the High Street; if so, it had been established in the previous century. Did it sell wine?

The second source is Nicholas Corsellis IV's rent book. In 1728 Mary Flack was renting "1/2 Woolpack" from him. The rent book also refers to *The Baytree*, *The Black Horse* and *The Cross Keys*. The manorial fief extended beyond Wivenhoe and all three ale-houses may not have belonged to the parish. However, a deed indicates that *The Cross Keys Tavern* belonged to the town.[45]

A third source of information is the ale-house recognisances, though few have survived before 1769, when they were formally and completely listed. One for 1764 names *The Rose and Crown*.[46]

The Register of Ale-House Recognizances for 1769 lists eight inns: *The Sun, Anchor, Rose and Crown, Falcon, Swan, Union Flag, Woolpack* and *Black Boy*. The Act of Union was passed in 1707 and The Union Jack devised soon after, which suggests that this inn opened early in the eighteenth century. In 1772, *The Register* includes, for the first time, *The Horse and Groom*, which was the successor to *The King's Arms*. Evidently, it had ceased to be a public house for sixteen years or so and was now reopened and renamed. The title indicates that public houses were, among other things, points of departure. In 1782, *The Woolpack* was renamed *The Ship at Launch*. A sign of the times; the clothmaking trade had now failed but in that year *The Inspector* was launched and very likely *The Comet* was already in frame.[47]

These were the centres of the community's sporting and social life. In 1766, the proprietor of *The Falcon*, Philip Lay, opened a bowling green. There was cockfighting at *The Anchor* in 1781. When a cricket match was held in July, 1771, dinner was provided for the players at *The Falcon* and *The Sun*, and *The Sun* was host to another match the following year. Incidentally, the first recorded cricket match at Wivenhoe was played on Wednesday, 3rd July, 1765, or at any rate it was if twenty-two men willing to subscribe five shillings and threepence apiece were found. Each member of the winning team received a wig bought out of the profits, so the game was evidently not played by the public at large. The 1771 match was played for hats and there was another attraction: a race for women. The winner would receive a holland smock, the runner-up a silk handkerchief. A match in 1772 was for hats, wigs or waistcoats, according to the fancy of the players. Thomas Corder, who at different times was proprietor of *The Falcon, The Sun* and, briefly, in 1764, *The Backus*, wherever that might have been, was also a brewer and sold beer by auction at this public house, besides farm animals and implements.[48]

During the second half of the century sales of boats and other property were frequently held at public houses, especially at *The Anchor, The Falcon*, and *The Rose and Crown*, and the public might pick up sale catalogues from these places. Financial matters were settled there, as when, in 1771, the creditors of the late George Wayland were bidden to meet at *The Rose and Crown* to receive a final dividend on his effects. The Wivenhoe Association, formed to make a stand against theft, held its annual meetings at *The Rose and Crown* and *The Falcon*.[49]

It is possible that when the Phoenix Company visited Wivenhoe to perform Sheridan's *School for Scandal*, on 9th July, 1798, that the venue for an extemporised theatre was a public house. However, commonsense suggests that since the event was sponsored by the freemasons attached to *The Angel Inn*, Colchester, and does not mention tickets, or indeed a venue, this was a private evening, perhaps under the aegis of the Rev. Nicholas Corsellis V at Wivenhoe Hall.[50]

The end of the century saw the rise of sport on the water. In 1783 there was a race for smacks in the Blackwater and a few months later another, off Mersea Island, with rules sufficiently detailed and precise to suggest that it was not the first of its kind. The course was from a buoy set between West Mersea Church and the Bradwell shore, to another whose position would be determined by the weather. Five boats entered, all fishing smacks, because this was before yachting as a hobby had developed generally. Wivenhoe entered *The Two Sisters*, the *William and Ann*, and the *Phoenix*, commanded respectively by George Wheatley, William Cole and Frederick Nicholson. A community described as "Hedg-row" entered the *Mayflower* and the *Tartar*. The *Mayflower* won and received a silver cup; the *Two Sisters* came second and received a suit of colours.[51]

There were similar races in 1782, 1786, 1787, 1792 and 1793, for smacks of ten tons and under. The course was from the Guard Boat opposite Brightlingsea Creek to the Wallet Buoy of the Spitway and back again. Entries had to be made at *The Rose and Crown*, which suggests that the races were organised by Wivenhoe.[52]

Fishing smacks were not originally designed for speed, but eventually the need to get down river to where the shoal had been sighted before anyone else became of prime importance and, as we have seen, there was sometimes a need to outsail the revenue cutters. Now the hard-won skills of the Colne fishermen were put to another use, for these races were the beginning of the local regattas, and would very soon be turned to profit as well, in the service of the rich men who owned the big yachts.

The leisure activities of the town also included an annual fair. The first reference I can find is in the *Ipswich Journal* for 1753, when we are told that it is held on St. Bartholomew's Day, 24th August, but would in that and subsequent years be held on 5th September; evidently, it was already well established.[53]

As in the seventeenth century the town had been disturbed by the Civil War and fears of a Dutch invasion, so the French posed a threat during the last two decades of the eighteenth. Would they come? If so, when and where? As we have seen, an East Coast attack was sufficiently probable to send the timider spirits scuttling out of Colchester in 1779, and Wivenhoe was doubtless relieved to provide winter quarters for a detachment of militia, the Pembrokeshire, over 1789-91.[54]

In May, 1781, the sound of heavy firing at sea was heard. However, the West Essex Militia, sister battalion to the East Essex whose history I have outlined in Chapter 3, was camped at Fingringhoe. It was given six twelve-pounder guns. Three were to be stationed in Beacon Field, on the south bank of the river, and three at Ballast Quay on the north. If the French appeared, their vessels would be raked from both sides of the Colne and if they landed the guns were to be spiked and the soldiers retreat in good order. On the Wivenhoe side of the river they must "obstinately dispute" the high ground.[55]

Such were the general's orders, but a suggestion made to me by Mr. C. M. J. Dunn leads me to think they may have been varied a little. Walk half a mile along the river wall downstream of the town and you come to an indentation.

Eighteenth Century

For no apparent reason the wall swerves inland to a spot now marked by a wooden seat. Mr. Dunn thinks that this might mark the site of a large gun, stationed to command a reach of the river and be as near to it as the Fingringhoe guns were on the other side. Then, when the downstream river wall was constructed, alongside the river, it was naturally taken in a little to include the existing earthen parapet.

When *The Rose and Crown* public house was built it was probably on land formerly belonging to Garrison House. If so, Garrison House was by now no longer one of the grander buildings in the town and could therefore be used to billet soldiers, perhaps the men of the West Essex who manned the three twelve-pounders on the Wivenhoe side of the river. Hence, surely, its name. The oral tradition that it was indeed used for this purpose is recorded in a book called *In Essex*, published in 1949. Far more credibly, *The Cottages of England*, published in 1929, states unequivocally that this was the former River Police Barracks, though whether the author is referring to the previous century or to Captain Daniel Harvey, does not appear.[56]

If a Wivenhovian of today were transported to the end of the eighteenth century much of the old town would be instantly recognisable, for the age had left its typical mark upon it.

When William Popps's ropery was auctioned in 1789 his house was described as "new-bricked".[57] This means that the original timber frame had been lately covered with what is called a Georgian facade, to make the building stronger, warmer and more imposing. This transmogrification was a sign of at least moderate wealth and since Wivenhoe has several such buildings we can assume that some of her citizens were reasonably well off.

As the century closed, the town included a fair cross-section of society. There were the grand people at the Park and the Hall; there were those who lived in houses with brick facades, tradesmen and schoolteachers; and there were the farmers and fishermen who lived in timber-framed cottages.

And there were the paupers, widows, elderly, chronically sick and orphans of the town, for which the parish, through the Vestry, now charged everybody a regular rate, as it was legally entitled to do. In 1726, a cottage on the Colchester Road, a single-storey building which it is thought dates from about 1700, was formally dedicated to the poor by Nicholas Corsellis III. By the mid-eighteenth century this was no longer adequate, so the Vestry borrowed £100 to build a workhouse. This was a place where the able-bodied poor could be given employment, generally spinning, which was good for their morale and helped to defray the running costs. On 9th October, 1750, the Vestry decided to levy a special rate of one shilling in the pound to pay back the loan and raise more capital.[58]

Mrs. Rebow, the chatelaine of Wivenhoe Park during her son's minority, was displeased. First she gave the overseers 13/4d and then they demanded another 16/-. So she consulted her solicitor, who advised her to pay. His opinion tells us that the money was "for the erecting and finishing of a Work House", though in fact the existing poor house was adapted, by adding another two storeys and a hipped roof. If this building was finished, what was erected? The answer would appear to be the house next door, which was where the master of the workhouse lived and where the bread was baked for the inmates.[59]

19. *The former Workhouse and, in the foreground, the former Master's house, now 14-17, Colchester Road.*

Photograph by Sue Murray, L.R.P.S., December, 1988

There was now accommodation for twenty people or so, of all ages, some of whom worked on the ground floor and all of whom slept on the floor above. If current practice was followed, single males would have slept at one end, single females at the other and families in between. From 1755 onwards the rent book already referred to in this section included pages of expenses relating to the workhouse, which suggests that it opened in that year, especially as the first few entries refer to the purchase and installation of a copper, in which the clothes of the inmates were laundered, a vital piece of equipment.[60]

Eighteenth Century

Here are some items from a bill run up between Easter and Midsummer, 1717:

		£ s d
April 15	For a pint of wine for old Brown	7
	For Gin and ale at his Death and burial	2 6
18	For 1 1/2 Yrds of Baise to wrap him in	3 –
	For the black Cloth	1 –
	For the Coffin	5 9
	For a Chaldron of Coals	1 8 –
	For a Load of Wood	5 –
	For mendg the workhouse bellows	8
23	To the Parson & Clark for the burial of Brown	5 6
26	For the boy Heaths Indentures	5 –
	For cloathing the boy Heath	1 10 –
May 12	For a new Gown and Mantle for Dame Knock	8 –
	For a new shift for her the making only	5
16	For cloathing the Girl Lock & Expences	1 1 10
June 18	For 18 oz of worsted & 4 oz of yarn	3 8
	For an Earthen Dish a Ladle & 2 Chamber pots	9

The inmates were treated humanely, even kindly. It is pleasant to record that on one occasion 6d was spent on "Children at the Fair".[61]

Not everyone who received assistance lived in the workhouse. In 1759, for instance, it is recorded that there were sixteen inmates and another twelve who were supported, though "out of the workhouse". Sometimes the parish paid the rents of the poor.

People continually came and went. Boys, for instance, were put into indentures, as apprentices, and there were odd cases of temporary poverty, as in 1759 when the workhouse took in Smith's wife and Gozard's family because these two gentlemen were serving with the militia.

Thus it continued into the new century, until legislation set up centralised workhouses for every hundred and Wivenhoe was governed in these matters by The Lexden and Winstree Guardians for the Poor. Now those who could not fend for themselves had to leave the town altogether, an obviously less pleasant arrangement. The former workhouse was divided up into three separate dwellings and thus remained until 1983 when it was bought by Mr. and Mrs. Peter Hill, who converted it into a single house.

The poor were also assisted by benefactions. Jonathan Feedham, a sailor, in his will of 1717, left £50 to buy land, the profits of which should be distributed on New Year's Day among poor sailors or their widows. Thomas Goodwin, a former rector, left a yearly payment of fifty shillings. Cox's Charity produced £2, and those of Potter and Kimpton £2 and £10 respectively.[62]

This century also saw the appearance of friendly societies, the first attempts to insure the sick and unemployed. There were two in 1795 and four in 1803.[63]

Altogether, it was far pleasanter to be poor in the eighteenth than in the nineteenth century. Moreover, those without great means had one benefit denied to later Wivenhovians. Beyond *The Flag* were some 540 acres of open land known as Wivenhoe Heath, which might be used by all. Here, for instance, a poor widow might graze a cow. In 1797 this land was enclosed and turned over to farming; it was the end of an era.

20. *A view of Wivenhoe Heath, taken from the map of Wivenhoe made in 1734 by Hayward Rush.*
From the drawing made by Harry William Hook in 1929

CHAPTER 5

Francis Slater and John Gurdon

Francis Slater, (1771-1845), the son of Richard Slater of Chesterfield, began his army career in a hard school. The Royal American Regiment, (60th Foot), raised in that country, principally from Swiss and German settlers, was later joined by deserters from other units, and criminals, including those who had become soldiers as an alternative to being hanged. In 1787 it recruited two more battalions and Slater, a seventeen-year-old ensign, accompanied it to the West Indies. In 1789 he was a lieutenant, in 1792 a captain; he commanded his regiment's grenadiers when Martinique was taken and, in 1794, St. Lucia and Guadeloupe. During this last action he was severely wounded in both thighs and invalided back to England.[1]

His marriage to Mary Hester Rebow in 1796 was of practical advantage to both parties. The groom obtained an estate and a large private income, and through them a far higher social rank. Within two months of the wedding he had hyphenated his wife's surname to his own and assumed her coat-of-arms, and in the following February exchanged the 60th Foot for the 2nd Life Guards where his career continued to prosper; in 1807 he became a lieutenant-colonel, in 1812 a major-general.

The estate now had a man in charge of it, one well used to command. Soon there were children. The first child, a boy, died in infancy; the second, Mary Emma, lived only seven years, but finally another daughter appeared, Mary Martin, to provide the estate with an heiress. When she was seven years old a struggling young artist from East Bergholt painted her portrait.

John Constable, a miller's son, grew up just the other side of the Suffolk border, attending schools at Lavenham and Dedham, where his burgeoning talent was noticed and encouraged. In 1799 he joined the Royal Academy as a pupil and three years later started to exhibit there. It was a difficult life, but his family was sympathetic. Aged thirty-five, he had now embarked on his long courtship of Maria Bicknell, whom he had known since she was a child. The

61

21. *General Francis Slater-Rebow (1771-1845).*

Essex Record Office at Colchester

lady was willing but her parents opposed the match, as did her maternal grandfather, Dr. Rhudde, the wealthy rector of East Bergholt. Fearing she might be cut out of the old gentleman's will, Mr. Bicknell forbade her to marry Constable.[2]

However, the lovers corresponded, and on 6th September, 1812, Constable told Maria that he was going to stay at Wivenhoe Park for a few days, to paint his small daughter, and later perhaps General and Mrs. Rebow.[3] He stayed there until 22nd September.

In November, Rebow was put in charge of the Household Brigade, which he accompanied to Lisbon, and there set about his duties so energetically that his own colonel and other officers threatened to resign. So he was given some leave, but returned to the Iberian Peninsula and stayed there until 1816.[4]

At the end of July, 1816, Constable paid another visit to Wivenhoe Park. On 17th August he called again and four days later wrote to Maria from East Bergholt:

My dearest Love,

I returned from my very pleasant visit at General Rebow's on Monday...

The General and Mrs. Rebow are determined to be of some service to me and at any rate their attentions are agreeable and add much to all that is respectable. I am going there again on Monday and shall stay a week there in all probability – do be so kind as to let me hear from you before you go to Mr. Lambert's.

I am going to paint two small landscapes for the General, views one in the park of the house & a beautifull wood and peice of water, and another scene in a wood with a beautifull little fishing house, where the young lady (who is the heroine of all these scenes) goes occasionally to angle.

They wish me to take my own time about them – but he will pay me for them when I please, as he tells me he understands from old Driffeild that we may soon want a little ready money. Both the General and his good lady are well acquainted with our history and they both hope to see us there <u>together</u>...

I am getting on as well as I can with my own pictures but these little things of the General's rather interrupt them and I am afraid will detain me here a week or two longer than I could have hoped... [5]

The two little things of the General's were *Wivenhoe Park, Essex, the seat of Major-General Rebow*, which was exhibited the following year at Somerset House and is now in the National Gallery of Art, Washington, and *The Quarters, Alresford Hall, near Wivenhoe*, which is in the National Gallery of Victoria, Melbourne.

On 26th August, Constable returned to Wivenhoe Park and on 30th wrote to Maria. His impending marriage was now a fact:

... I have been here since Monday and am as happy as I can be away from you – nothing can exceed the kindness of the General and his Lady – they make me indeed <u>quite at home</u>. They often talk of you, because they know it will please me, and I am sure they will show you the same attentions they do me. I feel entirely comfortable with them, because I know them to be sincere people – and though of family and in the highest degree refined, they are not at all people of the world, in the common acceptance of the word...

I am writing this in a most magnificent drawing room looking over Colchester and a beautifull evening – and hourly attended by a little dear girl whom I once painted – she has just put me down a wafer with "There Mr. Constable – did you not say a black one?"

This house is full of dogs, and some of them are very great beauties. I live in the park and Mrs. Rebow says I am very unsociable. We are now going a walk with the little lady. Adieu.

J. C. [6]

The Wivenhoe commission was finished on 17th September. On his return to East Bergholt, Constable wrote to Maria to say that, "We shall meet in a few days, to part no more for ever ... " They were married on 2nd October.[7]

The next few years of Constable's life were probably his happiest. His first child, John, was born in 1817, followed by other children to complete a large family. Many of his famous landscapes date from this time, including the most famous of them all, *The Haywain*.

Two drawings indicate that the Constables must have visited General Rebow in August, 1817, and Constable may have returned on his own two years later, for in a letter to The Rev. John Fisher, dated 13th August, 1819, he says: "I am under an engagement to paint the portraits of General and Mrs. Rebow at Wivenhoe Park about this time. I have written to him to know if it is still his wish & when I have his answer you shall hear from me again".[8] This is the letter the General wrote to Constable on 28th August:

My dear Sir,
I really am vexed that it has not been in my power to fix a time for having the pleasure of seeing you here, but our arrangements have been so perverse as to defy every attempt of doing so, & I have therefore allowed your letter to remain unacknowledged all this time.

First now however let me thank you very sincerely for it, offering at the same time our warmest congratulations upon Mrs. Constable's safety & your little girl's well doing, both I conceive from what you say may be now about going to Putney – & if in your Bachelor state you would come to us for a few days it would give us great pleasure.

I cannot however absolutely promise that it will be in our power to set to you, as our house is, & will be until we go from hence on the 15th September quite full – but if you come prepared we can see about it – I think we should prefer a group in one picture in preference to portraits.

If you will let us hear from you in reply we can receive you at any time. Accept our united good wishes & regards & believe me,
My dear Sir, very faithfully yours

F. S. Rebow[9]

No portraits of the General and his lady by Constable have survived and it would seem, for lack of evidence, that this visit was never made. In the autumn of that year Constable became an associate of the Royal Academy and he continued to exhibit there until his death in 1837, but it was many years after that before his work was generally admired. To many of his contemporaries the merits of his lyrical, informal, almost impressionistic style were not apparent. I think it is possible to infer from the above letter that the General valued him as a man rather than an artist.

22. *John Constable (1776-1837), by R. R. Reinagle, c. 1798.*

The Story of Wivenhoe

23. and 24. Two sketches by John Constable. Top: Wivenhoe Park, 29th August, 1817.
Bottom: Wivenhoe Park, 27th July, 1816.

Victoria and Albert Museum

Rebow was evidently sociable and public-spirited. John Hanson of Great Bromley Hall recalls in his diary that towards the end of the eighteenth century a dining club met every Saturday at the King's Head, Colchester, whose members included Colonel Bullock of Faulkbourne Hall, Colonel Rigby of Mistley Hall, John Round, Nicholas Corsellis V and General Rebow. In 1798 Hanson raised and commanded a troop called the Tendring Volunteer Cavalry. His first cornet was Frederick Nassau of St. Osyth's Priory, his second General Rebow.[10]

The General returned from the Peninsular War with some cork trees which he planted beside the lawn and settled down to spend the rest of his life as a local grandee. He became a magistrate and deputy lieutenant of the county, and took an interest in good causes both national and domestic. He was involved in the railway line to Harwich and gave £100 towards the new Colchester Town Hall which opened in 1845.[11]

On 6th July, 1857, there was a ploughing competition at Wivenhoe Park. Afterwards, beer and prizes were presented inside the house. Then everyone drank the general's health in a glass of "sound October" with three times three. The *Essex Standard* approved; it was reminded of former times when an English gentleman lived among his tenants and dependants, and made it one of his chief delights to promote their welfare and happiness by acts of judicious benevolence:

> *... Too much cannot be said of this and other instances of regard for the poor of his neighbourhood, which have been exhibited by General Rebow; they cannot fail to secure, as they deserve, the respect of his neighbours, and the blessings of the humble recipients of his bounty.*[12]

This contrasts with an incident the previous summer. The General had discharged one of his bailiffs, Samuel Goymer, and refused to give him a reference. Goymer, aged about forty and with a family, soon received an order to go into the workhouse. While in his cups at *The Bucks Horns*, Colchester, he threatened to shoot the General, who was told of this and immediately charged him. However, as the prisoner was penitent, so the General was lenient:

> *... To assure the prisoner he was not afraid of him, (for said the General, I never was afraid of any man in my life yet, thank God) ... I will not press the charge against him".* The prisoner said the General might rest satisfied for he never intended harming him.
> *The General: If you were to attempt it, I would shoot you, for I am always prepared for you.*[13]

On another occasion a tenant of the General's told him of two men who had ferreted for rabbits on his land; they received six weeks hard labour in the House of Correction.[14]

There was also the case of the church rate. One of the General's last public appearances was as churchwarden of St. Mary's, on 9th October, 1840, when it was known that the Dissenters were spoiling for a fight.

Boldly, the Dissenters indicated their faith and their independence by walking into the church with their hats on their heads. Then they challenged the church rate, money levied from them but used to pay for the upkeep of St. Mary's. The rector's churchwarden moved, and the General seconded, a motion that a rate of 6d in the pound be levied. The Dissenters moved an amendment, the General demanded a poll and the rector held one. 114 people voted for the church rate, 63 against. Again, the *Essex Standard* approved:

> *We congratulate the Churchmen of Wivenhoe on their successful resistance of this iniquitous attack upon the Church... We are glad to see General Rebow coming forward on this occasion to give the support of his vote and the influence of his example to the cause of this the first – best institution of the country. The violence of the enemies of the Church will, we trust, have the effect of uniting more closely all supporters of order, good government, and religion. Some of these may call themselves Whigs, as we believe the worthy General does (and the Rector too); but in spite of themselves, every day they become more and more Conservative. For several years there has been going on – it is progressing still – a sifting of political creeds, a trial of the spirits of men; and each successive movement in the political world urges on the process, which will end in knitting together the good men and true of all classes against the revolutionary designs of radicals and schismatics...* [15]

This was not the end of the matter. The 6d rate produced £90, of which £6 was due from the rate resisters. Five of them, led by an innkeeper, George Chamberlain, refused to pay and in the following March appeared before the local bench. However, Chamberlain had by now paid the twelve shillings due from him, another defendant had dropped out and the other three were not represented, so an order was made for the defaulters to pay up.[16]

It is possible that the Dissenters were opposed, not to the Church of England, but to General Rebow. In a history of the Wivenhoe Congregational Church, published in 1896, the author recalls being told that Charles Riggs, who was minister from 1851 to 1854, had been horsewhipped by "a somewhat notorious character, who was very bitter against dissent", and a later history of the same church assumes that this character was the General.[17]

I wonder if it was. At the time of the assault the General was in his early sixties and as a magistrate bound to uphold the peace rather than dispense an arbitrary justice of his own. On the other hand, the old martinet might have regarded dissent as mutiny. It is possible that Charles Riggs, an energetic and popular minister, appeared as a rival, but I doubt if the General would have thrashed him had he not been specifically provoked.

The lively little girl whom Constable took for walks grew up to marry a soldier. Sir Thomas Ormsby's career was not unlike that of his father-in-law. At seventeen he was an ensign with the 85th Light Infantry in North America. At twenty-four he became a major and married Mary Martin Rebow. Nine years later he died aboard his yacht, at Cowes.[18]

His funeral cortège included the carriage of " – Gurdon, Esq.", as a newspaper report put it; this may have been John Gurdon, the Etonian son of a Norfolk parson who married Sir Thomas's widow two years later, or any of his four brothers.[19]

The Gurdons traced their family to the Conquest and beyond. At the time of this, his first marriage, John Gurdon was about thirty-six and his bride five years younger. It may have been a condition of the marriage that he should add Rebow to his own surname, for he applied to do so very soon after and his application was backed by the General. So for the second time in forty years the name Rebow was artificially preserved at Wivenhoe Park. Sometimes the press hyphenated it on to the preceding Gurdon and sometimes not; the latter form is correct. Taking advantage of her former marriage, Mrs. Gurdon was known as Lady Ormsby Rebow.[20]

The General, who incidentally lost his wife in 1834, may have been looking out for a successor. At any rate, the new Rebows lived at Wivenhoe Park, and surviving correspondence indicates that John Gurdon Rebow, as we must now call him, was very soon in charge of its affairs, which the General, who finally became an invalid, may have been glad to relinquish.[21]

Rebow and his father-in-law shared many of the same interests and their names are often linked in press reports. Evidently, the General began to find getting about difficult, for more than once Rebow apologises for his absence at public meetings. On one occasion he speaks "on behalf of his father", a pardonable error, for he seems more like an adopted son than a son-in-law. He was certainly being trained, or training himself, to take the older man's place and he used Wivenhoe Park to launch himself as a prominent local figure, which he was for over three decades.[22]

He took part in many activities. There was the social round. The first mention I can find of the name J. Gurdon Rebow is when he appears, wth Lady Ormsby Rebow by his side, at the Colchester Fair Annual Ball on 24th November, 1836. In 1844 he chaired a dinner given by the Essex and Suffolk Hunt at *The Cups Hotel*, Colchester, to honour the retiring master, Carrington Nunn. When the cloth was removed he produced the brush of a newly killed fox, which the company greeted with a "View Halloo", then weighed into a panegyric couched in exactly the right vein:

> Having now got fairly out of cover with a gallant fox before us and a good scent, I will give you a toast for which I see you are already prepared; and in so doing I would bid you be in readiness for a gallant burst...

and so on, working up to the moment when Mr. Nunn was presented with a gift of silver plate.[23] The hunt frequently met at Wivenhoe Park and when it did was suitably regaled.

Besides social pleasures, there were social duties, which were doubtless also pleasures. In March, 1840, there was a meeting at the Shire Hall, Chelmsford, to present addresses of congratulation to Queen Victoria and Prince Albert on their marriage. Rebow said that while travelling abroad he had discovered Prince Albert was considered by the people of Saxe-Coburg, "to possess those noble principles which are so well calculated to endear him to her Majesty's subjects in general".[24]

He worshipped at St. Mary's, Wivenhoe, of which he was a benefactor and for many years churchwarden. Nor was he content merely to worship. At a public meeting to raise money for the Essex Asylum for Idiots he declared that the rise of public charities was due to Christianity "developing itself in real practical religion".[25]

No doubt it was this sentiment which prompted his hard work in the educational field: in promoting the Wivenhoe National School which was closely allied to the church; in becoming a trustee of the Colchester Royal Grammar School; in helping to set up reformatory schools in the county and create a public library in Colchester; and his association over several years with the Colchester Mechanics' Institute.

Like many another grandee, Rebow was a magistrate. From 1835 until his death he appeared on the Thorpe and Mistley bench, and at the Moot Hall, Colchester, and he was a regular attender at county assizes and quarter sessions.

Another of his principal interests, as befitted a man who owned 3,000 acres, was agriculture. We find him in 1837, already a vice-president of the Colchester Floral and Horticultural Society; at the Tendring Hundred Agricultural Association, in 1840 and 1841, he presented two sovereigns apiece to the labourer who had brought up the largest number of children without parish relief and the labourer who had brought up the largest number of children with the least parish relief. (All the children to be born in wedlock.)[26]

The 1838 harvest was a bad one and to provide enough cheap bread for everyone the government wanted to repeal the duty on foreign corn, although this duty provided an excellent financial protection for the English farmers.

Naturally, the farmers were extremely agitated, and they held public meetings everywhere. Rebow spoke at several. In February, 1839, he reminded the East Essex Agricultural Association, whose principal object was to oppose that repeal, what everyone present knew already, though he made it plain that his own opposition was not entirely selfish:

> ... *Why, gentlemen, we who are embarked as owners and occupiers of land would be deprived of a fourth, a third, or half of our properties; but we are not the most important class of the community that would suffer; no, gentlemen, it is the labourers. We may be deprived of one of the greatest blessings arising from the possession of owning property – that of doing good; but gentlemen, the labourer will be deprived of his all. (Hear, hear). The labourer who has hitherto had nothing but his occupation on the land as his best means of subsistence would then be deprived of his all – for his labour is his capital* ... [27]

Lady Ormsby Rebow died, childless, in the autumn of 1842. Rebow's second wife was a daughter of the Earl of Norbury, Lady Georgiana Toler, another catch for Wivenhoe Park. The wedding, on 2nd December, 1845, at St. Peter's, Belgrave Square, was impressive but brief. The bride and bridegroom caught an early train back to Colchester, very likely to acknowledge the crowd that assembled in the High Street to welcome them, despite the rain, while the bells of two churches rang out. At Wivenhoe the bells of St. Mary's were rung throughout the day, ships in the Colne decorated and a group of the more important people met at *The Rose and Crown* to drink the healths of the newly-weds.[28]

The first Mrs. Rebow accompanied her husband to events which women were allowed to attend; now and then she had a stall at a bazaar or made a small donation to a good cause. The second Mrs. Rebow was consistently associated with education. She sent a cheque to help build the Wivenhoe National School, was hostess at the school treats which were held at the Park and financed a new school at Crockleford Heath.[29] At the time of her marriage she was about twenty-five years old; her husband, forty-seven. On 11th September, 1846, she produced an heir for the estate, Hector John, who was followed by two more children, Georgiana and Mary.

Soon after his second marriage, Rebow began the reconstruction of Wivenhoe Park to designs by Thomas Hopper, (1776-1856).

Hopper, an energetic teetotaller from Rochester, designed and redesigned many country houses in contemporary Jacobean, Tudor and Gothic. It may be that he caught Rebow's eye when he produced a gaol for Chelmsford in Grecian Doric.[30]

Hopper wanted to pull down Reynolds's mansion and build another, but

25. *Lady Georgina Gurdon Rebow, neé Toler, drawn by John Hayter, engraved by W. & F. Hall.*

National Portrait Gallery

Rebow refused. Instead, the exterior was reclothed in red brick with stone facings, windows and entrances remoulded, chimney stacks rebuilt, a large bow window added to the west facade and a rectangular block to the east. Inside, rooms were altered, doors rehung and given new architraves, marble fireplaces put into bedrooms and a grand main staircase created. The entrance hall was given a particularly elaborate ceiling and its vast fireplace surmounted by the quartered arms of Rebow, Gurdon, Brabazon and Toler, with carved figures of Elizabeth I and the Earl of Leicester on either side.[31] A certain W. Nesfield, probably William Andrew Nesfield who did similar work at Kew, produced designs for new lawns and gardens.

In September, 1847, Rebow escaped from the builders with his wife and baby son, to take a holiday in Italy, but numerous bulletins, chiefly from his brother William, a local judge, kept him up to date. The Rebows returned in May, 1849, accompanied or followed by some Italian treasures that included a marble bust of Rebow and a full-length portrait of Lady Georgiana by Hauser of Naples.

Rebow acquired other beautiful and valuable chattels. In his new library to the right of the entrance hall, originally Lady Georgiana's boudoir, was a Grinling Gibbons carving, *The Stoning of St. Stephen*, now in the Victoria and Albert Museum. In the south drawing-room the family portraits of the Rebows and Captain Matthew Martin, were joined by a Van Dyke, *King Charles on Horseback*, presumably a copy, and Lely's *Moll Davis*.[32]

By March, 1849, the conversion had already cost Rebow the best part of £10,000, to say nothing of the furniture and other decorations, and after it was finished the builders returned for other jobs, including a large conservatory, until 1860.[33]

A man who lived grandly and appeared at grand occasions, gave freely to charity and took a close interest in the community would sooner or later be invited to stand for Parliament, as was John Gurdon Rebow, who fought his first election while his house was being transformed. In 1847 the North Essex Division M.P., Charles Gray Round, decided, at short notice, to stand for his old university, Oxford, and Rebow took his place. "I have no wish for public life, or to stand", he said, "but sooner than you would be without a candidate I will be put forward . . . "[34]

At this point we ought to look briefly at nineteenth century politics, to see how this candidate fitted into them.

I believe that among the issues of those times: Free Trade, Education, Dissent, the Irish Question and the rest of them, one quietly predominated. It was not often mentioned, for it was embarrassing, yet it lurked in the public subconscious and accounted for a great deal of what was said and done.

Occasionally, it *was* mentioned. Here is a politician speaking at Colchester in 1851: "It is one fruit of this great Conservative principle . . . that we have held together while all the rest of Europe has been revolutionised . . . "[35]

At the end of the previous century the French establishment had gone up with a bang and the same thing might have happened here. Moreover, as the French Revolution receded into history so other revolutions kept the possibility alive. 1848, for instance, was a lively year on the Continent. At home, the wholesale exploitation of men and women in mines and factories was a potential powder keg, while such people as Charles Bradlaugh, and such movements as Chartism – which at one time had a branch at Wivenhoe – made rich men uneasy.

No man could be an M.P. unless he *was* rich; and no man could vote unless he was moderately well off. Had there been a revolution both candidates and electorate would have lost their all – never mind the labourer. Yet to voice that fear publicly would brand the speaker as frightened and selfish.

How, then, was one *not* to be revolutionised? There were two main lines of defence.

The Conservatives maintained and proclaimed, as firmly and loudly as possible, the established order of things. Hence, their enormous public dinners and other rituals, grand set pieces with patriotic songs, patriotic speeches and loyal toasts sacramentally drunk with three times three and four times four, a wealth of incantation to exorcise the demon in the basement. Reread, in the present chapter, the quotations from the arch-Conservative *Essex Standard*, which was founded in 1831 to trumpet defiance at the terrible Reform Bill. There, in two or three nutshells, are the Conservative hopes and fears.

The Liberal defence was pragmatic. Change there must be; better reform than revolution. Extend the franchise, encourage literacy, give the working classes higher wages and better living conditions; give an inch and an ell might not be taken.

On one point the two parties were united: nobody should enter Parliament unless he contributed generously to local charities and took an interest in local affairs. It was no longer respectable to be a man of leisure. The great blessing arising from property was that of doing good, so one must sit on committees for building this, founding that and reforming the other, and when a subscription was raised for whatever it was, outgive the other givers. Behind the long lists of donations to schools, hospitals and asylums which appeared continually on the front pages of the *Essex Standard* can be glimpsed the spectre of revolution, discreetly prodding the nineteenth century to put its house in order.

Rebow told the electorate in 1847 that he believed in the Crown, the Church, and "those principles which have been established for a long period of time".[36] So – he was a Conservative, in the exact image of the woodcut at the top of the *Essex Standard*, which incorporated a bible, sceptre and crown.

Not so. There was still room for "moderate reform". Though a Protestant, he believed in liberty of conscience, but not to the extent of endowing Roman Catholics and Dissenters out of public funds. Only five per cent of criminals were literate, so educaton, as a moral influence, was vital. It ought to be paid for voluntarily, but if this system did not produce a high enough standard the state should help out. He had vigorously opposed the repeal of the corn laws, but now that this had been done the alteration must be given a fair chance. He had never been a party man, so he was standing as an Independent. The *Essex Standard*, however, called him a Whig.[37]

There were two Conservatives: Sir John Tyrell and Major Beresford. Rebow accused the latter of being a stranger to Essex because he owned no property there, which seems unfair since Rebow himself had become propertied in Essex only two years earlier, on the General's death. A fourth candidate, Harrison, was also Independent. Major Beresford was returned, to the single available seat, with 2,290 votes.[38]

When Rebow visited the Great Exhibition of 1851 he was struck by the good behaviour of the crowds. It was probably with this in mind that he opened the grounds of Wivenhoe Park on 31st July, to raise money for the Colchester Mechanics' Institute. It was estimated that between 3,000 and 4,000 people attended a rural fete which included cricket, football, archery, quoits, vaulting, boating and refreshments. There were also some electrical experiments, and demonstrations using the lakes, in one of which a ship was sunk and then blown up by remote control. The £100 profit was doubtless put towards the Mechanics' new premises in Colchester High Street, which included a public hall. They were opened in style, on 14th October, 1851, with Rebow, as President of the Institute, on the platform.[39]

In August, 1852, there was a second rural fete for the Mechanics and later in the month a school treat at which five hundred children were given a high tea at Rebow's expense, followed by races, cricket, football, trap-bat and other games. That same year Rebow was made High Sheriff for Colchester and helped to found the Essex Archaeological Society. In 1853 the rural fete and school treat were joined by a third public event, a review of the local volunteer force, the Essex Rifles, which included a field exercise in the Park. Rebow further encouraged the Essex Rifles by lending them the Park for drill and rifle practice, for he was as ardently and militantly patriotic as the next Victorian.[40]

On 21st April, 1856, Colchester turned out to see Prince Albert, who was presented with an address of welcome at the Town Hall and inspected the

26. *Prince Albert arriving at Wivenhoe Park on 21st April, 1856. This woodcut was made for the Illustrated London News, where it first appeared.*

Colchester Castle Museum

military camp. Meanwhile, the public streamed towards Wivenhoe Park. Rebow and his brother William received the Prince at the lodge gates and escorted him to the level ground outside the house, where local troops were drawn up. The Prince made an inspection, took a salute from the new iron balcony outside Lady Georgiana's boudoir, watched some exercises and departed. Rebow then entertained local celebrities.[41]

At the beginning of 1857 the resignation of a borough member caused a by-election at Colchester, and Rebow returned to the hustings. He was now a full-blown Liberal and in a far more professional frame of mind. His platform included improved education on a religious basis and the extension of the franchise to all taxpayers. "I believe", he said, "the present improved state of education and increased intelligence of the class to be enfranchised will render such an extension perfectly safe".[42]

There were orignally four candidates, but one of the two Conservatives dropped out, and the Independent, W. R. Havens, was a mere buffoon. So it was a straight fight between Taverner John Miller for the Conservatives and Rebow for the Liberals. Rebow won handsomely. Within a month there was a general election, but with Rebow, Miller and Havens competing, this time for two seats, the result was a foregone conclusion.

Early in 1859 the House of Commons rejected certain clauses in a bill for electoral reform, which Rebow publicly denounced as a sham, and the government appealed to the country. There were two Conservative candidates for the Borough: Miller was joined by P. O. Papillon. They were both returned. After the declaration, Rebow, without disguising his feelings, told the electorate that he was a disappointed candidate. However, before the year was out he declared that he would stand again. He was now a firmly committed politician.[43]

He maintained a close connection with St. Mary's and its rectors: the Rev. E. T. Waters, who came in 1846, and John Baillie who succeeded him. His relationship with these men was like that of the chairman of a trust set up to run a theatre or art gallery, and the administrator he employs. The advowson still belonged to the lord of the manor, but the Corsellises had by this time leased Wivenhoe Hall to strangers; in their absence Rebow became St. Mary's figurehead and chief ornament. He gave £500 towards rebuilding the church; it was by far the largest single donation he ever made.

The candidates for the general election of 1865 were those who had stood in 1859: Miller, Papillon and Rebow. Rebow was returned, with a handsome 691 votes, also Miller.

By now, Lady Georgiana had succumbed to mental illness and left Wivenhoe Park. She had evidently taken but a small part in her husband's interests, either because her illness was already manifest or because she did not share them.

Indeed, it may be that she was driven mad by being married to a zealous, public-spirited, mid-Victorian philanthropist and politician old enough to be her father. In all Rebow's surviving letters there is hardly a reference to her and no suggestion that they belonged together. Was she, perhaps, just one of the things in his life that he arranged to his own satisfaction?

By the end of 1864 Georgiana Rebow was a recluse in London, attended by a single nurse. Two years later, she was formally certified. She was sent to a private home in Middlesex and there she stayed until she died, in 1900, having outlived her husband by thirty years.[44]

At the 1868 general election, the Irish Question was to the fore. Rebow favoured disestablishing the Irish Church, which he thought would strengthen the Church of England. In this he backed Mr. Gladstone, to whom he pledged his support. Perhaps his brother Brampton, another M.P., who happened to be Gladstone's private secretary, influenced him.[45] The Reform Act of the previous year had greatly increased the electorate; on 17th November, Rebow was again, and finally, top of the poll, with 1,467 votes.

During the last two years of his life, he was as active as ever. The public fetes at Wivenhoe Park continued, as did work on the local bench, and as the year 1870 opened, he was President of the Essex Agricultural Society, with which he had been closely connected since its foundation. By the beginning of October he contracted a serious, but unspecified, disease, later supplemented by diphtheria. On 12th October, aged seventy-one, he died.

We know little about Francis Slater, but that little brings him to three-dimensional life. Although the public life of John Gurdon, who became John Gurdon Rebow, was reported in great detail, we can only construct a general picture of his personality.

As we have seen, he came from a reasonably distinguished family and married a rich, titled woman through whom he acquired a country mansion and over two thousand acres of farmland. He rebuilt that country mansion and filled it with works of art, entertained there, often lavishly, attended public events and eventually married a second titled woman who produced him an heir. Isaac Martin Rebow would have done no less.

However, this was the nineteenth century; social history was on the move and the old way of life under threat. So, like many of his contemporaries with money, chattels and rank, he loudly championed the established order, the Church, Crown and tradition generally, but thought it safe, or even politic, to extend the vote and have a secret ballot, educate the working classes, build public libraries and schools, tolerate Dissenters, admit Jews to Parliament and keep reasonably calm about Roman Catholics. He believed in progress, (but not rapid progress), and reform, (moderate reform). He suppported the things he liked and believed in with a generous dispensation of his time and money, and he liked and believed in a good many things. His was a happy metaphysic that embraced everything from God, tactfully referred to in public as Providence, downwards.

He worked hard, as did many of his contemporaries and, as it seemed, to good purpose, for things were evidently coming right in the world. Here he is in typical Victorian vein, addressing a conference in 1861 on "The present state of the labouring classes ... with the best methods of improving their material, social and religious condition".[46]

Rebow told the conference that an increased demand for labour elsewhere had reduced the number of farm-workers, thus ensuring those who remained on the land more permanent employment and raising their "social condition". This led them to save money through benefit societies, sickness clubs and the like, which in turn promoted further prudence and morality. It was a virtuous circle.

"The residences of the labouring classes" had improved considerably, but there was room for further improvement and they ought by law to be built to a required standard:

> *Better internal arrangements are sure to be soon followed by improved attention to other temporal comforts. The wife becomes more tidy, the furniture is better cared for, and the husband returns after his day's labour to a home which has attractions for him, instead of seeking them in the neighbouring beer-house.*

Beer-houses were too often the resort of bad characters, so licences should cost more, but a nominal one should be issued for the sale of beer, "not to be drunk on the premises". The labourer would buy his beer, but take it home where it would be drunk by the whole family.

Football and cricket were to be encouraged because:

> *they bring the several classes in a parish together; they promote order, a desire to excel, and so tend to civilise.*
>
> *Harvest home, when given, should always be on the farm. They will then be conducted in an orderly manner, and be a creditable thank-offering for mercies vouchsafed, instead of degenerating into a low debauch, as is too commonly the case when held at a public-house.*

He concluded by mounting his favourite hobby-horse. When he was young a parish school was a rarity; now, only six per cent of children were not educated. And education was working wonders: crime had diminished, the labouring classes were becoming regular church attenders, most cottages now had a bible and prayer book, *and the examples set by our gracious Sovereign and her Court, descending through the higher and middle classes of society, of increased religion and morality, is producing its natural effects on the improved habits and feelings of the working classes.*

It may not be the happiness of this generation to see fully realised all the benefits of their exertions to improve the material, social and religious condition of the labourer, but they will have the consolation and reward of knowing that the talent committed to their charge has not been unprofitably employed.

27. *John Gurdon Rebow (1799-1870).*

Essex Record Office at Colchester

Does this all sound intolerably pompous and patronising? If so, I suggest that you read it again, putting it into contemporary language as you do, and remember that at that time not only did the man up at the big house genuinely and sincerely think of himself as the leader and patron of the poor people in the area, but the poor people thought so as well. Moreover, they were both right. The farm labourers who worked on Rebow's estate were in no position to make their lives pleasanter; but Rebow himself was and, given this moral mandate, it was to his credit that he used it.

Further, the suggestions are good ones. If the Wivenhovians of those times had had bigger and nicer houses they would have been soberer and, perhaps, happier. The idea that the labourer should drink his beer with his family is intelligent and tolerant compared to the wholesale condemnation of alcohol and public houses rife at that time. We would all, surely, agree that universal education is, in principle, a good thing.

The greatest blessing arising from the possession of Wivenhoe Park was for John Gurdon Rebow, no less than for Isaac Martin Rebow, to enjoy living there in the style of a country gentleman of leisure, but in order to maintain that status the nineteenth century squire was obliged, as the eighteenth century squire was not, to give ground to his fellow men and consider their needs. We, who look over John Gurdon Rebow's shoulder, can be amused at his failure to realise the self interest behind his charitable deeds. Yet for all that we can credit him with sincerity and dedication.

At his death the tributes paid to Rebow by his brother magistrates and the local press stressed his generosity, integrity and, especially, his pleasant manners. He was variously described as hospitable, genial, courteous, affable and a good neighbour. The Rev. John Baillie stressed the late squire's religious toleration and "unsullied integrity". Though he had possessed no striking gifts of eloquence that only made him more like the average, honest Englishman.[47]

Eloquence Rebow never lacked. He always knew what to say and the idiom demanded by the occasion, whether political, jingoistic, post-prandial or whatever, and unlike many of his contemporaries stopped speaking when he had said it. Moreover, he obviously thought before he spoke. The rector probably meant that he lacked the gift of rhetoric.

Was there absolutely no scheming about him? Were his early involvements and disbursements not designed as the pedestal for a political career? I think not. A man who wanted to be an M.P. would have stood before he was forty-seven and it is worth noting that after the first rural fete and the opening of the Mechanics' Institute he ignored the general election of 1852. His speeches, which state precisely where he stands on various issues, have an honest ring about them. I am even inclined to believe the 1847 declaration, "I have no wish for public life, or to stand . . . "

His career shows a natural development, from the youngish man who made a nest for himself, to the older man who became involved with the world around him at a national level. "I make agriculture my amusement", he told the 1847 electorate,[48] which sounds eighteenth century, a world away from the disciple of Gladstone. A poem of Sir John Betjeman's speaks of certain Victorians as "men who never cheated, never doubted". We may suppose that John Gurdon Rebow was such a man.

Yet he knew that he neither cheated nor doubted. "If you should again do me the honour of sending me to Parliament as your representative", he said in 1868, "I should continue to follow in that upright independent career which has gained me your suffrage on several previous occasions".[49] I think this was true. He gained votes because he was trustworthy – and he knew that he did.

Yet one aspect of his life was not of a piece with this upright posture. For whether he noticed it or not the fortune amassed by Sir Isaac Rebow from Flemish weaving, the South Sea Bubble and the dowries of three rich brides was dwindling rapidly. Officially, Rebow spent £125 on the first of the two 1857 elections, £393 in 1859 and £901 in 1865. To this must be added the cost of a town house, (111, Eaton Square), and everything else connected with his work as an M.P. "Mr. Miller ... ", said the *Essex Standard* meaningfully at one election, "has a good income and a large heart", to which Rebow declared that he had subscribed to every Colchester charity.[50] It is believable.

On top of this there was the gratuitous rebuilding and refurnishing of Wivenhoe Park. There was entertaining: the elegant collations, sumptuous banquets, excellent repasts and other synonymous titles used by the press to describe the endless dispensing of food and drink. There was the upkeep of two homes, subscriptions to three London clubs, a good deal of travelling and such incidentals as his first wife's lavish funeral, his second wife's incarceration in a private asylum, and his son's schooling at Eton and Guards commission. Despite the lofty intentions, there is something ironically rakish in the way Sir Isaac's fortune was disbursed.

And if the money had indeed run out? Would the geniality, the courtesy and the unsullied integrity have been able to accept the situation? By 1870, however, the money had not run out; that showdown was reserved for the next generation.

CHAPTER 6

The Big Yachts 1801-1881

1 The Dawn of an Era: Philip Sainty and Pearl.

There was a Wivenhovian at Trafalgar: James Martin, an able seaman gunner aboard H.M.S. Neptune, who wrote an account of the battle in a small pocket book.[1]

He returned to Wivenhoe where, according to family tradition, his money was consumed in lawyers' fees as he attempted, vainly, to prove that he was descended from Captain Matthew Martin and by that token heir to some or all of the family wealth, including Alresford Hall.[2] It is conceivable that since neither of Captain Martin's surviving sons produced male heirs, the Captain produced one of his own and made legal arrangements to secure his inheritance. It is equally conceivable that his lawyer son, Thomas, contrived, with his own interests in mind, to defeat his father's wishes. It is conceivable – and utterly unprovable.

There was a keen amateur yachtsman at Waterloo: the Marquis of Anglesey, who commanded the British cavalry. He was an equally distinguished statesman, for he rose to cabinet rank and was a memorable lord lieutenant of Ireland, one of the few Englishman to leave that country with his reputation enhanced. And no man did more to make yacht racing popular. When he commissioned Philip John Sainty to build him the cutter *Pearl* he inaugurated the Colne's century of pride, splendour and mystique, of international fame and comparative prosperity.

Sainty was born at Wivenhoe in about 1754 and died here in 1844. He built commercial vessels, but as he himself was a smuggler probably designed other boats to outsail them, which was only a step from building boats with speed foremost in mind. The Marquis first commissioned him to build a yacht called *Emerald*, which was manned by a local crew and used for racing, then another, the *Liberty*.

83

28. *The Marquis of Anglesey, drawn in 1808 by H. Eldridge.*

National Portrait Gallery

The Big Yachts 1801–1881

The story of Anglesey's next commission, though tall, is credible, for it derives from an account written by a customs officer who was stationed at Colchester during this period. He tells us that Sainty smuggled contraband from Holland in a vessel with false sides. A Colcestrian called Brown was imprisoned there for uttering forged coins. Sainty managed to bring him back to England, whereat Brown promptly told the authorities where Sainty's smuggled goods were hidden in order to claim a reward. Sainty, his son John, and his brother were all sent to Chelmsford Gaol, apparently for life. After the Napoleonic War, the Marquis needed Sainty again and when he learnt he was in prison is supposed to have declared that, "if he were in Hell he would have him out". He visited Sainty and asked him if he could build a better yacht than *Emerald*. Sainty said he could build a yacht which was unbeatable. So the Marquis approached the Regent and an order for his release was made. However, Sainty was both a cool and a fly character. The order was made out in his second name, John, and when it arrived he allowed his son to leave the prison. He had judged his patron correctly. The Marquis was sufficiently anxious for his services to arrange for another order to be made. So Philip was released and when he said he could not do without his brother a third order was made. Although Sainty's brother Robert was a fellow smuggler, this may have been his brother Mosely who was apparently closely involved in his designs.[3]

Pearl was built, so the customs officer tells us, "about a mile out of Colchester", and other boatbuilders from "all parts" came to inspect her progress. No doubt they did, for at 113 tons she would be the biggest cutter-rigged yacht afloat, save one, a 116 tonner called *Atlanta*. Morally speaking, *Pearl* was the first of the big racing yachts and her captain, William Ham of Wivenhoe, the first of the Colne skippers. The day she was launched, in 1819, marked the beginning of an era in which Rowhedge, Wivenhoe and Brightlingsea vied to produce the best boats, crews and facilities for laying-up, and the Colne was a legend among seafaring men.

Though built for racing, *Pearl* was a well-appointed cruising yacht and made trips to the Baltic, the Mediterranean and, of course, Ireland when the Marquis became Lord Lieutenant. At first she won races because there was no boat of a comparable tonnage to oppose her. However, there presently appeared the 120 ton schooner *Hussar* which she beat in a race round the Isle of Wight in 1821. In 1825 she raced the 85 ton *Arrow* and the Marquis declared that if she did not win he would burn her. Happily, she did, by a slender ten-and-a-half minutes, and survived until 1902. The great days of racing had begun.[4]

The Marquis paid Sainty a retainer of £100 a year not to build boats for anyone else, but must have thought it highly unlikely that the agreement would be honoured. Nor was it. The most memorable of Sainty's many yachts were probably the 124 ton *Swallow* and the vast, 188 ton *Arundel*, both for the Duke of

29. *The cutter Pearl, built by Philip John Sainty in 1819.*

National Maritime Museum

Norfolk. The latter was specifically designed to race the mighty *Alarm,* which at 193 tons was thought unbeatable. Sainty disproved this.

As we have seen, the shipyard upstream of the town was apparently unused during the last decade of the eighteenth century, but in 1802 a Colchester timber merchant, William Hawkins, who lived at Alresford Hall, launched a 17 ton smack, *Union,* and a 149 ton brigantine, *Venus,* there, and in 1803 nine more smacks. When Sainty launched his own *Venus,* a 25 ton smack, at Wivenhoe the following year, it was almost certainly at the same place, for the names of these two men are sometimes linked. Sainty remained at Wivenhoe until at least 1809, in which year he produced the ill-fated cutter smack *Morning Star,* which was lost on a voyage to Flushing. Later, he moved to Colchester, but by 1823 was back at Wivenhoe.[5]

His final decade as a boatbuilder was remarkable. In addition to a string of 30 to 40 ton smacks, he produced 100 to 150 ton schooners and several individual vessels which should be mentioned.

The Big Yachts 1801–1881

30. *The sloop-of-war Pearl, built by Philip John Sainty in 1828.*

National Maritime Museum

The Marquis of Anglesey was so pleased with *Pearl* that he kept her for thirty-one years and even persuaded the Royal Navy to build a man-of-war to the same design. The sloop-of-war *Pearl*, last of the big naval warships to be built at Wivenhoe, was designed and constructed by Sainty. She was 558 tons, carried eighteen guns and with a draught of 15′ 8″ it is not surprising that her launch was attended with difficulty. She was due to enter the water on 3rd March, 1828, but Sainty observed that the earth beneath the cradle which was to guide her down the slipway was beginning to move, and to prevent a disaster that might have claimed the lives of the two hundred people aboard her, postponed the launch for a fortnight.[6]

On 17th March she was duly launched, amid general acclamation, and went to Woolwich for fitting out. However, unlike her civilian namesake, this *Pearl* was not a success. Neither the Saintys, Philip and Mosely, nor the Navy, were pleased with her. In the course of a peaceful career which took her to Lisbon, the West Indies and South America, she captured a Spanish slaver. For two years she was commanded by Lord Clarence Paget, one of the Marquis of Anglesey's sons. She was broken up in 1851.[7]

In 1829, Sainty produced a snow, (a small sailing vessel with two masts), of 202 tons, *Cupid*, in 1830 a cutter yacht, *Water Witch*, for Sir Thomas Ormsby, General Rebow's first son-in-law, in 1831 a three-masted barque of 196 tons, the *William and Mary*, for William Hawkins, and in 1833 a brigantine of 105 tons, *Fancy Lass*.[8]

It is probable that he built this last vessel not on his own account but for Thomas Harvey, to whom he sold the shipyard in 1832. It is typical of Sainty that he should have ended his brilliant, but hand-to-mouth career by going bankrupt, as he had already done on more than one occasion. It is also typical of boatbuilding. His goods were auctioned at *The Rose and Crown*. They included a house, shipyard, workshops and lofts, boathouse, paintshop and "various sheds with three good tenements", also three houses in Bath Street. After this his name disappears from public record. His son, Philip Moseley Sainty, was also a boatbuilder, but we know little of him save that one of his vessels, *Leading Star*, was launched in 1856 and that he owned commercial boats.[9]

It is recorded that in 1836 a fifteen-year-old son of Philip Sainty's had a copper bolt knocked through his hand. To produce a son at about sixty-seven argues a reasonable virility. Tradition credits Sainty with a large family and polygamy.[10]

During his regime there was at least one other shipyard in the town. In 1800, Joseph Cole, who had been working at East Donyland, came to Wivenhoe and set up a yard in which his father-in-law, Samuel Cook of Rowhedge, had left him an interest. Its site is unknown, but since Sainty occupied the open ground immediately upstream of The Quay it is not unlikely that Cole occupied the ground immediately downstream, an obvious place for boatbuilding and which indeed has been used for that purpose almost to the present day. He died in 1815 and was succeeded by his eldest son, Daniel. Between them, the Coles built over a dozen 20 to 50 ton smacks. Their yard closed in the 1820's.[11]

Besides building boats, crewing and laying up yachts, and fishing, the Colne seamen also salvaged, saving lives and goods from vessels stranded on the sandflats at the mouth of the Colne, often without turning the latter over to the proper authorities. So far as we know they were not wholesale wreckers as, say, Cornishmen were, yet there is reason to believe that now and then buoys were misplaced and lights extinguished. Indeed, they had no reason to be, for a stiff gale would drive a large number of boats ashore.

Besides, many of them owned, or part-owned, the cargo boats which carried goods round the coast. Between 1786 and 1875, the names of Wivenhovians who owned either smacks or cargo boats included Baker, Bennett, Blyth, Brooke, Chamberlain, Denton, Goodwin, Ham, Harvey, Heath, Madder,

The Big Yachts 1801–1881

Munnings, Neal, Penney, Pittuck, Pratt, Price, Sainty, Sandford, Stacey and Wadley. From 1806 to 1815 there were twenty such. The number plummeted after the Napoleonic War, but rose to a peak in 1856-65, when fifty-five Wivenhovians owned vessels with a combined weight of 7,554 tons.[12]

The town had its own fleet based at The Quay. Apart from twenty-five or so smacks, there were nine or ten colliers of about 80 tons, known as "billy-boys", and a dozen larger brigs, brigantines, ketches and the like, of which the fastest, handiest and most celebrated was the brigantine *Jesse Annandale*. She alone could sail up the Colne with a head wind. Coal was the principal cargo delivered to Wivenhoe and a good deal of it was spilled into the river, whence it was gleaned by children at low tide. These vessels plied between Wivenhoe and the North of England as colliers, but the larger ones roamed farther afield, to Quebec, for instance, and Jamaica. These bigger ships, unable to sail without a ballast, used to leave Wivenhoe with sand or gravel excavated from the area that is now the Dene Park Estate.[13]

Eventually, the railways appropriated the coastal trade until investing in cargo boats was no longer profitable. So the fleet disappeared; in 1885, the *Jesse Annandale*, the last of the big colliers, landed her final cargo.

2 Grandees and Tradesmen.

Nicholas Corsellis V had eleven children; his eight sons went into the Army, the Navy, the East India Company and the Church. On his death, in 1826, the contents of the Hall were sold and it was leased. The second son, Joseph Goodall Corsellis, was presented with the rectory, though he was never rector, but another member of the family, John M. Corsellis, was rector from 1814 to 1837.[14]

The eldest son, Nicholas Caesar Corsellis VI, joined the Navy as a midshipman aboard the *Roebuck*, which took part in the storming of New York, Philadelphia and Charlestown. After the American War, he served in the *Triumph*, commanded the gun brig *Furious* and saw the execution of Parker and his companions off The Nore. In 1803 he was stationed at Dungeness, to keep a sharp look out for the French fleet.[15]

Nicholas VI rose to captain and finally settled at Benson, near Oxford. His wife, Mary, the daughter of an M.P., produced no family, but a certain Sarah Plampin bore him eight illegitimate children. A contemporary Corsellis has sent me a family tree; opposite Miss Plampin's name is written, "A gypsey?" His eldest son, Nicholas Caesar Corsellis VII, who inherited the manor, became a doctor and practised at Benson.

Of the Hall's first tenants we know virtually nothing. A certain George Savill gave £5 to the Inhabitants of Starving Ireland in 1851; the goods of the

31. *Captain Nicholas Caesar Corsellis VI, R.N. (1763-1833).*

Loaned by Mr. E. H. C. Squire

Hon. A. Capel were sold in 1840; in that same year Stephen Brown had a spot of bother with a neighbouring farmer whose son went shooting over the manor without his leave. However, by the summer of 1858 Sir Claude de Crespigny, Bart, had moved in with his family and he proceeded to take a lively part in local affairs.[16]

Sir Claude was a genial, gregarious, extravert Old Wykehamist with a talent for knockabout comedy and a family of four sons and seven daughters. He devoted much of his time to the volunteer movement, becoming initially a captain and later a lieutenant-colonel of the 6th Essex (Colchester) Corps.

His soldiering was mixed with pleasure. In January, 1861, the 6th Essex made a route march to Wivenhoe. About a mile from The Quay its path was barred by a phalanx of fishermen with a huge ship's gun. A local sea captain advanced with a flag of truce and demanded to know if the Corps was friend or foe. Sir Claude, on horseback, announced that the Corps was friendly and with the utmost good humour the march continued, the local fishermen falling in behind. Then everyone trooped down to *The Anchor,* where Charles Heath, dredgerman and oyster merchant, produced Colchester natives. William Hawkins, who had come over from Alresford Hall, was elected chairman and healths were proposed and drunk. At 5 a.m. the volunteers marched back to Colchester, while their colonel treated the reception committee to John Barleycorn. This route march was probably staged to whet the public appetite, for later that month Sir Claude formed a Wivenhoe contingent.[17]

Sir Claude was much in evidence. He was a steward at public balls in Colchester and appeared at the Oyster Feast, and whenever he made a speech was sure to sing the praises of the volunteer movement. Evidently a friendly, approachable man, he sometimes allowed his tenants free coursing over his estate, and his eldest son, another Claude, played cricket for the town.

In 1858, this son, then a naval cadet, succeeded to the baronetcy and three years later was bankrupt with debts of over £3,000. However, he survived to emerge as Sir Claude de Champion Crespigny of Champion Hall, Maldon, who slew wild animals in every corner of the globe, engaged in every dangerous sport known to man, from steeplechasing to ballooning, and was a total law unto himself. "Evidently a 'survival'", said the local press when it was known he had assisted the hangman at Chelmsford Gaol.[18]

Captain Henry Tyler, the Chief Inspector of Railways, may have decided to live here when he examined the new line from Wivenhoe to Weeley. At any rate, he succeeded the elder Sir Claude at the Hall. A former officer in the Royal Engineers, he commissioned John Harvey to build him a yacht called *Sea Belle,* rode to hounds on a horse called *Locomotive,* accompanied by his daughter and three sons, and explained the use of the telephone to an Easter Day tea party at the Grosvenor Hotel. In 1877 he was knighted for his services to the railways and about two years later moved from the Hall.[19]

Then, briefly, the lord of the manor came home. Nicholas Caesar Corsellis VII, the Oxfordshire doctor, bequeathed the manor to his nephew, Nicholas Caesar Corsellis Lawton. Lawton moved into the Hall, became president of the new Wivenhoe Cricket Club, and no sooner had he settled down than he died, in May, 1881, aged forty-two.

Opposite Wivenhoe Hall, on what is now the top of Park Road, stood

32. *George Bryan Brummell (1778-1840), engraving by John Cook.*

National Portrait Gallery

Wivenhoe House, described by Thomas Wright in 1836 as "a handsome modern white brick mansion".[20] Its owner, William Brummell, an alumnus of Eton and Oxford, married the daughter of a governor of Bombay by whom he had two daughters, both of whom made good marriages, and died, aged seventy-eight, in 1853. At Wivenhoe all that we know of him is that he voted at elections and attended vestry meetings.[21]

However, we have all heard of a neckcloth folded with supernatural art and above it a basilisk gaze that shrivelled men and their habiliments into dust, "D'you call that thing a coat?", "Who's your fat friend?" and so forth. In fact, what we know of William's younger brother, George, is wide of the mark. This was no icy perfectionist, but an amusing, light-hearted companion. For how else could a man without birth gain entry to the highest society in the land?

The Big Yachts 1801–1881

"Brummell", said one of his fellow clubmen at White's, "your brother William is in town; is he not coming here?" "Yes, in a day or two; but I have recommended him to walk the back streets till his new clothes come home".[22] The reply was not to be taken seriously, though this perpetrator of myths and hoaxes would have liked his contemporaries, and us, to think so.

Did Brummell ever visit Wivenhoe? His many poses included a contempt for his relations and a contempt for the countryside, but I think he may well have done, though I can find no reference to such a visit. Writing of William Brummell, the local historian, Gerald Rickword, said that he, "was fond of clothes but did not indulge in the wild extravagances of the other, (his brother), who used to visit him at the little Colneside town ... "[23] Whether he, in turn, relied upon oral or textual authority I do not know.

During this century the gulf separating the Rebows and the Corsellises from their fellows gradually narrowed. The owners or occupiers of the Park and the Hall remained at the apex of the social pyramid, influential because they possessed most of the land near the town and employed farmers, gamekeepers and domestic servants. Yet not so very far behind was the rector, with his large rectory, which was rebuilt in 1835 to provide a reception room that could, and often did, contain a hundred people, the village hall of its day. There was also William Brummell, and his successors at The Nook, the property built on the same site, the lessee of Wivenhoe Lodge, (later known as Lower Lodge Farm), and, from about 1870, John Girling and his successors at Ballast Quay House, the mid-Victorian mansion at the top of Anglesea Road. I should also mention Edmund Round, the barrister who built the pleasantly modest Elaine Cottage, named after his yacht, in Park Road during the middle sixties. These were the people who chaired public meetings, patronised good causes and were accepted as the leaders of the community. As the century wore on, so social differences were modified. The grandees became increasingly accessible and the grounds of their houses were used oftener for public functions.

The town's social centre was St. Mary's Church. The office of churchwarden, so disliked three centuries earlier, was now enviable. The rector's warden was always a grandee, the parish warden an important tradesman. In the latter post, John Green Chamberlain, boat owner and merchant, Lloyds agent and deputy serjeant to the Admiralty Cinque Port, was succeeded by William Browne, the rope-maker, and Isaac Blyth, a butcher. John Martin-Harvey has left us a description of this last-named worthy and his wife:

> Here in the bow window, which has been thrust out above the front door of a neat house in "The Street", in order that she may keep watch upon the doings of her neighbours while she plies her knitting, sits Aunt Bligh. A busy life she and her husband "Ikey" Bligh lead, for there is not an irregular corner in the doings of the village into

which their inquisitive noses will not explore, not a small delinquency which they will not discover. On Sunday Aunt Bligh is at her most awe-inspiring. Now she is in her wide and billowing lavender silk which creaks and rustles as she marshals us into her small drawing-room for biscuits and sherry before we follow her in majestic procession to church.[24]

Before it was called the High Street, the central road in Wivenhoe was known as The Street, or Wivenhoe Street. West Street was once called Hog Lane, and East Street Love Lane. I am pretty certain that the Blyths, or Blighs, as their nephew called them, lived at what is now No. 35, whose upstairs window commands an excellent view of the High Street and churchyard. Talking of delinquency, in 1848 Isaac Blyth was summoned for using incorrect weights.[25]

The mill at the corner of Rectory Road, which belonged to the lord of the manor, was still a thriving concern. When the lease was sold in 1848 it was described as a post-windmill driving two pairs of French stones, with a round house, piggeries and sixty acres of land. In 1882 it was destroyed by fire, but was later rebuilt and was producing corn after the turn of the century. It was dismantled between the two world wars.[26]

In those days it paid to diversify, as did William Sandford, an oyster merchant who also owned a farm and warehouses. He had many regular customers. Some, such as General Rebow, Nicholas Caesar Corsellis V and William Brummell, were local grandees, but he sent his barrels to Lord and Lady Waldegrave, Lord Sherborne and the Marquis of Salisbury. He was also supported by one or two local tradesmen, such as the brewer, Samuel Bawtree, and Mrs. Blyth. He leased coalyards and warehouses, and his farm produced useful timber. He sold his oyster fishery in 1827 to his brother, Thomas.[27]

The Sandfords, Chamberlains, Brownes, Blyths, Harveys, Heaths and their like, the richer tradesmen who owned property, were next in standing to the grandees and if anybody could be said to run the town it was they.

The doctor was on the same social footing. In 1805 the parish agreed to employ a surgeon, Benjamin Smith, for £12 a year, to attend the paupers, with a guinea for each childbirth and two guineas if the midwife was unable to cope and he had to assist. Philip Havens, whose father owned East Donyland Hall, practised for many years in the town. We have already met his brother Rawdon and Philip, like the rest of the family, was reputed to be eccentric. During his reign the town succumbed to the 1849 national epidemic of cholera, not surprisingly in view of the primitive sanitation. He was joined latterly by Samuel Squire, and Squire's nephew, W. S. Ling, later became his assistant. At the end of the seventies, Dr. Ling's brother, Charles, also practised here.[28]

There exists a calfbound ledger in which successive Wivenhoe doctors recorded the payments made to them, quarterly, by benefit societies and other groups in Wivenhoe, Rowhedge, Fingringhoe, Alresford and Elmstead, from 1855 to 1935. The first entry shows sums of money ranging from 23s 6d to £17 2s 6d, in respect of nineteen different groups, a total of £92 3s 6d. Most of them were associated with public houses. Thus, there was *The Black Boy* "Prosperous" and *The Black Boy* "Durrells", *The Ship at Launch* "Benefit" and *The Ship at Launch* "Surgeon's". The other four villages never seemed to have more than one group at any one public house. Evidently the scheme was based on this town.[29]

Thus it continued, the quarterly sum rising to almost double the first entry by 1884 and declining, with fewer groups subscribing, in the new century. After 1900 the names of public houses start to disappear until finally there are just the five villages named as such. In 1930 they all join the Essex Public Medical Service, but evidently still pay their contributions through the local doctor. Thus the poorer people insured themselves against ill-health.

Besides the grandees and the tradesmen, there was another, new social class to be reckoned with: the captains, the men who held the tillers of the racing yachts, winning the town a golden reputation and themselves comparative affluence. We shall look at them more closely in the next chapter.

3 Education and Religion.

These years saw the rise of organised education, spurred on by the rivalry between church and chapel.

The second chapel was built in 1805, to the north of West Street, (now the premises of the fish merchants, Ken Green Ltd.). In the following year the pastor, James Hyde, opened a school there, probably to augment his stipend. Soon after, a proper schoolroom was built, sufficient for twenty children, with assistance from the newly formed Essex Congregational Union.[30]

This was the British School; in reply, the Church of England founded a National School in 1814, one of many set up at this time with assistance from the National Society. Its second anniversary celebrations were evidently a show of strength against nonconformity, for the pupils marched to church preceded by a regimental band, the bells were rung and flags displayed everywhere. A report of 1818 says that the 135 pupils were divided into a boys' and a girls' school. It was supported by £12 from school pence, (the money paid weekly by the pupils), £6 from girls' work and about £40 from voluntary contributions. Out of this the master received a salary of £139 per annum, the mistress £15. The rent of the schoolroom, a tiny, noisome place at the foot of the town, was £8 8s 0d. The British School, though with fewer numbers, was doing better at this time.[31]

In 1839, the rector, James Ind, reported on the state of the National School to the London Diocesan Board of Education. There were now only 117 pupils, of whom ninety actually attended, and it was very difficult to maintain. The master and mistress had themselves not been properly educated, which is perhaps why the pupils were disinclined to learn. The parents, though willing for their children to be taught, were apt to keep them away without good reason.[32]

Two of Mr. Ind's predecessors had tried to raise funds for a new schoolroom, but without success. In 1841, he himself applied to the National Society for a grant, which was offered. This, with promised subscriptions of £200, might have raised the necessary £380. Unfortunately, Mr. Ind retired to Madeira for the sake of his health and the correspondence was passed to General Rebow. By now Charles Riggs had left the town and the Nonconformist day school had closed, else the General might have pursued the matter; instead, he told the National Society that the idea of a new school had been dropped, declined the grant and quietly snuffed it out.[33]

According to the Archdeanery Return for 1841, there were four hundred Dissenters in Wivenhoe and some 365 who were "divided, doubtful or . . . irreligious, altogether 40 per cent of the population". Some of the doubt and division was probably mopped up when a branch of the Swedenborgian Society was founded in the town. Simple, noisy and mystical, this was a religion well suited to men who risked their lives in the pitiless North Sea.[34]

The Brightlingsea branch of the Society, founded in 1813, became a centre for the movement. By 1848 Wivenhoe was holding its own services and receiving regular visits from the Rev. David Goyder, of Welsh descent, who became its pastor. It is recorded that a Church of the New Jerusalem, as the Society called its meeting houses, was opened or, more likely, found itself a proper home, at Sun Yard, Bethany Street, (doubtless so named at this time), in 1849, where its evening services attacted congregations of about sixty.[35] One of the pastor's earliest and most stalwart converts was the boatbuilder, Thomas Harvey, whose son, John, married Mr. Goyder's daughter, Margaret.

Very likely Harvey, the upstream boatbuilder, helped to finance the Sun Yard meeting house. However, when the Society built itself a church at the top of Alma Street, in 1864, it was entirely paid for by the downstream boatbuilder, James Husk. This plain, tall building, (now Dean's Antiques), contained a meeting room for two hundred people with good acoustics which by night was lit by a corona of gas jets.[36]

The advent of the railway, described later in this chapter, was preceded by the navvies who built it, in the spring of 1864. These rough, powerful, nomad labourers made life unpleasant for the communities in which they lodged, for they habitually thieved, fornicated, drank and brawled. However, the railway's Inspector of Works, Henry Ruffell, also lodged here, and he and his wife, Martha, determined to provide these men with religion. A barn, lent by a sympathetic farmer, was fitted up as a chapel and used for two Sunday services which soon attracted good congregations, including about a dozen navvies, and at harvesttime the worshippers obtained the use of a warehouse. Later, they went to the clubroom at *The Greyhound*, which was not large enough, even with two Sunday services.[37] The flock was now in the charge of a young evangelist from Kerry, George Carter Needham.

In 1865 the aforementioned barn was dismantled, but a larger one built in its place, which Needham inaugurated with a service attended by six hundred people. In the following year the group rented the Swedenborgian Chapel for six months, changing its name to The Gospel Hall. I assume that the Swedenborgians returned, for David Goyder was certainly living at Wivenhoe in 1871 and John Martin-Harvey, who was born in 1863, tells us, "Services were held in a large room in Alma Street, and if my memory is correct, the music was supplied by the village band, whose discordant trumpetings were my special delight". He would hardly have been taken to the chapel at the age of three. One Wivenhovian recalled that a reading room opened in 1871. Very likely this was at the former Swedenborgian Chapel, for it was certainly there before the century was out. However, this was not the end of Swedenborgianism in Wivenhoe, nor indeed in Brightlingsea and Colchester where it flourishes to this day.[38]

33. *The former Swedenborgian Chapel in Alma Street, now Dean's Antiques.*

Photograph by G. Martin

34. *The former Congregational Church in Quay Street.*

Photograph by Sue Murray, L.R.P.S.

Needham also conducted open air services. One pleasant evening in May, 1866, after his flock, assembled on The Quay, had sung the hymn, "What vessel are you sailing in?", he started to address them when a man fell off a barge into the river and was drowned. In the congregation was a young man, Nathaniel Harvey, nicknamed Satan because of his colourful language. He had come to heckle Needham, but the incident evidently affected him, for not long after he was converted.[39]

Needham attempted to build a proper hall for his flock, but could not raise enough money and early in 1868 set off on an evangelising tour of America.[40]

We know about Needham principally because his ministry was recorded in a Methodist magazine, but it seems he was never a Methodist minister. Yet the Methodists had arrived by this time, indeed had been active for many years already. Three of their factions were based on Colchester and two, the Primitives and the Wesleyans, started sending out preachers early in the century. The first record we have of Methodism in the town is supplied by a list of officials on the Colchester Wesleyan Circuit for 1823, which tells us that a class of six members here was led by John Grimes. The Primitives resolved that Wivenhoe should be included in their preaching "plan" as early as 1837. In the years that followed the parties vied with each other to secure the town and, later on, build a chapel.[41]

The latter may have been inhibited by Needham, for if he attracted a hundred or so Wivenhovians, and the Congregationalists and Church of England did likewise, it left very few potential worshippers for anyone else. However, on 29th December, 1870, the Primitives resolved to secure land and on 5th January, 1871, two of their number were sent to open a preaching room. Was this, perhaps, the Swedenborgian Chapel?

On that same day the Wesleyans decided to buy two plots of land above the new railway cutting. It turned out that one of them was not the owner's to sell, but the other quickly became the site of a new chapel which was opened on 23rd February. Evidently, there had been a race and they had won. Unfortunately, in their haste they erected little more than a clapboard shed. Cold in winter and hot in summer, it only seated 162 and was altogether inadequate. Within ten years they were agitating for a new chapel, even though the debt on the first had not been paid off. The second and present chapel was opened on 24th October, 1901. The first, barely recognisable under its coat of rendering, still stands. It is called The St. John's Ambulance Hall.

The Congregationalists were given a fillip when Thomas Sandford, whose oyster layings and other investments had prospered, paid £2,400 for a new chapel. Designed in an Italian style, with six hundred seats, it was built at the corner of West Street and Quay Street. It opened on 28th April, 1847, and remained a chapel until it was sold by the church in the winter of 1961. (Externally, it is unchanged; internally, it is now luxury flats above and offices below). Another member of the family, John, converted the earlier chapel into a new British School for three hundred pupils in two classrooms, one above the other. This opened in September, 1847.[42]

Had General Rebow been alive he might have regretted his earlier inaction. However, in 1846 an energetic new rector, E. T. Waters, arrived. He told the National Society:

> *The present school is a mere cottage tenement, with boarded walls, containing two rooms capable of holding only sixty children each, whereas our school now nearly amounts to two hundred children. It is confined in its situation, being in a small dirty yard, it has no playground, there is but one Privy for the schools and for six families who reside in the yard and the spot is unhealthy and inconvenient.*[43]

Overcrowded and unhygienic it may have been, but it was probably replaced only because of religious rivalry. Although the site, in the High Street, alone cost £207 and the total needed was over £1,000, the money was quickly raised. £623 was promised locally, £75 donated by the National Society, £24 by the Diocesan Board of Education and £276 by the Committee of Council. The school opened on 26th October, 1848. There were 250 pupils, but room for

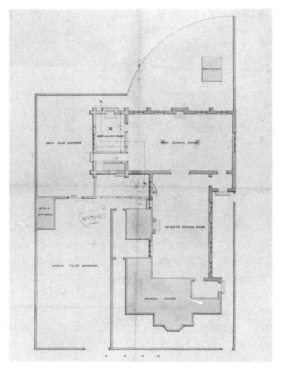

35. *Above: Watercolour of the National School built in 1841.& 36.*
   Below: A groundplan of the same with the addition proposed in 1873 by F. Evelyn Morris.

Essex Record Office at Chelmsford

400. Needless to say, John Gurdon Rebow favoured the project, though he made it plain he did not object to nonconformists.[44]

James Ind had wanted to start a lending library; the trustees of the National School set up a reading room there in 1861, which upon the death of the Prince Consort was christened the Albert Reading Room. Under its auspices Wivenhovians attended lectures on poetry or readings from Dickens. The school was also used as a public hall. It was here that Sir Claude de Crespigny appealed for volunteers and the Wivenhoe Gas Company was formed.[45]

Until 1859 the parish church of St. Mary's looked much as it had done since the Reformation. However, the stools had now disappeared and the congregation sat in tall, square pews and two galleries on the north and west sides of the nave. It was a plain, lofty place, "a barn-like arrangement", as John Gurdon Rebow put it, and was falling into extreme disrepair. Perhaps this had a bad effect on the congregation. In 1839 a service was delayed for ten minutes or so because two young men, John Taylor and William Chapman, were misbehaving in one of the galleries. Taylor apparently asked a girl to sit on his knee and people were laughing. The parish warden, John Green Chamberlain, tired of this sort of thing, made an example of them. They were brought before the local bench and sent on to the Assizes.[46]

Now, in the course of a year, the building was not only repaired, which involved a complete reroofing, but "gothicized". The chancel was lowered and extended thirteen feet to the east. A south aisle was added to balance the north one. The east windows of the chancel and north chancel aisle were filled with stained glass. Oaken pews and doors were installed, together with a font, pulpit and altar rail of stone. The nave was surmounted with a pitched roof and under it were placed bosses representing Christ and the Apostles. Fortunately the committee overspent its funds by £500; had it not it would have removed the charming cupola, which was added to the tower in about 1805, and substituted a steeple.[47]

The church had been hitherto "void of all architectural interest or of church-like propriety", but possibly a homely, friendly place; now it was a suitable vehicle for church parade as conducted a century ago, where nobody would think of asking a pretty girl to sit on his knee, even if it were physically possible.

The National School prospered, its numbers rising, so that in 1850 a separate Infants Department was created and in 1874 a Girls Department, and more accommodation added on to the original building in the form of an upper storey. In 1880 there were 330 pupils on the books, 270 of whom attended fairly regularly, by which time the three principal teachers had assistants, including senior boys and girls.[48]

The tale of school life in the High Street, on the site of the present public library, is taken up for us in the year 1868 by the first of eleven thick, squat school logs which have been kept from that day to this by the reigning principals.[49]

The first is entitled *Wivenhoe Infants School*. Miss Eliza Jones was in charge of the five to seven-year-olds and it was evidently all she could do to make them come to school, let alone educate them. "School rather thin", we read, "some of the little girls going round the village as May Queens", or, "School very thin and the 5th (of November) scarcely any present in the morning..." Naturally; as the girls went May-ladying, as it was called, so the boys went out with their guys. Circuses were a natural attraction, of course, as was the annual fair, a launching or even a funeral. Nor, without parental support and in the days before compulsory education, was there much that Miss Jones and her successors could do, save to strike the names of persistent offenders off the register and send them home.

The weather was a perennial hazard. A wet day sent the attendance down dramatically because a fair number lived at Elmstead, Alresford and The Cross, and of course everybody walked to school. Even in fine weather the journey was difficult for the few who had no shoes. During the winter the infants who lived at these places did not come at all. "Several babies left for the winter", we read, as if they had hibernated, as indeed they had, to their local dame schools.

It took a long time for the country children to return after the summer break, for they were needed on the farms, gleaning for peas and beans, gathering acorns for pigs or blackberries for their parents. Natural disasters, such as shipwrecks, left families destitute and unable to afford the modest fees. A depression at the shipyard sent families out of the town in search of work. The fewer the children, the fewer the fees to pay for the school; so the early ledgers are very much concerned with attendance.

Diseases struck at the under-nourished frames of these children, and their teachers, practically all the year round. Then, as now, there were the severe colds which we call influenza, together with mumps, measles, chicken-pox and whooping-cough; then, unlike now, there was croup, scarlet fever and diphtheria, the two last-named often killing their victims. Even a headache could keep a child from school in the days before aspirin. The children's heads were often verminous, and they had scabies and sores, problems the authorities had not yet begun to tackle.

So the attendance figures fluctuated wildly; on one day Miss Jones might have fifty or fewer children to teach, on the next 170.

It was not easy to keep the school open. Apart from the holidays and half holidays, such as the regatta and the Queen's birthday, the building was often required for an election, a revision of the electoral register, a concert, masonic function or meeting of the trustees. So the school year was much longer than it is now, but if there were not too many epidemics and falls of snow the equivalent of forty-two weeks tuition might be achieved within the space of a year.

It was difficult to teach because all the infants were in one room, inadequately heated by stoves in winter and often stiflingly hot in summer. Sometimes the children shivered, sometimes they fainted. Nor was there generally enough staff to provide each of the four or five forms in the department with a teacher apiece.

Yet teaching was accomplished. The children learnt their letters with the aid of slates, also some simple arithmetic. They sang songs, such as *Once There Was A Little Kitty* and *When Father's Daily Work Is O'er*, performed simple physical exercises and had object lessons about such things as a Donkey, a Rabbit or a Potato. The older infant girls did needlework.

As the school was under the aegis of the Church of England, the rector or his curate came twice a week, and sometimes oftener, to hear the children recite the Lord's Prayer and the Creed, and give instruction on stories from the Old and New Testaments.

The first Boys Department log starts in 1888, which is for the next chapter, but the first Girls Department log starts with the department itself, in 1874. The work is more sophisticated, of course, but the problems, particularly of getting seven to fourteen-year-old girls to school, are the same.

There was also private education. James Ind's report of 1839 tells us that there were nine private schools at that moment, two of them, he thought, "a little above the rest, the children in them, paying, I believe, one shilling weekly". Of the two hundred children attending, about fifty were at dame schools or middle schools, the rest at "schools for the Higher Classes".[50]

They came and went, these schools. In the forties, for instance, H. N. Bransby ran the Colne House Academy where boarders paid eighteen to twenty guineas a year. There was F. Read who took two of his pupils to sea in order to make "scientific observations upon the sun", but their boat was wrecked and the party scrambled ashore at Mersea Island. And there was Edward Caston who bought £100 of furniture for his school, went bankrupt, fled from his creditors, had his house stripped by them in his absence, returned and was prosecuted for "vile conduct" towards his pupils.[51]

Gradually they dwindled; in 1871 there were reckoned to be only seven, with 139 pupils between them. However, the teaching probably improved. Miss Jane Hyde, formerly employed at the British School, set up for herself at premises behind the White House in the High Street which still exist. She taught from about 1870 to 1885. Miss Isabel Proctor came to Wivenhoe as a governess for John Martin-Harvey and in 1874 started a school in a double-fronted house in West Street, opposite *The Shipwright's Arms*. These were the two most important teachers in Wivenhoe at this time.[52]

4 Thomas and John Harvey.

Thomas Harvey, who succeeded Philip Sainty at the upstream shipyard in about 1832, was born in 1803. Having lost his mother at an early age, he was brought up by a Mrs. Todd. It is believed that he worked as a house carpenter and joiner with a man called Todd, doubtless this lady's husband or uncle. If this is the William Todd who built the smack *Liberty* in 1813 we can guess that he also trained Harvey as a shipwright, for Harvey once said that he had built a smack when he was twenty-one. For several years he was landlord of *The Black Boy*. Then he started to work in Sainty's old yard on his own account and soon acquired an excellent reputation for building boats that were light, swift and durable.[53]

Among his early successes was a series of small schooners used to bring fresh fruit to this country. This was before the days of effective refrigeration, so these vessels were heavily canvassed and designed for speed, rather on the lines of racing yachts. Four of them, launched between 1836 and 1839, suggest a touching of the forelock: *Lady Rebow*, *Gurdon Rebow*, *Slater Rebow* and *General Rebow*, for the Rebows were not financially involved with them.

The launch of the fruit schooner, *Prospero*, on 27th December, 1840, was a curious affair. One of the owners' wives, a Mrs. Johnson, came from London to christen her and was suitably instructed by Captain Joseph Blyth. The great moment arrived and she stood beside the slipway holding a bottle of wine which was attached to the *Prospero* by a rope. However, as the vessel moved towards the water the bottle was jerked out of her hands by a sailor on board, John Howard, and hauled rapidly inboard where it was publicly consumed by a crowd of sailors. In the scramble for the bottle, the men who should have prevented the ship from running into the opposite bank failed to do so and she foundered on the Rowhedge shore, breaking her rudder and cracking her sternpost. Captain Blyth was aggrieved. On the first day of the new year he caught up with Howard on The Quay, and first hit him and then flogged him with a rope's end. The local bench tacitly condoned the assault, for it fined Blyth a nominal sixpence and called Howard's behaviour "unsailorlike".[54]

The whole incident was extremely unsailorlike, for sailors are superstitious and if a bottle fails to break across the bows of a newly-launched ship it is considered a bad omen. Moreover, this was no jest on the spur of the moment, but a carefully contrived insult. Nor, in normal circumstances, would the sailors have allowed the ship to be damaged. There must have been bad blood in the shipyard at this time. Perhaps the sailors were underpaid, for in 1859 forty of them struck for higher wages. It would be interesting to know how the big employers of Wivenhoe, the Sandfords, Chamberlains, Harveys and their like, were regarded by their employees. Was this insult aimed at Thomas Harvey? He was certainly a forceful character and unlike many of his fellow

The Big Yachts 1801–1881

37. *Thomas Harvey (1803-1885).*

38. *Mrs. Thomas Harvey.*

39. *John Harvey (1830-1901).*

40. *Mrs. John Harvey, née Goyder d. 1871.*

boatbuilders a good businessman, for he prospered sufficiently to open a second yard, at Ipswich, in 1848. Was he tightfisted? In that same year a timber carter recovered £14 7s 7d from him in the Colchester Small Debts Court which might be a straw in the wind.[55]

At any rate, the torch lit by Philip Sainty was handed on. After the 25 ton *Prima Donna*, launched in 1845, proceeded to beat some of the best yachts of the Thames Yacht Club, the cups she won were exhibited in the window of Wallis's ironmonger's shop and the town shone with a reflected glory.[56]

At about this time, one of Thomas's sons, John, became actively involved in the firm. Born in 1830, his interest in yacht-designing started early. At fifteen he was apprenticed to his father and four years later helped to design the 48 ton cutter *Volante*, which was launched at Ipswich in 1849.

Two years later, the *Volante* and sixteen other English yachts raced the United States schooner *America* for a £100 cup presented by the Royal Yacht Squadron. The *America* beat all her rivals. Such was the beginning of the America Cup and of Great Britain's continual and unavailing efforts to win it. In 1852 John Harvey designed for himself, so that he could learn to race, the 10 ton *Kitten*.

Besides smacks and other commercial vessels, including a large number of brigs, (general cargo ships with a rig comprising both square sails and fore-and-aft), Thomas Harvey also built several yachts. When, in about 1857, he took John into his firm and renamed it Thomas Harvey & Son, racing and cruising yachts became a speciality and soon its reputation in yachting circles stood very high indeed. At Wivenhoe, father and son between them built over fifty yachts.

One of their earliest and most prestigious customers was the Marquis of Anglesey's fifth son, Lord Alfred Paget. Between 1857 and 1865 they built him two cutters: *Resolute* and *Snowdrop*, and two yawls: *Waterlily* and *Xantha*. Lord Alfred was a goldmine to the boatbuilding industry; he commissioned over forty yachts from different yards.

The launches became important social occasions. When, for instance, the 120 ton *Ione*, built for Richard Blanchard of Walton-on-the-Naze, descended the slipway, on 4th September, 1860, the local grandees, including John Gurdon Rebow and his young son, Hector, and Lady de Crespigny, were present in force. After the ceremony, forty ladies and gentlemen had a champagne luncheon in the Harveys' moulding loft.[57]

The river wall downstream of the town had for many years prior to this been used for laying up yachts, and the business of bringing the sails ashore and cleaning them, renewing such items as rigging, repainting and refurbishing the hulls, and generally looking after them for the six months between September and April, was now an integral part of the town's economy.

In 1862 the Harveys built a 12 ton schooner for a gentleman of leisure who

41. *The crew of the Waterlily, August, 1864.*

Loaned by Mr. John Leather

spent his time visiting, translating, keeping up with the arts in London and sailing round the Suffolk coast. Edward Fitzgerald was fifty-three and had recently printed his translation of a poem by a twelfth century Persian, *The Rubaiyat of Omar Khayyam*, as yet generally ignored by the public. Fitzgerald kept the *Scandal*, as he named his new boat, for eight years and often sailed her between Lowestoft and the mouth of the Colne.[58] In 1855-6, the Harveys were commissioned by the government to build four mortar vessels for the Crimea, ships, that is, from which mortars were actually fired, the launching pads being situated amidships, supported by eighteen solid pillars so that the ship could withstand the recoil.[59]

Thomas Harvey closed his Ipswich yard in 1864 and in the following year retired from Wivenhoe, apparently after becoming insolvent, making over the yard to John, who now called himself John Harvey & Co. Before Wivenhoe House was demolished, in about 1860, he had bought the mansion and twenty acres of the surrounding parkland, which he divided up into small building plots. It proved an excellent investment, for Wivenhoe was seriously overcrowded and needed to expand northwards. Then he retired to Brightlingsea where he made similar and equally successful speculations.

Disdaining the railway, he used to walk the seven miles to Wivenhoe with a spline, the five foot rod used by carpenters for measuring timber, in his hand. He died in 1885.

The elder Harvey, a creature of instincts and emotions, remained a member of the working class. His son John was essentially middle class. We can tell this by the simple fact that he sailed – for pleasure. He designed yachts on mathematical principles, read papers to the Institution of Naval Architects, of which he was a founder member, and helped Lloyds to establish a formal method of classifying yachts according to their measurements. This was no supplier of bespoke yachting to the gentry, but a man on a par with most of his clients.

The elder Harvey established a thriving shipyard which was principally known to the world of commerce; the younger Harvey put the town firmly on the social map and rivalled the best designers of his day. In this respect the sixties and seventies were wonderful years for Wivenhoe.

The most spectacular commissions were the *Dagmar*, a 33 ton cutter, and the *Alexandra*, a 39 ton steam yacht, both designed and built for the Prince of Wales, and launched in 1865 and 1869 respectively. Yawls were a speciality. There was the 80 ton *Druid* (1868), and the 148 ton *Rose of Devon* (1869) which won a silver cup at Le Havre shortly after her launch. Harvey and E. H. Bentall designed the famous *Jullanar* (1875); it was a tribute to the former's prestige that though built at Heybridge she was fitted out at Wivenhoe. A wealthy stockbroker, Theodore Pim, commissioned the 49 ton *Syren* in 1872 and three years later an 88 ton yawl, the *Rosabelle*, which he raced for a short while before taking up cruising. Pim's association with Wivenhoe was to be long and lucrative, also prestigious, for he was commodore of the Royal Thames Yacht Club.

Press reports indicate that at the turn of the sixties, Harvey's, in addition to commercial and government work, was generally building four yachts at any one time, with perhaps another eight undergoing repairs. Nevertheless, despite increasing, and increasingly well-heeled, custom, half way through his tenure of the shipyard John Harvey was declared bankrupt, an event somewhat eclipsed by the fire which preceded it.

On Thursday, 22nd August, 1872, a new yacht, *Softwing*, was launched and two days later her owner, J. M. Courtauld, gave a celebratory dinner in the shipyard to eighty of the workmen. The premises were clear by 10 p.m. and an hour later George Pryer, a draughtsman who joined the firm in about 1870 and later became John Harvey's partner in all but name, looked round to see that all was well. Shortly before midnight, Harvey's sister-in-law, Mrs. Joseph Harvey, who lived at *The Shipwright's Arms*, just outside the shipyard, saw that the building in which the dinner had taken place was alight. Her husband, who was walking on The Quay, also saw the flames. A horseman galloped to Colchester and by 1 a.m. the first fire-engine had arrived. It was low tide and to draw water from the river suction pumps had to be placed on the ferry hard, which made pumping more difficult, while the small fire-engine on the premises was itself overtaken by fire. By 5 a.m. the situation was in hand, but the firemen were kept at it all that day.

The blaze destroyed offices, warehouses, building sheds, houses belonging to John and Thomas Harvey, and several other cottages. One smack was saved by launching her, another by filling her hull with water, which actually boiled. Afterwards, John Harvey decorated his house with abstract sculpture: molten glass in which copper bolts, screws and the like were embedded.[60]

The rector immediately opened an appeal to replace the workmen's personal tools, which had been destroyed, and Harvey wrote to the *Essex Standard* to emphasise that this was urgent. It had been reported, he said, that the shipyard was insured for £17,000, but he held policies for only £3,400, including those on neighbouring property. In November of that year, he and his brother Thomas, who were business partners, were declared bankrupt.[61]

The bankruptcy proceedings revealed a good deal. John Harvey stated that his father "came to grief" and that his creditors were satisfied by William Hawkins of Alresford Hall, who then gave him enough money to get started. As soon as he did so, clients advanced money. "A man did not want capital to commence yacht building if he had got a good name". Though the business was run on a somewhat hand-to-mouth basis, there was no trouble, apparently, until John, with evident reluctance, admitted his brother Thomas as a partner in 1870, after the latter had filed a suit in Chancery. Presumably his father had promised Thomas a share of the business and he thought he could prove as much. John, as he put it, "gave way", and after that the firm went rapidly downhill. He tried to stop Thomas signing cheques, but without success, and had no idea what the firm's profits were. At the hearing the brothers were represented by different solicitors and John made it plain that he had no opinion of Thomas whatever.[62]

The fire benefited John Harvey, for it precipitated an inevitable bankruptcy and eliminated Thomas Harvey. At the bankruptcy proceedings he said he thought the fire had been started deliberately. It seems likely. He himself was absent at the time which is always suspicious. George Pryer had the best opportunity and it is conceivable he thought it best to have the bankruptcy early rather than late. As an accountant he would have known exactly how the firm stood. Again, the hypothetical arsonist might have been merely a workman with a grudge. All this is pure conjecture.

John Harvey's incombustible talent rose like a phoenix from the flames. On 21st March, 1873, the *Essex Standard* announced that a limited liability company had been formed, chaired by Edward Round, who, like his cousin Edmund, was a lawyer and a yachtsman. One of the first orders was from the Khedive of Egypt, who wanted two steam launches. At the beginning of May it was reported that Wivenhoe had few idlers. This was good news, for the town largely depended on the shipyard, which not only employed over 150 men but promoted a host of ancillary trades. Throughout that year the premises were rebuilt, and far better than before.[63]

Before his bankruptcy, John Harvey was personally responsible for the large, precarious concern which bore his name: thereafter, the finances rested with the directors, who employed him as manager, and with no loss of face for, in obvious tribute to his commercial value, the firm was named The John Harvey Yacht and Shipbuilding Company. His son tells of friction between Harvey and the directors, the artist versus the business world, but it may be that his father's exceptional talents needed the discipline of a boardroom.[64]

In the seventies, Wivenhoe reached the zenith of its fame and prestige, as indicated by *The Field* in the spring of 1874:

> *Every year something or other very good, and sometimes very original, is launched on the Colne, and the banks of the river during the long winter months are as closely packed with yachts as the more fashionable Medina or Haslar Creek. The Harvey firm have, and always had, a happy way of achieving exactly what they have set to do . . .* [65]

The article names, in alphabetical order, forty-one boats which had spent that winter at Wivenhoe. The smallest was the 5 ton cutter *Adela*, the largest the 565 ton bulk of the massive *Sunbeam*. Her owner, Thomas Brassey, M.P., ennobled in 1887, was a dedicated sailor who became Secretary to the Admiralty, obtained a Board of Trade Masters' Certificate and sailed the *Sunbeam*, with his wife and family aboard, all round the world, an achievement which Lady Brassey chronicled for the public.[66] The story is told that during one heavy storm at sea the crew were aloft, taking in the top gallants or performing some similar task. They could hardly see for the blinding wind and rain. One of them, a Wivenhovian called Jim Husk, turned to the man on his right and, referring to his employer, said: "The old bugger ought to be up here now". "The old bugger *is* up here!", replied Lord Brassey.[67]

"But", continued the article, "there are other yacht-building yards at Wivenhoe . . ." In particular, there was Husk's, which occupied the site immediately downstream of The Quay from the late 1840s. James Husk was a blacksmith who built a fishing boat. She "proved a clipper", so he built other smacks and yachts. In 1872, he produced the 14 ton cutter *Surge* and at the time of this article had just launched a cruising yawl, the 54 ton *Crusoe*. James Barr flourished in the seventies. He built a smack, *First Fruits*, behind *The Greyhound*, and a number of yachts at premises of his own near Husk's, among them the schooner *Snowflake* (1874), the cutter *Whydash* (1876), the yawl *Curlew* (1876) and the cutter *Kittiwake* (1878). One November evening in 1878 his yard caught fire. Happily, the Wivenhoe engine was soon in attendance and since his premises adjoined the brook the fire was extinguished in under four hours. Nevertheless, he lost everything except a blacksmith's shop. It is recorded that G. R. Lardner, a master at the National School, built a yacht called *Silver Spray* in 1882. It is unrecorded, but we can assume, that other Wivenhovians built themselves small smacks and dinghies.[68]

The article reminds us that many Colne fishermen crewed during the summer. The winter of 1875 had been unprofitable for them owing to gales, and "the late disturbances in the commercial and financial world" meant that fewer yachts would be put into commission, so the summer would be less profitable for them as well. Even as the yachting seasons rose to their zenith, life was not easy for the average Wivenhovian.

Closely connected with the shipyards were the sail-making and rope-making industries. The former were represented by Samuel Goodwin, who flourished for forty years from about 1820, and by the firm Madder & Son which started in the middle of the century in succession to the Durrell family.[69] Near The Cross, Browne's Ropery produced goods as prestigious and, in their own way, as highly regarded, as the big yachts they graced. The manufacture of rope involved machinery from an early date; on one frosty morning in 1855 it was the cause of a fatal accident.[70]

At 10.30 a.m., on Monday, 19th February, a steam boiler, a cylindrical affair made of plating two thirds of an inch thick, split into three pieces with a mighty bang which could be heard two or three miles away. The explosion shattered the engine room in which the boiler stood, strewing bricks and timber up to a distance of one hundred yards. None of the fifteen to twenty employees of the firm was injured, but three youths standing near the boiler were killed outright. What exactly happened is not clear, but at the inquest it was more or less agreed that the water inside the boiler evaporated and in consequence the boiler became red hot, so that when some other water reached it, probably from a steampipe which was beginning to unfreeze, an explosive gas was produced. Another, unofficial, and quite unprovable version, which eventually found its way into print, alleges that the explosion was caused because a heavy weight was hung on the safety valve in order to increase the pressure inside the boiler.[71]

Some ten years later the county magistrates received complaints that the ropery had caused several accidents. The principal feature of the factory was a gigantic rope walk, five hundred yards along, which stretched from Ropery House along The Avenue near to the present Harvey Road. The ropes were spun by machinery which travelled up and down the walk in an overhead

42. *The Ropery in the Avenue, with the factory chimney on the right, c. 1900.*

Loaned by Mr. E. H. C. Squire

gantry and small boys risked their lives by taking joy rides on the cables. However, the accidents had nothing to do with this. It appeared that the sight of the machinery made horses shy. So Mr. Browne screened his machinery from the public and the bench was satisfied.[72]

Wivenhoe built the big yachts, crewed them, laid them up and fished.

Sprats and oysters were landed on The Quay in abundance and if fish were scarce or unmarketable fishermen would dredge for a form of limestone known as septaria, which was used as a cement in building, or for copperas, (ferrous sulphate), which was used for dyeing, tanning and making ink.

Starfish, known as "five fingers", were another perennial. They were put in vats, where their decomposition was assisted with sulphate of lime, then ground up and mixed with dried clay procured from Ipswich, to be sold as manure.

At the beginning of the seventies a man called Charles Hamilton conducted this operation in a warehouse ten to fifteen yards from *The Black Boy.* Rotting starfish have a most unlovely and a most penetrating smell. The reek from Mr. Hamilton's warehouse, normally almost intolerable, was, on 27th July, 1872, literally so. Dr. Squire was woken in the small hours by the stench, John Polley, a shopkeeper, was unable to eat his breakfast, and Thomas Goodwin, the landlord of *The Black Boy*, actually left his premises. These people, and others, testified to the magistrates at Colchester, but at the end of five-and-a-half hours the case was dismissed. A letter from five irate Wivenhovians to the *Essex Standard*, accused the defendants of perjury and impugned the integrity of the bench. Since no action was taken against them they were probably right.[73]

5 Sporting and Social.

It was during the years covered by this chapter that Wivenhovians discovered that the Colne could be a source of pleasure to them, as it was for the owners of the big yachts.

Regattas became more numerous and better organised. There was a Colne Regatta as early as 1849, at Mersea, when a Wivenhoe boat won the race for smacks under 25 tons. From 1856 onwards it was held annually. In 1868 there was a rowing race between Colchester and Wivenhoe, followed by a sculling race for youngsters, and in 1869 a proper Colchester and Wivenhoe Regatta, based on rowing races for ships' and smacks' boats with, as its climax, a race for four-oared galleys. Originally a galley was a large, open boat of a kind favoured by coastguards and customs officers, but these were proper racing fours. One of them was specially built by John Harvey for this race. Coxed by George Pryer, it won easily and having done so the boat and crew were lifted bodily from the water and carried in triumph along The Quay.[74]

In 1870 there was an enlarged regatta, enlivened by The Wivenhoe Alexandra Band and fireworks. Before the day ended the committee dined at *The Black Boy* and having done so founded The Colne Boating Club, later known as The Colne Yacht Club. Edmund Round, whose yacht *Elaine* always graced the regatta, was the first commodore. The following year's regatta was held under its auspices.[75]

The 1872 regatta was cancelled because of the shipyard fire, but the 1873 was the biggest yet, with a race for yachts belonging to any recognised yacht club. As the seventies wore on, so the regattas continued to develop and in the last year covered by this chapter, besides rowing and sailing races, there was a punt race, aquatic derby race, swimming match and duck hunt shovel race, while ashore there was a circular rope walk, shooting gallery, swings and the usual fireworks.[76]

The first nineteenth century reference to cricket in Wivenhoe I can find is the report of a match played on Tuesday, 17th August, 1856, which "commemorated" the formation of a club. The Rector's XI played that of Sir Claude de Crespigny at the Mill Field, and the players included Dr. Philip Havens, George Chamberlain, William Browne, Master de Crespigny and

Master Gurdon Rebow. The father of the last-named was chairman, presumably at the "handsome repast" which punctuated the event.[77]

Next year there was a match between teams captained by Sir Claude and a Mr. Daniels. The spectators included "the gentry of the neighbourhood" and there was "a capital luncheon, tastefully arranged in a tent decorated with flags and flowers", provided by Sir Claude. In proposing the health of the host, the Secretary said that they were indebted to him for the formation of the club, "and he trusted the day was not far distant when it would be as flourishing . . . as the Wivenhoe Club in days of yore".[78]

So much for John Gurdon Rebow's assertion that cricket brought "the several classes in a parish together". These matches brought the grandees and the rich tradesmen together at times when everybody else was at work. The festal atmosphere, reminiscent of Dingley Dell's encounter with All Muggleton, was now old-fashioned and suggests that these were occasional events, and if the club had no opponents outside its own ranks it must have been somewhat exiguous. When this club was founded, or when the previous one existed, has not yet been discovered.

It evidently continued as long as Sir Claude reigned at the Hall, and indeed matches were played there. Not surprisingly, when The Wivenhoe Cricket Club, (now The Wivenhoe Town Cricket Club), was founded in 1879, N. C. C. Lawton was its first president and he was succeeded by the Hall's next tenant, James Jackson.[79]

By now, however, things had changed. The man at the Hall loaned the pitch, but the club was run by tradesmen and the players were the best cricketers in the town, irrespective of social class. The first recorded fixtures included Brightlingsea, Great Bentley, The Colchester Town Cricket Club, The Colchester Conservative Club and The Royal Grammar School.

As in any community, there were people with character and people who were characters. John Martin-Harvey gives us a few vignettes of the Wivenhovians he remembers when he was a lad in the seventies:

> . . . *Here comes John Jones, the giant Welshman, with his great white beard and patriarchal hair streaming in the wind, a veritable Charon, who plied the ferry-boat across the river to the opposite bank . . .*
>
> *And here is Polly Kent, the old crazy fishwife, whose articulations, in the absence of a roof to her mouth, are difficult to follow, and whose strange idiosyncrasy it is to throw herself into the river at every spring tide.*
>
> *There stands old Jack Gardiner upon the threshold of "The Rose and Crown", whose answer to your morning salutation will imply a courteous correction, "Good morning to you, sir". Backwards he will turn for the liquid refreshment which his nature demands, and more frequently as the day draws to its close . . .*

And here, swaying and lurching between his crutches, for he has lost both legs, swings Billy Cole. Down and out, my father set him up with a donkey and cart to carry parcels between Colchester and Wivenhoe. To see Billy, his donkey stabled for the night and the reward of his merit squandered at " The Black Boy", roaring drunk, his red eye-balls fixed and glaring, navigating his legless trunk uphill on the starboard tack, in a stiff east wind, was as gruesome a sight as even a Robert Louis Stevenson could hope to describe.

And now hops into memory the alert and charming little hunchback who keeps the store in our Shipyard – Arthur Sainty, son of the builder of the Pearl. His pinched but eager face radiates a quick intelligence. He will take one, if greatly favoured, into his small parlour, where hangs a portrait of himself, as a child, before the fall which dislocated his spine . . . [80]

Martin-Harvey also reminds us that smuggling was still rife in the town. He tells of one captain who, as he was carrying casks of rum ashore from the Harveys' own boat, was approached by a customs officer who demanded that duty should be paid on them. The captain thereupon carried the casks back aboard and invited the adult male population to a rum party, which invitation was joyfully accepted.[81]

To this man the incident was a glorious joke, but other Wivenhovians, especially in the early part of the century, were more seriously involved. Daniel Sutton, born in 1797, was young enough to have learnt about smuggling in the pre-Napoleonic era, and though he was Town Clerk of Colchester and built a quay at Wivenhoe, owned a number of boats, notably the lugger *Fox*, that engaged almost brazenly in the trade.[82]

I have been told, and disbelieve, tales of underground passages linking the church with public houses. However, Wivenhoe did contain a number of hiding places. At the shop that is now The Village Delicatessen, on the east side of Anchor Hill, it was discovered that in one room the skirting board could be removed in sections to reveal storage space behind. In The Storehouse, on The Quay, is a large cavity between two rooms that was once used for storing contraband silk. I have been told, and believe, that each public house on The Quay adopted a different smuggled spirit, gin at one house, brandy at another, and so on, with a tacit agreement not to poach on each other's preserves. Occasionally, there was a conviction. One of General Rebow's retainers, a woodranger called John Smith, was sent to prison after twenty-seven gallons of brandy and almost as much geneva had been found in his house.[83]

Crime was the immediate responsibility of the town constable. Until about 1850 he was able to put petty criminals into a temporary lock-up, The Cage, still situated in a corner of Anchor Hill. It a was useful place for drunks, but fell into disrepair about the middle of the century and was demolished near the end of it. Yet the name lingered on. Up to the Second World War, if you went to West Street via the tiny alleyway at the top of Anchor Hill you went "through The Cage".[84]

The eighteenth century Wivenhoe Association was revived in 1855 with the title The Wivenhoe and Elmstead Association for the Protection of Property and the Prosecution of Housebreakers and Thieves, and for many years its annual meetings, held at various public houses, were followed by convivial male evenings, though it also did some work.[85]

As Sunday morning church parade defined human relationships, so the public house expressed them. Here, male Wivenhovians gossiped, joked and sang. Many were frequently drunk, not a few were always drunk, and many a time the best of friends would fight each other in their cups and be friends the next day if they even remembered what had happened.

Those mentioned in Chapter 4 were now joined by others, after The Beerhouse Acts of 1828 and 1830 enabled householders to sell beer on and off their premises. In the latter half of the century, Orbell George Green produced "Wyvenhoe Ales and Stout" at his brewery in Paget Road, which might be bought at the nearby *Brewery Tavern*. I can find references to the brewery between 1867 and 1874. Then it evidently closed; the building itself was demolished in 1966.[86]

As in the previous century, the principal public houses were used for other purposes. For instance, when George Carrington, a carpenter, hanged himself in a fit of depression, the inquest was held at *The Anglesey Arms.* Having returned a verdict of temporary insanity, the jury, twelve important tradesmen with time on their hands, trooped round to *The Shipwright's Arms* where they considered the case of seven-year-old George Aldridge who was drowned while playing in some boats on The Quay. The coroner said, tritely, that boys ought not to be allowed to play about in boats, but in those days the odd drowning, whether of a child in the river or his father at sea, was part of life.[87]

Here, also, the lord of the manor exercised his residual rights concerning property, which were not formally extinguished until 1922.

Public houses were often used for auctions, and to follow the advertisements in the local press is to glimpse an aspect of social life that was always changing. In the 1830s and 1840s the auctions are for boats, and the stores, fittings and timber of wrecked boats. The auction is usually held on The Quay, but sometimes at *The Rose and Crown* or *The Ship at Launch*, or, up to about 1850, The Cinque Port Admiralty Warehouse, while wood surplus to Thomas Harvey's requirements is sold at The Shipyard. In the 1850s wrecks fall off as the Colne and the surrounding waters are better buoyed. *The Anchor* and *The Black Boy* join the list of venues. The early sixties see a swing from boats to houses and land. The Brummell estate was largely disposed of in Wivenhoe. Now *The Rose and*

Crown and *The Ship at Launch* fade out and *The Grosvenor* and *Park Hotels* fade in. Wood, no longer surplus, but battens and deals which arrive in bulk from abroad, is sold at The Shipyard. Meanwhile, the public houses continue to develop as social venues, where committees meet, celebratory dinners are held and trophies presented, places of male ritual and good fellowship.

As the century wore on, the social life, including its pleasures, became more organised. It was probably the rivalry between the two schools which ordained that their respective summer treats were preceded by formal processions to whichever garden or meadow was being loaned for the occasion. In August, 1867, the British School was accompanied by the Wivenhoe Alexandra Band, which was formed in 1863, the year the Prince of Wales married, and it was soon customary for this, the official town band, to be present at all treats, fetes, launchings, regattas and other important events. What the standard of playing was like we do not know, but a hint may be disclosed by one of the rules which has survived: "That any member blowing or beating his instrument before commanded to do so by the bandmaster be fined 1d and a penalty be 3d for any larking or nonsense".[88] The Wivenhoe Band continued until the end of this chapter; thereafter it was called The Wivenhoe Town Band.

6 The Railway.

As we have seen, most Wivenhovians were involved with the river, so when Peter Bruff, a prominent local engineer who was in the thick of the burgeoning railway industry, produced, in 1842, a scheme for a canal along the north bank of the Colne, from Wivenhoe to the Hythe, with a floating basin at either end, it must have aroused considerable interest.[89]

It was a bold, imaginative plan. The Paving and Channel Commissioners, the Colchester committee empowered to look into such matters, was interested and there were encouraging letters in the local press. The Admiralty, however, which sent two officials to look at the river, was unenthusiastic. Five years later The Colchester Navigation Bill was passed. Nevertheless, the scheme came to nothing. Evidently, Colchester was afraid of risking such a large sum of money. In 1854, however, there was a compromise solution: the channel up to the Hythe was made deeper.[90]

This scheme was, of course, designed to facilitate the passage of cargo boats up to the Hythe, in lieu of a branch line from Colchester to Wivenhoe, which Bruff thought would do Wivenhoe but little good and Colchester a lot of harm.

Nevertheless, after the main line from London to Colchester opened, in 1843, a branch line from Colchester to the Hythe was built, for which Bruff was the engineer, and in 1859 The Tendring Hundred Railway Company was formed, whose intention, and achievement, was to carry the line on to Clacton. The

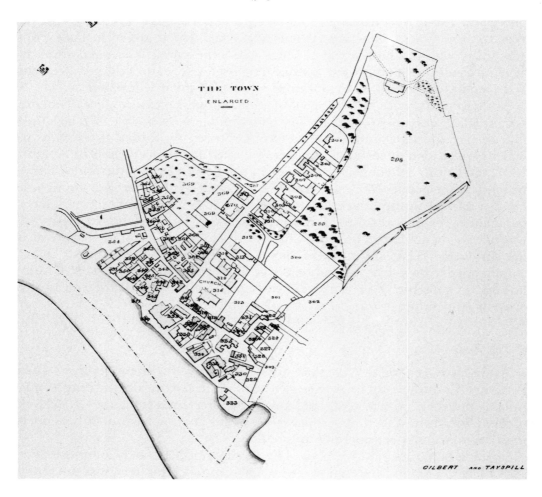

directors included J. C. Cobbold, whose family is now associated with beer, and Sir Claude de Crespigny.

At the beginning of 1862 it was announced that construction would shortly begin and on 2nd May, 1863, a deputation from the Great Eastern Railway met a deputation from the Tendring Hundred Railway and together they inspected the new station and dined on oysters in the new goods shed. The buildings were nominal, with neither a bridge nor a signal box and remained so for the next twenty-three years. However, there was already a spur of track down to the river. Now sprats could be landed directly on to railway trucks from the smacks; henceforth this area was known as the Railway Wharf, or the Railway Quay.[91]

The Big Yachts 1801–1881

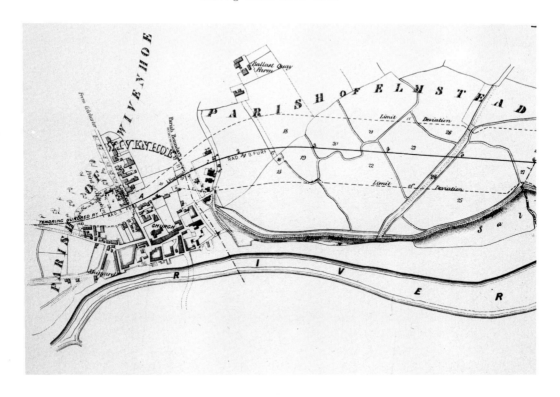

43. *Left: Map of Wivenhoe before the railway, made by &* 44. *Gilbert & Tayspill, Surveyors.*
44. *Right: Map of Wivenhoe showing the proposed railway, but without the branch line to Brightlingsea.*

Both from the Essex Record Office at Chelmsford

On Friday, 8th May, 1863, without ceremony, the line was opened. A single track carried six passenger trains daily in each direction between Wivenhoe and Colchester. The first was the 8.30 a.m. from Wivenhoe, the last the 6.30 p.m. from Colchester. At a shareholders' meeting in October of that year it was announced that the line was already doing well. In the eighteen-and-a-half weeks from 8th May it had carried 11,575 passengers and 1,460 tons of goods, mostly fish.[92]

Naturally, the Tendring Company wanted to build the five mile extension line to Brightlingsea, but had been forestalled by a north country solicitor and entrepreneur, George Bradley of Castleford, Yorkshire. Bradley convened a public meeting at the *Duke of Wellington*, Brightlingsea, at which he met the

119

45. *The Station Hotel, c. 1900.*

Loaned by Mrs. Claire Weston

46. *The railway station, c. 1900.*

Loaned by Mr. Brian Oakley

The Big Yachts 1801–1881

47. *Where the railway line branched off to Brightlingsea, with a signal box, c. 1905.*

Colchester Castle Museum

48. *Alresford Bridge, c. 1900.*

Loaned by Mr. E. H. C. Squire

locals and talked abut the railway as if work on it might begin the following morning. However, Parliament did not sanction the project until the following July.[93]

On Monday, 21st September, 1863, work was ceremonially put in hand. The directors arrived by the 11.27 a.m. train and were greeted with *See The Conquering Hero Comes* from The Wivenhoe Volunteer Band. They proceeded to Brook Field, presumably adjacent to Brook Street, where Sir Claude de Crespigny, who had gone over to the enemy by leaving The Tendring Hundred Company and buying a large number of shares in the new one, made a speech. Then he handed a tiny steel spade, its handle ornamented with a white satin bow, to the rector's wife, who cut the first sod. The company then repaired to the new, and as yet unlicensed, *Park Hotel*, where there was a banquet and more speeches. Sir Claude, perhaps jokingly, quoted the contractor, William Munro, as saying that the line would open in six months' time.[94]

In fact, it took much, much longer and as month succeeded month The Tendring Company became restive, for it wanted to extend the main branch line to Walton, but until the smaller company had completed the first section of track to the point where the Brightlingsea line branched off to the right it was unable to do so. Eventually, it gave The Wivenhoe and Brightlingsea Railway Company an ultimatum: either the first section of track was completed by November, 1864, or it would do the work itself.

And, indeed, this is just what happened. The Wivenhoe and Brightlingsea Company itself was also concerned at the slow progress; early in 1865 Munro was dismissed and Bruff took his place.

Although the original estimate for the line was £25,000, Bradley himself talked of the cost being contained within £40,000 at a shareholders' meeting early in 1864, and towards the end of the following year the company applied for a bill to raise more capital. In November, 1865, the line was inspected and official consent for its opening withheld; very likely it still showed the effects of a landslip near Alresford Creek.[95]

Meanwhile, the Tendring Hundred line from Wivenhoe to Weeley opened on 1st January, 1866, and the extension to St. Botolph's on 1st March.

On 17th April, 1866, Sir Claude and his fellow directors were at last able to make the ceremonial journey from Wivenhoe, to eat oysters and speechify in the new goods shed at Brightlingsea.[96]

Thus was the railway line extended eastwards from Wivenhoe Station to bisect the High Street. Looking at this rather ugly cutting one might imagine that several houses in the High Street and elsewhere were sacrificed to make it. Not so. There was already a gap in the High Street at this point; to the west was Joliffe's Garden, to the east the lower part of the Brummell estate. The only

The Big Yachts 1801–1881

houses to be demolished were some old cottages – to make way for the station.

The railways changed the Colne radically. Brightlingsea, which had visions of becoming an East Anglian Grimsby, anticipated the boom by building larger smacks. From 1857 onwards, Aldous, instead of building the usual 13 tonners, started producing 20 to 40 ton vessels. So did boatbuilders at Wivenhoe and Rowhedge. In 1874, 132 smacks of 15 to 40 tons were registered at the port of Colchester.[97]

In March, 1865, the chairman of The Tendring Hundred Company, William Hawkins, gave his shareholders some extremely good news about the Wivenhoe railway wharf. From the opening of the line to the end of 1864, 2,462 tons of fish and oysters had left Wivenhoe for London and 1,630 for local stations. 73 tons of fish had left the town in the first two months of 1864, 383 tons in the first two months of 1865. One interesting freight was Scotch oysters, which were delivered to London by steamer, sent to Wivenhoe by rail, put into the Colne for a few months and then sent back by rail to the London market. On one exceptional day no fewer than sixteen tons of oysters had arrived at the station. Coal was unloaded at the new wharf and would be in far larger quantities were it not for Mr. Corsellis. By no financial inducement could he be persuaded to part with more land for a larger wharf. Eight thousand more people had used the line than in the corresponding period of the previous year.[98]

Meanwhile, trucks containing rails, sleepers and ballast were moving over the track to extend the main branch line to Walton. On 17th May, 1867, the whole extension was opened.

7 Mid-Victorian Expansion.

Wivenhoe was now far, far more accessible to the rich men who owned the big yachts and correspondingly more attractive to them – and indeed to everyone else. The new station had hardly opened before *The Station Hotel* and *The Park Hotel* appeared, obvious billets for commercial travellers, and by 1866 they had been joined by *The Grosvenor Hotel*. Thanks to the St. Botolph's extension, Colchester was now within easy reach of Wivenhovians, and for a somewhat daunting 6/9d they could reach London on a third class ticket in an ordinary train. A first class express ticket cost exactly twice as much.

The railway accelerated the expansion of the town, which had been moving northwards since the death of William Brummell in 1853. In the following year Wivenhoe House was bought for £6,000 and two years later the house, garden and twenty-five acres of parkland were auctioned in Colchester. Thereafter, bits of the estate were sold off, year by year, for building. Wivenhoe House was

49. *Sir W. S. Gilbert at the wheel of his s.y. Chloris.*

demolished in 1861 and Park Road established through the site, north to south. A few acres were used for a new, medium-sized house, The Nook.[99]

In 1863, a vestry meeting decided to pay £200 for a road from the station to the High Street on land donated, no doubt willingly, by the railway.[100] Station Road was soon built, and Clifton Terrace which emphasised the disfiguring gash made by the railway line across the original pattern of small streets. Socially and economically, the railway was a great boon to the town; visually, it was and remains, an intrusion.

The Big Yachts 1801–1881

Slightly grander houses started to fill in the east side of the High Steet opposite the high brick wall, built in 1841, surrounding Wivenhoe Park. Gothic House appeared in 1870; then, it was "a desirable residence", now, it is sometimes called "the Hitchcock house". Beside it, in Rebow Road, the foundation stone of six pretty little almshouses was laid in July, 1873, and two months later they were ready for completion. They cost £5,000; the donor was Mary Ann Sandford, sister of Thomas who built the Congregational Church. Her beneficiaries had to be spinsters or widows, over sixty and with no means of employment.[101]

At about this time several other houses covered their timber frames with Victorian facades, and the reigning, though absent, lord of the manor contributed some new buildings. The initials N.C.C. and a date in the seventies appeared on Anchor Hill and the outhouses of several farms in the neighbourhood.

Almost opposite the chapel, on the corner of Alma Street and Hamilton Road, was a piece of land which fetched £35 when it was auctioned at *The Anchor* in 1863; six years later a warehouse had been built there with sail lofts on three floors. This building, 30, Alma Street, was to serve many different purposes over the next century or so, as indeed was the former Swedenborgian Chapel.[102]

Alma Street cannot antedate the Crimean battle of 1854 and was probably begun soon after. The architecture of Alma Street, and of Station Road, Clifton Terrace, Denton's Terrace, Colne Terrace, Paget Road and 1 to 11, Anglesea Road: box-like accommodation without gardens for people too busy to tend them, (save, fortuitously, in Clifton Terrace), and long, protruding lofts on the first floors, or passageways running from front to rear for sails and spars, is typical of the Colneside sixties.

The mid-Victorian picture is completed by the arrival of gaslight.

The Wivenhoe Gas Company Ltd. was formed at the beginning of 1861, under the patronage of Sir Claude de Crespigny, John Gurdon Rebow and the rector. It issued a thousand £1 shares, sold them all and built a gasworks in St. John's Street; by New Year's Day, 1862, some shops and houses in the town were lit by gas. Soon after, the streets were also.[103]

During this chapter the population of Wivenhoe rose, though erratically, from 1,093 in 1801, to 2,280 in 1881. There was a slight fall in the 1800's and a sharp one in the 1830's, but the success of the shipyards and the advent of the railway sent the numbers up thereafter. Rowhedge grew fairly evenly, from 370 to 1,272 and Brightlingsea, apart from a drop in the 1840s, from an estimated 807 to 3,311. So the census returns tell us, but they cannot be totally accurate. Then, more than now, people were reluctant to divulge information to the authorities.

8 The End of an Era: John Harvey and Chloris.

When *The Field* visited Wivenhoe in 1879, it found no "new forms" to study in Harvey's shipyard, but took note of familiar ones and thought they were as good as anything afloat. Harvey and Pryer, whose names appeared side by side at the top of the firm's headed notepaper, were now more involved with commercial craft. They had two steamers in hand, of 507 and 300 tons, also a 400 ton auxiliary brig, a 70 ton torpedo boat and a 4 ton sailing boat, while Husk was building and altering small boats, and Barr occupied with a 10 ton racing yacht, "something of the Jullanar type".[104]

Harvey did, however, produce one more, moderately large yacht, the *Chloris*, for the dramatist and librettist, W. S. Gilbert.

Not long after his first play was produced, Gilbert commissioned Ratsey of Cowes to build him the 38 ton schooner *Pleione*, in 1867; his next boat was the 28 ton yawl *Druidess*, which was built at Dartmouth. He was already a well-known playwright when *H.M.S. Pinafore* made Gilbert-and-Sullivan a household name. Its successor, *The Pirates of Penzance*, opened in April, 1880. Perhaps this second huge success, the knowledge that *Pinafore* was not a fluke, encouraged Gilbert to commission another and larger yacht.

Over the winter of 1880-1, the *Chloris* was built in Harvey's yard. She was a 60 ton steam yacht, rigged as a yawl, 85 feet long, with a draught of 10′ 6″, a comfortable, practical, handsomely appointed, but neither luxurious nor ostentatious vessel, one well suited to its owner's tastes and disposition.

Harvey kept his client posted as to the yacht's progress. On 4th April, 1881, he proposed that the *Chorlis* – the name had perhaps not yet been settled – should be launched exactly a fortnight later, at 3.20 p.m. Perhaps she was, though I can find no record of this in the local newspapers; it is possible that Gilbert, always a gentleman, asked for a quiet launch. The name *Chloris* is also typical in that it refers to none of his stage successes.[105]

After the launch there was more fitting out to be done and Harvey wrote to Gilbert about the side light and the lavatory and the mirrors for the berths and the stove-tables and the steerage lamp and the folding chair ... A letter at the end of April begins, "Following your several letters of 21st, 22nd and 24th and your Telegram of 25th I beg to say ... " Gilbert evidently took as meticulous an interest in his yachts as he did in the production of his operettas.

Eventually, the yacht left Wivenhoe and for three summer months her owner took her in and out of harbours on the South Coast.

Even as John Harvey built the *Chloris* he probably knew that the firm which bore his name would have to close. It was not his only worry. There was his son, John Martin, a short, moody youth, now rising seventeen, with a penchant for collecting things, personal adornment, reading, writing and day-dreaming, but little interest in the family business to which he was apprenticed.[106]

Young John was born at a house in the shipyard, on 22nd June, 1863, the fourth of seven children, three of whom died in infancy. The other survivors were his sister, May, and brothers Charles and Goyder. Not long after his birth, the family moved to Quay House, at the foot of Rose Lane.

Mrs. Harvey was never well and what with her absences in search of better health and her premature death when John was only a boy, the family was often split up. However, John spent a fair amount of his youth at Wivenhoe. It was at Quay House that his father first introduced him to the theatre. Here he made his debut in a children's play, *The Frog and the Princess.*

His father would have liked John to design boats, but though the younger Harvey appreciated the aesthetic side of the trade, he was not attracted to the routine work. Relations between father and son became extremely strained until one day John's future was settled. His father asked him if he would like to act, John said he would and from then on it was simply a matter of finding a suitable opening. Naturally, Gilbert's assistance was invoked. He suggested that John should take lessons from an actor, which he did. Later, he gave him an audition in London and encouraged him.

Later that year John Harvey's shipbuilding firm was put into voluntary liquidation; evidently there was not enough work to keep the yard going. However, his second bankruptcy, like his first, did him no financial injury. He emigrated to America where his reputation kept him in constant demand. Very likely George Pryer might have succeeded him at Wivenhoe had he not died, in September, 1880, aged forty-two. John Harvey finally retired to England, but before his death, in 1901, he had the great satisfaction of seeing his son John become an actor-manager.

John Martin-Harvey records that things were changing at the shipyard:

Iron was then displacing wood for ship-construction, and the sound of the adze, the ring of the caulker's mallet, and the hum from the saw-pits, were giving way to the strident rattle of the riveter's hammer and the lurid work of iron furnaces.[107]

Evidently, the yard was beginning to adopt the new medium and its techniques, but John Harvey was essentially geared to wood. Happily, for the survival of the yard – and the town – a complete change was made. For a few years later a shipbuilding firm from the Thames took over the yard and a steel age was begun.

The Story of Wivenhoe

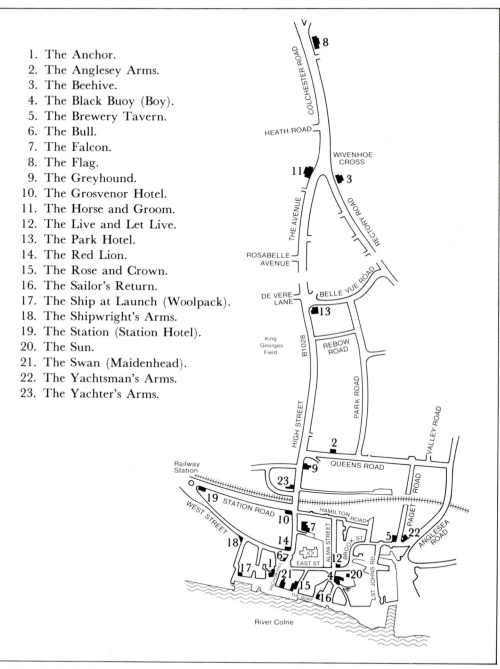

1. The Anchor.
2. The Anglesey Arms.
3. The Beehive.
4. The Black Buoy (Boy).
5. The Brewery Tavern.
6. The Bull.
7. The Falcon.
8. The Flag.
9. The Greyhound.
10. The Grosvenor Hotel.
11. The Horse and Groom.
12. The Live and Let Live.
13. The Park Hotel.
14. The Red Lion.
15. The Rose and Crown.
16. The Sailor's Return.
17. The Ship at Launch (Woolpack).
18. The Shipwright's Arms.
19. The Station (Station Hotel).
20. The Sun.
21. The Swan (Maidenhead).
22. The Yachtsman's Arms.
23. The Yachter's Arms.

50. *Wivenhoe Public Houses, past and present.*

Map specially drawn by Vince Rayner.

CHAPTER 7

Late Victorian and Edwardian 1881-1914

1 The Earthquake.

At 9.18 a.m., on Tuesday, 22nd April, 1884, the worst earthquake that has ever reliably been recorded in this country was felt over an area of 53,000 square miles. The shock waves reached as far north as Cheshire, as far south as the Isle of Wight, as far west as Somerset and to the east at Boulogne and Ostend. It was not a very severe earthquake, but within seven seconds it damaged between 1,200 and 1,300 buildings. The epicentre was to the south east of Colchester, in the Abberton, Peldon and Langenhoe areas; here the worst damage was wrought. The most extensive damage, however, was at Wivenhoe because there were more buildings.[1]

It was a little after high tide. Lord Alfred Paget had just boarded his 300 ton *s.s. Santa Cecilia*, which was moored against the Rowhedge bank, opposite *The Anchor*. All at once the vessel pitched violently and a low rumbling was heard, so that her owner thought the boiler was about to blow up. He was flung against the rigging, which he grasped firmly, and thus obtained the finest possible view of the destruction as it moved swiftly along The Quay from east to west.

It was a tidal wave expressed in terms of bricks and mortar. The houses rose up, then fell back, gently and slowly pitching and tossing, like small craft acknowledging a passing liner. The roofs rippled and most of the chimney pots fell into the bedrooms beneath, while showers of tiles descended in a gigantic cloud of dust. At the east end of the town the fifty foot chimney of the gas works collapsed over eight houses owned by John Green Chamberlain. He and Isaac Blyth, another large property owner, suffered severely. At the west end, Edwin Wilkins was standing in the shipyard near the stern of the 180 ton schooner, *Medora*, hauled up on the slipway; he saw that vessel rear and plunge, as did other boats, though none of them fell over, while cracks appeared in his office buildings and their chimneys collapsed. The Rev. John Baillie was in his churchyard; he saw the church tower make obeisance, first to the south east,

129

51. *Quayside Cottage, Maple Cottage and Trinity House, bandaged up after the earthquake.*

Colchester Castle Museum

then to the north west, while several tons of masonry fell from the battlements and with such force that pieces were deeply embedded in the ground. A huge crack appeared in the tower, from the top to the middle. The Congregational Chapel lost much of its balustrade and cornice; the centre of the ceiling fell and with it the gas chandelier. Wivenhoe Hall lost a gable on the north end and several chimneys. Rooms were filled with soot and rubble, so James Jackson temporarily moved out, as did Colonel Bowen from The Nook and George Harvey from Gothic House. Other Wivenhovians were luckier. At Elaine Cottage, Edmund Round escaped almost unscathed. The chimney pots of the almshouses "started", but stayed where they were. At the National School the children panicked, but the headmaster, Mr. Collins, realising what was happening, calmed them and dismissed them. The Infants' headmistress, Eliza Jones, compared the earthquake to "a terrific rumbling noise, as if wheels were heard underground". Not a single child was injured.[2] The nearer to Colchester, the less the damage. Wivenhoe Park, whose owner was abroad, lost some

52. St. John's Road, or Gas Road as it was then known, after the earthquake, photographed by Philip Damant.

Colchester Castle Museum

chimney pots but was otherwise unharmed. As The Quay shook and shuddered, so a huge wave swept across the Colne. The craft afloat tossed violently and fishermen working aloft were casually shrugged off into the water.

The earthquake lasted for no longer than six or seven seconds. Boats and buildings were again motionless, and as a pall of dust rose from The Quay, so did the cries of the panic-stricken and wounded. They streamed out of their houses, fearful that this was the beginning of a more frightful disaster. The men left their nets or the shipyards and quickly returned to their homes, to rescue and comfort their wives and children, tend injuries, survey the damage and start to clear the debris.

Wivenhoe looked as if it had been shelled. Many houses were uninhabitable and their contents largely spoiled or destroyed, yet the words "wreck" and "ruin", which appeared frequently in the press reports, were overstatements. Had the earthquake lasted a few seconds longer, the mediaeval timber frames would have been as denuded of bricks as they were of tiles. The timing was also

53. *The destruction as viewed from the s.s. Santa Cecilia, photographed by Philip Damant.*

Loaned by Mr. Bernard Polley

very fortunate. Had the earthquake occurred, say, three hours earlier, several Wivenhovians would have died in their beds; instead, the townsfolk had the rest of the day in which to absorb the shock, gossip, commiserate, extemporise bedrooms on ground floors or seek sanctuary elsewhere. The weather, too, was merciful. Heavy rain or a high wind would have multiplied the damage. The east end of the town had a narrow escape. As the employees of the gas works fled the choking fumes issuing from fractured pipes, one man had the presence of mind and courage to pause and turn off the main cylinder. An explosion would have surely killed several people.

In fact, Wivenhoe claimed a single victim. Emily Betts, a spinster of forty, who lived with the Browne family at The Ropery, was in bed, recovering from a stroke. After the earthquake she had a relapse and died later that day.

Dr. Squire was kept busy for some time, bandaging up his practice. The houses were likewise bandaged, their wounds covered with tarpaulin. Most of the interim repairs had been achieved by Friday.[3]

It is not recorded that Wivenhoe suffered any lingering physical or mental damage, though the schoolchildren were on edge for a week or so. The real damage was financial. The houses could be repaired fairly easily, but the cost was often beyond their owners' means. Widows, especially, were hard hit.

The grandees realised this and quickly took action. A deputation of notables waited on the Lord Mayor at the Mansion House the following Saturday, with John Baillie and James Jackson representing Wivenhoe. There was oratory and an *ad hoc* exhibition of photographs taken by Philip Damant.[4]

There were public meetings in London, Chelmsford and Colchester, and more speechifying. A relief fund was set up, to which Edmund Round and

James Jackson gave £50, and John Baillie £20. Mr. Jackson was dissatisfied with its progress; he thought that more money would have been raised if the disaster had occurred in Timbuctoo. However, by mid-June almost £10,000 had been collected. The final reference to this fund I can discover is on 2nd August. The earthquake, a nine days' wonder, which had brought a host of sightseers to the town, was now over.[5]

This disaster should be compared with the failure of Messrs. Mills, Bawtree & Co's bank in 1891. This affected hundreds of Wivenhovians, some of whom lost their lives' savings. Though an infinitely less noticeable disaster it may have been the greater of the two.[6]

2 Wivenhoe Park: Hector Gurdon-Rebow and Charles Gooch.

When he inherited Wivenhoe Park in 1870, Hector John Gurdon-Rebow was twenty-four; two years later, probably because he was in the Guards, he leased the property to another gentleman farmer, Abraham Garrett. Though he evidently lived in London, Gurdon-Rebow donated small sums to local charities, hunted with the Essex and Suffolk, built cottages for his farm labourers and adopted some new methods of agriculture. In 1873, he married his cousin, Judith Gurdon, and two years later they had a son, Martin.

In the autumn of 1880 Mr. Garrett surrendered his lease. Hector Gurdon-Rebow was now thirty-four and ready to squire it at Wivenhoe Park. Apart from his military training he had served an apprenticeship in a brewery and when Daniell & Sons became a limited company he was made chairman. He was also chairman of Essex and Suffolk Life Assurance and had other directorships. He was a magistrate, a lieutenant in the Essex Rifle Militia, a deputy lieutenant of the county and, in 1882, High Sheriff. He played cricket, for Colchester and East Essex, also football and tennis. Somebody who knew him described him as "a cheery companion, a good friend, a generous landlord and a popular sportsman".[7]

In 1884, he was paid a unique and extremely flattering compliment. It so happened that the Colchester Town Council at that time comprised twelve Conservatives and twelve Liberals, so whenever it disagreed the matter could never be decided by a vote. Happily, a recent statute enabled it to co-opt an outsider as mayor, which it did, for the first and only time. Needless to say, the outsider had to be politically independent, reasonably well-informed and a good chairman, and it appears Gurdon-Rebow was all these things.

If his father had no striking gifts of eloquence, he had none whatever, which was just as well, for besides presiding over the full Council he also chaired every single one of its fourteen committees. During his term of office he helped to create the Recreation Ground at Old Heath and chaired two important public

54. *Hector John Gurdon-Rebow (1846-1930).*

Colchester Borough Council

meetings: one produced The Albert School of Science and Art, (now The Colchester Institute of Higher Education), the other considered the depression in trade and agriculture.

This triumphant mayoralty was followed by Gurdon-Rebow's financial ruin, the sale of the Wivenhoe Park estate and his retirement into complete obscurity.

There were three factors which led to his undoing: his father's profligacy, the depression of the eighties and his inability to appreciate or to handle his social and financial position. A hundred years later it is not easy to assess their relative importance; but the last was surely decisive.

It is possible that the estate was encumbered to some extent when he inherited it; when he sold it, in 1902, the purchaser was told that the vendor would receive no money at all. Had the agricultural depression of the early eighties not intervened, a prudent and businesslike man might have paid off the mortgage, if one existed. However, such evidence as we have indicates that Gurdon-Rebow was not that sort of man.

He was a "generous" landlord. Does that mean soft? In 1884, when the depression had already appeared, he took a trip abroad for four or five months. Did he think he could afford this? What did it cost to be mayor of Colchester, and later an alderman of the Essex County Council? He was not reckless with money, but should he have entered local politics at all?

In 1899, when he joined the Essex County Council, time was already running out, for in the following year he declined re-election. His fellow councillors regretted his departure. So did the School Board in Wivenhoe, when he resigned the year after that. At this point his name disappears from the local press. I suppose he went to live at his town house, 92, Eaton Place, for it was from here that his youngest sister was married in 1895.[8]

In March, 1895, he let Wivenhoe Park for three years to Sampson Hanbury, a retired businessman, who died there in 1900. The Grinling Gibbons carving of *St. Stephen* was sold to the Victoria and Albert Museum in 1897; very likely it was then that the other art treasures in the house were sold or auctioned. In August, 1900, more than 1,200 acres of the estate were sold off. There were two more short lets and on 7th July, 1902, the remaining 2,381 acres, comprising the house, park and fourteen farms, were auctioned in London, but withdrawn at £57,000, having failed to reach the reserved price. A month or so later, so I am credibly informed, a lady who was looking at the property advertisements in *The Times*, said to her husband, "Oh, Charlie! I know that place. I've been there. Let's buy it!" And they did.[9]

Even as Gurdon-Rebow's financial problems were coming to a head, his son took a commission in the Grenadier Guards, for whose social life he would have needed ample funds. One day young Martin would have had to resign his commission; instead he died in South Africa. On 17th September, 1901, he was in charge of a patrol which was surrounded, in a farmhouse, by an overwhelming number of Boers. He refused to surrender and was shot dead at close range.[10] His parents donated a brass altar cross to St. Mary's Church in his memory; it stands there to this day.

In 1908, Gurdon-Rebow was sued by a Mr. N. Cohen of The Yorkshire Receiving Office, for £110; he had been declared bankrupt earlier that year and was being pursued by another money-lending company. Altogether, he owed friends and money-lenders over £19,000. Nevertheless, he was still living at Eaton Place, employed a groom-valet and had recently quitted a prestigious address at Windsor. The court learned that he was writing cheques and had assigned shares in breweries of which he was a director to his sister, which he was not supposed to do, and moreover without telling his creditors. Like his

55. *Charles Edmund Gooch (c. 1870-1937) and his wife, Eleanor (1868-1918), outside Wivenhoe Park.*

Loaned by Mrs. Patricia Gooch

father, he evidently lived beyond his means, without knowing, or wanting to know, that those means were fast running out, and without knowing, or wanting to know, what he should do to avoid ruin. Was this ignorance, vanity, or simply his upbringing?[11]

Some time later, he and his wife retired to Woodhall Spa, Lincolnshire, their whereabouts known only to a few friends. He died in 1930. His retirement suggests that once his role as a gentleman of leisure was over so was his effective life, for he had no other role to play. Like a captured piece on a chessboard, he was out of the game.

Gurdon-Rebow was succeeded at Wivenhoe Park by another Old Etonian gentleman of leisure, Charles Edmund Gooch, (1870-1937).

His daughter-in-law thinks that he bought the estate because of the game, since he was a good shot. He certainly spent a good deal of time running it and personally farmed the Home Farm immediately north of the Park. He was particularly generous to his tenants.[12]

Mr. Gooch was a punctilious churchgoer; on Sundays he and his family would walk to the Wivenhoe or Greenstead parish church, or be driven to Elmstead, where he invariably read the lessons.

He was an enthusiastic campanologist. He could be charming, and effectively helpful to those in trouble, but at the same time was autocratic, especially with his children, Charles and Marguerite, whom he brought up strictly, not allowing them to mix with other children or even sending them to school. He kept up his house and grounds properly and maintained a full staff of servants: butler, footman, cook, kitchenmaid, scullerymaid, head housemaid, second housemaid, between maid, nurse, under nurse, ladysmaid, tutor, governess, coachman, under coachman, one or two grooms and a boy who cleaned the boiler and helped in the garden. Though not particularly sociable, there were dances and parties at the Park. He was a pillar of the Conservative party, an ardent patriot, a magistrate and county councillor. For his spare moments he had an excellent classical library, while his wife, Eleanor, a large Scotswoman, played the piano. One Wivenhovian who remembered the Gooches described them to me as "the true sort".[13]

Up to the First World War and for several years thereafter, Wivenhoe Park was in capable hands, those of the last owner who could afford to maintain it as a country gentleman's seat.

3 Wivenhoe Hall: James Jackson, Claude Egerton-Green and Alexander Barlow.

Wivenhoe Hall, meanwhile, was sliding into a state of extreme disrepair. Tenant succeeded tenant, but with gaps between the lets, and the town must have begun to wonder what would happen to the old pile.

In August, 1881, after the death of N. C. C. Lawton, an Australian who had been at Eton with Hector Gurdon-Rebow, James Jackson, moved in. He was president of the Cricket Club and commodore of the regatta, while Mrs. Jackson sold Zulu assegais at a bazaar held to raise money for a new church organ, and taught at the Sunday School. In 1885 the Jacksons moved to Lexden Manor, on the other side of Colchester, but Mr. Jackson stood for the Harwich constituency in that year. The boundaries had been redrawn and for the first time included Wivenhoe, as they did until 1983.[14]

By the spring of 1887 he was succeeded by a young sprig of the local Green family. Claude Egerton Egerton-Green began his tenancy by marrying. When

56. *Claude Egerton Egerton-Green (1863-1904).*

Colchester Borough Council

he returned from his honeymoon his carriage was met at The Ropery by a party of locals on horseback, boys from the National School holding flags and the Colchester Town Band. Then it was drawn by hand to the Hall, where there was a triumphal arch with God Bless The Happy Pair on it. This suggests that he was already popular. He certainly took a leading part in local affairs, becoming a captain, not a mere figurehead vice-president, of the Cricket Club, patronising other clubs and societies, helping to found The Colne Lodge of Freemasons in the town and running a soup kitchen in the winter months, which may have been connected with his evident desire to shine in politics. For he became a county councillor when the Essex County Council was founded in

1889, and a Colchester town councillor in 1892. Twice mayor, his star was still rising when, in 1904, he fell off his bicycle and died of a heart attack, aged forty-one.[15] Alexander Kay Barlow, a rich Old Malvernian of forty, who succeeded him in the summer of 1896, was content to be a big fish in a small pond. He was the first and longest-serving chairman of the Wivenhoe Urban District Council and he often entertained his fellow members and guests at the Hall and chaired smoking concerts. During his tenancy social events were frequently held in the Hall grounds and the brick wall bounding the High Street was used for graffiti by Barlow himself. He owned a succession of boats and belonged to several yacht clubs. He had recently married and three of his four children were probably born at the Hall. Barlow was described to me as "a terrific character, rather a naughty old thing", and his wife as down-trodden. He could certainly be tricksy and temperamental.[16]

Before he moved into the Hall, Barlow rented it, for a modest £84 a year, but paid over five times that sum in repairs. He finally bought the property from the lord of the manor, a young man with the same name as his father, Nicholas Caesar Corsellis Lawton, who was living quietly with his mother at Ballast Quay House.[17]

The graffiti, the casual hiring, the money spent in repairs and even the sale of the Hall, all suggest that it was in bad physical shape, which indeed it was. In 1906, Alexander Barlow appeared before the local bench, armed with a fragment of windowcase which was crumbling into powder, and demanded a reduction in his rates. His request was granted.[18]

The Corsellis estate was now in the hands of a receiver and the only recorded gesture by the young and impecunious lord of the manor was to present a tree to the fremasons of the town. In 1896 he married, discreetly, at Elmstead Church, though Wivenhoe put up bunting and some boats were dressed overall. On 16th March, 1899, the lordship and the estate, which the Corsellises had owned for two-and-a-half centuries, was sold, to a Colchester estate agent and auctioneer, Ernest Stanley Beard, who doubtless recouped his investment from the houses which now started to appear in and above Belle Vue Road.[19]

After the new century opened, the Methodist Church, the Foresters' Hall, the Masonic Hall, the Co-Operative Stores and after them a row of private houses, moved northwards along the east side of The Avenue opposite the corrugated iron fence which bounded the vast orchard, while modest terrace houses began to mark out Ernest and Stanley Roads. With this development came a social distinction. Hitherto, it had been more respectable to live above the railway bridge than below; now the town divided itself into "Upstreeters", those who lived above *The Park Hotel*, and "Downstreeters", the poorer and often poverty-stricken families, a rivalry that persisted until the end of the Second World War.

57. North facade of Wivenhoe Hall, c. 1900.

Colchester Castle Museum

58. Wivenhoe Hall from the south. Behind the large, first-floor window is the "Justice Room" where meetings of the manor court were held. c. 1900.

Loaned by Mr. E. H. C. Squire

Later in 1899 the lordship was resold, to George Frederick Beaumont, a Coggeshall solicitor. In 1954, various lordships were auctioned in London and Wivenhoe's was bought by Mr. Harry Hutchinson, a retired house furnisher from the North country. It was bought from him, in 1961, by Professor R. H. Graveson, Q.C., of Gray's Inn, for the sake of sundry documents that went with it, including some manorial court rolls which at one time were used as stage properties by the Colchester Repertory Company. The present lord of the manor has visited the town on more than one occasion.[20]

After the estate was sold, Ballast Quay House was bought by an Old Carthusian, John Bawtree Hawkins, whose father was mayor of Colchester four times, and he remained there, with his wife and family, until the end of this chapter. He had an uncle in William Hawkins of Alresford Hall. Young Hawkins was thirty when he came to Wivenhoe. He founded and commanded a volunteer regiment in the town, took a leading role in several societies, was a county councillor and a pillar of the Harwich Conservative Association.

The Nook was also important during these years. Alexander Trotter, who supervised the upstream shipyard from 1888, lived there for three years until his death. His successor, Henry Rice, was a brewery manager.

These individuals, together with the richer shop-keepers and publicans, and the yacht captains, were the obvious and acknowledged leaders of the community. There was also the rector.

4 John Sinclair Carolin.

In 1890, the Rev. John Baillie died and was succeeded by a domineering, hot-tempered Irishman with a talent for self-advertisement, John Sinclair Carolin (1856-1922).

Whereas Baillie had set his face against Sunday trains and amateur theatricals, Carolin believed that Sunday, apart from church, should be a day of recreation. He favoured early evening services so that his flock could listen to the town band afterwards, and personally promoted and took part in theatricals, concerts, smoking concerts and other diversions.

Carolin described himself as a Christian Socialist. He chaired meetings of the Liberal party and preached Liberal sermons, in an accent that was not a full brogue, to a packed church. "The day is long past", he once told his flock, "when we used to say, 'God bless the squire and his relations, and keep us all in our proper stations' . . . ", at which point, so the story goes, Charles Gooch rose and left the church, never to return.[21]

There is no evidence that Charles Gooch ever presumed on his position, but from the outset Carolin was nothing if not squirearchical for he tried to run his church without consulting either his churchwardens or parish council.

141

59. *The Rev. John Sinclair Carolin with the choir of St. Mary's Church, c. 1910.*

Loaned by St. Mary's Church

His earliest recorded clash was with the Wivenhoe School Board, of which he was a member and irregular attender, in 1893. He had twice used the school for concerts and dances, but without asking permission, without paying the proper hiring charge and, on the second occasion, leaving it in a mess. Dick Ham, the auctioneer, was frank with Carolin: "My experience since you have been in Wivenhoe", he said, "is that you have always wanted your own way, and if you call that self-sacrifice, I say it is not". However, after Carolin had cut meetings for six months the board was able to dismiss him and he retaliated with a sarcastic letter.[22] The chairman of the board, Dr. Samuel Squire, refused to have any truck with Carolin and worshipped at Rowhedge; John Hawkins, who lived only up the road, went to Elmstead.

Carolin could never work within a team, but if he were captain then all was superficially well. He soon formed The Wivenhoe Lawn Tennis Club, with himself as president, which survived until he turned to cycling. In 1895 he founded The Friendly Society. This was what was known as an "improvement" society. The members met to discuss new ideas, read papers, play music and even organise theatricals. A letter to the press suggested that instead of

Friendly Society it should be called Bullying Society, for when a lady had questioned the election of the president she had been shouted down and when a gentleman had risen to say that the minutes were inaccurate and should not be signed, the rector had signed them nonetheless.[23]

There were some enterprising choir outings. In October, 1912, for instance, the choir caught the 8.07 a.m. train to London, attended morning service in Westminster Abbey, visited the Houses of Parliament, lunched at Lyon's Corner House in Piccadilly, secured front seats for a matinee of *Drake* at His Majesty's Theatre, had tea at Straker's in Piccadilly, saw Sarah Bernhardt in *Phèdre* at the Coliseum and had a fish supper near Liverpool Street Station before catching the 12.05 a.m. train home. The day was a Saturday, so choir and rector had to be up betimes the next morning.[24]

From sermons and a stream of letters to the local press, the public learnt that Carolin opposed vivisection and capital punishment, and of his views on such things as phrenology and the long hours served by a Clacton shopgirl. The local column often carried news of his relations. His wife, Elizabeth, a pacifist well before her time, also wrote to the press. When the Carolins first arrived she appeared in concerts; later, she was confined to a wheelchair.

The rector took trouble with the church music. His organist and choirmaster, Frederick J. Lax, was a professional musician who also accompanied at dances, concerts and public-house smokers. He conducted the Wivenhoe Town Band and formed a Wivenhoe Choral Society. So people were displeased when, in 1901, Carolin abruptly dismissed him. The churchwardens, who had not been consulted, rebelled and declined to pay the salary of the new organist, Miss Elizabeth Barker. The rector invited his flock to take the matter up with the bishop.[25]

There was a similar eruption in 1909. One of the wardens, William Wadley, was organist for six months and then discovered that the rector was trying to replace him behind his back. He flared up at a vestry meeting and during a heated discussion told the rector, "You can't help insulting anyone, that's your nature. You are often criticised, you and your sermons too", and the meeting ended without either wardens or sidesmen being elected.[26]

So there was a second vestry meeting, at which the rector appointed Charles Gooch as his warden, even though Mr. Gooch had stopped coming to church. At yet another meeting the rector climbed down and begged Mr. Gooch to be warden again. Mr. Gooch drily consented, "if the rector thought he was worthy to fill the office", but he would not promise to attend church.[27]

Apart from his arrogance and bad temper, there was something crude, even for those days, in the way Carolin patronised his fellows. If somebody died there would be public commiseration from the pulpit. A couple who had lost their daughter were told that "the Heavenly Gardener had only transplanted their beautiful flower from the fields of this world to the Garden of Paradise", which was further reported in the press.[28]

The man who patronises his inferiors and quarrels with his equals is likely to venerate those above him. So it proved here. When Gladstone died, Carolin preached on the text, "There were giants in the earth in those days", and at Queen Victoria's death quoted extracts from her favourite poem, *In Memoriam*.[29]

The man who practises an extreme independence is likely to appeal to the established order from which that independence is derived. So it proved here. Carolin might govern his church without churchwardens, but when a motorcar skimmed past him at twenty miles an hour, as he was bicycling near Wivenhoe Park, he was incensed and, naturally, wrote to the press. However, he was not a reactionary. He eventually owned a motorcycle himself.[30]

5 Edwin Wilkins and Forrestt's.

In the previous chapter I mentioned a minor grandee, Edmund Round, an Old Harrovian barrister for whom John Harvey built the 38 ton cutter *Elaine*. He left the bar because of failing health, but patronised football and cricket, was commodore of the regatta and the Colne Yacht Club, chaired Conservative meetings and gave generously to the poor of Wivenhoe and Rowhedge from 1874 to his death in 1891. His obituary tells us that he saved local shipbuilding, "when it was in danger of extinction".[31] It looks as if he set up Joseph Edwin Wilkins at the shipyard, which was closed for a year after John Harvey left, an interesting parallel with 1873, when his cousin, Edward Round, put Harvey back on his feet.

Wilkins was a pupil of Harvey's and a marine architect in his own right. He was a superintendent of the Sunday School for several years and a churchwarden from 1889 to 1893, and since he was also involved with the regatta, the Colne Yacht Club and the Conservatives, Round would have known him well.

So the upstream shipyard was called Wilkins' Yard. Work began again there in 1882 and continued quietly during his five year reign.

In 1884 he rapidly built four 35 foot "Nile" boats which left by rail for Khartoum where General Gordon badly needed assistance. The boats were completed ahead of schedule but not in time to save Gordon from the Mahdi. Wilkins also produced nine deep-sea trawlers and several small yachts. He designed, and E. J. Gardiner built, the *Kara*, which Sir Henry Gore-Booth, Bart. commissioned for cruising in the Arctic. There was also the usual round of repairs, alterations and overhauling, enough to keep a fair number of Wivenhovians busy.[32]

Late Victorian and Edwardian 1881-1914

60. *A launch at Forrestt's, c. 1895.*

Loaned by Mr. Don Smith

Theodore Pim, the owner of the *Rosabelle*, might have taken his custom elsewhere when Harvey left; instead, he gave his next commission, the 130 ton yawl *Elfreda*, to Wilkins who both designed and built her. This was the highwatermark of Wilkins' tenure of the yard and the last really important yacht to be built at Wivenhoe. On 3rd July, 1886, a lovely day, with the shipyard and its environs hung with bunting, she slid into the water in the presence of Mr. Pim, his skipper, Captain Henry Harlow, James Round, M.P., and Hector Gurdon-Rebow, after Mrs. Pim had failed to break a bottle of wine across her bows. Pim told the company over luncheon at *The Anchor* that his next yacht would also be built at Wivenhoe. So it might, had not Wilkins left the yard.[33] He, too, could not make boatbuilding pay.

Pim was as true to his word as he could be. His fourth *Rosabelle*, of 460 tons, was designed by Wilkins and though built at Leith, was launched with Captain Harlow in charge of her and brought round to Wivenhoe for fitting out. This was in 1897. Thereafter, she was based at Wivenhoe. So was her successor, the fifth and final, 640 ton *Rosabelle*, after which Rosabelle Avenue is named, though she, too, was built at Leith, in 1902. As, in the new century, the big yachts deserted the river wall, one by one, she still remained, the final relic and symbol of an era.

After his tenure of the upstream shipyard, Wilkins was employed locally as a designer, but became bankrupt in 1894 and finally left the town.

In January, 1888, it was announced that Messrs. Forrestt & Son would take over the upstream shipyard and build a dry dock.

As we have seen, steel was displacing wood; now steel took over. No longer was the plank the building unit, but the metal sheet, cut to a convenient size and bolted to its fellows with rivets.

A rivet is a bolt without a thread, and three men were needed to insert it. First it was heated red hot in a stove on the ground, for only thus could the metal be worked. Then it was thrown up, by the rivet heater, to a colleague, the catcher, who caught it in a sort of funnel, before placing it, with a pair of tongs, in a hole that ran through two plates of overlapping metal. While the catcher held the rivet in place, the third man, the riveter, beat the protruding end of the rivet flat over the hole. The rivet cooled and in so doing drew the two sheets of metal firmly together. Thus were boats, noisily, assembled.[34]

On 21st March, 1888, Forrestt's inaugurated its regime with a public relations exercise: a dinner for 150 in the moulding loft. Frank Schneider, the firm's managing director, presided, and with him was Alexander Trotter, his local administrator, A. G. Mumford, whose engines, made at his factory in the middle of Colchester, invariably graced the boats from the yard, representatives from Messrs. Cox & King, a firm of yacht brokers now associated with the town, Edwin Wilkins, and captains from Wivenhoe and Rowhedge, the Barnards, Carters, Cranfields, Ennews, Fosgates, Hams, Harlows, Munsons, Pennys and others, those cunning and courageous men who made the Colne famous. The room was decorated with union jacks, there was music on piano and violin, songs and speeches, and everybody drank the health of everybody else. Yet even as Mr. Schneider felicitated the company he must have known that his commissions would be mostly for working boats, that the shift from pleasure to commerce would continue.[35]

So it proved. It was announced at the end of 1890 that the yard would build a yacht for the Bishop of Melanesia, but the bishop quickly corrected this. What would a man in his position want with a yacht? This was a mission boat for his immense and scattered diocese in the Pacific. The following May the 386 ton *Southern Cross* was dedicated "to the glory of God and the advancement of the Kingdom among the heathen", with a surpliced choir and numerous clergy in attendance.[36]

As the *Elfreda* ended one era, so the *Southern Cross* began another. Here was a boat designed for a specific, esoteric purpose in a foreign land. Forrestt's would build many another. So, with interruptions, would their successors, upstream and downstream, until 1986.

Other commissions included a 140 foot passenger steamer. She was bolted together, and then dismantled, every piece carefully marked and numbered. This done, her plates and angles were crated, loaded on to railway trucks and

Late Victorian and Edwardian 1881–1914

61. *The auxiliary schooner, Southern Cross, launched in 1891.*

Colchester Castle Museum

62. *The paddle steamer Tern, built by Forrestt's and sent as assembly kit to Lake Windermere.*

Photograph by Anthony Faulkner, 1988

sent direct by rail to the shores of Lake Windermere, where she was riveted together under supervision from Wivenhoe.[37]

This vessel was *Tern*, one of the first boats ever to be sent to her owners as an assembly kit. Her long, elegant hull with its distinctive, canoe-shaped prow, joined her sister ships, *Esperance, Raven, Cygnet, Teal* and *Britannia*, later that year; she has been taking passengers and holidaymakers up and down Lake Windermere ever since.

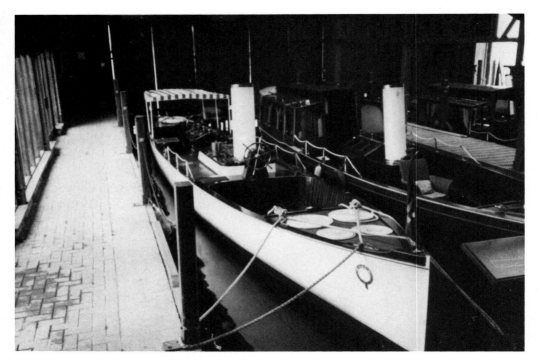

63. *The steam launch Otto in the Windermere Steamboat Museum.*

Photograph by Anthony Faulkner, 1988

Tern not the first vessel to go from Wivenhoe to Windermere; James Husk had earlier taken the 20 ton yacht *Manola* there, on a lorry driven by two horses, a twelve day journey. However, it was very likely *Tern* that drew the attention of the Sladen brothers, Alfred and Mortimer, rich young Cambridge graduates, to Wivenhoe. In 1894, Alfred Sladen commissioned Forrestt's to build him a slim, 65 foot launch, *Elfin*, to his designs, and in 1896 the 43 foot *Grebe*, later rechristened *Otto*, both for his brother. *Elfin* was capable of 25 m.p.h., then a very good speed. She survived until 1926; *Otto* is now in the

Windermere Steamboat Museum. Both, of course, were construction and re-erection jobs. A third launch designed by Sladen and built by Forrestt's was *Pearl*, for a Mr. H. R. Kirk of Leeds. She was last heard of on the Thames in 1939. In 1897, the Sladen brothers bought the *s.y. Gunilda*, then lying at Wivenhoe.[38]

Also in hand at Forrestt's in May, 1891, were three submarine mining launches for the War Office, three steel whale boats, (two for expeditions up the Congo), three vedettes, (small warships used for scouting), for the Admiralty, and several sailing boats. The yard was prosperous and its employees working overtime.[39] The Wivenhoe fishermen were less fortunate; 1891-2 was a disastrous season for sprats and stowboating.

One of the first things Forrestt's did was to build a dry dock, the only one between Lowestoft and London, which was completed early in 1889. In about 1898 a galvanising plant appeared. When the *s.s. Vanadis* turned on a powerful searchlight in the Colne, in April, 1894, the new form of illumination alarmed many; on 28th November, 1900, Forrestt's was lit by electricity for the first time.[40]

The final decade of the nineteenth century was a busy one at the upstream shipyard. Much of the work was for overseas; assembly kits large and small were sent to every corner of the known world. Sometimes the boats arrived as bundles of plates and angles, sometimes in sections, like tree trunks sawn into logs. For instance, the *Advance*, a 28 foot vessel with several pairs of oars and a lugsail, for the explorer, H. M. Stanley, was despatched to Africa in twelve sections and for journeys overland was dismantled, each section carried by a pair of natives. Another explorer, the Marquis of Dufferin and Ava, was provided with a 22 foot sloop, the *Lady Hermione*, packed with ingenious devices, including a charcoal stove beneath the cockpit to keep the owner's feet warm.[41]

For negotiating shallow waters, especially in Africa, the firm produced shallow draught vessels propelled, at their sterns, by paddle wheels. In 1896 Lord Kitchener was provided with three 140 foot sternwheel gunboats. Equipped with searchlights and bristling with guns, they proceeded up the Nile at a stately 14 m.p.h. Other steamers, such as the 50 foot *Pyefleet*, for the Colne Fishery Company, had their paddles conventionally at their sides.[42]

The firm also built numerous screw-driven steamers, single and twin, for home and abroad, launches, barges, lifeboats and, for the Admiralty, gunboats, Admirals' barges and a host of rowing boats, sailing boats, cutters and pinnaces.

There were other unique, esoteric commissions: a grotesque, squat, caisson diving bell barge, which the Navy needed to lay the moorings of large ships at Gibraltar; a sternwheel bucket dredger for Ceylon; a fire extinguishing and disinfectant steamer for the Mozambique government; two canoe sledges for an Arctic expedition which could be used alike on the ice and in the water.

64. *The Advance rowing boat, built for H. M. Stanley by Forrestt's.*
Colchester Castle Museum

65. *The paddle steamer Pyefleet, built for the Colchester Oyster Fishery by Forrestt's.*
Colchester Castle Museum

Late Victorian and Edwardian 1881–1914

66. *The stern paddle steamer Ndoni, built by Forrestt's for trading on the rivers of Northern Nigeria.*

Colchester Castle Museum

Pleasure craft were fewer and smaller. Some racing cutters descended the slipway: *Creole*, in 1890, which won 104 races in fourteen years, and in 1904 three examples of a South Coast One Design. In 1895 Forrestt's was building twenty-three boats of the Dabchick class for the Lower Thames Yacht Club. There were many similar smaller commissions.

The first vessel to enter the new dry dock was the *s.s. Walrus*. Thereafter it was usually occupied, especially by those perennial giants of the river wall, the *Elfreda, Island Home, Valfreyia, St. Kilda, Gunilda* and, of course, *Rosabelle*. On the adjacent slipways, repairs and fitting out kept a large number of men busy.

With little over a year of the nineteenth century to run, there was a grand, sentimental, patriotic, optimistic, empire-building setpiece: the launching of the twin screw *s.s. Cecil Rhodes*, destined for Lake Tanganyika. The yard was hung with bunting; a large party of ladies and gentlemen came up from London by special train. Cecil Rhodes' sister, Edith, was present; so were the directors of Tanganyika Concessions Ltd., which had commissioned the vessel. Photographers turned up in strength and a local newspaper reckoned this was the first event in Essex to be "cinematographed".[43]

After preliminary trials on the Colne, the *Cecil Rhodes* was dismantled and packed into parcels, each weighing no more sixty pounds, which travelled by sea to the mouth of the Zambezi and thence, via one of its tributaries, to the foot of Lake Nyasa. A sailing ketch, *The Lady of the Lake*, another Forrestt's assembly kit, carried the fragmented steamship to the top of the lake, where each parcel was loaded on to the shoulders of an African, some 150 of whom carried her on the last leg of her journey, save for three pieces of machinery which were carted. The route to the lake was over 250 miles of rough country and the trek averaged five miles a day. By September of the following year she had reached her destination; three years after that she was wrecked on the shores of Lake Tanganyika.[44]

In 1892, Forrestt's became a limited company, but over the following six years made a loss, principally at the Limehouse yard, which was given up in 1897. 1898-1901 showed a small profit; then followed a collapse. For two years the firm was in the hands of a receiver; then it was bought up and renamed Forrestt & Co. Ltd. The new enterprise brought in workmen from the North of England and found houses for them; in 1904 four cottages called Forrestt Row, were auctioned by Beard & Co. The dry dock was extended.[45]

As before, there was laying-up and fitting out, and the commissions flowed in: home and foreign, commercial and private, including the first and last submarine to be built at Wivenhoe.[46]

Initially, the Admiralty disdained submarine warfare. Underwater was underhand, ungentlemanly. However, by 1901 it realised that such craft were essential and early experiments included the midget, 17 ton *Volta*, designed by A. Hilliard Atteridge for the British Submarine Company, but actually sponsored by a firm called Marryat & Scott whose various electrical devices filled the vessel.

Two electric motors, connected in tandem, gave her a forty mile run before their batteries needed recharging, with a top speed of about eight knots. Running fore and aft along the base of the submarine's interior was a set of rails upon which a weight, normally amidships, could be moved either forwards or backwards, also by an electric motor. When the submarine wished to submerge, the weight was sent forwards, so that her bows pointed downwards, and simultaneously the main ballast tank was flooded. To surface, the weight was sent aft and the tank emptied. A 10 cwt weight was attached to her keel; if she was unable to surface in the normal way this could be detached and she would immediately rise.

Volta had a crew of three. Her captain stood with his head inside the conning tower, whose portholes gave him a good, all round view, while he steered his vessel by means of horizontal and vertical rudders. He was assisted by an engineer, who faced the main switchboards, the controls between his knees, and

67. *The submarine Volta.*

Colchester Castle Museum

there was a torpedo-man. The noise of the vessel's nine electric motors was so loud that the crew could only converse through speaking tubes. The submarine was 34 feet long, with a diameter of 6′ 9″, small enough to be carried on a railway truck, or aboard a battleship whence she could be lowered by davits for duties such as harbour work.

She took over a year to build. Her construction, in a boarded-off corner of Forrestt's largest shed, was shrouded in secrecy and as work neared completion government officials kept a close watch on the premises.

She was launched on 5th June, 1905, and after diving tests had been carried out in the dry dock and the emergency surfacing procedure in midstream, went down the Colne for further tests, but not before a Customs House officer had come aboard and refused to leave until he had received a written assurance that *Volta* would not leave the country without the knowledge of the authorities.

And now the submarine's Achilles heel was revealed. For her nine electric motors generated magnetic fields which effectively neutralised that of her magnetic compass, so that it was quite impossible to steer her. However, that difficulty was later overcome by fitting her with a gyrostatic compass.

There is no record of the *Volta* entering Naval service, and where she went and what became of her nobody knows. However, one Wivenhovian who worked on her, Albert Simons, believed that she was shipped to America, via Liverpool. Apparently, the man in charge of her construction was an American, known as "the Professor".

There were other novelties, notably a craft built in 1908 to recover treasure from the frigate *Lutine* which had lain shrouded in sand at the mouth of the Zuider Zee since 1799. It comprised a large pontoon through which there descended a 103 foot tube, down to an eight foot square workroom where portholes disclosed the sea bed lit by powerful reflectors. The equipment included centrifugal pumps designed for sucking up sand which, it was reckoned, they could do at the rate of 40,000 tons in twenty-four hours. However, this salvage vessel never went further than Brightlingsea, where she stayed for the next thirty years and finally, as scrap metal, made her contribution to the Second World War.[47]

The boats were now generally larger. The sternwheel steamers *Centipede*, *Polypode*, *Milliped* and *Kapelli* were all 100 feet long and the mighty *Sudan*, launched in 1908, 180 feet. Seemingly the company was doing very well, but when it went bankrupt it appeared that the managing director, H. D. Swan, a pillar of local cricket who had come to Wivenhoe via Uppingham and Oxford, had been given the company by his father to set him up in business, but though Swan himself poured the best part of £9,000 into it he could not make it pay.[48]

Fortunately, help was at hand. Messrs. G. Rennie & Co. closed their shipbuilding operation at Greenwich and transferred part of their plant and skilled workforce to Wivenhoe, just as Forrestt's had done twenty-five years earlier. The Rennie Forrestt Shipbuilding, Engineering and Dry Dock Co. Ltd. was formed in February, 1912.[49]

Trade picked up. In March, 1913, the work in hand included launches, steamers, tugs and lifeboats. There were three especially important commissions that year. In the spring the firm produced a training ship for the Metropolitan Asylums Board, the three-masted auxiliary schooner, *Exmouth II*. In the autumn there was a triple-screw motor yacht *Mansa Kila Ba*, mosquito-proofed throughout for service in Gambia, with accommodation for a hundred passengers. Shortly before Christmas the *s.s. Beacon* was launched, commissioned by the Board of Trade to service lighthouses in Ceylon, which at 900 tons was very likely the largest vessel yet built on the Colne.[50]

Throughout this chapter the upstream shipyard was the biggest single employer of labour and upon it the town depended. The employment was

Late Victorian and Edwardian 1881–1914

68. & 69. *Above: the fire float Beta. Below: the stern paddle steamer Sudan, built for the Sudan government in 1908. Taken from Andersen's brochure.*

Both from Colchester Castle Museum

70. *The auxiliary schooner, Exmouth II.*

Loaned by Mr. Brian Oakley

never secure; but from 1888 it never ceased. It is estimated that 300 to 350 men worked there.

Downstream of The Quay, Cox & King was on one side of the brook and Husk's on the other. James Husk, son of the firm's founder, established himself in the early nineties. Besides repair and maintenance work, he produced sundry gigs and cutters for large yachts, and some small yachts of his own, such as the 6 ton sloop *Ala* for W. F. Cockrell, the manager of Browne's Ropery, and a 38 foot cutter, *King Coel,* for Alexander Barlow who raced her locally, both to their owners' designs.[51]

The transition from wood to steel naturally affected the fortunes of the rope-making and sail-making firms in the town. When Forrestt's arrived, Browne's Ropery was still flourishing, but in 1896 the firm became a limited company, presumably to avert closure, for in 1899 close it did. The premises, save for the house fronting the main road, were demolished not long after. Madder & Son was doing well at the turn of the century but closed after the First World War.[52]

6 The River or the Shipyard?

During the years under discussion most Wivenhovians worked on or beside the water; they had three main professional choices: fishing, fishing-and-crewing, and shipbuilding.

The fishermen, who caught soles and dabs throughout the winter, sprats from mid-November to mid-February, dredged for oysters in the spring and trawled for shrimps, mussels and starfish in the summer, needed courage, skill, physical strength, resourcefulness, luck and a thorough knowledge of the coast. Apart from the perils of sandbanks and strong tides, it was difficult to find fish in the water and buyers ashore. At times sprats were unwanted even as manure, and left on The Quay to rot.

Life was always near the bone for these self-employed men, the toughest, hardiest members of the community, yet they were their own masters and some declined to surrender their independence by crewing in the summer. Nevertheless, the competition for places aboard the big yachts was fierce.

Crewing had several advantages. First of all, there was a regular wage, which in a racing yacht might be doubled or even trebled by prize money.

The crewman had two important perquisites: he was clothed and fed. Every season each man was kitted out by the owner. His uniform would last the rest of the year and used or unwanted items be passed down the family or given away. When a fisherman left home he took most of his larder with him. The wife whose husband crewed, and was therefore away for the season, could expect to feed their family properly.

Life aboard a cruising yacht was, of course, much easier as, except for the

Late Victorian and Edwardian 1881–1914

71. *The Quay, c. 1900.*

Loaned by Mr. Glendower Jackson

72. *The upstream end of The Quay showing Bath Street and The Ship at Launch public house which was demolished in 1914.*

Colchester Castle Museum

captain and engineer, the crewman was more of a domestic servant than an athlete. Like a good servant, he made himself useful at all times. Like a good servant, he was blind to things it was not his business to know. One crewman recalled an owner who was a stockbroker. His wife and children were given a fortnight's holiday aboard his yacht, but at other times he was joined by his mistress, nominally his secretary. The crew, reared on a totally different moral code, had to accept this in silence. "Funnily enough, she was always very good to us", he said, as if she might have been Jezebel in person. Another crewman recalled that a young lady, the daughter of a rich and important man, thought nothing of bathing in the nude. The crew might be present, but since they were only crew the lady was alone.[53]

Yachts generally visited pleasant places, ports in the Mediterranean, for instance, where the crew would spend a good deal of time ashore. There was no close season; the summer voyage might well be followed by another. The *Rosabelle, Rannoch, Vanessa* and *Venetia*, among other yachts, often went to Scotland for the shooting.

Crewing had its mystique: the thrills of competing in a prestigious sport, of adding to the town's considerable reputation, of escaping from the Colne estuary, seeing different places and people, and returning with souvenirs and stories.

It had one very special attraction: that of becoming a captain. If a man was seen by an owner to be smart, diligent and sober, then he might be promoted to mate and thence, probably with the assistance of a captain's reference, to captain. He now held the tiller during races and picked crews to win them. Like a modern football manager, he would remain a captain so long as he *did* win races.

Of the seagoing men, the captains alone were secure. For besides a basic wage of £5 a week they were paid a £2 retainer throughout the winter. This was only right, for they looked after their yachts all the year round, indeed the yachts were laid up at Wivenhoe to be near their skippers.

Because the captain chose his men and because of his unquestionable skill and experience, he had considerable authority over them. The crew might include younger relations, but the captain was "Sir" and at election time they might have to sport his colour, or that of the yacht's owner, which was more likely to be blue than yellow. The captains retained their Essex burrs but might be on first name terms with their employers. If they wanted to show off they swanked about The Quay in their peaked caps, hands in their pockets, or went to the Captains' Promenade, the area now occupied by Mr. Lewis Worsp's greenhouse, but then reserved for the captains, and they alone, or visit one of the larger public houses which had a captains' room, there to sit in their personal chairs and drink from their personal mugs. In the days when *The Rose*

Late Victorian and Edwardian 1881–1914

73. *The Forrestt's Workforce, c. 1910.*

Loaned by Mr. Don Smith

and Crown was divided into bars, the Captains' Room included the bow window that overlooks The Quay.

1 to 11, Anglesea Road was known as Captains' Row, for this was where many of them lived, but several owned properties in the High Street or built houses in Belle Vue Road. Their wives were often obliged to keep their homes as immaculate as their boats and, up to a point, in the same manner. Doors were picked out in gold leaf and steps covered in brass, like the bows and gangplanks of the big yachts. When Captain William Harvey was due home his wife would go over the house, fearful that it would not pass his inspection. Well she might be, for he was captain of the *Varuna*, known as "the floating palace".[54]

These men had triumphed in a harsh world and were accorded a tremendous prestige, just like the public school prefects and first eleven cricketers of those days.

A chief engineer or steward might also be paid a retainer over the winter months. At about the turn of the century a crewman received thirty shillings. After the First World War this was 45/- or even £2 10s 0d.[55] A Wivenhovian who came of age in 1930 recalled a wage of £2 15s 0d, of which seven or eight shillings was given to the cook for food. On top of this he received 3/6d for

159

74. *The crew of the 50 ton s.y.* Alexandra, *which John Harvey designed and built for the Prince of Wales. She was launched in 1869*

Loaned by Mr. John Leather

entering a race, £1 for winning it, 15/- for coming second and 10/- for coming third.[56]

A comparison with wages earned in the shipyard before the First World War, referred to later in this section, is instructive. A crewman's basic wage was lower than that of his artisan colleague at Forrestt's, but if his boat prospered it was considerably higher. On the other hand, although he might return to Wivenhoe with plenty of money at the end of the racing season, if the fishing was poor that winter he would be poverty-stricken by the following spring. Moreover, the fishing-and-crewing year generally had two gaps of a few weeks, in April and September.

In the early years of the present century there were about twenty boats laid up against the river wall. On the opposite shore, on either side of the ferry, were the *Lady Blanche* and the *Rannoch*. Most of them were steamyachts. They were generally moored parallel with the river channel, from Husk's to the first stile, connected by a network of pontoons improvised from sections of old masts topped with planks. In contrast to these glittering toys was the stern black bulk of Lord Brassey's *Sunbeam*. She, and she alone, occupied the first berth below Husk's, which was known as Lord Brassey's dock.

Between seasons each yacht's personal gear would be taken out and stored in a multitude of places along The Quay and elsewhere. Come the spring and the crews would be hard at work fitting out the yachts, which involved thorough and elaborate redecoration. The very dinghies had to be rubbed down and revarnished, and experts at french polishing were imported to deal with the wooden panelling. The owners themselves rarely came to Wivenhoe. Instead, their yachts would go down river with enough provisions for an initial voyage to Southampton, where they would stock up properly and then, probably still without the owner, make for Cannes and Deauville where he and the "company", as they were known, would join for a Mediterranean cruise.

The mother of a Wivenhoe boy whose father worked in the upstream shipyard wondered if she should send him to sea or not. She consulted her brother-in-law, a coastguard. "If he asks to go, let him", was the verdict, "but if he doesn't ask to go, say nothing to him".[57]

The sea meant adventure; it also meant insecurity. That youngster never did ask to go to sea, so he had a safer, but far duller career in the shipyard.

The shipyard was, of course, less dangerous, though heavy sheets of metal and red hot rivets had their perils and a trolley was always ready to carry injured men to the doctor's. The wages were as secure as the yard itself and if the yard closed its skills could be employed elsewhere. However, to learn them a man had to serve a seven year apprenticeship, starting at fifteen. In his first year his wage was five shillings a week, which rose annually by a shilling or so. When trained, the money was reasonable. Platers, the most highly skilled workmen, earned 36/- in Edwardian times. At the other end of the scale, unskilled labourers appear to have been paid little over a pound.[58]

The trade unions afforded rudimentary protection. Metal workers joined The Amalgamated Society of Boilermakers, Iron and Steel Shipbuilders, which formed a Wivenhoe branch in 1890. Shipwrights, who worked in wood and were now far fewer in number, joined The Shipwrights Society. It seems that membership was soon compulsory, but in the early days the unions were like benefit societies. When apprentices joined they attended a meeting at *The Greyhound* which frightened the lives out of them. As the rules were explained the poker in the fire was allowed to become red hot, the implication being that they were to be branded with it.

Despite the unions, the management had the upper hand. There are reports of shipwrights striking in 1896 and joiners in 1910, but not of the unions backing them up. On the latter occasion most of the places were soon filled with other men.[59]

As the captains were the prefects of Wivenhoe, so the foremen were the sergeant-majors. It was they who hired and fired men, and watched them as they worked. The long haul towards acquiring a trade began by asking one of these men for a job. "Can't do anything for you, today, lad. Come again tomorrow", was the reply to the son of a shipyard worker who presented

75. *Philip Chamberlain's boot and shoe shop where every year a gang of cobblers made wooden studded shoes for the crews who manned the big yachts. It is now No. 52, High Street.*

Loaned by Mrs. Pamela Dan

himself at the gates of the shipyard one morning in 1912. So the boy appeared the next day and received the same reply, and for several days thereafter. At the end of two or three weeks the foreman asked him who his father was and where he worked. Then he was taken on as an apprentice. The foreman evidently wanted to know if he had the stamina to rise early.[60]

An apprentice learnt one of the skills used in the shipyard under a man called a mechanic. He might learn plating, engine-fitting, joining, drilling, riveting, carpentry, painting, rigging, caulking or building wooden boats as men had done on that spot for untold centuries. Some of the workers, platers in particular, worked in gangs of four, five or six and would stay together as a team until a particular job was finished. Others worked individually. The work was supervised by foremen, who were generally feared and respected, but not hated. The foremen drove their men hard, as well they might, for the yard often went bankrupt. They dismissed men for slackness, also redundancy, which kept their workers up to scratch. Some foremen instilled a love of doing a job well for its own sake into their apprentices and were remembered with gratitude on that account.

Men who thought ahead tended to work in the shipyard and for this reason I think were socially a slight cut above the seagoers. Yet there was one important difference between the shipyard workers and the yachtsmen-fishermen. The former might be strangers from outside the town; the latter were Wivenhovians to a man.

Late Victorian and Edwardian 1881–1914

7 The Social Scene.

If one takes a bird's eye view of the years 1881 to 1914 it is easy to see that social history is on the move. Two trends, in particular, are clearly discernible. As the community becomes more literate and mobile, and receives protection from the secret ballot and the old age pension, so it becomes less dependent, emotionally, socially and financially, on the people who live in the big houses. The other trend is from the simple to the sophisticated. The adventurous but precarious life of the sailor begins to be supplanted by the safer but duller life of the shipyard worker and the social scene is marked by more, and longer-lived, and better organised, groups for promoting the welfare and recreation of the townspeople.

Wivenhoe functioned as a unit. It mourned when the grandees, rich men, captains and important tradesmen died, shutting shops, pulling down blinds and lowering colours to half-mast for their funerals; when they married, especially if they were well-liked, then yachts were dressed overall and bunting displayed, even if the wedding was not in the town. Thus, when two female relatives of Edmund Round married on the same day in London, bunting was hung out at several public houses and he himself marked the occasion by treating fifty-five widows of the town to a dinner at *The Grosvenor Hotel.* Unimportant deaths and marriages were less regarded. A Boxing Day couple was pelted with snowballs and when Sinclair Carolin intervened he was snowballed himself and had his hat knocked off.[61]

The mystique of birth and class still obtained. The public automatically looked up to the people in the big houses who, in turn, unselfconsciously patronised them. For instance, in 1881 Edmund Round gave soup, 250 pounds of beef and twenty-four pairs of blankets to "the six poor women in the almshouses". It was also the third year of Mr. Oaksey's Irish stew dinners, which took place on Thursday mornings during the winter. A formal dinner for the Poor and Aged was started in 1906 and continued annually until 1914. Note the lack of embarrassment at giving or receiving charity. The poor, old and widowed were invariably described as such.[62]

To alleviate poverty and illness, many Wivenhovians belonged to trusts or friendly societies. The Oddfellows and Foresters had branches in the town; so, from 1891, did The Ancient Order of Buffaloes. Sometimes *ad hoc* committees were set up to deal with a particular crisis, such as the terrible stowboating season of 1892-3.[63]

Social events included the Parish or Easter Tea, and the Yacht Captains' and Tradesmen's Tea. "Tea" merely indicates that these formal stag parties, comprising a meal followed by speeches, toasts and songs, started at about 6.30 p.m. The Easter Tea, given by the Parish Council, shortly after the annual Vestry Meeting in April, was generally held at *The Grosvenor Hotel* The

76. *Part of the 1902 Coronation Procession.*

Loaned by Mrs. Pamela Dan

Captains' Tea was originally held to celebrate the end of the yachting season, but in 1883 switched to January. It was attended by captains from the other Colne ports and such notables as the local M.P. In most public-houses there were laying-up suppers which turned into smoking concerts and smoking concerts that concluded annual general meetings or raised money for good causes. The annual meetings of The Wivenhoe Association for the Protection of Property continued, but I can find no record of one after 1889.[64]

Thus the gentlemen got together, but apart from the school there was no venue for mixed and juvenile occasions, until the town built itself a public hall.

The idea of the hall was first raised at a meeting held on 1st March, 1889, chaired by Alexander Trotter. A committee was appointed to investigate the matter and that was that.[65]

Sinclair Carolin, a warm advocate both of a public hall and a recreation area, spoke on behalf of the former at a meeting of the School Board in 1892. In 1900 the new Urban District Council considered a site in Belle Vue Road and a plan was drawn up. After the failure of a £2,500 appeal, it was agreed to

Late Victorian and Edwardian 1881–1914

77. *The 1902 Coronation Committee. Back Row, left to right: William Wadley, (master mariner), Walter Pullen (boilermaker), Thomas Williamson, (tax collector), James Heath, (oyster merchant), Alexander Barlow, (Wivenhoe Hall), Henry Rice, (brewery manager), Fred Brown, (landlord of The Brewery Tavern), John Rice, (son of Henry Rice), John Goodwin, (builder), Philip Ewing, (manager of Forrestt's), Dick Ham, (undertaker and auctioneer), and Henry Bow, (landlord of The Grosvenor Hotel). Middle Row, left to right: William Wadley, (schoolmaster), James Moore, (grocer), John Felgate, (farmer), Arthur Garrett, (draper – his shop is now The London Delicatessen), Philip Chamberlain, (bootmaker). Front Row: Percy Rowe, (chief clerk at Forrestt's), Bob Ross (at Forrestt's), Billy Towler (at Forrestt's) and Stacey Wood (grocer – his shop is now Green's).*

Loaned by Mr. Don Smith

produce plans for a hall costing £1,500, but this scheme likewise foundered. However, before that year was out a shed near the station, formerly used by the Methodists, was christened the Public Hall, but the venue for most social occasions remained the school in the High Street.[66]

Then, on 13th October, 1904, The Ancient Order of Foresters opened the Foresters' Hall in The Avenue. It contained a main room, 64 feet by 30 feet, and two small anterooms. Wivenhoe now possessed a more or less adequate public hall.

Open air events united the whole town. The annual fair was now held on three days. The first nineteenth century account of it I can find is for 1883. It started on Monday and the regatta was on Thursday, "most of the inhabitants making a general holiday of it since Monday... the streets were lined with bazaar stalls, fruit hawkers, Aunt Sally, cocoa-nut throwing, and other similar attractions. Most of the inhabitants decorated their houses..." As early as 1884 there were shooting galleries and a roundabout, "Barker's steam circus", on Coker's Field, where the Wivenhoe Centre now stands. As time went on the

78. *The exterior of the Foresters' Hall. The building still stands, barely recognisable after the alterations of 1987-1988 which changed it into maisonettes.*

Loaned by Mrs. Claire Weston

79. *An unidentified event at the Foresters' Hall, c. 1904-1914.*

Loaned by Mr. R. O. Richardson

sideshows became more numerous and varied. When the new school was built, Coker's Field disappeared and in that year the stalls left the High Street. From that time on, we are told, attendances declined. The fair moved from one site to another, including the saltings, but in 1906 was at The Cross, where it remained.[67]

I find the first press reference to Guy Fawkes Night in 1884. Then, as now, there were several guys which the "small fry" paraded round the streets and, then as now, they asked for money. However, in those days the approach was not the simple, "Penny for the guy". Instead, the children used to knock on doors and recite the traditional rhyme, "Please to remember, the Fifth of November . . . " The revels started early, even at 7 a.m., until the children went into school. In the evening a huge guy was paraded round the town with squibs and crackers. The bonfires were originally on Anchor Hill and later in this period on the Broom Field.[68]

One nocturnal, torchlit, fancy-dress parade with an effigy was followed by another: Lord Mayor's Day. I can discover two dates for it, 9th and 10th November. We first hear of it in 1884: "In the evening the Wyvenhoe minstrels paraded the streets in all manner of costumes, followed by large numbers of the smaller fry". In 1889 the Lord Mayor's effigy was accompanied by twelve cavaliers dressed as such, with music and fireworks. The following year there were effigies of a lady, a gentleman and a baby; the correspondent did not know who they were. We are told that the event had been "for several years past".[69]

The last we hear of The Fifth is in 1906 and of Lord Mayor's Day in 1905.[70] The crude, vigorous, noisy, colourful, occasional character of these events suggests to me that the people who organised them were yachtsmen rather than shipyard workers. Certainly, the processions, minstrel concerts and, of course, regattas, all took place when the big yachts were laid up.

By the 1900's there were two bands: The Volunteer Band, in succession to the Town Band, (which finally became the Wesley Guild Band), and the Salvation Army Band. The latter organisation now had its citadel at the former Swedenborgian Chapel in Alma Street. Some bandsmen belonged to both. They played at regattas, fetes and other social occasions, and for the processions of which the town was now very fond, including those of the Sunday School treats.

There were four Sunday Schools in the 1900's: Church of England, Congregational, Wesleyan and Salvation Army. The treats, which comprised an afternoon of organised sports, followed by tea, generally took place in the grounds of The Nook. When they were over the children would leave by a pair of stout black gates in Park Road and form up. Here they would be joined by one of the bands and the procession would move off, up Park Road, along Belle

80. *The Salvation Army Band in 1911.*

Loaned by Mr. Glendower Jackson

Vue Road to the High Street, thence to the appropriate church headquarters where the children would each be given a small present. One Wivenhovian specifically remembers these as torchlight processions, with the musicians reading their music by the light of big acetylene lamps on poles held by assistants who marched beside them.[71]

There is a distinctly male flavour about these festivities, but St. Valentine's Day, with its mysterious exchanges of cards and gifts, was an essentially female occasion, and once a year a May Queen was chosen by ballot at the Girls' School. The Queen and her maids of honour, all decked out with flowers, and the former encompassed with a hoop similarly decorated, would come to people's doors and sing a little song:

> *Please remember the May Lady,*
> *My father has gone to sea.*
> *My mother has gone to fetch him,*
> *Please remember me.*

Then one of the girls would say, "Coo, coo, Coo, coo", which was an invitation to the householder to give them a penny.[72]

Before we leave this section I must mention the rising star of John Martin Harvey. He joined Henry Irving's company in 1882 and stayed with him for fifteen years, though he played nothing of importance. However, he and some colleagues formed The Lyceum Vacation Company, which toured the provinces while the main company rested. The last of these tours, in 1894, visited the Theatre Royal in Queen Street, Colchester, for three nights. As coincidence would have it, Harvey's elder sister, May, had also gone on the stage, and she also visited the Theatre Royal, three months before her brother, playing for six nights in a production of *Caste*. Both the Harveys received favourable notices.[73]

Martin Harvey, as he was now known professionally, mounted his adaptation of Dickens' *A Tale of Two Cities*, which he entitled *The Only Way*, with himself as Sydney Carton, in 1899. He was now an actor-manager and in the town's eyes a great man. His company paid two flying visits to the Hippodrome, Colchester, in 1908 and 1909, with single matinees of *A Cigarette Maker's Romance* and *The Breed of the Treshams*, which, next to *The Only Way*, were his most famous productions.

8 Bayard Brown and the Sporting Scene.

During these years organised sport made considerable headway.

There was no regatta from 1886 to 1888, probably because the shipyard was doing badly. However, in 1889 The Colne Yacht and Boat Club was formed, and Alexander Trotter, who had arrived with Forrestt's to run the shipyard, became its first commodore.

The club started auspiciously. Before the regatta that year there were two preliminary ones. The first of these, in July, had four rowing races. Afterwards the committee and its guests retired to *The Grosvenor* for a cold collation. Among those present was the American owner of the 735 ton *s.y. Valfreyia*, which had dropped anchor off Brightlingsea a few weeks earlier, McEvers Bayard Brown. Responding to a toast, Brown said he was very pleased to be in the Colne and hoped he might remain there for some time.[74] He did, until he died, thirty years later.

The *Valfreyia* was then, and for many years thereafter, one of the largest and most luxurious chattels afloat. Because he had the money to buy and maintain that chattel, the Colne knew Brown as a rich man and by that token, though illogically, a great man, for in those days the modest tradesmen and impoverished smacksmen accepted such people as their natural leaders. Rich he certainly was, but like many another millionaire, had no more idea of how to

81. & 82. *Regatta Scenes, c. 1895-1905.*

Both loaned by Colchester Castle Museum

Late Victorian and Edwardian 1881–1914

83. & 84. *Regatta Scenes, c. 1895–1905.*

Above: Loaned by Mrs. Dorothy Chaney
Below: Loaned by Mr. Don Smith

spend, share and enjoy his wealth than an infant and quickly succumbed to the unpleasant dottiness that breeds in money bags.

He tipped recklessly; porters and cabbies received the equivalent of four weeks' wages. So naturally he soon became the target for people with hard luck stories, true or invented. The *Valfreyia* was moored in the middle of the Colne at a point where it is about half a mile wide, so the ferrymen used to row these individuals out to the yacht and there they would wait, often for many hours, in fair weather or rough, until the great man deigned to appear. When he did, he might receive the suppliants on board and reward them, or drop sovereigns into the dinghies, or drop sovereigns into the water, or drop sovereigns heated in a frying pan into the outstretched hands, or pelt his visitors with lumps of coal from the ship's boiler, or flatly refuse to hear or pay anyone, just as the fancy took him. This ritual continued year after year, while the *Valfreyia*, with steam up, always ready to set off on some wonderful cruise, remained rooted to the same spot.[75]

Most of these dinghy people were women, usually heavily veiled and muffled, who were often entertained on board. Some were professional prostitutes; other were women forced into temporary prostitution by poverty and there are tales circulating Brightlingsea to this day about Brown's illegitimate descendants.

Not everyone, however, was biddable. One day a man and a boy were doing a carpentry job aboard the *Valfreyia*, when the boy, John Canham, noticed a sovereign on the deck. The man told him not to touch it. There it remained for several days, a natural temptation, until finally Brown came along and asked, "What's that sovereign doing there?" "Oh, it's your's", said the man. Brown tried to pick it up, but discovered that his employee had drilled a hole through it and screwed it firmly to the deck.[76]

Yet Brightlingsea had good cause to like Brown, as had Wivenhoe. During the terrible stow-boating seasons of 1890-2, when the sprats disappeared, his bounty was invaluable. Whereas Edmund Round and Alexander Barlow habitually gave £5 to the poor at Christmas, or the equivalent in goods, at various Christmasses between 1893 and 1900, probably all of them, Brown gave £50 to Wivenhoe alone. Thereafter his bounty dwindled, but it continued, and when he died he bequeathed £100 to the rector and £500 to be invested for the poor of the parish.[77]

By the end of 1889 The Colne Yacht and Boat Club had acquired ninety-two members. Its opening regatta, the first of the new series, was called The Colchester and Wyvenhoe Regatta and was patronised by leading Colcestrians. There were four sailing matches, including one for smacks, several rowing matches, a race for steam launches and a duck hunt. The following year the club organised at least four days of racing before the official regatta, but that is

Late Victorian and Edwardian 1881–1914

85. *A Cyclists' Club in The Avenue, c. 1905.*

Colchester Castle Museum

all we hear of it, for then, apparently, it went down river to become the present Colne Yacht Club at Brightlingsea. It would seem that Wivenhoe could support a regatta, an annual, domestic affair involving fishermen, yachtsmen and other locals, but was not yet ready for a sailing club with races throughout the summer.[78]

When Alexander Trotter died, in 1891, he was succeeded as commodore by William Johnson, who was also his successor at the shipyard, and then, from about 1907 to 1913, by Alexander Barlow.

In 1891 the event was called The Wivenhoe and East Donyland Regatta, and thereafter The Wivenhoe and Rowhedge Regatta. It was held at Wivenhoe and Rowhedge alternately.

Meanwhile, The Cricket Club continued, with the goodwill of Wivenhoe Hall, to use Tenacres. When Thursday was made early closing day, in 1897, there was sometimes more than one match a week. The Lawn Tennis Club, founded by Sinclair Carolin in 1891, voted twelve ladies on to its committee

173

86. *Tennis, c. 1900.*

Loaned by Mr. E. H. C. Squire

two years later, as much a social as a sporting development. It was wound up in 1897, "because cycling had taken its place", but was revived in the new century, again with the rector as president. The Cycling Club must have been well established at this time because in 1897 there was a race for a gold medal, presented by The Tom Tit Cycle Club, which started and finished in Wivenhoe. In 1888 I find the first reference to a Quoits Club. This sport was played between public houses; it flourished up to the First World War. In 1900, *The Falcon* had a billiards saloon; the game was played at *The Rose and Crown* the following year.[79]

By the early eighties football was reported regularly in the local press. In February, 1886, there was a match, "said to be the first... ever played at Wivenhoe". It was nominally prestigious: Wivenhoe beat Colchester United by two goals to one.[80]

In November, 1888, a meeting to form a football club, chaired by Claude Egerton-Green, was held at the school. Edmund Round, who presented the first ball, was elected president, and Alexander Trotter vice-president. Twenty members were recruited. Two years later there was a second meeting to form a football club, this time at *The Park Hotel*, chaired by Sinclair Carolin, with a far better attendance of important people. Again, Claude Egerton-Green was made president; the vice-presidents were Edmund Round, Alexander Trotter, Hector Gurdon-Rebow, Sinclair Carolin and Bayard Brown. The captain was Charles Scofield, a painter who was also landlord of *The Brewery Tavern*; the secretary was Alexander Trotter. Evidently, it was no good forming a club or

Late Victorian and Edwardian 1881–1914

87. *A cricket team, c. 1905.*

Colchester Castle Museum

88. *A gymnastics team, c. 1905.*

Loaned by Mr. and Mrs. Don Mason

89. *An unidentified football team, c. 1905.*

Colchester Castle Museum

90. *St. Mary's Football Club 1913-1914. The photograph was taken at Smith's Corner, probably by "One-Arm" Smith.*

Loaned by Mr. Glendower Jackson

Late Victorian and Edwardian 1881–1914

91. *McEvers Bayard Brown (?-1926).*

Loaned by St. Mary's Church

society unless the people who got things done – the important tradesmen and captains – received moral, and perhaps financial, support from the grandees. The venue may be also significant. Public houses were the places where people met to do business and *The Park Hotel*, already the regular venue for the Cricket and Quoits Clubs' annual general meetings, was a general sporting centre for the town.[81]

Three football matches were reported in the spring of 1891. Further matches were reported up to 1900 when a second club was formed from the local volunteer corps which may have stifled the first one, for in 1905 a meeting was held at *The Pointer*, Alresford, with John Hawkins in the chair, to form a combined club with that village. In 1907, The Wivenhoe United Football Club, as it was called, and The Wivenhoe Volunteers Football Club, were amalgamated as The Wivenhoe Town Football Club, again under Hawkins' presidency. In the 1900's football was played on a field lent by a Mr. Watsham at The Cross.[82]

As life was rougher in those days, so the feeling between local villages was not always friendly. One Wivenhovian remembers that the rivalry between Wivenhoe and Brightlingsea was very keen and that on occasion, when men had more than enough to drink, there were fist fights.[83]

There was a Wivenhoe Gymnasium Club in 1904, but in September, 1906, The Wivenhoe Athletic and Gymnastics Club was formed, with a membership of fourteen young men. In 1908 we hear of a Wivenhoe Athletic and Cycling Club which was hoping to acquire a proper gymnasium and in the following year was reported to have a swimming section. In 1913 a hockey match was played between Alresford and Wivenhoe; the contestants were all women.[84]

9 Education.

In the eighties and nineties the scope and framework of formal education in the town changed radically. The National School in the High Street, recently enlarged, had room for 133 boys, 133 girls and 112 infants, but was no longer big enough, so in 1886 the architect to the trustees, J. W. Start of Colchester, conferred with the Education Department in London about an extension. As we have seen, this school belonged to the Church of England and was supported by voluntary contributions. In a jeremiad, the *Ipswich Journal* advised Wivenhoe to build an extension before the Education Department turned it into a Board School, that is, one with an elected board of governors supported out of the public rates. As if to forestall this there was a ratepayers meeting the following year at which it was decided to transfer the school to the parish. The ancient civil war between the British School and the National School was now ended.[85]

Late Victorian and Edwardian 1881–1914

92. *The Infants at the Board School in 1911.*

Loaned by Mr. F. P. Reed

Nevertheless, on 23rd April, 1888, the school became a Board School. Ten men competed for five places and in a low poll John Goodwin, a builder, came top with 293 votes, followed by Hector Gurdon-Rebow, Alexander Trotter and then T. C. Goodwin, the landlord of *The Black Boy*. These four were all Church of England, but the fifth member of the new board was the Rev. William Tyler, the Congregational minister. Tyler began his ministry in Wivenhoe at the age of twenty-six, in 1883, and ended it forty-four years later.[86]

The new board elected Gurdon-Rebow as chairman and considered a pile of 207 applications for master of the Boys' School. Its choice, a Mr. John Jenkins of Pembrokeshire, was not a happy one, for by January, 1891, he was under notice to leave, and he did, suddenly. "His departure is sincerely regretted by most of the tradesmen in the place as well as by several in Colchester", hinted the *Essex Standard*, "especially as he has left no address". Soon after, the foreman of the schools likewise disappeared leaving several unpaid bills.[87]

The next task was to accommodate 150 children. The Board, mindful no doubt of the ratepayers who encountered them on at least one stormy occasion, wanted to extend the existing buildings, but the Department of Education insisted on new ones. Plans were prepared by Mr. Start, and then, because the tenders were all too high, more plans. Eventually, Mr. Dupont, who had just built the dry dock for Forrestt's, was accepted, at £4,790. Land was bought

93. *The Girls at the Board School in 1911.*

Loaned by Mr. F. P. Reed

beside the railway line, in Phillip Road. The whole project was to cost £6,000 or so, and the ratepayers, who thought this was too high, sent a petition to the Department. Nevertheless, the new school, for girls and infants, was built, and it opened on Wednesday, 16th September, 1891, before all the furniture had arrived.[88]

Sixty-six Wivenhovians had asked the School Board to retain surplus land next to the new school for a recreation area. The Board agreed, but later reneged on its promise and the land was sold for housing. Perhaps this was because it was difficult to pay the architect following the collapse of Mills, Bawtree & Co's bank.[89]

In the previous chapter we looked at a couple of School Logs. As this one opens, Eliza Jones has transferred to the Girls' Department and her sister, Emma, is in charge of the infants. Apart from the difficulties already mentioned, Miss Jones evidently suffered from chronic ill-health, yet for all that I think her daily record protests too much. Too often she rails at the parents with their unending excuses for the truancy of their progeny and at the rival dame schools that send on illiterate children to her. It is therefore not surprising that after an unenthusiastic Inspector's Report in 1895 she was given notice and even less that she swept prematurely out and wrote several long, self-justifying letters to the press and the school board. Yet give her her due, even at Phillip

Late Victorian and Edwardian 1881–1914

Road conditions were far from easy. Of the four classes in her department, the youngest had eighty-five children.[90]

Yet things were improving and continued to do so. Education was now compulsory and the parents knew it. Things certainly improved for the infants when the strict and thorough Miss Polly "Pi" Kent, who wore a boater and stumped about with a stick, took over their department in 1900. Attendances rose and the inspector reported: "the children are very happy and are taught with success".

Don Mason, who was born in 1906, told me about his schooldays.[91]

The infants occupied the half of the Phillip Road nearest the High Street. They learned reading and writing with slates, for they had no pens and ink, and arithmetic. They also did a good deal of painting in watercolour. There was a maypole, round which patterns with coloured ribbons had to be woven. If this was not done correctly Miss Kent sternly reproved her young charges.

At seven the sexes divided. The girls moved to their own school under the same roof; the boys went up the road. The headmaster, William Wadley, who took over in 1888, has left us a sober, straightforward account of his forty years at the school. He seems to have been efficient, if not particularly inspiring nor an innovator.

Don Mason learnt to write a copperplate hand with a special school pen suitable for thin upstrokes and thick downstrokes. Pencils and rubbers were used and each boy had his pencil box which was collected at the end of the day by a monitor. English Literature pursued a central path, with Shakespeare and Dickens very much to the fore. The boys learned poems, such as *The Loss of the Royal George* and *The Eve of Waterloo*. Arithmetic was sufficiently advanced to involve graph paper. There was history, "kings, wars, 1066 and all that sort of thing". There was geography, with a globe and a map of the world, much of which was red, divided into hemispheres; once a week the pupils copied a map of their own from an atlas and coloured it. A Mr. Barrett attended from time to time to give a lecture on Alcohol and the Human Body, though the effect of the former on the latter was something his hearers had every opportunity of observing for themselves.

The boys were divided into six classes called "standards". It was expected that a boy would move up a class each year of his school life, though he had to take a test to do so and the duller ones were left behind. Each member of the staff taught two forms simultaneously. Standards One and Two, taught by the headmaster, were upstairs; the others were on the ground floor.

There were external examinations, but now and again an inspector would ask the boys questions. The brighter pupils might take an examination for the Colchester Royal Grammar School; there was no equivalent examination for girls.

The school day began at 9 a.m., with an assembly at which the register would be made up and the names of absentees noted. There were prayers, including the Lord's Prayer, and a hymn accompanied by a member of the staff on the piano or harmonium. The hymns the boys sang were simple ones for children, such as *There is a Green Hill Far Away*. At noon the pupils went home to dinner and returned at 1.45 p.m., though some, including those who came from Alresford, ate sandwiches on the spot. The afternoon session ended at 3.45 p.m.

Both the morning and afternoon sessions included a fifteen or twenty minute break. "It was absolute Bedlam in the playground", Mr. Mason told me and he described one particular game which his contemporaries used to play. It was called, as I think I heard him say on a somewhat used tape, Jacking and Towing the Line. The players were divided into two teams. One member of the first team stood against the wall to act as a buffer and his colleagues would hold each other round the waist and bend forward to present a series of arches. The most agile boy from the opposing team would take a run, put his hands on the back of the first arch amd try to get as far over the wall as he could. So, in turn, did his colleagues. "And the last boy, usually the smallest one of all, would be the last one to come and he'd hang on to the last back. It was all right if everyone landed fairly, but if they landed on the skew you can imagine what happened. You finished up with a heap". He thought it a wonder nobody was killed.

There were indeed accidents from time to time, such as dislocated fingers, for which the doctor's help was needed, and sometimes violence would flare up into a fist fight. "You know where to finish that off", Mr. Wadley would say on these occasions, and they did, behind the Co-Operative Stores. The boys formed a ring, the offended parties fought it out and shook hands; two or three hours later they were friends again.[92]

The boys had hoops of iron, made by the blacksmith, Mr. Jones, at his forge up at The Cross, for 1/6d. The girls also had hoops, but wooden ones. The boys played marbles; the girls played similar games but with beads. Tops, spun with a whip, were common to both sexes. Mr. Mason remembered seeing thirty or forty boys and girls in the High Street at one time with tops.

There were no properly organised school games, but if a match, say, with the scouts was arranged, Mr. Wadley would pick a team. Other, informal games included raiding the vast orchard above the Hall, in which the wits and celerity of such adventurous spirits as young Ernest Hatch, were pitted against those of the local policeman and gamekeeper. The boys used to look for chestnuts in the Wivenhoe Wood, then privately owned.[93]

There was no school uniform, but most of the boys wore linen or celluloid collars three inches deep. The boys whose parents were fairly well off wore grey flannel trousers and blazers over a clean white or blue shirt. The poorer ones wore their fathers' blue serge trousers cut down so that they came just below the knee, and much-darned pullovers.

Discipline was a problem, for the classes were large and, then as now, some boys made themselves very difficult. Mr. Mason recalled one contemporary who was caned almost every day by Mr. Wadley; after this individual had kicked the headmaster once or twice in front of the class he was punished privately. "But there was never any parental trouble. They didn't interfere. If you got the cane, well you got the cane. You deserved it, and that was that". There was a good deal of truancy because this was before parents realised the importance of literacy. If a boy went absent and reappeared without a note to explain why, the Schools Attendance Officer, "Circumference" Goodwin – he went round and he *was* round – would visit his parents. Repeated truancy would lead to a summons.

Don Mason left the Boys' School when he was twelve because he went on to the Technical College, now the Colchester Institute, to study engineering. Had he not done so, he would have stayed there for another two years.

Mrs. Etta Dan, who recorded her impressions of life in Wivenhoe for a research student at the University of Essex, was born in 1891, so the Girls' School she remembered was a decade or so earlier than the Boys' School recalled by Don Mason. She, too, started at the Infants' School before graduating next door:

> And honestly that Girls School was a most marvellous school. There was the most marvellous woman there, headmistress. I have never seen anybody like her in all my experience of hundreds of teachers I have seen. When we were in the Top Class, you know, we used to do English . . . equal to O Level English and A Level English![94]

High praise, because when she left the Girls' School Mrs. Dan would have been only fourteen, or even younger, and she went on to train as a teacher herself. This headmistress was Mrs. Eliza Wright, whose husband taught at the Boys' School. The Wrights lived next door to the Boys' School, in what was called the School House; their daughter, Mabel, was an assistant teacher at the Girls' School.

Mrs. Wright, who took over in 1883, kept her logs beautifully. It was evidently no chore to write up the details that the inspectors and governors needed to know, but a labour of love, and her pages, with their use of red and black ink and headings with wavy underlinings, are a visual delight. Her style is matter-of-fact, but now and then there is a touch of emotion, when, for instance, a pupil dies suddenly.[95]

She was a disciplinarian. If her pupils were not on time she stood at the door of the school with the bell in her hand; in form they sat upright, their arms folded behind them. Her attendance figures, generally well above 90 per cent after the turn of the century, show that she established schoolgoing as a way of life for her pupils.[96]

There were seven standards in her department; she taught the top two herself and only girls who tried hard were admitted to them. Grammar was taught formally, with parsing and analysis. The girls learnt to tell an adjectival clause from an adverbial one. They wrote compositions and did a good deal of spelling. They read poetry and memorised it. When they recited, Mrs. Dan thought they "spoke well", that is, without their native Essex accent, as if there were some merit in losing it. Arithmetic included neither algebra nor geometry. Music was read from sight and the girls sang part songs. When she returned to teach at the same school, Mrs. Dan taught her pupils in the same way. The girls danced, in a style that was neither folk nor country; they drew, painted and did a good deal of needlework. They learnt about hygiene, the importance of ventilation in bedrooms and brushing one's teeth.

In 1902, Mrs. Wright adopted the ceremony of choosing a May Queen as a school custom. Until 1915 there was a formal ballot among her pupils every year; the girl with the highest number of votes was May Queen, the six or eight runners-up her attendants. It so happened that no girl was ever elected more than once.[97]

As the boys had their personal games, so the girls played rounders, which they called baseball, improvising bats from bits of old wood. They played verbal games as well, such as I Sent A Letter To My Love, seated in a ring on the ground. Mrs. Dan's parents took an interest in her progress at school and would see the work she brought home, but there were neither reports, open days nor speech days.[98]

The clever girls trained to become teachers. Mrs. Dan graduated to the Technical College for this purpose and so did Mr. Mason's mother, Millie Goodwin. Mrs. Mason recalled that there were about 225 girls at the school and that four classes were taught simultaneously in a single room. She, too, had praise for Mrs. Wright: "a wonderful woman, very clever, thorough and interesting". Later, after an apprenticeship at Wivenhoe, she taught at Fordham. For three years she cycled there and back, a round distance of twenty miles, and coped with her family and the household chores as well.[99]

"There are no less than seven dame Schools most conveniently centred in the different corners of the town, that prevent nearly all the young children from attending this, until they are between six and seven years of age", Emma Jones recorded grimly in 1882. Conceivably, their existence had something to do with her own performance, but as the physical conditions of her school improved and a form of free education was established so, doubtless, their number decreased. However, in the years before the First World War Miss Proctor still flourished in West Street.[100]

Late Victorian and Edwardian 1881–1914

94. *A view of the town from the church tower. To the left of The Black Boy is The Nottage Institute.*

Colchester Castle Museum

95. *A contemporary scene at The Nottage Institute which is now on The Quay. Left to right: Mr. Don Smith, Mr. Lewis Worsp and Mrs John Worsp.*

Essex County Newspapers

Another private school taught some fifteen to twenty children of all ages up to fourteen in a tiny hall, which still exists, tucked away behind the Post Office. It was run by "Dimmy" Smith, who achieved a good standard; he, too, kept going until 1914.[101]

In the nineties, Wivenhoe acquired its own technical college. Captain Charles Nottage was a wealthy Londoner whose extremely successful racing yachts, *Boarhound* and *Deerhound*, were skippered and crewed by men from the Colne. He died, prematurely, in 1894 and left money to found an institute, either at Brightlingsea or Wivenhoe, where navigation could be taught. It was also to be a club, with either a reading room or library. He bequeathed £3,000, and a further £10,000 on the death of his wife.[102]

Within two years a board of trustees put his intentions into effect. On 11th November, 1895, it met in London and decided that the institute should be established at Wivenhoe, because this was more central. On 29th April, 1896, the committee met at *The Black Boy*. Claude Egerton-Green, then deputy mayor of Colchester, presided, and Captains French and Cranfield were present. Wivenhoe was represented by Captains William Ham and William Wadley, also the landlord himself, T. C. Goodwin. That same autumn The Nottage Institute opened, in premises next door to *The Black Boy*.[103]

Now the enterprising young seaman had his own night school, where he could forward his career in the Merchant Navy. Men came to its classes on the Rowhedge ferry, on the branch line from Brightlingsea and in traps from as far afield as Tollesbury. However, as the years passed so the character of The Nottage changed. To this day it gives classes in navigation and seamanship, but to men for whom sailing is a hobby. At any time the ground floor of the premises on The Quay, to which it transferred in 1947, contains dinghies in various stages of construction and on the floor above is a lecture room that contains a permanent exhibition of Wivenhoe's maritime history, with a small library at the back. Everyone who lives here should, sooner or later, pay it a visit.

10 Politics and Amenities.

In December, 1894, Wivenhoe elected its first parish council. There was a pleasantly informal meeting at the School, chaired by the rector, who opined that these new parish councils would be a bond between classes and that people would henceforth take a greater interest in local affairs. Eleven men were elected on a show of hands, but it was felt that a proper poll was needed, so one was held. About 70 per cent more votes were cast and the results were similar. Captain William Wadley and a solicitor, John Watson, who had tied for first place in the informal poll, with 73 votes apiece, now tied again, with 107. The other nine councillors comprised three shipwrights, two captains, two builders, a bootmaker and a joiner.[104]

Thus the town acquired an organ of local government composed of its own inhabitants. However, this was merely the prelude to the slightly smaller Wivenhoe Urban District Council which came into being on 1st April, 1898. The public showed little interest; out of an electorate of 500 to 600, only 231 voted. The results were as follows:

Elected:
Alexander Barlow	118	Gentleman of Leisure
William Wadley	113	Master Mariner
James Heath	103	Oyster Merchant
Thomas Williamson	102	Tax Officer
John Felgate	101	Farmer
John Watson	97	Solicitor
John Goodwin	91	Builder
Dick Hamm	83	Builder and Auctioneer
Walter Pullen	82	Shipbuilder

Not Elected:
Henry Rice	71	Brewery Manager
Charles Ellis	69	Master Mariner
Sinclair Carolin	63[105]	Clergyman

The man who topped the poll was a straightforward Conservative and the man who came last an avowed Liberal, but I would guess it was popularity, not politics, which determined the voting. Was the rector offended? He never stood again.

On 13th April, 1898, the new Council met for the first time, at premises in the High Street. Later it moved to Little Wick, the Georgian house on the southern corner of the High Street and Alma Street. There was a little difficulty in electing a chairman. Walter Pullen proposed Alexander Barlow, he having topped the poll, but Captain Wadley was aggrieved:

> *He must say, though he was not ambitious of office, he felt it very much that after the three years' service he had rendered to the parish and having been, he thought, principally instrumental in obtaining these urban powers, not one of his old friends had the pluck to get up and second his candidature. After the work they had done in the Parish Council, he thought it bad treatment, and they could not very well expect very much from him.*[106]

They soothed him down by giving him the vice-chair. This was the first display of temperament in the Council Chamber; it was very far from being the last.

Claude Egerton-Green was invited to be treasurer, perhaps because he was a banker who had occupied Wivenhoe Hall, or a banker who had been popular, or both. The Council acquired a temporary medical officer and a temporary sanitary inspector, and talked about finding a scavenger.

Before the month was out the Council held its first routine meeting, from which we can gather a rough idea of its powers and activities.[107]

It felt it could do nothing about the overcrowding of the Rowhedge ferryboat. It refused to pay a bill presented by the rector for work done in the churchyard. It permitted Forrestt's to open up a road in order to tap a well in West Street. It gratefully accepted the gift of a strip of land at the side of Belle Vue Road offered to it by N. C. C. Lawton. It took over the functions of the former Burial Board. Four Colchester solicitors, all anxious to earn an extra £40 a year, wanted to be Clerk to the Council; C. W. Denton was chosen. A medical officer and an inspector of nuisances were appointed, and it was resolved to appoint a surveyor and a rate collector. A case of diphtheria was reported and that of an old man who had died and been found covered with vermin. Shops were said to be choked with dust in the summer and residents unable to open their windows because of it.

Hitherto, the lack of a proper water supply, proper sewerage and made up roads, with the dirt and disease which accompanied them, had not been generally regarded as problems because nothing could be done about them. They were simply part of life. In 1888 and 1892 the Council's predecessors, The Overseers of the Parish, had been compelled by The Rural Sanitary Authority of the Lexden and Winstree Union to call public meetings with a view to doing something about unemptied privies and open cesspools, under pain of the Rural Authority bringing in its own scavengers and levying a rate for so doing. These matters were publicly discussed, but nothing seems to have happened. However, things were changing. Roads could be tarmacadamed, holes bored for fresh water and sewerage pipes installed. At the Council's first routine meeting, Alexander Barlow said that "the health of the place should be the Council's first care", and for the next decade or so it was.[108]

Barlow himself secured a regular water supply for much of the town by making borings in the grounds of Wivenhoe Hall, connected to standpipes in the High Street, whence it could be obtained free of charge. Up till now Wivenhoe had obtained its water from the brook after which Brook Street is named. Before school, children did what was called their "burden". They fetched two bucketfuls of water from the brook, using a frame that kept the buckets away from their legs as they walked home with them. Grown-ups used

Late Victorian and Edwardian 1881–1914

96.   *The Water Tower, which was opened in 1902.*

Photograph by G. Martin

yokes and chains, as if they were milkmaids. Water could also be obtained from Jimmy Munson who used to sell it at a halfpenny a gallon.[109]

Meanwhile, the Council planned a waterworks, for which it borrowed over £6,000, and eventually 6,000 gallons of water an hour were discovered at the bottom of Queens Road. The Council bought a site there from Henry Rice and a waterworks was built which pumped water to a tower near The Cross.[110]

This tower was built in a year. It is about 77 feet high, contains some 143,000 bricks, and the tank at the top holds 50,000 gallons. It was formally opened on 3rd July, 1902. Within a year the Council was serving notices to people not connected to the mains; some three years after that the waterworks was connected to fifty-two houses. Almost overnight the town was far cleaner and healthier. Meanwhile, the Council had bought two acres from Ernest Beard for a sewage works, but this problem was not solved until after the First World War.[111]

By the time the water tower had opened, the High Street and the spinal route had been made up and, one by one, the other roads followed suit, all save Anglesea Road, which looks as it has always done because the parish and borough boundary runs down the middle and nobody can decide which authority should deal with it.

To lay the dust in the roads, the Council acquired a dustcart. Pedals operated by the driver of this horse-driven vehicle sprinkled water over the road. Children took off their socks and shoes and ran behind. The driver flicked his whip at them but they swarmed back like flies, until he operated a device that sprayed them from head to foot.[112] The cart and its two horses were kept at the Council Offices.

So, after 1909, was the barrow, with its buckets and hoses that comprised the equipment of the Wivenhoe Fire Brigade; before, there was a fire station at 30, Alma Street. When a blaze was reported, a maroon was fired at the Council Offices, whose noisy report summoned not only the brigade but all Wivenhoe, particularly the youth, who were not otherwise engaged. The first two firemen trundled the barrow to the blaze and everybody else gave unsolicited help, until the firemen, in desperation, turned their hoses on the youngsters who were crowding round.[113]

The town already had one amenity that others lacked. For almost thirty years Wivenhoe had possessed gas lamps, which provided useful goalposts for street football, and practically every house used this service for domestic lighting. Shortly before the First World War it was available for cooking, though the quality and quantity were both poor and it took an age, say, to boil a kettle.[114]

The gas was made by baking coal in ovens called retorts, and then purifying it, before it was fed into two sizeable gasometers, and a smaller one used to run

Late Victorian and Edwardian 1881–1914

97. *The gasometers in Gas Road at some time between the two World Wars.*

Loaned by Mr. E. G. Barnes

the plant itself. There were no pumps to send the gas round the network of underground pipes, so the gasworks was situated at St. John's Road, in the lowest part of the town, whence it rose by gravity, being lighter than air. High tides not infrequently flooded the premises and extinguished the retorts. After the gas had been extracted, the resultant coke was sold to the public; it was good quality because the temperatures used in the retorts were not high enough to complete the process. The tar formed by the gas as it cooled was also sold; an excellent waterproofing, it was used, among other things, to seal the bottoms of boats. There was a curious piece of folklore to the effect that the peat earth used at the plant, after it had been made extremely pungent in the purifying process, was good for asthma, (which indeed Wivenhovians suffer from a good deal). People used to bring their children to inhale it.[115]

At about the turn of the century the telephone made its appearance. Don Mason's grandmother, a Mrs. Mitchell, was the first caretaker/operator

98. The High Street c. 1900. To the right is the wall surrounding Wivenhoe Hall which was built in 1841. A few years after this it received the graffiti: IN THEFT THEY TRUSTED, IN PECKHAM THEY BUSTED, evidently a jibe at the Liberals.

Loaned by Mr. Mick Glozier

99. The High Street c. 1900. To the right is the entrance to Wivenhoe Hall of which a relic remains as the front of No. 97; to the left can be seen the Board School, where the Library now stands.

Colchester Castle Museum

Late Victorian and Edwardian 1881–1914

100. The Avenue, before the Co-op appeared on the left or Cedric's Garage on the right.

Loaned by Mr. E. H. C. Squire

101. Below: The Avenue, with the new Methodist Church on the right and a long corrugated iron fence on the left.

Loaned by Mrs. Claire Weston

employed in the town by The National Telephone Company. For a wage of £1, with coal and light included, she was on call twenty-four hours a day, coping with the requests of seven subscribers. The exchange was sited at 88, High Street. Two years later there were seventeen subscribers and in 1925 over fifty. Five years after that, when Mrs. Mitchell retired, this number had trebled.[116]

Thus was the town crier displaced. This official, who was established by the eighties, went round the town with a handbell and after he had rung it announced forthcoming events or items of importance. For instance, on Christmas Eve, 1889, he had this to say: "Oyez! Oyez! Lost, stolen or strayed, a sailor's bag, belonging to one of the crew of the yacht *Valfreyia*. Whoever will take the same to No. 1, Blood Alley, High Street, Wivenhoe, will be handsomely rewarded. God save the Queen!"[117]

The last man to hold this office, from 1909 to 1934, was William "Shreddy" Currell, a stoutish man with a stentorian voice. He wore no livery, but made his rounds in shirtsleeves or a Norfolk jacket according to the season. He ran a carrier's business with a man called Billy Cole and he could dance a traditional boot dance as performed by fishermen wearing fly boots. It was supposed to represent the ritual hosing down of the boots to clean them.[118]

The spate of development that opened the twentieth century very nearly included a bridge between Wivenhoe and Rowhedge. In fact, this had been authorised by an Act of Parliament at the beginning of the nineteenth century and the matter had been raised again from time to time. It was needed for two reasons: to provide access between the two communities and to promote the commercial development of the neighbourhood.

In 1901, the Fingringhoe Parish Council approached John Hawkins, who had just become a county councillor in a straight fight with Alexander Barlow. He was enthusiastic. Three years earlier, Messrs. Pearson & Son had planned a railway link between Wivenhoe and Mersea including, of course, a bridge over the Colne. They now produced plans for a bridge on its own, with a revolving central pedestal, which cost just over £5,000. However, the Colchester Town Council insisted that the bridge should be manned at all times, lit at night, take no longer than two minutes to open and that no tolls should be charged.[119]

The scheme hit a snag. The bridge was to be sited on the saltings upstream of The Quay, either at the ferry or opposite Regent Street in Rowhedge. So the road to the bridge lay across the saltings and the committee had to buy this strip of land, and the owner, who happened to be Alexander Barlow, wanted £1,000 for it. This meant that when public bodies were approached to fund the scheme they would be put off by the outrageous price placed on a mere two acres of marshland. For outrageous it was; Barlow paid only £657 for the whole thirty-two acres of saltings, so he was holding the committee, of which he was incidentally a member, and the public, to ransom.[120]

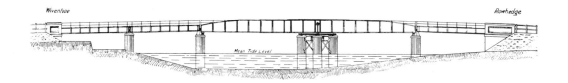

102. *The design for the proposed bridge over the Colne taken from a plan made by J. M. Meldrum for John Hawkins of Wivenhoe.*

Colchester Public Library

There was a lull of two years. In the spring of 1904 it was variously reported that 1,500, 2,000 and 4,000 householders had signed petitions favouring the bridge. The County Council was approached, but refused to consider the matter until Colchester had modified its original provisions, while Colchester refused to modify its conditions until the County *had* considered the matter. So that was that. Barlow declared that if a suspension bridge was built he would give land for the site, and roadway, free of charge; whether he was serious or skittish is not apparent.[121]

In 1904, Barlow abruptly resigned as chairman of the Urban District Council, allegedly because somebody said in the House of Commons that chairmen of urban district councils were generally bad magistrates, but rejoined two years later. However, in 1907 he was not re-elected.[122]

Henry Rice reigned in his stead and as president of the Cricket Club found himself in difficulties because Barlow refused to let the club use Tenacres. F. Watsham, who befriended the Football Club, lent the cricketers a field at The Cross adequate for a private pitch, but there were no home matches in 1908. In 1912, the club again sent a deputation to Barlow, who had just rejoined the Council, having topped the poll with 220 votes. Evidently this deputation was no luckier than the first, for in the following year two members were sent to ask John Hawkins for the loan of a pitch at Mill Field.[123]

General elections were extremely lively, but essentially good-natured affairs, and Election Day itself was a gala, with posters everywhere, and strings of blue flags and union jacks across the streets. The town was overtly more Conservative than Liberal, so blue favours predominated over yellow, which everybody wore just like football supporters. For the children it was a holiday because polling took place at the School. So they roamed the streets, singing political ditties. The leading Conservatives: Charles Gooch, John Hawkins, Dr. Samuel Squire, John Felgate and James Heath, lent their carriages to voters, some of whom had to cross over from Rowhedge. Gothic House was their

The Story of Wivenhoe

103. *The Conservative headquarters at Gothic House, probably in 1906 or 1910.*

Loaned by Mr. Brian Oakley

104. *The Liberal Headquarters at the White House in 1906. The voters are pointing at the winner, Levy Lever, M.P.*

Loaned by Mr. Philip Dan

headquarters and a banner with electric lights stretched across the High Street at that point. The Liberals had their champions too, notably Sinclair and Elizabeth Carolin, the Rev. Franklin Tyler and Captain William Wadley.

We have seen that pressure was put on some Wivenhovians to vote in certain directions. Besides the political allegiances of the skippers, there were the pressures of family and religious tradition. Wesleyans, for instance, were known as a class to be Liberal.

Each candidate usually managed to address at least one public meeting in the town. Up to 1904 the venue was, of course, the School, and then the Foresters' Hall. The candidate would be introduced by a chairman and then make a speech which would be robustly heckled by those of the opposite persuasion.

Wivenhoe, now part of the Harwich constituency, returned the Conservative James Round in 1885, 1886, 1892, 1895 and 1900, on the last occasion unopposed. In 1904, Round was succeeded by H. K. Newton. However, for a rural county Essex is fairly left wing and in 1906 Newton was beaten by the Liberal, Levy Lever, who received 5,530 votes to his 5,308. In 1910, Lever lost to Newton and the Conservative victory was greeted by rockets fired from several of the large yachts that were laid up.[124]

Then, as now, Members of Parliament were rarely seen in Wivenhoe except at election time; then, unlike now, the winning candidate reappeared shortly after the election and his supporters gave him a victor's welcome.

11 The Wivenhoe Flier.

We can gauge the public attitude to people and events by the incident of *The Wivenhoe Flier*.

Jack Humphreys was a member of the Aero Club and a partner of a firm called British Aeroplanes Syndicate Ltd., and he wanted to build an aeroplane that could take off from water. Over the winter of 1908-9, a machine described as an aero-hydroplane was constructed to his designs in a large, corrugated-iron shed on the saltings, near the Rowhedge Ferry, and on Saturday, 27th March, 1909, a large crowd assembled to see this craft, already christened *The Wivenhoe Flier*, make her appearance. It was disappointed. However, the following Saturday she was wheeled out early in the morning and put on a cradle, prior to being launched from the river bank. At noon, with Jack Humphreys as pilot, launched she was, but quickly keeled over and deposited her progenitor in the water. The *Flier*, stranded on the mud by the receding tide, was rescued when she refloated at midnight.[125]

Her second appearance was on 15th April. She was launched successfully, then a gearbox snapped. On the morning of Sunday, 18th April, she was launched and towed downstream behind James Heath's *Dreadnought*, which had

105. *The Wivenhoe Flier.*

Loaned by Mr. L. W. Kemble

some prominent Wivenhovians on board, including Alexander and Mrs. Barlow, to Alresford, where the engines started up "with a loud scream" and she began to move independently of the tug. Then the engines stopped and the aeroplane, which apparently needed a rudder, drifted towards the Alresford shore. The engines were restarted, but the same thing happened. It seems that not all the cylinders were firing and that the gearboxes were acting as brakes, so that a lifting speed could not be obtained.[126]

The *Flier's* fourth and last appearance at Wivenhoe was on 14th May. She was launched at 7 p.m. and towed down to Alresford Creek. Her air boxes, which were situated along the lower part of the structure, had been replaced by two small canoes, each with a rudder operated from the cockpit. The six-cylinder engine started and the propellers revolved; there was a loud bang, which seemed not to matter, and Humphreys detached the aeroplane from the tug and moved forward. However, he was again unable to achieve a lifting speed; it was thought that his propeller was not strong enough.[127]

Before he left the town, Humphreys attempted to win *The Daily Mail's* prize of £1,000 for the first circular mile flight in the United Kingdom by a British pilot in an all-British aeroplane, not in the *Flier*, but in a monoplane with a 35

106. *The monoplane which I assume was the successor to the Flier and failed to win the prize offered by The Daily Mail.*

Loaned by Mr. G. Martin

h.p. engine which cost £300 to build. At 5 p.m., on Saturday, 9th October, the river wall skirting the saltings was packed with spectators. Twelve sailors with union jack armbands kept the public away from the route to be taken by the aeroplane. At about 5.30 p.m., accompanied by loud cheers, Jack Humphreys walked to his machine. At a signal, five men who were holding it, let go and it moved forward. The pilot taxied forward about a hundred yards and hit a ditch over which he had intended to skim, which broke his propeller and ended his flight. He was not too upset; that same evening he made a political speech to a crowd in Falcon Yard. On 18th October this aeroplane left for Blackpool in a pantechnicon and the aviator, sitting beside the driver, acknowledged the cheers of the locals as he left. Well might Jack Humphreys be cheered. He had employed Wivenhoe labour in an age when employment was uncertain; moreover, it was believed that British Aeroplanes Syndicate Ltd. would set up a factory at Wivenhoe.[128]

In April, 1910, a third aeroplane, built at Wivenhoe, left for Brooklands. The next year Humphreys' monoplane, presumably this one, flew at Brooklands, though not with Humphreys as pilot.[129]

All this contrasts with the announcement, in the spring of 1909, that a firm

199

called Nitro-Compounds Ltd. wanted to manufacture nitro-glycerine on a site not far from Lower Lodge Farm. Charles Gooch and Alexander Barlow disliked the idea, but when they organised public meetings to protest, found they were very much in the minority. "We want work and we'll have it", was the cry and after one meeting, "the crowd followed the speakers up the High Street vigorously hooting". However, when Nitro-Compounds applied for a licence from the Colchester magistrates it became obvious that the firm was a myth and that the real intention was to buy a parcel of land, obtain a licence for a factory in respect of it and then sell it again at a much higher price.[130]

107. *The Flag at the turn of the century.*

Colchester Castle Museum

Late Victorian and Edwardian 1881–1914

108. *Dr. and Mrs. Samuel Squire in their donkey cart with their three sons on bicycles. One of them, E. H. C. Squire, helped me with this book.*

Loaned by Mr. E. H. C. Squire

109. *Robert Wyatt, the carrier.*

Loaned by Mr. R. O. Richardson

12 Spoiling for a Fight.

Wivenhoe's reaction to the Boer War was lively and positive. When Spion Kop was captured, in January, 1900, some open ground between Belle Vue Road and The Avenue was christened Spion Kop and so called until it was built on. Patriotic items started to appear in concerts given by the Friendly Society and there was a Children's Penny Fund for wounded soldiers. The relief of Ladysmith provoked a day of intense, spontaneous rejoicing. Flags flew everywhere, cannon were fired, the church bells rang and after the children in school had sung *Rule Britannia* and *God Save The Queen*, there was a half holiday. That evening a torchlight procession passed through the main streets of the town headed by The Wivenhoe Brass Band and The Drum and Fife Band, with men of the Naval Reserve drawing a model of a cannon on a carriage. At the rear was "a corps of youngsters who admirably acquitted themselves", or in other words marched. There were fireworks at the Mill Field.[131]

These patriotic feelings were soon put on a more formal footing. At a public meeting on 6th March, K Company, 2nd Volunteer Battalion Essex Regiment was formed, under the enthusiastic patronage of John Hawkins, who became its commanding officer, supported by Henry Rice, William Johnson, Franklin Tyler and Sinclair Carolin. Mrs. Carolin had bitterly criticised the Indian Frontier War; it is possible that her husband's militancy caused friction at the

110. *2nd Battalion Wivenhoe Volunteers, photographed on 1st September, 1900.*

Loaned by Mrs. Dorothy Chaney

Late Victorian and Edwardian 1881–1914

Rectory. In August the company left for its first camp, with The Wivenhoe Band in attendance; its first annual parade was held in October, its first prizegiving at the end of the year.[132]

Wivenhoe provided some professional soldiers for South Africa. Clifford Goodwin, a son of T. C. Goodwin, went out early in 1900. He was followed shortly after by Arthur and John Goodwin, sons of the builder and town councillor John Goodwin, who were attached to St. John Ambulance. John Goodwin died of enteric fever at Bloemfontein. When David Joyce, who was wounded at Paardberg, returned, he was given a smoking concert in his honour at *The Greyhound*.[133]

When Mafeking was relieved, the town went wild. The men at Forrestt's downed tools and roamed the town singing popular songs, the High Street was draped with red, white and blue. Again, cannon were fired, the church bells rung, flags hoisted everywhere, ships dressed overall, while the torchlight

111. *The Mafeking Celebrations. Part of the parade in the courtyard of The Falcon.*

Loaned by Dr. William Dean

procession that night and the fireworks evidently outdid any previous celebrations. Outside Philip Chamberlain's shoe shop in the High Street hung a strip of leather with the inscription, "British-tanned Boers' hide".[134]

One Wivenhovian did not return from South Africa. John Goodwin died of enteric fever on 7th June at Bloemfontein. His brother Arthur wrote home to his father:

> *Dear Dad,*
> *You will have received my cable and letter telling you the sad news by the time you get this, but do not know what I said as I was so upset then. He died in the arms of Col. Richardson's wife, who was most kind to him, and I have had to give her his scissors in remembrance of him. Everybody has been most kind to me in my troubles, and my officer patients told me to a man that if they could do anything for me I was to tell them. Sister Wilkinson, who is in charge here, offered to pay half funeral expenses, but I knew you would not like me to let her. I had him buried in a coffin covered with black cloth and black plate, splendidly written, and put in a separate grave, as I knew you would not like him buried in a blanket, and put in a pit with others. I have received no pay that was due to him. Capt. Hobson is bringing some things home for me. I am in the best of health, but shall be glad to get away from this death-trap . . .*[134]

There was a memorial service for John Goodwin at St. Mary's; Arthur Goodwin was given a complimentary dinner at *The Park Hotel*.[135]

The entry of the British into Pretoria occasioned another procession and a formal dinner at the School, followed by a soirée which lasted into the small hours. That autumn the regatta fireworks included portraits of Lord Roberts, General Buller and General Baden-Powell.[136]

Sixty to seventy Wivenhovians danced away the old century at the School to the music of a string band, with *Auld Lang Syne* and the National Anthem at midnight. On 22nd January, there were theatricals at the School arranged by by Mr. and Mrs. John Hawkins. "The evening's enjoyment was only marred by the news, which arrived before the finish, of the sad death of our noble Queen . . ."[137]

The six bells that had hung for a century in St. Mary's belfry were wearing out and four of them were cracked, so in February, 1903, it was decided to raise money for a new chime. The bell fund committee received a curious offer. An anonymous donor would give £10 provided the new bells were first rung on 9th November, 1904, at noon, 3 p.m. and 6 p.m., each time for an hour, in memory of the dead, and, with uncanny prescience, on 11th November the big bell must be tolled at noon and 6 p.m., each time for half-an-hour, also in memory of the dead. The offer was accepted and one Wivenhovian recalled a bell being tolled because an old lady had provided money for this purpose. The donor's name was never revealed; I guess it was Mrs. Carolin.[138]

Late Victorian and Edwardian 1881–1914

112. *A church parade shortly before the First World War.*

Loaned by Mr. Brian Oakley

113. *Church Parade on 20th April, 1913.*

Loaned by Mrs. Claire Weston

114. *Empire Day, probably 1906, at the Boys' School. Mrs. Gooch has just raised the Union Jack.*

Loaned by Mr. Brian Oakley

Late Victorian and Edwardian 1881–1914

Numerous building lots, in Stanley, Ernest and Rectory Roads were sold off in 1902 and 1903, and year by year the owners built on them. At the same time, as we have seen, the town's amenities increased and improved.

The 1900s also saw a rise in militarism and nationalism, described at the time as patriotism.

Lord Roberts stumped the country pressing for rifle clubs, which sprang up obediently in his wake. K Company had formed The Wivenhoe Rifle Club by 1903 and was soon taking part in competitions throughout the area. Presumably this was for the exclusive benefit of the Company, for in 1911 J. B. Hawkins founded a miniature rifle club, that is, one that fired .22 bullets, called The Wivenhoe and District Rifle Club. The first reference I can find to a Wivenhoe Gymnasium Club is at a volunteer fete, which suggests that this, too, was a military offspring. The gymnasium, equipped with a trapeze, punching ball, horizontal bars, boxing-gloves, dumb bells and Indian clubs, was at 30, Alma Street, where K Company kept its rifles and heavy greatcoats.[139]

In 1903 a church parade is first mentioned. On Sunday, 27th September, members of The Boilermakers' Association, The Shipwrights' Society, The Oddfellows and Foresters, marched from Tenacres down to St. Mary's, preceded by the band of K Company, formerly The Wivenhoe Town Band. In 1905, the procession passed through all the principal streets before arriving at the church and in that year the centenary of Trafalgar was celebrated with decorated yachts and minute guns fired continuously from 2.30 p.m. to 4 p.m.[140]

On 24th May, 1906, Empire Day made its appearance. This was for the rising generation. At the Girls' School the pupils performed what was described as "a character sketch", to show "how Great Britain and the Colonies combine by means of commerce, industry, education, science, art and religion to make the greatness of our vast Empire". Up the road, the boys marched past the Union Jack, saluting it, and sang patriotic songs. The flag and flagpole were donated by Mr. and Mrs. Charles Gooch.[141]

Two years later the event was well established. First the infants and girls marched up to the Boys' School, where patriotic notables were assembled. Rudyard Kipling's *Recessional* was sung and then Henry Rice exhorted everyone "to try and prove themselves worthy of the great empire of which they were members". Mrs. Gooch unfurled the Union Jack "amidst hearty cheers" and this was followed by the National Anthem. While the boys performed military drill the girls and infants returned to their school where Mr. Gooch gave them another exhortation, and there were songs and recitations and a play showing the greatness of the Empire. Finally, the National Anthem was sung a second time and everyone broke up for a half holiday.[142]

The boys' drill was organised by an assistant master, H. L. Wright, who became scoutmaster to the 1st Wivenhoe Troop of Boy Scouts, founded in 1909, two years after the movement itself. Scout meetings, held on the top floor of 30, Alma Street, always seemed to coincide with raids on Daniel Chapman's neighbouring apple orchard. Military drill made its appearance at the Boys' School as early as 1903. The teachers' logs indicate that both Mr. Wadley and Mrs. Wright approved of these ceremonies and I have the word of at least one participant that they were taken extremely seriously.[143]

In 1910, Charles Gooch became president of an association designed to promote more scout troops in the area, and chaired, and spoke at, two meetings of the National Service League. He talked about defending the country against invasion. Compulsory military training was advocated and slides shown of the Franco-Prussian War. Invasion was also the theme of a Red Cross Society meeting chaired by John Hawkins. An army officer showed how to tend the sick and wounded should invasion occur.[144]

The coronation festivities of 1910 were more formal than those of 1902. In the morning there was a Coronation Service at which the lesson was read by Charles Gooch – it would seem that squire and rector were at least temporarily reconciled – and which concluded with the National Anthem. A procession of

115. *The townspeople on their way to the Coronation festivities at Tenacres in June, 1911. Very likely this photograph was taken by "One-Arm" Smith from his house in The Avenue.*

Loaned by Mr. F. P. Reed

important organisations, including the Urban District Council, together with the scouts, schoolchildren and Sunday schools, accompanied by the band of the Wesley Guild, marched round one or two streets at the lower end of the town, then up to Tenacres. Here, with everyone still lined up, the National Anthem was sung and three cheers given for the King and Queen. The afternoon was devoted to sports, the band playing the while. Some of the items in a long list, notably a four mile marathon, were specifically for scouts. Between 600 and 700 children had tea, then there was a scout display, a prizegiving and, to conclude, a formal procession down the High Street where the National Anthem was sung yet again. The town, and indeed the country, was becoming dangerously fond of that melody. Later in the year Ralph Herd had to explain that its omission from an orchestral and ballad concert was not due to disloyalty.[145]

In May, 1912, H Company 5th Essex Regiment paraded through the town with scouts distributing leaflets, then held a recruiting drive at the Foresters' Hall which produced twelve conscripts. By the following year the Wivenhoe Red Cross Voluntary Aid Detachment had been formed. The first record of a whist drive I can find, in October, 1912, was to raise money for the Red Cross.[146]

116. *An unknown festivity shortly before the First World War.*

Loaned by Mr. R. O. Richardson

So the little victims played. The historian, seated at the microfilm reader, relishes, sadly, the dramatic irony of the situation unfolding, for he knows that before another hundred copies of the *Essex County Standard* have rolled by, the holocaust, one of their own devising, alas, will be upon them.

1914 arrived. In February, a meeting of the National Service League in Colchester was poorly attended and in the Wivenhoe column accounts of quasi-military activity are notably absent, save that the church parade of 17th May seems to have been the largest and longest of its kind. Headed by the Wesley Guild Band, it marched down from the Foresters' Hall to St. Mary's via Station Road, West Street, East Street and Alma Street. Afterwards, the procession returned, just as tortuously, to the Foresters' Hall, via the High Street, Belle Vue Road, Rectory Road, The Cross and The Avenue.[147]

That summer, Charles Gooch was occupied with other things than the National Service League. He had been called a sweating landlord and he defended himself vigorously from the charge at an open-air Conservative meeting in Elmstead. In his twelve years at Wivenhoe he had not received a farthing's profit from his property because the rents did not cover the expense of keeping the farm buildings and cottages in order.[148] However, this was challenged by a Liberal agent in a letter to the *Essex County Standard*:

> *The wages question had got to be settled. The farm labourers are entitled to a living wage and liberalism means to see that they get it . . . The labourer must be paid before the landlord, or even the parson, and until the labourer gets a fairer share of the wealth that his labour does so much to create there will be no peace in agriculture . . . A change is inevitable, and the sooner Mr. Gooch realises it the better for his sense of humour . . .* [149]

Four more copies of the *Standard* to go, but perhaps the blow may not fall after all . . . !

In his final, pre-War Wivenhoe column, James Moore had four items to report. The Brotherhood, a fairly new, male, nonconformist group, had met the previous Sunday afternoon. William Green, the son of James Green, had obtained his master's crtificate at a Board of Trade examination at Grimsby. Four young ladies who had been taught the piano by Miss Bellman-Taylor of Belle Vue Road, had gained certificates. At the annual meeting of the Football Club held at *The Park Hotel*, its president, John Hawkins, had been thanked for the use of his ground at Ballast Quay; in return, he said it was a great pleasure to encourage good English sport.[150]

Such was the state of play at the beginning of August, 1914.

CHAPTER 8

Into the Slump and out of It 1914-1965

1 1914-1918

Though the War started abruptly, the transition from civil to military was almost instantaneous. In the first week the banner of the Red Cross flew over the Infants' School, which had been requisitioned as a hospital, and it was estimated that over a hundred Wivenhovians left to join the Naval Reserve.[1] On the morning of Sunday, 9th August, the Territorials, already stationed in the town, marched to church attended by the Wesley Guild Band. More troops arrived. On August 15th, a detachment of the Royal Army Medical Corps camped at Ballast Quay. To supply it with a necessary 500 gallons of water a day, the Fire Brigade lent it a hose. A hundred blankets were provided, mostly from the *Rosabelle* and *Lady Blanche*. By mid-October, between eighty and a hundred men were billeted in the town.[2]

There were troops, and their horses, everywhere. Tents appeared in the grounds of the Park, the Hall, on Spion Kop, the Mill Field, and on the present Valley Road and Dene Park Estate. Soldiers were even billeted in the yachts' stores and, of course, compulsorily on the inhabitants, though the elderly, sick and widowed had EXMT, for Exempt, chalked on their walls. Mrs. K. G. Everitt remembers that her widowed mother chose to billet soldiers and was given two despatch riders, who delivered messages on bicycles. She was paid a little money to keep them and every week they brought their rations to her: four large loaves, a large frozen piece of meat, a pound of very rancid margarine, some tea and some "frightful jam in a big tin".[3]

The Mill Field was used for sports; an area of Spion Kop, between the new cemetery and Rectory Road, became a mass of trenches, with troops practising to go over the top and jabbing at straw dummies with bayonets. They were entertained by The Allies Concert Party at the Foresters' Hall. The Congregational Chapel was opened to them as a reading and writing room, and the Upper Room of the School turned into a recreation area, with papers and

The Story of Wivenhoe

117. *October, 1914. These recruits belong to D Company, 5th Service Battalion Essex Regiment. Back: (left to right), Pte. Blundon, Pte. Dann, L/Cpl. Reed, Pte. Turner, Pte. Franklin. Front: (left to right), Pte. King, Drummer Adams, Pte. Bridges.*

Loaned by Mr. F. P. Reed

118. *Regimental Sports Day at the Mill Field, on 29th April, 1915.*

Loaned by Mr. Brian Oakley

Into the Slump and out of It 1914–1965

magazines, but the headmaster was displeased when soldiers used the walls of the School as an *ad hoc* urinal.[4] However, a proper urinal was built for them at the Council Offices, in Alma Street, which remained until 1973. F. W. "Plumber" Smith, who had bought 30, Alma Street in 1912, installed six baths there, which the troops, and residents, used at 2d a time.[5]

In October, there was a recruiting meeting, though it appeared that all the able-bodied young men had already left, and after stirring speeches by Alexander Barlow, Charles Gooch and H. K. Newton, six more men joined up.[6]

Other Wivenhovians favoured the Navy. At least three captains of yachts were commissioned in the Royal Naval Reserve. Some boats were called up, too. On 7th August, the *Venetia* was requisitioned, as was the *Vanessa*, and with all her crew, who volunteered to a man. Early in 1915, the *Rosabelle*, with her skipper, Captain Wenlock, was requisitioned, also the *Miranda* and the *Lady Blanche*. These yachts became armed patrol boats; they were painted grey and equipped with six and twelve pounder guns.[7]

Although the men at Forrestts' were initially put on three-quarter time, the shipyards were soon in full swing. Admiralty contracts included a special

119. *A trawler of the Strath class, which was built at Wivenhoe, the William Fall.*

Colchester Castle Museum

service vessel, *Wave*, launched in 1914, a minesweeper called *Pirouette* and sixteen trawlers of the Strath class, all built between May, 1918 and November, 1919. These 215 ton ships had an overall length of 123 feet, carried a crew of up to eighteen and cost about £18,000. The Navy sold them all two or three years after the War.[8]

In June, 1915, the R.A.M.C. left, but other troops came, including the North Staffordshires. The public dinner which opened 1916 was given to the 350 N.C.O.'s and men of the 29th Provisional Battalion.[9]

With the spring of 1916 came conscription for all males up to the age of forty, and a network of tribunals was set up for those claiming exemption. Wivenhoe's comprised six men chaired by Alfred Tapling of Wrawby House, formerly Elaine House, with an army officer and the new Deputy Clerk to the Council, Frank Byles, in attendance. The employers of the thirty men interviewed often spoke on their behalf, but the tribunal nevertheless conscripted three butchers, two carpenters, a baker, a farmer, a grocer, an ironmonger, a tailor, a stoker, a stockman and an oyster dredgerman. It could not afford to be soft, for the Essex Appeal Tribunal, in Colchester, was able to reverse its decisions. The most embarrassing case must have been that of Arthur Vinson, the chairman of the Urban District Council, for facing him were three of his fellow councillors. The tribunal accepted that baking was a certified occupation and Vinson was granted conditional exemption. His case appears to conflict with that of Ernest King who, his employer declared, was baking bread on a government contract; King was conscripted.[10]

The ancient problem of a bridge over the Colne was solved by the military, for they built one for their own use, linking Rowhedge with the Ferry Road. The first man to cross over was King George V. He motored into Wivenhoe on the afternoon of Friday, 14th July, and all the schoolchildren lined the High Street to see him. As the boat owners had feared, progress up and down the river was retarded and more than one skipper was summonsed for failing to stow his sails and warp his vessel through the bridge. After the War there was talk of keeping it, but it was sold and demolished.[11]

Yet the bridge, as a possibility, remains and every so often flashes, comet-like, across the public horizon. In 1937, Councillor William Loveless declared at a public inquiry that it was vital to the town's development. Half a century later, Mr. Michael Roots, a former town and borough councillor, wanted it built with Common Market money to take the traffic out of Wivenhoe and it appears in the network of roads proposed by the 1987 Fraenkel Report.[12] In June, 1916, Elizabeth Carolin died and an article she had written, offering little comfort for the future, was printed under an account of her funeral. After Germany was worsted they would have to fight the German on the industrial front. They would have to prepare for harder times . . . [13]

Into the Slump and out of It 1914–1965

120. *Photography strictly forbidden but an illicit box brownie snapped King George V as he walked over to Rowhedge on 14th July, 1916.*

Loaned by Mr. Brian Oakley

Harder times arrived swiftly. In the summer and autumn of that year the casualty lists soared, and higher still were the lists of youths rising eighteen who appeared at Colchester to protest their unsuitability to share their fate, for the most part vainly. Others tried to dodge the holocaust with less subterfuge. In the early summer of 1917 a Wivenhovian called Percy Pike was charged with failing to present himself for military service. He said he did not know his age, but he was not eighteen, he was sure of that, and his mother confirmed that he would be eighteen on 20th May, a day or so after the court hearing. The court consulted the parish register and discovered that Pike had been eighteen since 26th February; it fined him £2 and handed him over to the Army.[14]

The War took a very heavy toll of subalterns and therefore of the grandees and their relations, who were automatically commissioned. In July, 1916, the last real lord of the manor, Lance-Sergeant N. C. C. Lawton, was killed in action. At the end of August, Captain John Hawkins, an adjutant with the British Expeditionary Force in France, died of pneumonia brought on by overwork. In September, 1917, Alexander Barlow lost his second son, John, a dashing young pilot of eighteen, who was forced into a nosedive when he took on six German planes simultaneously.[15]

On the home front life became practical and austere. Charles Gooch ran a volunteer regiment to teach the over-forties how to use rifles. By the beginning of 1917 the Council had acquired a War Agricultural Committee. Henry Rice

121. *Munition workers at Forrestt's.*

Loaned by Mrs. C. G. Scofield

let it have five acres near the waterworks pumping station, which was cut up into eighty allotments, most of which were taken up by March. Then a co-operative pig-keeping scheme was started. The Council built four sties, stocked them with ten pigs and by the end of the year made an 80 per cent profit. A War Savings Association was set up. There was a food economy campaign; sugar was rationed and oats sown in the cemetery. The Council declared war on vermin. 2d was offered for a dead rat, 3d for a dozen dead sparrows. It was

122. *The unveiling of the War Memorial, 19th June, 1921.*

Loaned by Mrs. Muriel Ryder

eventually discovered that some rat-catchers were receiving 2d at Wivenhoe and 1d at Elmstead for one and the same rat. There were collections for wounded soldiers, but the soldiers themselves seem to have left, for we hear no more of them after 1917.[16]

In the midst of all this activity there was still time for temperament in the Council Chamber. When, in 1917, Herbert Wright was elected chairman, William Husk exploded:

Well, gentlemen, I don't want any office, and I don't want to be chairman. It would be just the same if I did because there is not a – one of you who would propose me. You talk about senior members. I have been fifteen years on the Council and you put me down as a bag of soot.[17]

The final year of the War arrived. Part of the graveyard was leased to a farmer for potatoes and more plots of land were cultivated in Stanley Road. John Hawkins' home, Ballast Quay, was bought by a Mr. H. W. Pawsey. The *Valfreyia*, for some reason unconscripted, moved to the river wall. In the summer there was a War Weapons Week; Wivenhoe saved over £7,000 and bought a weapon it christened the Wivenhoe Gun. Mrs. Gooch died in June; her coffin was taken to the cemetery on a farm waggon.[18]

When the Armistice was signed bunting was hung out and the church bells rang; the church clock chimed again and everyone had a holiday.[19]

It took another year to shake off the War. 1919 opened with a general election and the Conservative, Major H. K. Newton, beat the Liberal, Commander Aylmer Digby, by a fair margin. In March, the Wivenhoe Town Football Club was reconstituted and in its first match beat the Medical Corps by thirteen goals to nil. The steamyachts *Rosabelle* and *Lady Blanche* returned to their places on the river wall.[20]

What form should the memorial take? Four ideas were proposed: a monument, almshouses, a cottage hospital and a recreation ground. It was decided to have a monument, perhaps because this was the cheapest. Wivenhoe had sent over four hundred men to the War; forty-six names are inscribed on the granite cross in the churchyard.[21]

2 Unemployment.

In June, 1919, two hundred demobilised soldiers and sailors were given a welcome home party at the Foresters' Hall. There was a procession round the town with the Wivenhoe Brass Band and people in fancy dress, and a fete at Tenacres by permission of Mr. and Mrs. Roland Morgan, the new tenants at the Hall, with sports and a huge tea. So everything would be just as before? Perhaps symbolically, the church bells were not rung on the day peace was signed; remarks were passed about this and the bellringers resigned in a body, so that for some months the bells were not rung at all.[22]

Happily the demobilised men came back to some work. Most of the big yachts, and the jobs they provided, had gone for ever, but Rennie Forrestt was in business. It was now amalgamated with two Scottish firms, as part of The Rennie, Ritchie and Newort Shipbuilding, Engineering and Drydocking Company. There were cargo vessels to be reconditioned, some from Germany as part of war reparations, and nine vast cargo ships to be built for the Maindy Transport Company of Cardiff. The first of these, the 1,400 ton *Maindy Transport*, was launched on 23rd March, 1920, with champagne and optimism. Intended for use as a collier, she was over two hundred feet long, the largest vessel ever built at Wivenhoe. Downstream, Husk's and Cox & King were still operating.[23]

In the Council elections of 1920, John Frostick, Labour, topped the poll with 242 votes, the first candidate ever to stand under a party label. He was a platelayer. When the new Council met, Captain Abraham Harvey received a

Into the Slump and out of It 1914–1965

123. *The Maindy Tower.*

Colchester Castle Museum

124. *A group of workers at Forrestt's shortly before the shipyard closed.*

Loaned by Mr. Philip Dan

The Story of Wivenhoe

wound which would never be healed because Arthur Vinson was elected chairman and not he. So they offered him the chair, but vainly. The die was cast and Captain Harvey would never get over it as long as he lived.[24] There was a Whit Sunday church parade in 1920, with the Council, Oddfellows, Buffaloes, Fire Brigade, Boy Scouts, Girl Guides and the Women's Institute, headed by the Wivenhoe Brass Band. It seems to have been the last of its kind. Empire Day survived the War, but is not recorded after 1931. The fire of pre-War jingoism had warmth in it yet; unfuelled, it finally burnt itself out.[25]

That autumn saw the last Annual Fair, the social ritual which had occurred spontaneously for well-nigh two hundred years at least, and the first Armistice Day, another social ritual and its polar opposite. It also saw the first post-War regatta. The Cricket Club, without a pitch, and without John Hawkins to agitate for one, took a long time to revive and it was several years before Wivenhoe found itself another recreation ground. The former Swedenborgian Church in Alma Street was opened as the Social Club, but did not last long. The

125. *"The White City" at Forrestt's as it looked in the early sixties. To the rear is the engine shed, which was made a listed building in 1988.*

Essex County Newspapers

church itself, installed at "Dimmy" Smith's former school, survived until 1933. The Salvation Army disappeared about ten years earlier. The Council started to build sixteen council houses in Rectory Road. Two more large cargo vessels were launched: *Maindy Tower* and *Maindy Keep*.[26]

One of the shipyard's employees at this time was young Don Mason, fresh from his engineering course at the Colchester Polytechnic. He started in the pattern shop. Pattern makers designed those parts of the vessels that were cast in iron or brass. The items were first modelled in wood and then moulds of sand were made. The pattern maker's art consisted in making a design slightly larger than the finished article, to allow for contraction when the metal, brass especially, cooled. For if it were too large it would waste not only metal, but the time taken to machine it down to the right size. It was three months before he was allowed to make a pattern, but eventually he made two. One was for the gigantic square bollards on the *Maindy* ships. They weighed, he thought, $2\frac{1}{2}$ hundredweight each.[27]

After six months there, Don Mason spent another six in the fitting shop, a concrete building called the White City, probably because of its colour. Here there were lathes, planing machines and similar equipment. Then he spent six months outside on the boats themselves, in particular working with marine engines and pumps. After that came six months on maintenance and he would have gone to the drawing office and perhaps stayed there, but the Depression intervened and he was laid off.

His career in the shipyard, that of a man who had already received specialist training, was unlike those of the men who arrived unskilled and were apprenticed there. He recalled that rivets, thousands of them in every vessel, were still put in by hand and enormous skill by men with long-handled hammers. The caulkers worked with a number of differently-shaped chisels. What with caulking and riveting the yard was extremely busy. Wood was only used for panelling the cabins.

1926 brought unemployment. At the January meeting of the Council the government grant for unemployment was mentioned only to be dismissed. However, as the year wore on so the numbers out of work rose, and although the fourth cargo vessel, *Maindy Cottage*, was launched, 150 men were idle by October.[28]

A vociferous mob waited on the Council meeting of February, 1922 and was sympathetically received. However, The Lexden and Winstree Guardians for the Poor, in Colchester, considered several cases and reluctantly gave relief to about a third of them:

> *Rev. Davies ... objected to giving a penny to Wivenhoe unemployed. Let them do as he had had to do, and travel the country for work.*[29]

126. Barrells' Sawmill and Timber Yard.

Loaned by Mrs. Dorothy Chaney

A fifth cargo vessel was launched in June, but that summer the town was struck two heavy blows. On 26th May, a timber yard at The Cross run by Ben and Martin Barrell caught fire, and flames rose high above the neighbouring water tower. Some thought the fire opportune, for the firm was not doing well, but it was largest single employer in the town apart from the shipyard.[30]

In June, Ritchie Rennie itself went bankrupt. It was estimated that 75 per cent of the two hundred men out of work at the end of 1922 had been employed there.[31]

In the middle of this general gloom came a piece of good news, albeit one that belonged to an age that was passing away: Captain Albert Turner, a Wivenhoe fisherman, was made skipper of the King's yacht, *Britannia*.

By the autumn of that year the situation was so bad that bi-weekly dinners for the children of the unemployed were provided at the Girls' School. Nevertheless, the Council's desire to push ahead with schemes for putting people into work was opposed by a highly voluble Wivenhoe Property Owners and Ratepayers Association, which quickly attracted eighty members. Its *raison d'etre* was to stop the Council from putting up the rates and borrowing money which, it believed, would bring the town to ruin, to say nothing of costing the ratepayers more money.[32] The largest of the Council's schemes was a main sewerage system, which would cost £15,000 and require a loan of £6,000. The Ratepayers protested and there was a public inquiry, in March, 1923. The

Into the Slump and out of It 1914–1965

127. *Aboard the Britannia in 1933. With Their Majesties, King George V and Queen Mary, is the present Queen Mother, then Duchess of York, with her back to the camera. The King talks to his skipper, Captain Turner. In the foreground is Captain Turner's son, another Albert.*

Loaned by Mrs. Ivy Turner

Council's doctor and its sanitary inspector argued eloquently for the scheme: that the only system at present was one of dead wells and buckets, which were cleared once a fortnight or even once a month; that there were outbreaks of diphtheria; that it was high time for a proper system. The Ratepayers contended that Wivenhoe was one of the healthiest places in England; that the present system was perfectly adequate; that the work thus provided for the unemployed would be only temporary; that some houses could never be connected to the system; that the rates would go up and the town become insolvent.[33]

Council elections were held every year, three of the nine members retiring in rotation. In 1923 the Ratepayers put up George Duncan, who topped the poll with 322 votes; in second place, Walter Salmon and J. Richardson, both Labour, tied with 222.[34]

By the autumn of that year some sewerage works had begun, though Councillors Richardson and Salmon were still urging the main one. Other schemes were seriously considered: the making-up of more roads and the Wivenhoe to Rowhedge bridge. In 1924, the Council set about converting the

223

street lighting to electricity. From this time we hear less about the privations of the jobless. It would seem that problem eased off a little and that by now the town was used to it. Nevertheless, times continued hard and remained so until the Second World War.[35]

In February, 1925, the upstream shipyard was acquired, for £22,500, by Otto Andersen, of Bergen, Norway, who called himself Otto Andersen & Co. (London) Ltd. He published a catalogue of the work he thought he could do, though in fact this was a catalogue of what the previous management had done. He tried hard, but failed. Between his arrival and June, 1926, his turnover was £5,898, of which almost half was the dock rent of the *Valfreyia*, which had moved to Wivenhoe during the War. His only commissions were two small boats and some pontoons for the War Office, though he also did some work on the rusty skeleton of the sixth *Maindy*, abandoned since 1922.[36]

Bayard Brown, a recluse on his dockbound yacht, died in 1926. On a stormy, wet afternoon Wivenhoe pulled down its blinds for him and turned out to line

128. *The Valfreyia in dry dock.*

Colchester Castle Museum

129. *Employees of Cox & King Ltd. outside the firm's premises.*

Loaned by Mr. Albert Scales

130. *Husk's building pleasure boats for Brightlingsea.*

Loaned by Captain R. J. Husk, R.N.

131. *The Kingwell family attends the launch of* Wyvern III *at Husk's in 1935.*

Loaned by Captain R. J. Husk, R.N.

the High Street and crowd St. Mary's, whose bells rang a muffled peal for a service attended by notables. The body was then taken to London and shipped to America for burial. The *Valfreyia* steamed down to the river wall where her crew received gifts of money under her late owner's will. Before the year was out she had left the Colne. She was bought by the Maharajah Jam Sahib of Nawanagar and rechristened the *Star of Asia*.[37]

The shipyard struggled on. Sir Frederick Rice, the town's Conservative M.P., pumped £1,000 of his own money into it. In 1926, Otto Andersen sold the White City to a firm called Pollock Anderson Oil Engines, which made semi-diesel engines and employed some twelve to fifteen fitters. This new organisation performed indifferently and it seems that both firms closed in 1930. In 1933, it was rumoured that the yard would be leased to John Brown, the mighty enterprise at Clydebank; in fact, it was taken for fifteen months or so by a London-based firm called Arthur R. Brown & Co., which built a tug called *Rodney*, also a small towing boat for Fiji.[38]

Downstream, things were a little better. Cox & King foundered in about 1923, but not before it had built a forty foot motor boat for a Mr. Burke of California in March of that year. I can find little other record of that firm, save that a Mr. Francis Pratt, trading as Cox & King, was the subject of a receiving order in 1934 at the suit of the Admiralty in connection with an uncompleted contract dating from the War.[39]

Husk's kept going quietly with smallish commissions. Shortly after the War it produced motor launches for the Sanitary Authority of the Port of London, and a Mr. G. T. Morris commissioned a series of six motor yachts at two to three year intervals, each larger than her predecessor. The sixth, a comfortable sixty footer, was launched in 1930. Other individuals commissioned motor cruisers and other light craft, such as the twelve ton auxiliary cutter for Major Edwards of Leigh-on-Sea, launched in 1935. The firm also built small sailing dinghies and motor dinghies, and even boats for a boating pool at Brightlingsea. In 1937, Husk's went into voluntary liquidation.[40]

3 The Changing Scene.

Meanwhile, Wivenhoe had lost Wivenhoe Hall. I have been told by Edward Squire, the doctor's son, who returned from the War to set up a small and not very long-lived motor-cycle factory in the town, that the property was bought by one of his uncles and later sold for demolition, but whether directly from Barlow or not I do not know. At any rate, the Morgans were joined at the Hall by Mr. Morgan's son-in-law, Frederick Nettleinghame, and his wife. He described himself as a financial organiser and in October, 1922, the press was invited to inspect some garden furniture made by a company called Rusticana.[41]

A case in the Colchester Police Court established beyond very much doubt that Nettleinghame was a rogue and it is likely that he had been appointed occupier of the Hall to burn it to the ground, for a fire there was, in the summer of 1925. However, the brigade dealt with it because, as one urban district councillor sarcastically remarked, it might have spread to a nearby bungalow. On 9th January, 1926, there was another fire, but again the brigade was too quick for it. Three fires in a row would have stretched the credulity of the insurance company too far, so the Hall came to a dignified end. It was sold for demolition on 17th March, 1927, at the Foresters' Hall, and dismantled during the summer of that year, while the estate was divided into building plots and also sold.[42]

At about this time the Foresters' Hall itself was also transformed. It had been sold, in 1921, for £1,000, to a Mr. F. W. Smith of Queens Road, who reopened it the following year. It was neither well booked nor well patronised. Then it was turned into the Foresters' Cinema.[43]

This venture began no later than November, 1927, when it was first patronised. The Hall was thoroughly transformed, with a sloping floor, wooden ceiling, stage tabs and a ten foot square projection box, made entirely of concrete, with a thick teak door. There were two projectors which, though motorised, were somewhat primitive. When they broke down the films had to be cranked through by hand. Though the cinema was lit by electricity supplied by Barrells', there was not enough power in the mains for arc lamps inside the projectors, so the cinema generated its own electricity in a small building attached to the Hall. This was the last decade of silent films, so there was a panatrope, run by two ladies, Grace Chaney and Zena Durrell, with records apparently borrowed locally, connected to loudspeakers behind the stage.

Films were shown on Mondays, Thursdays, Fridays and Saturdays at 6 p.m., with a Children's Matinee on Saturday at 2.30 p.m. The programme, which was changed twice weekly, comprised two feature films, with a ten minute intermission during which the audience could buy sweets, cigarettes, chocolates and monkey nuts. Altogether, the programme lasted three hours. At the end of the week the films were collected by Film Transport Ltd. in "a rough old truck" and new ones delivered. The cinema acquired a projectionist, electrician, maintenance man, publicity agent and cleaner in the person of 21-year-old Cecil Riches, who came from Halesworth in Suffolk. He was paid 55/- a week, but earned more by doing electrical work for the town in his spare time. He delivered posters for the cinema on his motorcycle and struck up an acquaintance with Cedric Peck across the road, for Peck's father ran Cedric's Garage, which opened with a flourish on 7th July, 1928. Riches' assistant was 16-year-old Jack Hatch, who projected the films and rewound them. The cinema made about £5 or £6 a night and it was Mr. Riches' final chore each

Into the Slump and out of It 1914–1965

132. *Cedric's Garage as it looked when it first opened.*

Loaned by Mrs. Claire Weston

night to take the train to St. Botolph's and deliver the takings to his employer, Albert Purkins, who ran *The Plough* public house there.

Purkins looked rather like Peter Lorre and Mr. Riches was a little frightened of him. Also involved in the enterprise was a man called Game who ran a motor-tyre business near *The Plough*, and Colonel Bell who wore a furry trilby hat, was physically very upright "and liked to bend his elbow". In April, 1929 the venture became the Wivenhoe Cinema Company.

It was Deecee Bishop's job to lock up the cinema, but one night young Riches was asked to do so. He discovered that in the ante room on the left hand front of the building, which had a wooden dado three feet high, there was a trail of combustible material stretching from the fireplace round the wall to the cupboard where the sweets were kept. Cinema in Wivenhoe was evidently not paying and the insurers were to be asked to make up the deficit. Mr. Riches moved the rubbish away from the fireplace and as soon as possible found another job.

The cinema had so few patrons in the summer of 1930 that it closed in May, intending to reopen in September, but never did so. One of the reasons given to the Official Receiver for its failure was that the return fare to St. Botolph's suddenly plummeted from 11d to 3d. However, it would not have lasted much longer, for the talkies were on the way and the necessary equipment was very expensive.[44]

There was now, incidentally, a regular bus service between Wivenhoe and Colchester. By 1920 a Silver Queen, with solid tyres, had made its appearance; it stopped outside St. Mary's Church, using Falcon Yard as a turning bay.[45]

No doubt the cinema was a revelation for young Wivenhoe, which in those days was generally obliged to improvise its amusements and found a good deal to keep it out of, and into, mischief. It was fun, for instance, to go to "Pug" Stebbing's general shop at the head of Quay Street, slap the sides of bacon there, call out "Pug!" and run like blazes; or go for a ride on the turntable in the upstream shipyard on which the engines reversed; or, regrettably, tease poor Miss Polly Havens, the pleasant but eccentric grand-daughter of Dr. Philip Havens, the Rowhedge doctor, who used to bowl a hoop about the street and lived with numerous cats in the house which is now Talisman's; or watch coffins being made in a shed at the foot of Hamilton Road and collect curls of plane-shavings; or watch the bullocks and pigs being killed in the slaughterhouse at the foot of Blood Alley every Monday; or simply gawp at any wedding or funeral.[46]

As Wivenhoe Hall disappeared, so another landmark was restored. Alderman Wilson Marriage, who lived at Alresford Grange, put Garrison House into good order and offered it to the Council as a Moot Hall.[44] The Council was pleased, but now that Wivenhoe Hall had gone, with most of the boundary wall, new premises were built on the west side of the High Street and the Garrison House was bought by The Society for the Protection of Ancient Buildings, who owned it until 1986.

In the spring of 1929 the street lighting changed from gas to electricity and the Council moved from Little Wick into its new and hideous Council Offices in the High Street.

As the captains and smacksmen retired or died and had few or no successsors, so a way of life ebbed gently away, year by year, and the Wivenhovian became a land animal. In the autumn of 1929, Theodore Pim, a direct and indirect benefactor to the town, who had laid up his yachts here for fifty-four years, died, and twenty-six members of the *Rosabelle's* crew attended his funeral. Happily, the yacht's new owner, Colonel Abraham, kept her at the river wall, where she remained until the Second World War. Every autumn, when she appeared off Brightlingsea, Wivenhoe was informed and at the next high tide the inhabitants flocked to see her move majestically to her resting place. Then the captain's barge was lowered and Captain Abraham Harvey was rowed in state up to The Quay.[47]

Into the Slump and out of It 1914–1965

133. and 134.   *Above: East Street looking towards Anchor Hill.*
Below: The Wivenhoe to Fingringhoe Ferry.

Both loaned by Mrs. Claire Weston

The Story of Wivenhoe

135. *The Rosabelle in dry dock.*

Colchester Castle Museum

The town shone with reflected glory from the last of the racing skippers. Like all captains, Albert Turner learnt his seamanship from fishing and possessed in enormous measure the supreme quality needed to win races, an iron nerve. For racing was largely a battle of nerves; the man who could hang on to his course until the very last safe moment was the man who won. This is what Turner was noted for as a youngster and it gained him his royal command. He raised a family of five girls and a boy, and lived, in modest grandeur, at Malting House in the High Street, but his head was unturned and he continued to fish during the winter. Wivenhoe respected him.

There was also some reflected limelight from one of the last actor-managers. At the outbreak of the First World War, John Martin Harvey, whose career was at its zenith, flung himself into the war effort with the literalness of a boy scout and his subsequent knighthood was evidently as much for this as for acting. Thereafter he hyphenated his last two names into a double-barrelled surname. It so happened that a daughter of Canon Frederick Langbridge, who helped to write *The Only Way*, married Alfred Tapling, the owner of Wrawby

136. *Sir John Martin-Harvey (1863-1944), as Sydney Carton in The Only Way.*
The University of Bristol Theatre Collection

House in Park Road. On at least one occasion the great man visited the Taplings and found time to greet old friends.[48]

Penury the town had always known; unemployment was a hazard that grew with the numbers working at the upstream shipyard, so that the fortunes of the town were ever more dependent on it. As we have seen, this fear now and then became a reality, but now it persisted and with the loss of the big yachts and the quiet erosion of the fishing fleet these years were wretched and demoralising for many people. One or two vignettes will make this plain.

Mr. James Harvey remembers his father crying during one off season. "What's the matter, Tom?", inquired his wife. "I can't get a bloody job, May". However, he did find the odd job. On one occasion he laid gas mains, on another was in charge of a brick kiln at Fingringhoe. Mrs. Harvey used her sewing machine to support the family. Robert Wyatt, the carrier, brought her pieces of alpaca from a Colchester clothing factory which she made up, working with one child on her lap, another on her back and a third tied to the treadle of her machine. At Christmas young James sang carols, literally for his family's supper. The Harveys lived in Smugglers Cottages, a row of dwellings jutting out from The Quay towards the river. They had earth floors and were frequently flooded.[49]

Mrs. Harvey also spent a good deal of time altering clothes, for her own and other families. People begged for cast-off clothes in those days, even for used tealeaves. Yet despite the scrounging and begging there were times when there was nothing left. Mrs. May Potter, who lived in Alma Street, never forgot the day when her two young daughters came to the tea-table and the cupboard was literally bare.[50]

The lower end of Wivenhoe had always been the slum end. Many of the dwellings, in East Street, West Street, Brook Street and Sun Yard, were pulled down by the Council before they fell down, and the present conservation area has a gap-toothed appearance. Those that remained, in particular The Folley, were noisome, fetid places, ripe to be condemned. Outside taps were shared between families; there was outside sanitation and the unholy reek of the nightsoil cart.

After the three worst years in the early twenties, unemployment receded a little but then returned, probably in 1929, when the number out of work was recorded at ninety-two and then 159. There was now a Labour Exchange in Alma Street; first it was at No. 10, then it crossed the road to a small hall once used by the Salvation Army, at No. 5. Here, the acerbic George Brooks, a former Army man, bullied his wretched clients like a sergeant major. When handed a card for a job, a man had to take it, or his dole, a mere pittance, was stopped. So Mrs. Ruth Munson's husband, who had lost the use of his left arm in the War, dug sewer trenches and went sugar beet harvesting. It was too much

Into the Slump and out of It 1914–1965

137. *Captain Eves, a barge captain who lived on The Quay.*

Photograph by John Tarlton, A.I.B.P., A.R.P.S.

138. *Two fishermen. On the left Arthur William Gunn, on the right his father, Charles Gunn.*

Loaned by Mr. Don Smith

for him, but he dared not give up. Mr. Leslie Kemble recalls that his father, after two years' unemployment, helped to build the ferry quay at Harwich. He rose at 5 a.m. and bicycled there. The line of unemployed, some three or four hundred, including men from Elmstead, Alresford and Fingringhoe, stretched back to Alma Street and round the corner to *The Grosvenor Hotel.* There, and on the railway bridge, they congregated, lounged and commiserated.[51]

In June, 1932, there was a meeting for the unemployed in the Congregational Schoolroom, and The Unemployed Assistance Committee was formed, with J. Mallet, chairman of the local Labour Party, as its chairman. Its intention was to raise money for the long-term unemployed. Over the winters of 1932 and 1933, there were weekly house-to-house collections. The Committee pointed out to the Council that on Fridays the men were attending the Labour Exchange twice, first to sign on and later for payment. Could the two operations not be combined?[52]

Unemployment was tackled in various ways and with some success. The Council applied to Wivenhoe Park for help. Would Mr. Gooch allow unemployed men to remove dead timber from his estate? Indeed, he would. So every week during the autumn of 1932, about a hundred men took away one or two hundredweight of wood apiece. The fishing industry was steadily declining and the fishermen who caught sprats often dumped them for lack of a market. In November, 1932, Lewis Worsp opened a sprat-canning factory on The Quay.[53]

North Sea Canners (Great Britain) Ltd. started in the former *Rosabelle's* store, now owned by Colne Marine. In this shed the sprats were spitted, smoked for twenty minutes with smoke from an oak fire, had their heads removed with a bandknife and were packed in tins with a vegetable or olive oil. They went all over the world, particularly to Fiji. Mr. Worsp had three smacks working for him and initially employed about twenty men and women, later fifty. In the off season his staff peeled shrimps or canned chickens, but when the firm moved along The Quay to the present Wilkins' stores, freezing apparatus made it possible to tin sprats all the year round.

Sprats, indeed, were invaluable at this time for whatever privations the average Wivenhovian endured, he could always count on a cheap, or even a free fish meal. Whenever the *Xanthe* or the *Maria* or the *Daisy* dumped a pile of unsaleable fish on The Quay the inhabitants helped themselves before the gulls arrived. For a nominal sum, or even nothing, the fishermen would fill a bucket with fish and, of course, they were sold in several shops. Mrs. R. J. McEune recalls that at this time a bloater cost a penny and so did a herring, while fish-and-chips was twopence.[54]

In 1935, 30, Alma Street was sold to the Colchester Manufacturing Company Ltd., and until after the end of the Second World War this firm,

Into the Slump and out of It 1914–1965

139. *Sprats up at the Tower.*

Loaned by Mr. Don Smith

140. *Sprats being unloaded at The Quay.*

Loaned by Miss Dorothy Skilton

237

which employed about twenty-five Wivenhoe girls, made alpaca coats and sports blazers.[55] Outside the parish, at Keelar's Lane, but staffed mainly by Wivenhovians, was The Wivenhoe Sand, Stone and Gravel Company, which supplied these three items to builders and roadmakers. Starting in the spring of 1920, with two wheelbarrows, two sieves and two men, it expanded until before the War it employed about thirty people. Meanwhile, horses and carts yielded to lorries and mechanical equipment of ever-increasing sophistication. In the thirties prices for these commodities fell drastically, but the quality of the sand and gravel found at this site evidently pulled the company through. The firm is now called Redland Aggregates. Its first manager, later a partner and managing director, was W. G. Loveless, who is remembered by one of his staff, Mr. Walter Wix, as a fair, even generous, man who looked after his workmen but would stand no slacking.[56]

At last, at long last, the sewerage scheme was constructed. It cost less than the anticipated £15,000, some £13,700, in fact, but was designed for a population of 2,500, Wivenhoe having now grown to 2,100 and likely to expand. It comprised a pumping station, near Anglesea Road, with three pumps to convey the sewage half a mile to the disposal works which were situated in the fork of land where the railway line to Brightlingsea branched off from the one to

141. *Employees of The Wivenhoe Sand, Stone and Gravel Company. W. G. Loveless stands on the left.*

Loaned by Mr. Walter Wix

Clacton. The work, which included laying 6,000 yards of pipes and making a hundred manholes, kept up to ninety men occupied for about a year. The pumping station was opened on 19th December, 1932. It was expected that the task of connecting up properties would continue to provide employment for some time to come.[57]

The Council had other problems besides unemployment, in particular that of electing a chairman. In 1921, it was agreed that one year's vice-chairman should be the next chairman. In 1930 it was the turn of Mrs. Bessie Richardson, an elementary schoolteacher, to move from the vice-chair to the head of the table. The widow of the former Councillor Richardson, she joined the Council in 1926, the first woman ever to do so. She was proposed as chairman by William Wadley. There was no seconder. Then Mr. Last proposed Mr. Hook, the current chairman. Mrs. Richardson erupted. The Council had deliberately insulted her, this was a plan to prevent her from being chairman, Council meetings had been arranged so that she would be unable to attend them and she would not have accepted the chair in any case, even it it had been offered with a salary of £10,000.[58]

Mrs. Richardson left the Council in 1935, in order, as she explained in a public letter, to leave a clear field for the re-election of Harry Bensley, to whom the electors owed a great debt, because he had helped her to straighten out the Council's finances and reduce the rates. She darkly hinted that she might at some future date publish her "unique and almost incredible" experiences as an urban councillor.[59]

Harry Bensley was a maverick who had acquired a bizarre notoriety by wagering that he would push a perambulator round the world wearing an ancient iron helmet. This feat was interrupted by the War.[60] After he had been discharged from the Army through sickness, Bensley came to Wivenhoe where at one time he worked as a collector to the Essex Public Medical Service. He stood for the Council as a British Legion candidate, unsuccessfully, was elected for Labour in 1931, but failed to get back in 1934. Then, perhaps due to Mrs. Richardson's support, he recovered his seat in 1935. However, shortly after this he succumbed to ill-health and retired to Surrey.

The straightening out of the Council's finances had something, probably everything, to do with the eclipse of its clerk, Frank Byles, who left it in 1931 to serve three years' penal servitude for embezzlement. According to him, his invalid wife had needed expensive medical care and this had swallowed up his salary. So he had borrowed money, at exorbitant interest and then, to keep up with the moneylenders, turned to fraud. For five years he had effectively doubled his salary. Mr. L. H. Martin, who remembered Frank Byles as "a tall, pompous-looking man with a bulbous face", recalled that when the Council moved to its new premises there was a bonfire of papers in the courtyard of

The Story of Wivenhoe

142. *Harry Bensley. One of the conditions of his wager was that he had to marry, so the lady is very likely his wife.*

Loaned by Mr. Glendower Jackson

Little Wick. "I can still see old Byles standing there with a smug look on his face", he told me, "and it wasn't long before Mrs. Richardson and Harry Bensley got on to the Council and turned things inside out, and Frank Byles was inside".[61]

The inter-War years, with the departure of the big yachts and perennial unemployment, were bleak, but not entirely so. Up through this barren soil rose some sturdy new shoots, the first signs of a more self-supporting society, one that was learning to do without the grandees.

We can see social life changing as we turn the pages of the School Logs. At the Boys' School, William Wadley's successor, Gustavus Baker, introduces the first Parents Day, in 1927, and in 1929 a Sports Day. In 1935, twenty-seven boys enter the North East Essex Music Festival.[62]

At the Girls' School, Mrs. Wright bows out just before the War ends. In 1925, Miss Ethel Smith arrives, and in 1926 Miss Betsy Grasby becomes her assistant. Santa Claus visits the infants. By 1930 there is an Old Girls Club. *Hiawatha* and *A Midsummer Night's Dream* are performed by the upper classes, (not standards).[63]

143. *A League of Nations pageant at the Girls' School in 1923.*

Loaned by Mr. Brian Oakley

144. *Wivenhoe County Boys' School, January, 1927.*

Loaned by Mrs. Dorothy Chaney

War is waged, and after several years won, against ill-health. Nurse Steele arrives, in 1917, to inspect heads. Very soon, she and her successors are examining heads and teeth, and eventually Miss Smith sends verminous children home. It is a struggle, for parents write abusive letters and even round on Miss Smith. However, they have to climb down. The Louse War, (1928-1933), has been won and, save for a short-lived insurrection in 1978, there are no references to vermin after 1937.

In 1936, Miss Smith is put in charge of all three departments. Meanwhile, Empire Day is eased out and an Armistice Day Service, if 11th November is a weekday, eased in. Some parents now contest the use of the cane. One father calls in the N.S.P.C.C., but it backs the school.

In the Autumn of 1938 the senior boys leave their premises in the High Street and go by bus to the Colne High School at Brightlingsea. Henceforth, all education takes place at Phillip Road.

Quietly, but persistently, organised sport made progress during this period. After the War, the Cricket Club, still without a pitch, put up with the saltings

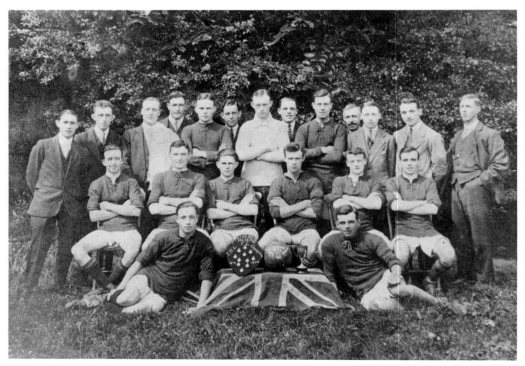

145. *The Wivenhoe Town Football Club Reserve Team in 1919-1920.*

Loaned by Mr. Mick Glozier

Into the Slump and out of It 1914–1965

for three or four seasons, while the Football Club used Spion Kop until it was built on. However, in the early twenties both clubs were accommodated on some rough ground off Rectory Road and in 1927, the Council, which owned this land, granted the exclusive use of it to the Cricket Club. The Club might have bought it for £150; later, the Council bought it for £250. By the close of 1930 the Club was agitating to buy "the back portion of land in Rectory Road", but the Council, though not unsympathetic, wanted to provide more houses for poor people and this was the only land it had. However, the Club built itself a pavilion in 1932, for £65 14s 2½d, and its president, William Loveless, who also ran a second football club for his employees, drummed away at the Council until, in 1936, the Club was allowed to buy the land at £25 an acre.[64] The former grounds of Wivenhoe Hall were now and then opened to the public by their owner, Charles Scofield, but he would not let the Council buy the land. However, Wivenhoe was expanding and had there not been banners at the 1935 Jubilee Celebrations with We Want Somewhere To Play on them, the Council would have soon applied for a compulsory purchase order. The land

146. *A Wivenhoe Town Football Club team in the early thirties.*

Loaned by Mr. Glendower Jackson

147. *Part of the Diamond Jubilee Celebrations in 1935.*

Loaned by Mrs. Ruth Munson

148. *The opening of the King George V Playing Fields in July, 1935. W. G. Loveless holds notes for a speech. Behind him stands his wife. At the back, with spectacles, is Charles Gooch. To his left is Mrs. Gooch. The rector is the Rev. G. W. Boothroyd.*

Loaned by Mrs. C. G. Scofield

was bought for £750, partly by public subscription, and on 28th July, 1935, The King George V Playing Fields were formally opened. Though the ground sloped, the Football Club now had a reasonable pitch.[65]

Tennis flourished between the Wars. In 1927, The Colne Social Bowls Club was formed, begotten by The Colne Social Club, but by this time a bowling green had been made for it, on land just inside the gates leading to the former cricket pitch at Tenacres. It opened in 1934 as The Wivenhoe Bowls Club. The Allotment Holders' Association was formed in 1931, a continuation of the allotment scheme started during the War: the allotments themselves were now at The Cross. In that same year The Wivenhoe Horticultural Society was revived; it held annual shows in the grounds of Wivenhoe Hall until 1939.

On Saturday, 15th May, 1926, ten sailing-boats raced between Fingringhoe Ferry and Alresford Creek. There were fourteen races that season and when he presented the prizes, Sir Frederick Rice, M.P., congratulated the new Wivenhoe Sailing Club on the progress it had made. During the first few years it had about thirty or forty members. The boats were kept at various berths along The Quay and social meetings held at *The Black Buoy*. Charles Scofield was the first chairman and others closely associated with the club included Arthur Vinson, Alfred Tapling, Lewis Worsp and Dr. Travers Kevern. Dr. Kevern was the town's medical officer from 1918 until his death in 1932. He was to have been buried at sea, his 14 ton yacht *Blonde* scuttled with his remains on board, but on the appointed day there was a gale and instead Dr. Kevern was buried at Wivenhoe.[66]

His successor, Dr. Walter Radcliffe, was also a yachtsman. He recalls that because the boats owned by the club members were of different sizes it was difficult to handicap races fairly and after one stormy meeting at *The Black Buoy*, the chairman, secretary and treasurer of the Sailing Club all resigned. So, with the assistance of Lewis Worsp, he produced a small sailing dinghy especially for Wivenhoe, the Wivenhoe One Design.

Dr. Radcliffe had two factors in mind: cheapness and convenience. So he designed a fifteen foot dinghy with a mainsail and two jibs, and a centreboard to keep it upright in the mud at low tide. The hulls were built by Parsons of Leigh-on-Sea. Hector Barr, a professional sailmaker with premises on The Quay, provided the sails and rigging. The boats cost £45 each. The first six of these half-decked sloops were built in the spring of 1935 and launched that summer.[67]

The laying-up supper that year was attended by Captain Albert Turner, the club's rear commodore. Up to the end of the 1932 season Captain Turner had secured 326 prizes for the King's yacht, including 216 firsts, sufficient prize money to cover the cost of building the *Britannia* in 1893. The King, in turn, gave Captain Turner a silver cream jug, sugar basin and tongs. It was

149. *Mrs. Hector Barr and Mr. James Bell in a Wivenhoe One Design Sailing Dinghy.*

Loaned by Mrs. Violet Page

Wivenhoe One-Design
Length 15 ft
Beam 5 ft 2 in

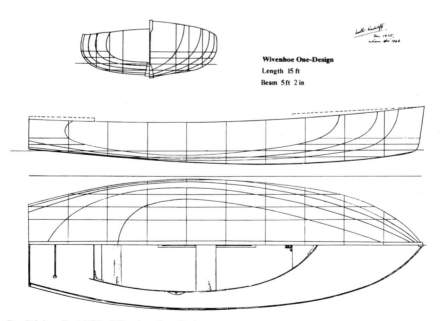

150. *Dr. Walter Radcliffe's Wivenhoe One Design.*

Loaned by Dr. Walter Radcliffe

151. *Captain Turner aboard the s.y. Britannia shortly before she was scuttled. On his right is the Chief Steward, Fred Mason, on his left his son, Albert, the Mate.*

Loaned by Mrs. Ivy Turner

thought that the *Britannia* would be converted to cruising before the next season; the King was evidently now too old to race. In fact, he died and Captain Turner attended the scuttling of his yacht.[68]

Thus ended Wivenhoe's contribution to the story of the big racing yachts, which had begun with the Marquis of Anglesey; thus, at roughly the same time, began a totally different sort of racing, not for national and international prestige, and not by men who were paid to do it, but a simple, domestic, middle-class pleasure enjoyed by men and women who were essentially landsmen. The Wivenhoe One Design was the most positive thing to happen in Wivenhoe between the Wars, and the most significant. Five members of the Wivenhoe Sailing Club put up the £30 needed to build a clubhouse on the hard. It was opened on Easter Monday, 1936, and stands to this day. The membership rose swiftly, from twenty-eight in 1934, to seventy-four in 1935, and 179 by the autumn of 1936. The club now possessed nine of Dr. Radcliffe's sailing-dinghies and when it visited Manningtree for a regatta the Stour Valley Club commissioned three more. Eighteen Wivenhoe One Designs were built before the Second World War.[69]

In 1936 the Sailing Club revived the regatta, but there had been none since 1920 and now it was different. It occurred not when the crews had returned from racing or cruising, for very few Wivenhovians did so now, but at the end of July. Instead of a band there was music broadcast over loudspeakers from a van, together with announcements, and stalls appeared on The Quay under the aegis of the Horticultural Society. Regattas were held from 1936 to 1939. Dr. Radcliffe, as commodore of the club, appealed to his members to make the last of these the best; it probably was.[70]

152. *A regatta scene in the 1930s.*

Loaned by Mr. Glendower Jackson

Stanley Holmes, M.P., Sir Frederick's Liberal successor, said he had found prosperity everywhere in his division except at Wivenhoe. However, he believed that the upstream shipyard would reopen at no distant date. Instead, it was bought by National Shipbuilders' Security Ltd., a firm which existed to close unprofitable shipyards so that the comparatively profitable ones should survive. And that was the end of shipbuilding until the War.[71]

Into the Slump and out of It 1914–1965

4 Charles Gooch the Younger.

The reign of the grandees was not yet over. In the early thirties Charles Edmund Gooch retired, for the sake of his health, to Petersfield, where he built himself a house. He died there in 1937 and was given a lavish funeral at Wivenhoe.[72]

It had been his wife's dying wish that their son, Charles, should not be sent to Eton because a relative had strained his heart while rowing there. The wish was honoured. Young Charles remained with his sister, Marguerite, at Wivenhoe Park and he bitterly regretted missing the rough and tumble of school life. However, he mixed with the Barlow boys and they went round on motorcycles together, and he was allowed to complete his scanted education at Jesus College, Cambridge, where he read history, obtained an M.A. and made up for lost time. He played the guitar and banjo, and sometimes the drums, so he became a member of The Footlights Club orchestra. When he went down he formed his own professional dance band, The Cambridge Nightwatchmen, which played at the Café de Paris in London, the South of France and as far afield as India. It was especially necessary for young Charles to go out into the world because he had been sheltered even from his own class, but there were ringing rows between father and son and Charles was disinherited, as was his sister when she eloped with a gentleman called Henry Cole.[73]

153. *Charles and Marguerite Gooch.*

Loaned by Mrs. Marguerite Cole

154. *Mr. and Mrs. Charles Gooch, with their children, Robin and Andrew, and their nanny, on the front doorstep of Wivenhoe Park.*

Loaned by Mr. and Mrs. P. L. J. Le Poer Power

Into the Slump and out of It 1914–1965

155. *The funeral cortège of Charles Edmund Gooch in Belle Vue Road. Charles Gooch the Younger walks behind the farm cart.*

Loaned by Mr. John Revell

Happily, there was a reconciliation, for at the end of 1932 Charles Gooch married Joan Spicer, an outdoor girl who raced motor boats, and in January, 1933, the newly-weds came to live at Wivenhoe Park which was made over to them. Anything that Charles did, he did thoroughly and he now dropped his band and took up farming wholeheartedly. The Park was run on a more modest scale than before the War, but the Gooches had a butler, housemaid, parlourmaid, cook, chauffeur, kitchenmaid, bootboy, nanny, nurserymaid and three gardeners. The huge house was icy in the winter, for there was no central heating. Nor, until 1935, was there electric light, and only one bath. Oil lamps and candles were used after dark; the first Mrs. Gooch recalls that it took a girl one whole morning just to clean the lamps.

The younger Gooch had few close friends and his manner was abrupt, even acerbic. Like many a squire, he used to say outrageous things just to shock people. However, he was a popular landlord and the men who worked for him liked him. He never put anyone out of a tied cottage and when the husbands died their wives were allowed to stay on. At that time the social life of the district revolved round the Garrison and the Gooches were part of it. There were parties and dances at Wivenhoe Park, and the Essex and Suffolk Hunt, to which Charles belonged, met there, though they never had hunt balls at the Park. His sons, Charles and Robin, were sent to Harrow and thereafter trained to farm, which they both do.

Because he owned Wivenhoe Park, Charles Gooch was invited to open functions in Wivenhoe and generally patronise the town. So we find him helping raise money for the church bells to be rehung, chairing a committee to receive ideas at the 1935 Jubilee and doing the things that squires are supposed to do.

5 1939-1945.

The First World War had been anticipated, in a general way, ever since the Boer War and, if you read between the lines of, say, the Wivenhoe column in the *Essex County Standard*, welcomed. Read the same column prior to the Second World War and a totally different attitude is revealed. This time, war was anticipated specifically. We knew where it was coming and how it was coming, but perhaps incantation might drive it away . . . ?

The first significant item refers to a National Peace Ballot held early in 1935; 96 per cent of the inhabitants favoured Great Britain remaining in the League of Nations. Under the pacific guidance of Dr. William Dean, who arrived to join Dr. Radcliffe in practice, there were meetings to debate such things as How Best To Avoid War, and subscriptions were forwarded to such causes as the Spanish Red Cross. Mrs. Munro from Boxted gave a lantern slide lecture on Munich and urged her audience to cultivate friendly feelings towards Germans and all foreigners.[74]

The Air Raid Precautions Act of 1937 was passed and soon Dr. Radcliffe was training his fellow citizens in its lore. In October, 1938, the rector, as A.R.P. warden, issued hundreds of gas masks to his parishioners at the Boys' School, which soon became the A.R.P. headquarters. Demonstrations on how to cope with incendiary bombs were given on Anchor Hill and at The Cross. By the end of the year arrangements were being made to teach auxiliary firemen, not only fire-fighting, but anti-gas techniques.[75]

Early in 1939 every household received a copy of the Government's scheme for National Service, the system of defence for the first stages of a war. At the Council meeting in February it was reported that 95 per cent of the populace was prepared to billet evacuees and help in every possible way. (What of the remaining 5 per cent?) Month by month, the town was becoming more and more war-minded, so that if historians had only the Wivenhoe column to guide them it would be impossible to tell that on 3rd September, 1939, war was actually declared.[76]

War, however, was not the only thought in people's minds. The Foresters' Hall was now rechristened The Lido, and thither the public came to see improving films presented by The North Essex Film Society, chaired by Dr. Dean. Dr. Dean's wife, Margery, wrote and directed two lighthearted revues which were performed there by a company called The Wivenhoe Wafflers.[77]

On 1st and 3rd September, 472 children arrived as evacuees, mostly from West Ham, though by mid-October 173 had returned home. The weddings that month were described as "quiet . . . owing to the international situation". Farmer Harold Dutton of Sunnymead Farm wrote to *The Times* to say there was still time to negotiate with Hitler and save the day. It so happened that Bernard Shaw visited the town at this time. Since John Martin-Harvey had recently appeared in his play, *The Devil's Disciple*, it is not unlikely that he broke his journey from Frinton, where he was staying when the war began, to look at the place for interest's sake.[78]

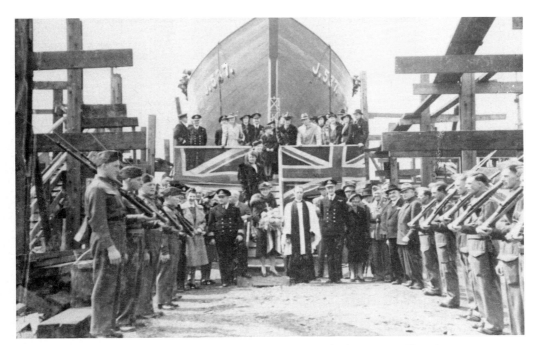

156. *The Home Guard attends the launching of a motor minesweeper in the upstream shipyard.*

Loaned by Mr. Brian Oakley

157. *Another launching in the upstream shipyard.*

Loaned by Mr. Brian Oakley

Before the year was out the news on the home front was distinctly cheerful: the upstream shipyard had been commandeered by the Admiralty. In January 1940, Wivenhoe Shipyard Ltd., an offshoot of Rowhedge Ironworks Ltd., started up. Many Wivenhovians, and some foreigners, were employed there. The motor minesweeper was the staple product; over two dozen of them were built using, not steel, but wood, to preserve them from magnetic mines. Each ship required about 250 oaks and elms, which were taken from Wivenhoe Wood and other local areas. The yard also built motor fishing vessels, motor torpedo boats, nine rafts called "skids", which were designed to explode magnetic mines, and four decoy submarines. Altogether, fifty-four craft were built. There was also maintenance and repair work, nothing very large, though on one occasion a patrol ship came to the dry dock. Her skipper, a lieutenant-commander, stayed with his wife at *The Park Hotel*. During the raids he bicycled down the High Street to man the guns aboard his ship and fire them. Starting with a workforce of fifty, the shipyard was employing about 350 men in 1944.[79] A firm called Vosper Ltd. came to the downstream shipyard in 1941. It had been bombed out of Portsmouth and wanted a site that was not too visible from

158. *Sir Winston and Lady Churchill in Wivenhoe Park.*

Loaned by Mr. and Mrs. P. L. J. Le Poer Power

the air. It began to build the first of fifteen motor torpedo boats on 16th July, and in October, 1943, started repair work. Thirty-five boats were repaired at Vosper's; 225 men worked there. The firm stayed until 1946.[80]

As in 1914, the *Rosabelle* steamed off to become an armed patrol vessel. She was sunk in the Mediterranean on 11th September, 1941; nine of her crew were saved. It was the end of a chapter in Wivenhoe's maritime history.[81]

As in 1914, Wivenhoe Park became an army camp, and the Gooches moved to Allen's Farm on the estate, where they employed a large number of landgirls. The first arrival was a regiment of Churchill tanks, which came to Wivenhoe by rail, thundered up to the Park, churned it into mud, frightened away the deer, which never returned, were inspected by their namesake, and after a fairly long stay left as they had come.[82]

Regiments came and went until finally the three hundred men of the Second Special Air Service moved in and were there when the War ended. Then, as now, the S.A.S. was refreshingly unlike any other regiment in the British Army, indeed was a private army on its own. The men trained, fairly rigorously, and went on missions, but when, where or how is still private

159. *No. 2 Squadron 2nd Special Air Service Regiment, October, 1945.*

Loaned by Mr. and Mrs. P. L. J. Le Poer Power

knowledge. This battalion, (and the First S.A.S., which was stationed at Chelmsford), fought according to their own rules and off duty entertained in a manner that possessed not a shred of wartime austerity. The two balls it threw at Wivenhoe Park were probably the most lavish occasions ever seen there.[83]

Unlike 1914, soldiers were not billeted in Wivenhoe and the evacuees gradually dwindled throughout 1940. The Council sent out 700 forms on the subject early in that year, but only forty-one were returned and not all of those were favourably disposed to more billeting.[84]

The early months of the War were a time of preparation for invasion from the air and by sea. Gas masks were issued to everyone, trenches dug and shelters built. The Council received a letter signed by sixty-one parents who wanted a shelter built at the school. The Chairman said the Council had no power to dig trenches or erect shelters on "educational" land, but it was agreed to bring the matter to the attention of the county education authorities. Considering what was at risk, the Council should have built a shelter itself forthwith. However, an air-raid shelter was built at about this time and frequently used. Between 21st and 23rd January, 1941, the pupils spent a total of seven-and-a-half hours there. The Surveyor reported that 134 householders had been contacted about air-raid shelters; most of them did not possess one or "they took no interest

Into the Slump and out of It 1914–1965

160. *Ambulance No. 1 Brigade.*

Colchester Castle Museum

161. *Wivenhoe's detachment of the Auxiliary Fire Service. Mr. Percy Chaney is the man in plain clothes.*

Loaned by Mr. Mick Glozier

162. *The Wivenhoe Home Guard, photographed by Douglas Went.*

Loaned by Captain R. J. Husk, R.N.

in the matter". Yet this was 1940 and the Luftwaffe as yet unvanquished. One Wivenhovian recalls seeing about 250 German aeroplanes flying up the Colne, evidently using the river to guide them towards London, with British fighter planes in attendance.[85]

The North Essex Film Society, hit by petrol rationing, a reduced bus service and the blackout, was wound up, but The Lido blossomed forth as a social centre. People wanted entertainment badly in those days. The town had its Home Guard, of course, but because many of its inhabitants were in reserved occupations, such as working in the shipyards, they were by no means all middle-aged men. They fired rifles in the sandpits at Alresford Creek; their weapons were kept on the first floor of the water tower. The fire brigade, or Auxiliary Fire Service, as it was called, now came into its own. The sail loft opposite *The Brewery Tavern* in Brook Street was commandeered as a fire station and manned twenty-four hours a day. No longer had it to make do with a barrow, but was equipped with two cars and an auxiliary towing vehicle with a trailer pump at the back. Later, in 1967, a proper fire engine arrived and has been there ever since.[86]

Various women's groups came together under the chairmanship of Mrs. Gooch to form a Wivenhoe War Working Party which produced a vast number of knitted woollen garments for the troops, especially socks. War Weapons Week, in 1941, aimed at a target of £7,500 and secured over £11,000.

Into the Slump and out of It 1914–1965

163. *A knitting party at The Nottage Institute.*

Loaned by Mrs. C. G. Scofield

A co-operative fruit centre was set up in Alma Street, to turn surplus fruit into home-made jam and sell it to the Government wholesale, which then retailed it back to the public via the local shops.[87]

When Hitler attacked Russia and Japan provoked America into action, it must have been clear to everybody that the War was won. It was certainly clear to The Malvern Group, which was formed no later than June, 1942, to plan a brave new world. The two doctors were members, so were Harold Dutton, Mrs. Loveless, Betsy Grasby and a former rector of St. Mary's, the Rev. R. H. Jack. On one occasion Mr. Jack told a meeting that after the war there would be no fees at primary, secondary or public schools.[88]

Dr. Dean was also involved with the Common Wealth Party, which was formed at Joscelyn's Café, Colchester, in July, 1943. "There must", said a speaker, "be a fellowship with common ownership of all the means of production".[89] This was radical politics, of course, but it was also idealistic and practical, a determination that the terrible slump of the inter-War years should

259

164. *Dr. and Mrs. William Dean.*

Loaned by Dr. William Dean

not be repeated. So Margery Dean, Harold Dutton and their friends embraced the Beveridge Report and sought eagerly to promote a state medical service, educational reform, better housing for the workers and the elimination of poverty and unemployment. And, surely, when the War ended, much of their Utopia was indeed realised?

Acting on a request by the authorities that people should spend their holidays at home, the two doctors, their wives and a number of leading Wivenhovians promoted a Wivenhoe Holiday Week, in August, 1942, which included a treasure hunt, open air whist drive, ladies' ankle competition, military dance at The Lido, challenging of mystery personalities and other amusements. At about the same time the Women's Institute showed edifying films from the Ministry of Information, such as *Physical Education* and *The Value of Vitamins for Young Children.*[90] Vitamins the schoolchildren of Wivenhoe did not lack. Every day each child was given a large spoonful of Virol, and in December, 1942, school meals were instituted. The authorities extended the search for lice into a general medical welfare that included an examination of eyes and teeth, and sundry weighings and measurings.[91]

In August, 1942, the Wivenhoe Savings Committee was inaugurated at the Council Offices and about a month later Wivenhoe had saved enough money to buy a tank. The following year the national Wings for Victory Week raised enough to pay for four Spitfires, or over £15,000. This last-named cause was attended with local events that included a Grand Scrounge, which involved collecting miscellaneous objects including a mouse, (dead or alive), a baby's feeding bottle, a pair of steel knitting needles, a note of Dr. Radcliffe's car number and a policeman's helmet.[92] It sounds as if everyone was thoroughly enjoying the Second World War. One small boy who certainly did was Glendower Jackson, whose father kept *The Grosvenor Hotel*. The town he remembers, that of the late thirties and war years, was, he told me, "the finest place on earth for a boy to grow up in". It had the river, the saltings, the woods, the sandpits and, because of the emergency, a special feeling of excitement. There was no doubt as to the outcome. "My Dad said we would win the War and that was good enough for me".[93]

The American Mustangs and Thunderbolts carried extra fuel tanks, long, cigar-shaped affairs made of strong aluminium. Glen Jackson and his friends used to buy them for 2/6d at The Hythe and bolt them in pairs, to produce safe and stable double canoes. The bolts were cadged or stolen from the shipyards, Mr. Lewis Worsp donated old fish boxes for paddles and some boys made sails and rudders. These boys, none much older than eleven, raced their improvised craft, or a party of twenty or so would paddle down river on the tide for a day at Alresford Creek, collecting winkles and cockles which their parents boiled. They swam, of course, a skill which Glen Jackson learnt in the sandpits, jumping off the railway bridge into the creek. They made mud slides down the banks of the little creeks. One boy would sit, curled up, at the top of a bank, holding a rope's end. Down he would slide, his body scooping away the mud, while a colleague on the opposite bank, who held the other end of the rope, would guide him so that he went from side to side in his descent. The result was a cresta run which, sloshed with water to keep it slippery, could be used by everyone. Sometimes they clambered on to the overhead machinery of The Alresford Sand and Ballast Co. Ltd., which carried sand down to the creek, and took a ride on it, just as their grandparents had done at The Ropery. Dangerous sports, but there were no grown-ups around to spoil the fun and nobody ever got hurt.

There was sport to be had in Wivenhoe itself. Glen Jackson used to tie string to doorknockers and make them rap from a safe distance or, as a variant, tie two knockers together. Clifton Terrace was a good venue for this activity, as it was for knocking the local policeman's helmet off his head. A piece of black cotton was tied to a drainpipe; the other end was held by a boy on the far side of the terrace, concealed behind the eight foot wall that bounded the King George V Playing Fields. The victim, P.C. "Tolly" Day, approached on his bicycle and as he did so the cotton was drawn taut so that it was on a level with the top of his helmet and would catch it. By the time that "Tolly" Day had recovered his helmet and raced round to the entrance of the playing fields the boys were far away. Mr. Jackson reckons he played this trick successfully at least two dozen times; it never failed and he was never caught. More formal games included cricket, with twenty or so to a side, and a sort of military exercise in which one side guarded a metal drum in the wood and the other had to capture it. On these occasions the boys divided into Upstreeters and Downstreeters, for the rivalry between these factions was fierce and indeed helped to create these games. Glen Jackson, living in Belle Vue Road, felt he could choose his allegiance and opted to become a posh Upstreeter.

Pocket money could be earned by helping the war effort. Blackberries, for dyeing service uniforms, fetched 1d a pound, acorns for the pigs 4d or 5d a sandbagfull. In the autumn the boys put sticks on the handlebars of their bicycles and went to the fields where horse-drawn binders were at work. Rabbits would dart out and might be caught with little effort, a useful addition to the meat ration. "You could imagine the joy and pleasure of marching into the house with a rabbit on a stick. Fantastic!"

There was school, of course, in Phillip Road, where the Misses Smith and Grasby presided. One was headmistress, the other her assistant; to Glen Jackson they were co-equal, a pair of tigers. There was also Mr. Plummer, a neat dresser and strict disciplinarian, Mrs. Etta Dan, whom everyone liked, "You could play her up", and Mrs. Ruth Munson, "She was a nice lady". Here, he learnt the three R's, folk dancing, craftwork and a game played with walking-sticks called shinty. The War was frequently visible.

Look up and you might see an enemy aeroplane, or later a V2, doodlebugs as they were called, a double cigar shape with a flaming tail, travelling no more than five hundred feet above the ground. Glen Jackson saw Hurricanes and Spitfires fly alongside doodlebugs and gently nudge them round so that they returned whence they had come or, in the more open country near the mouth of the Colne, turn them over so that they fell and exploded harmlessly.

Look down and you might see an anti-personnel bomb, "butterfly bombs", as they were called, brightly coloured little devices dropped by the enemy to attract children and injure them. The police earnestly warned the children about them; Glen Jackson and his friends threw stones at them so that they exploded harmlessly.

Sometimes Glen Jackson went to Peck's Garage and filled up the Churchill tanks which lumbered down from the Park; sometimes he went up to the Park itself. His favourite regiment was the S.A.S., the "Sausage and Spam" boys, as they were christened by his friends. They allowed the boys to ride in their jeeps and watch them train. Sometimes there were many of them about, sometimes only a handful.

And once he saw an enemy. A German pilot had baled out at Alresford

Creek and was waiting on Wivenhoe Station to be taken away, so Glen Jackson went to have a look at him. "And, do you know, I was disappointed. I expected him to have two heads or pointed ears or a tail. I expected him to look bad, but he looked just like everyone else".

Not everybody was contented. A letter to the press from "Justice" wanted to know why, since the majority of Wivenhovians had surrendered their iron gates and railings to the war effort, certain people living on The Quay and elsewhere had been exempted. Farmer Bowes of Ballast Quay Farm was displeased. His son, whom he needed to help him, had been called up and the next day The War Agricultural Committee sent him a youth, who for some unknown reason had been granted deferment, to cut grass with a sickle. Did the W.A.C. call this playing the game?[94]

All this while, the upstream and downstream shipyards were making a direct contribution to the war effort. And then a firm called Dorman Long covered an area of the upstream saltings with concrete, and employed over forty welders and several cranes to make two, strangely-shaped pontoons, eighty feet by sixty. They bore the codename Whale and nobody knew what they were or what they were for, not even when they were towed downstream. On 6th June, 1944, one of them may have appeared at Arromanches on the French coast; the other is part of a pier at Southampton used by the Isle of Wight ferry to this day. Wivenhoe's contribution to Mulberry Harbour was a pair of tank landing buffers.[95]

With the Normandy landings, the War moved into its final phase and Wivenhoe prepared to face the pleasures or horrors of peace, and to welcome back its 310 serving sons and daughters. In the autumn of 1944 the Home Guard bowed out. The Council planned to build twenty-four houses in the year after hostilities and twenty-four the year after that.[96]

Early in 1945 it was announced that there would be at least limited sailing on the Colne and Blackwater that summer, and when the summer came sailing indeed there was, with a regatta that had a post-War euphoria all its own. The programme included two races for the makeshift canoes mentioned above, manned singly and in pairs, and among the contestants were men of the S.A.S.[97]

"The long nights, black as hell . . . ", is how the Prime Minister recalled the War which had just ended. Yet it had not been hell for Wivenhoe.

The War made life simple and straightforward. There was an objective which everybody believed was absolutely right. Everybody had his post, and thanks to rationing everybody was fitter for his post than in any succeeding generation. Unlike its predecessor, this war had a shape to it. After the Battle of Britain and the Invasion of Russia we knew we would win; after El Alamein we knew we were winning; after Normandy only an endgame remained. It was a

165. *A Victory Tea-Party in Park Road.*

Loaned by Mrs. Dorothy Chaney

far safer war than its predecessor; between 10 and $12\frac{1}{2}$ per cent of the Wivenhovians in uniform died during the First World War, only $2\frac{1}{2}$ in the Second – eight more names for the War Memorial. Thrown back on its resources the town made its own pleasures, evidently very real ones, and some of its inhabitants creditably planned a better and brighter future for their offspring. For those at home the Second World War was surely the happiest period in the whole history of Wivenhoe.

6 Brave New World.

Was there to be unemployment all over again? On the whole, not. Vosper's left in February, 1946, but after fourteen idle months the downstream shipyard was acquired by James W. Cook & Co. Ltd., a long-established firm of tug and barge owners from the Thames. Meanwhile, the Admiralty had more work for the upstream shipyard. The Lido became Gainsboro Products Ltd., a clothing factory.

As 1945 brought the Labour Party to power nationally, so it produced five Labour councillors for the urban district council, including Margery Dean, who topped the poll with 584 votes. Yet within two years there were no Socialists on the Council, not because the mood of the electorate had changed

Into the Slump and out of It 1914–1965

166. *Prefabricated houses in Rectory Close on the site of the present Stuart Pawsey House.*

Essex County Newspapers

but because the Socialists were no longer interested in standing.[98] Councillor Margery Dean went into business. She converted the former Swedenborgian Chapel, which was now falling into disrepair, into an antique shop which opened in April, 1950. It is now run by her children.

The Council built houses, starting with six prefabs called Rectory Close, off Rectory Road. Meanly utilitarian dwellings, they nevertheless survived for forty years. Rosabelle Avenue and Britannia Crescent were created at the same time. The upstream shipyard built some more minesweepers, including the 152 foot *Calton*, but in July, 1947, following the launching of a Trinity House pilot vessel, *Valonia*, it was announced that the shipyard would build no more. However, it continued to do repair work until 1960.[99]

In the dry dock was the hulk of the 295 ton, three-masted, barquentine *Cap Pilar*. Built at St. Malo for the Newfoundland cod trade at the turn of the century, she acquired fame when a crew of young, and fairly untrained, sailors took her round the world from October, 1936 to September, 1938. In the summer of 1939 she appeared at Brightlingsea and would have been used to train Jewish cadets had the War not broken out. Then she was taken up to Wivenhoe. After the War there was talk of putting her into repair. Vainly, for by now she was totally unseaworthy.[100]

The upstream shipyard was moribund, the downstream one was not. Cook's, now well-established, produced a stream of tugs, tankers and, assuming the mantle of Forrestt's, esoteric craft for special purposes, often for other climes and countries. In 1950-51, it produced nine pontoons for the Festival of Britain.

167. *The Cap Pilar.*

Loaned by Mrs. Pamela Dan

They were towed round to the Thames. Four of them went to the Battersea Pleasure Gardens and the rest to the South Bank.[101] In 1952, Mr. Guy Harding founded The Colne Marine and Yacht Company, whose offices, a wooden hut on stilts, occupies the site of *The Sailor's Return.* His premises comprise the yard immediately downstream, where the Customs House lookout tower stood until it was demolished in 1946, and the shed immediately upstream which at various times has stored coal, corn and the gear of the *Rosabelle.*[102] Having cut his milk teeth on a dinghy Mr. Harding assembled a team of locals and was soon producing four or five yachts a year. The first was the largest. The 51 foot *Tugrador* was begun in January, 1955, and launched in June the following year and she was followed by about twenty-six other yachts. Unhappily, in 1970-71 fibreglass arrived and Mr. Harding's stream of commissions dried up; from that day to this he has had to be content with repair work, laying-up and hoping the public will become as disenchanted with fibreglass as he is.[103]

168. *Cook's Shipyard.*

Loaned by Mrs. Gail Cross

In the fifties the town lost the Wivenhoe to Fingringhoe ferry. At one time the locals used to bid for the lease and the ferry house that went with the job, but as the number of car owners rose steeply, so the number of passengers dropped and when Arthur Bell retired in 1950 there was only one applicant. Mr. D. Carroll struggled valiantly, but in 1952 his average number of fares was three a day and the Colchester Town Council, which owned the ferry, decided to close it in September of that year.[104] There was an outcry. Local councils discussed the matter and 286 Fingringhovians signed a petition demanding that the ferry be reopened. In the event, Colne Marine came to the rescue and made an arrangement with Colchester whereby it undertook to run the ferry on an hourly basis. The ferry opened in March, 1953, but closed, for lack of passengers, in November.[105] Fingringhoe joined forces with Wivenhoe when in March, 1955, the Lord Chief Justice, no less, considered an action brought by Mr. Derrick Allen, a Fingringhoe shipbuilder, against the Colchester

The Story of Wivenhoe

169. and 170.   *The Herald, one of Guy Harding's yachts. Above: In frame, Below: The launching.*

Both loaned by Mr. Guy Harding

171. *The Herald.*

Loaned by Mr. Guy Harding

Corporation, for failing to maintain the ferry. Lord Goddard, who had visited Fingringhoe, was sympathetic, but thought that Colchester could not be compelled to run a ferry at a loss. So that was the end of the ferry and although it made life a little difficult for a handful of people who came over to work in Wivenhoe, it is hardly missed. For some reason, Wivenhoe's connections with Fingringhoe, and indeed with Rowhedge, have become of little or no importance. People neither need, nor desire, to travel from one side of the river to the other and the ancient rivalries have been totally forgotten.[106]

Of a piece with the loss of the ferry, was the loss of the branch railway line to Brightlingsea. This, too, was threatened by the motor-car from the end of the Second World War, and in 1953 the authorities were given an opportunity to close it down. For in the first hour of Sunday, 1st February, 1953, the East Coast was inundated by a mighty tide which made 21,000 people homeless. The view from The Quay, disclosed by the moon in the small hours of that day, was of a lake stretching to the foot of Fingringhoe Hill, which completely concealed the marshland. Only one family was homeless in Wivenhoe, the occupants of the Toll House on the Rowhedge Ferry Road. Forewarned of the tide, the shipyards had raised dynamos and electrical equipment well off the ground, but the generating plant of the North Sea Canning Corporation was submerged. The railway line between Wivenhoe and The Hythe was flooded and put out of action, but trains were running again by Monday evening.[107]

172. *The toll house and the Rowhedge Ferry shed on the upstream saltings at the time of the 1953 floods.*

Loaned by Miss Dorothy Skilton

Into the Slump and out of It 1914–1965

173. *Mr. Ernest Hatch, (left), and Mr. Jack Burnham, (right), at Wivenhoe Station.*

Loaned by Mr. Ernest Hatch

However, the damage along the Wivenhoe to Brightlingsea line was more serious; two miles of track were washed away. In April it was announced that the line would not reopen.[108] Again, the public was too strong for the authorities. The impetus came from Brightlingsea, led by Mr. Charles Johnson, and on 9th June there was a public inquiry at Liverpool Street Station. The matter was hotly pursued by the locals and after The Central Transport Users' Consultative Committee had considered it and agreed to give the line a three year trial, there were extensive repairs and it reopened on 7th December, amid general rejoicing. Yet the plain fact was that the line was no longer economic and sooner or later close it must. It fell a victim to Dr. Beeching's axe on 14th June, 1964.[109]

Meanwhile, the main line had been electrified and London was now, in theory, barely an hour away. Many more people were commuters now, to London, Chelmsford and, indeed, Colchester. The town was expanding rapidly, the land between The Avenue and Rectory Road filling with houses and the population soaring.

174. *The Wivenhoe Ferry. The ferryman is Mr. Arthur Bell, his passengers, left to right, Barry Eves, Mrs. Coralie Clarke and John Harris.*

Essex County Newspapers

At the beginning of the sixties, Wivenhoe stood at the crossroads. Was it to become a suburb of Colchester? No. For in 1961 Wivenhoe Park was sold to the new University of Essex, which drove an effective green wedge between the two communities. Was it to become an annexe of the University? No. For the University never achieved the figure of 12,000 students it envisaged.

Thus a major threat was averted, but it was followed by another which has not been resolved to this day, for at the end of 1965 a firm from Stratford, London, J. Gliksten & Son Ltd., applied to use the upstream shipyard for warehousing and open storage of timber.[110] Social history was very much on the move.

CHAPTER 9

The University of Essex

1 The Making of a Troublespot.

How shall we recall the Sixties? Perhaps by the title it gave itself, the Swinging Sixties. Just as the Twenties are prescriptively carefree, though in defiance of facts such as unemployment, so the public may accept that the Sixties were swinging, but again in defiance of the facts. Surely this was not a generally happy time?

What happened in the Sixties? There was a man on the moon. There was coloured television. There were The Beatles, transcendental meditation, flower power, flared trousers, long hair, hippies, yippies, permissiveness, drugs, drop-outs, the murder of President Kennedy, the Vietnam War, protests, demonstrations . . . and, of course . . . . . . the University of Essex!

For, among other things, this was an age of Thinking Man. The individual who between 1961 and 1970 had a textbook in his hands was, by that token, respectable. The number of universities in Great Britain rose from twenty-two to forty-six, the number of students from just over 100,000 to 220,000.[1]

The Student. Who has not heard of his worthy penury and study-bedroom, his grant, concessions and privileges, his National Union and politics, his strikes and sit-ins, his hatred of forms, ceremonies, conformity and the established order, his uniform blue denims and uncut hair? He is still with us, of course, but now we take him for granted. In the Sixties he was a Colossus with the ball at his feet and, because new and unknown, feared.

Sussex acquired a university in 1958 and soon other counties were clamouring for them. The Government decided to support six more; to ensure that Essex was one of these the Essex County Council set up a University Promotion Committee chaired by the Lord Lieutenant of the County. The Government's University Grants Committee favoured universities of 3,000 undergraduates and upwards, on sites no smaller than 200 acres, preferably away from towns. This was reasonable, for the Robbins Report of 1963

175. *Wivenhoe Park.*

The University of Essex

predicted that by 1980 there would be 500,000 boys and girls in higher education, 60 per cent of them at universities.² The local committee was initially torn between Chelmsford and Colchester. Four sites were proposed: Hylands Park outside Chelmsford, and Gosbecks Farm, Mile End Fruit Farm and Wivenhoe Park, all near Colchester. The U.G.C. favoured Colchester because it was farther from London, so there would be less temptation to desert the campus at weekends.³ This was also reasonable; a university should be a genuine community. In May, 1961, Colchester was chosen and the town, according to the *Essex County Standard*, was euphoric. The *Standard* certainly was:

> *Shopkeepers will be affected in a big way... For example, take hairdressing. Another thousand or so girls wanting a hairdo regularly will keep several new salons occupied. As for books, the town's trade will be revolutionised. The sales of cigarettes and confectionery will boom; the number of coffee-bars, already growing rapidly, will grow even faster; the record shops will find sales charts shooting up. The University will probably save the Repertory Theatre if the company can hang on long enough. The cinemas, which have not been doing roaring business, to say the least, in recent months, will have a shot in the arm. The new swimming-pool planned for the town will be a necessity...* ⁴

By December the site had been chosen: Wivenhoe Park.

What were the owner's feelings? Typically, Charles Gooch made the decision to part with his home without consulting his family. Some people said he sold the Park knowing that if he did not it would be acquired compulsorily, others, that he saw a good bargain and it was he who approached the local committee. Publicly, he welcomed the University, facilitated its arrival and even made gifts to it, such as the marble fireplaces in the house. On the one occasion I met him, a few years after it had opened, he was at pains, at too great pains I thought, to assure me that he thoroughly approved of it.

I should imagine his real feelings were mixed. Sixty years earlier, Hector Gurdon-Rebow had retired from the Park bankrupt, nor could his successor make it pay. Though the younger Gooch worked hard he must have found the cost of running a mansion prohibitive and staff hard to come by after the War. Besides, the Big House was now a social anachronism. There was a third consideration. Colchester was expanding. In 1945, there was talk of the borough acquiring the Park as a leisure centre for the town. Charles Gooch intimated he was not prepared to sell and the idea was dropped.⁵ Yet if the town continued to expand, surely this moral imperative would have loomed ever larger? How could one family enjoy all those acres when thousands needed room in which to live and play? What if light industry continued to move down the Colne Valley? What would the view be like with factories all along the railway line?

On the other hand, this was not only Charles Gooch's family home, but the visible centre of his public persona, that of a landed country gentleman. To surrender it, and to a totally different regime, one which knew and cared nothing about landed country gentlemen, must have seemed like a defeat or an abdication.

Although he was born and bred there, Charles Gooch's feelings about Wivenhoe Park were unsentimental, but I believe that at heart he was deeply committed to the idea of the Big House. For when he did sell the Park, Raymond Erith designed him a mansion, in a style described as neo-Palladian, comprising a central square block with elegant flanking wings. Wivenhoe New Park, as it is significantly named, is a country seat. Charles Gooch might have retired to one of the farms on his estate. Instead, he chose to reaffirm his class, education and background.

It was the second time he had turned a defeat into victory. He was not an easy man to live with and after the War his first wife left him for a Special Air Service officer, Peter le Poer Power, whom she met when he was stationed at the Park. A few years later Charles Gooch married her sister, Patricia. He invited the le Poer Powers to the Park and generally behaved very pleasantly to them. They now, incidentally, live at Wivenhoe.

176. *Wivenhoe New Park.*

Essex County Newspapers

Yet this second victory was not complete. For there is one thing fundamentally wrong with Wivenhoe New Park; it is invisible. The Big House, the place which proclaims its owner's status, must be seen to do so, else the gesture is futile. Wivenhoe New Park, hidden by a curtain of evergreens on the north side of the Clacton to Colchester Road, is as unknown to the University as it is to Wivenhoe. When Charles Gooch moved there he might just as well have left the district. He died there, in 1983; three years later the house was sold.

Wivenhoe Park was sold on the first day of 1962, for £75,000.[6] Before he left, his eldest son, Charles, married Annabel Greene, a niece of the novelist, Graham Greene, and there was a society wedding reception, held in the sure knowledge that the social ambience of the place would soon be entirely changed. Mr. and Mrs. Charles Gooch now live at Tye Farm, near Elmstead Market, the present headquarters of their estate. Mrs. Gooch has told me she would have liked the opportunity to live at Wivenhoe Park but, with respect, I think she is lucky not to do so. A century ago, that barn of a house was already proving unruly; today, the rates, repairs, heating, lighting, staffing and safety precautions would quickly beggar anyone but a multi-millionaire.

Having secured an existence and a site, the University appointed a vice-chancellor, for which purpose an Academic Planning Board was set up, chaired by the Provost of King's College, Cambridge, Lord Annan. Various large firms had already donated money to the University, so these, too, were consulted. In July, 1962, it was announced that the vice-chancellor was a professor of modern languages from Liverpool University, Dr. Albert Sloman.

The appointment was imaginative. Dr. Sloman had taught at Berkeley College, California, where he met his French wife, Marie-Bernadette, run Spanish studies at Trinity College, Dublin, then moved on to Liverpool where he became Dean of the Arts Faculty. However, this was far from all. While an undergraduate at Wadham College, Oxford, just before the War, he had learned to fly. In 1940 he became a night pilot and saw action continuously from 1941 to 1945 with 209 Beaufighter Squadron, in North Africa, Malta, Salerno and Anzio. Against the odds, very heavily against the odds, he had outlived the War. He was still only forty-one, but with a wealth of experience. Who better to instruct and inspire the Attlee babies than a man who had courageously and repeatedly risked his life for their better future?

Dr. Sloman's task was to create a university and administer it. It was two years before the first students appeared, two years in which the new ruler of Wivenhoe Park had his kingdom to himself and, in a honeymoon of public optimism and approval, time and freedom to plan his pupils' education.

His masters had given him guidelines. The University was to be large, with three, six, perhaps twelve thousand undergraduates and graduates; even twenty thousand was mentioned in those early, heady days. It would concentrate on a few large departments. Computer studies, electrical science and engineering would be taught, also solid state physics and inorganic chemistry, because this sort of knowledge, it was thought, would be needed by the mushrooming communications industry, which in turn might invest in the University. The Board also favoured economics, social administration and sociology, "because the social sciences have been the Cinderella in all our universities and because we need to understand how our own and other societies work today more than ever before..." At a fund-raising luncheon held at the Grocers Hall, London, the vice-chancellor echoed these views and added a third branch of knowledge, comparative studies, which would include languages, literature, politics and history, but with the emphasis on foreign literature and politics, and recent rather than ancient history. "All our subjects are of immediate interest and concern today", said Dr. Sloman. "Essex stands for modern studies..."[7]

177. *Lord Butler of Saffron Walden.*

The University of Essex

With him was the new chancellor, Lord Butler of Saffron Walden. This was a clever appointment. On the one hand, Lord Butler was an ageless pillar of the Establishment and generally revered as such. On the other, his Education Act of 1944 was the gateway of the new, post-War, subsidised learning, albeit one that had he not opened would have been flung a good deal wider by his Labour successors in office. A third recommendation was that his home, at Saffron Walden, was within easy driving distance of the University. In 1965 he was appointed Master of Trinity College, Cambridge, which in turn reflected glory on Essex. Lord Butler rose to the occasion and made a speech in which the old and the new, John Henry Newman and the Robbins Report were united.[8]

To the 204 acres in which Mr. Gooch's cows were still grazing peacefully, thousands, several thousands, of men and women were coming to study and live together. Boys and girls, singly and in pairs and groups, casually, anonymously dressed, would stroll, book-laden, across this landscape; move purposefully with heads bent against the wind; trudge briskly through rain and snow; trot out to the football field and the tennis court; reel about in their cups; and finally pose, in gowns and mortarboards worn only once, for their parents' photographs. The air would be filled with lively bickerings; politics, national and domestic, would be endlessly discussed. Invisible, but almost palpable, would be that idiotic heresy which obtains at all universities: that the intellect is the only faculty, that men exist from the neck upwards. And the place would have a mystique – because it was a university.

All this the new vice-chancellor might have expected; but not that the boys and girls for whom he had fought the Luftwaffe would clamour for his removal, and that to several generations of them he would be a figure of totemistic scorn; not that the Cinderella of sociology would be off to the ball with a vengeance; not that the University would soon be a national symbol and byword for dissent and unrest, indeed a national joke.

The University of Essex . . . . . . !

For such is its reputation, in the wake of sixties and early seventies. As we shall see, there are many good reasons why there should have been unrest, but which of them actually did provoke that unrest, and to what extent, is hard to say; besides, we must never forget that student rebellion was at that time a worldwide phenomenon. Why, we should rather ask, was the University of Essex, in these generally troubled years, so particularly troubled?

When things go wrong in an organisation the first place to look is at the top. What sort of man, therefore, was Albert Sloman, who from 1962 to 1987 was the University of Essex's chief administrator and apologist? He was pleasant-spoken and affable, and from all accounts and evidence technically competent, with no difficulties about deskwork, committees, making appointments and generally running his organisation. He was a good fund-raiser and, particularly as chairman of the Committee of Vice-Chancellors and Principals, a champion and spokesman for higher education. Yet many of his pupils neither liked nor trusted him. The phantom chancellor, they called him. He was not noticeable, either physically or socially, but I think that the soubriquet, unconsciously wise, cut a good deal deeper. As we know, for four years he was under a terrible strain, of a kind that can cause the form of nervous breakdown known as battle fatigue. Throughout the War he knew that his chances of survival were slim as, one by one, his companions died quick, horrible deaths, spiralling down out of the sky for the sake of freedom. The man who survives such an ordeal frequently sacrifices part of his emotional capital and I think this is what happened here. Had it not been for this experience we may guess that he would never have survived the years of student unrest; equally, had it not been for this experience he would never have provoked that unrest, would have been more outgoing and caring. There is something missing in the centre of his personality; his pupils disliked him because they could not understand him.

178. *The newly-appointed vice-chancellor, (left), Dr. Albert Sloman, and architect, (right), Mr. Kenneth Capon.*

Photograph by Des Blake

Months before the first students appeared, two hostages were offered to fortune: the designs for the new university and the B.B.C.'s Reith Lectures for 1963, the latter written and broadcast by Dr. Sloman and later published as *The Making of a University*.⁹

The architect, Kenneth Capon, was appointed in September, 1962. He and Dr. Sloman, who had travelled widely to look at contemporary academic architecture, worked closely together on the designs. Together, they produced a scheme for fitting 20,000 students into 204 acres.

From the lakes a small stream runs down the cleft in the valley on the west of the site. This was chosen as the central axis. High on stilts above this cleft were placed five linked quadrangles and around them the teaching and administrative buildings, also the bars, restaurants and shops, so arranged that access from one department to another would be easy. Dotted round this central block was the student accommodation: twenty-eight apartment blocks, or tower blocks as they were soon called, each fourteen storeys high. The

179. *A model of Kenneth Capon's designs for the University.*

Essex County Newspapers

University is fairly compact and one merit of this scheme is that it frees the higher, level ground for sport.

A scale model was unveiled to the public in the autumn of 1963, for the vice-chancellor and his architect planned their conception slowly and carefully. "The University will be strikingly beautiful", said an early brochure, "a harmonious composition of towers and terraces, floating in the lap of its wooded valley".[10] I have yet to meet anybody who agrees with this encomium; most people think it is strikingly ugly. However, let us remember that what we see, two-thirds of the central complex and six towers, is something essentially incomplete. At the very least the architect has produced a house style. There is nothing quite like it, even at other universities.

The architecture is without facades or decoration; it is essential stuff and it wants you to know it. Approach it from the lower road and you enter a gloomy, dirty, subterranean chasm in which the University's viscera, the pipes that carry water, gas and electricity, are all visible; ascend to one of the quadrangles and the views of the Park and countryside are pleasant enough. People today live in small compartments and the University is composed of them. No lecture room is bigger than it needs to be and the degree day ceremony is only accommodated by opening up a partition between the two largest. One corridor is exactly like another and it is easy to get hopelessly lost.

180. *A study-bedroom in one of the tower blocks.*

Essex County Newspapers

The University of Essex

The tower block was a new conception in those days; it had not yet been discovered that its inmates tend to become lonely, neurotic and insecure, and that it is not even an effective space-saver. The architect cannot be blamed for introducing them, but he and the vice-chancellor are very much to be blamed for producing tower blocks of this particular design.

On each floor live up to sixteen students of the same sex. Each has a study-bedroom, 11′ long, by 6′ 6″ wide and 7′ 6″ high, with a bed, desk, cupboard, shelves and two chairs. Each room discloses park-like views and, most of them, a very long drop to the ground, save for those on the bottom floors whose occupants can be inspected as if they were animals in a zoo. They have brick walls on which it is impossible to hang pictures and are connected by narrow, brick-lined corridors. The washing and lavatorial accommodation is inadequate. In the middle of each floor is a central living area, half kitchen, half lounge, which is also inadequate. Besides a lack of space, the main problems are noise, not from adjoining rooms but above and below, and the one or two members of each commune who leave the place in a mess. The lifts, two to a block, are frequently out of order and always covered in graffiti. Though each tower is built round a core of reinforced concrete, enough bricks have been added to make a housing estate. The external ones are black because they have been baked hard, so that those at the foot of each tower can support the weight of those above. On a fine day these featureless monoliths are depressing; on a bleak one they lower. There is a grim, penal quality about them; if this were not a university it would surely be an open prison.

What excuses can be made for them? Cheapness in the light of a strict budget fails on two counts: firstly, because the blocks were expensive to build, as they are to service; secondly, that at the time the first two were rising, a vice-chancellor's lodge was built which, with six bedrooms and three bathrooms, amply satisfies its owner's needs. In an interview, the architect said, "We wanted to create little cells, aloft, remote, where you could be alone, quiet. I suppose it sounds corny. We wanted the elemental quality of monastic cells. A place with the traditional qualities of withdrawal. Bare walls and ceiling, roof to floor slit light . . . " He was, seemingly, bemused by the hill towns of Italy, in particular San Giminiano with its high towers. However, in a more practical vein, he tipped his young son's Lego set over a contour model of the site and modelled his buildings from that.[11] I distrust, I disbelieve, his talk of monastic cells and Italian hill towns; his brief, and his intention, was to do the job as cheaply and plainly as possible. Though neither compassion nor a concern for human dignity weighed much with either the architect or the vice-chancellor, commonsense might well have done. For, all other things being equal, which boy or girl would want to attend a university that looks like this? From the very beginning Essex chose itself a place at the bottom of everybody's list.

The Story of Wivenhoe

181. *The first four of the six tower blocks: Keynes, Tawney, Rayleigh and William Morris.*

Essex County Newspapers

A commission as large as this was certain to contain a few howlers, but there are some at Essex which a trained and sensitive architect should have avoided. Kenneth Capon might have known that his series of quadrangles would act as a wind tunnel; that it would have been better to put windows in the restaurant, where everyone would want to look out, than in the Library, where everyone would want to concentrate; that buildings are looked at from every angle, not just the air, as in a scale model; and that many of the views which the students would have of his functional architecture – particularly the underground entrance and the tower blocks – would send the hearts of the impressionable young deep, deep down into their boots. I recall the case of a girl who joined the University a few years after it had opened. It depressed her, horribly. She told her parents she could not go back. They sympathised and suggested she should spend the weekends at home and go there only for lectures and classes. She tried this, but succumbed to misery and finally fled. That same term she was admitted to St. Hugh's College, Oxford, where she was perfectly happy. She was by no means the only student to be overwhelmed by this place.

The Reith Lectures for 1963 are the literary complement to Kenneth Capon's designs. The six half-hour talks concern themselves with the physical

The University of Essex

design of the University and the subjects to be taught there, and how the two interrelate. Of the social, moral, artistic and spiritual ambience of the University, or what universities are for, or what role they should play in the late twentieth century, there is hardly a word. We are given a definition: "The university ideal... is of a self-governing community concerned with advancing and disseminating knowledge", but the idea that they exist for anything more than this receives but a lick and a wipe:

> *Apart from its formal teaching the university ought to have allowed him (the graduate) the chance to think and argue about the fundamental problems of life, and to stand on his own feet; it should have given him a respect for learning and for people, and developed his character; and it should have made the arts accessible to him in a way that they may never have been before.*[12]

A principal of a technical college would have said no less. Given the superb opportunity that was offering and the stakes at risk, these lectures are hardly less feckless than irresponsible. They should have made people extremely uneasy. One passage certainly did:

> *The segregation of men and women in separate buildings, we believe, is no longer feasible. It has never asssured good morals. And it is against the whole spirit of the day. We rather hope the proximity of men and women in our towers will have a civilising effect!*[13]

For the most part the lectures are written in the first person singular. Who is the "we" that takes upon itself the responsibility of putting boys and girls together and lightens this responsibility with a jest and a merry exclamation mark? I asked Dr. Sloman and he told me that "we" means "The University – the policy approved by the Council".

In those days people still found the idea of pre-marital sex shocking and it seemed to some Wivenhovians that the vice-chancellor was encouraging loose behaviour. In plain terms he was saying:

> *We all know that students sleep together and there is nothing that can be done about it; indeed, with efficient contraception, no awkward results should follow, so we are going to wash our hands of the whole matter.*

He should have had the moral courage to put it in plain terms.

So the students were packed into tower blocks, in alternate layers of boy and girl. The shape of the blocks, visible for many miles around, suggested that a snook was being cocked at conventional morality, and since by common consent they were hideous a moral ugliness was suggested as well. It was unfortunate that the lectures were delivered on Sunday evenings.

285

Other passages suggested interesting possibilities to would-be students. Dr. Sloman told his listeners that the traditional ends of a university would have to be sought by new means, that since a new university had a clean slate, the plans would be "freer, more daring, more experimental".[14]

These youngsters believed, or thought they believed, that Dr. Sloman was hinting at total equality, though he said nothing to seriously support this view. One particularly disillusioned young man, David Triesman, told me after he had been sent down:

> *The plan was beautifully idealistic in spirit, but the goods were seldom delivered. The book (of the lectures) was a lie. He had no power to do what he wanted. We worked for change through the legitimate channels. After two years it became apparent that the power structure prevented us bringing these into being . . . We were bitter because we had put in so much.*[15]

Here was a vice-chancellor soon to be caught between two fires. To many people, he already seemed irresponsible, even licentious, but when his first pupils realised that he and they were not going to run the place together they considered he had broken his word. Months before the first of them arrived, the seeds of trouble had been sown.

Meanwhile, the money was rolling in handsomely. The central complex was to be paid for by the University Grants Committee, which incidentally had had a good deal to do with choosing the site, and the student accommodation by the public. Several large firms, including Carreras, Plessey, May & Baker, Unilever, Woods of Colchester and Anglia T.V., were generous, particularly Ford of Great Britain, which gave £200,000, and many individuals made donations large and small. The £127,800 which had been raised by September, 1961, rose to £1,100,000 by March, 1964.[16]

Sixteen students on fourteen floors in twenty-eight towers gives us 6,272 boys and girls out of the projected 20,000, and before the first of them arrived Dr. Sloman told the press that the University would be one-third residential. That is to say, he assumed that his pupils would spend only one year out of three on campus and that the neighbourhood would billet 14,000 of them.[17] Before the nineteenth century educationalist who lived at Wivenhoe Park sallied forth to improve the condition of the Labouring Classes, he transformed his own home into a passing likeness of Hampton Court; as his twentieth century successor packed boys and girls into cells hardly more luxurious than those at Wormwood Scrubs and chucked an even larger number at the surrounding countryside, he secured a very comfortable billet for himself. Between the times of John Gurdon Rebow and Albert Sloman, human society has changed out of all recognition; human nature not a whit.

2 The Troubles Begin.

The University of Essex opened on 2nd October, 1964. 122 freshmen, 77 boys and 45 girls, arrived at Wivenhoe House, to be greeted by, and photographed with, the vice-chancellor, and then told to find themselves diggings, as no accommodation had been built. This was unwise and could easily have been avoided by providing demountable study-bedrooms.[18]

It seems that in the first two years, while the builders were at work in the valley and the University was based on the Victorian mansion, everybody, from the professors to the cleaners, was on Christian name terms and there was a pioneering spirit in the air. In a very short while clubs were formed and social life was under way. The first term produced a Students Council, a magazine called *Wyvern*, the Theatre Arts Society and a debating society, also an Anti-Blood Sports Association in whose name five students demonstrated at Boxford on 21st November; the incident caught the attention of the local press. In March, 1965, there was a rag week and the police were cross when helmets were taken from Queen Street Police Station. However, no harm was done during the first academic year.[19]

There were three hundred more students in the autumn of 1965 and a serious lodging problem, which should have been solved before the three hundred more students arrived. Work had now begun on the Library. *Wyvern* attacked the University for telling freshmen they would find facilities, including study-bedrooms, which were non-existent. However, during that year students started to move into the first tower block, to discover that the rooms were tiny and work elsewhere still noisily in progress. In the spring of 1966 the vice-chancellor's lodge, austere but dignified, which straddles the lake beside Wivenhoe House, was completed, for the sum of £20,000. Work was begun on the lecture theatre block designed by T. Cadbury Brown, the only successful piece of architecture in the University.[20]

As the students moved into the towers, so the honeymoon ended and life became inevitably more formal. Instead of one young man saying to another, "I'll examine you in sociology on Friday, if that's convenient", there were noticeboards and memoranda. For those who had founded the University there was a natural chill of disappointment; not only was the pleasing informality at an end, but they were working – or trying to work – above the noise of construction, in a jumble of mud and concrete that would not be socially viable until they had gone down. Moreover, they discovered that one important facility was never to be provided. There was to be no union building, nowhere, that is, which the students could call their own and from which they could run their affairs.

If these grown-up men and women had no specific place and business it followed logically, either that they were ciphers, or that their place and business was the whole of the University. No wonder Mr. Triesman and his friends thought they had come to what they called a "syndicalist" university and felt betrayed when they found it was not.[21]

One of the earliest confrontations occurred when the staff met in a lecture room to discuss some administrative matter and were promptly followed in by a party of students. The vice-chancellor, as chairman, thereupon walked out and the meeting was not held.[22]

From the spring of 1967 dates the sort of behaviour for which the University was soon to become famous. The fees for overseas students were raised, so the Minister of Education, Mr. Anthony Crosland, was received with boos and slow handclaps when he paid a visit. Classes were boycotted and the students marched, for the first time, through the streets of Colchester. They had another cause for discontent; the police had raided the campus to look for drugs.[23]

The lecture theatre block was not yet complete, so the installation of Lord Butler as chancellor and the bestowal of an honorary degree upon the Prime Minister, Mr. Harold Wilson, took place at the Colchester Moot Hall. Unfortunately, to Mr. Triesman and his friends, Mr. Wilson was "most unacceptable" and some students thought the ceremony a misuse of £3,000. So a demonstration was planned. When Dr. Sloman heard about it he said, "For God's sake, let them demonstrate. That's what they're here for". (But could he have prevented it?)[24] Thirty or forty students barracked Mr. Wilson and there were clashes with the civil and military police.[25]

Mr. Enoch Powell was given a rough reception in February, 1968. "I have visited most of the new universities", Mr. Powell said, "and have never found a lower standard of conduct". The University Disciplinary Committee put six students on charges, but other students threatened sit-in strikes unless the charges were dropped and when Dr. Sloman tried to interview the six he was prevented by an occupation of his office.[26] By this time the University was receiving plenty of coverage in the national press.

The next incident rocked the young campus to its foundations. On 7th May, 1968, Dr. T. D. Inch, a lecturer at the Porton Down germ warfare establishment, visited the Chemistry Department to give a lecture. The students as a whole wanted to question him about germ warfare and when they realised they would not be allowed to do so they prevented him from giving his lecture. Dr. Inch was barricaded in the department by a hundred chanting students and left under police escort. Without investigating the matter, Dr. Sloman rusticated three of the ringleaders: David Triesman, Raphael Halberstadt and Peter Archard. To pass judgment without hearing the evidence is always unfair; under the University's seeming charter of liberalism it was unthinkable. The students and staff, many of the latter only a few years older than their pupils, held a six hour meeting. It was decided to boycott lectures and take over the Hexagon Restaurant. It appears that such powers as there were at the University in those days were not very strong-willed and it may have been simple pusillanimity that led the Senate, the ruling body, to lift the rustication unconditionally, which action was celebrated by the students with a bonfire and dancing. However, Dr. Sloman was supported by the chancellor, also the chairman of the local Conservative Association, Lord Alport, and Colchester's Conservative M.P., Mr. Antony Buck, as he then was.[27]

It must be remembered that there was student unrest everywhere at this moment; at Berkeley, California, where students were fired on and killed; at The London School of Economics which, like Essex, had a large sociology department; at Boston, New York, Warsaw, The Sorbonne and West Berlin.

Happily, the incident led, not to more unrest, but a series of public debates which were chaired by a strong-minded sociology student. They were attended by staff and students alike, the vice-chancellor and even the general public. The nature and purpose of the University were discussed at great length, sometimes into the small hours. Meanwhile, its life and work continued without occupations or confrontations. This, surely, was putting the place to its proper use. It is a pity that later generations have not felt moved to discuss the rationale behind higher education.

At about this time the physical appearance of youngsters, especially boys, changed radically. Hair and beards were uncut, clothes totally casual and there was a brief fashion in the late sixties for dressing up. The scarlet military coats, solar topees and so forth of bygone ages, reappeared in public, but not with dressing up faces, which were sullen, even belligerent. To the public, even to their parents, students seemed like creatures from another world; never had the generation gap been wider.

It was doubtless to provide the University with a now much-needed veneer of respectability that the public was invited to join The University of Essex Association, as it was eventually called. Members attended special lectures and meetings, and, as the title implies, were formally identified with the University. This piece of adroit window-dressing still survives.

The fifth academic year, 1968-69, was memorable. It began with the students heckling Dr. Sloman while he addressed the freshmen. An anti-Vietnam procession marched twice round the centre of Colchester and thirty-eight students were arrested. The next foreign cause to attract attention was Biafra; there was a two-day strike in support of that country and a Biafra "starve-in" outside the Colchester Town Hall. In December, forty students were expelled from The House of Commons where they protested against the Nigerian Civil War.[28]

In mid-January two dozen students occupied the computing centre for twenty-four hours. Raphael Halberstadt had been sent down for failing his examinations and they wanted to see him reinstated, but their action was condemned by a petition which attracted 420 signatures. February produced an event as bizarre as anything Peter Simple dreamed up for Stretchford University: a Festival of Revolution. Twenty-two universities sent representatives, as did The London School of Economics, but it seems to have been a lighthearted affair and the only damage done was the ritual burning of a car.[29]

The University now acquired a reputation for drugs and harbouring dropouts. The *Daily Express* discovered a malingerer called Danny Matthews who left school without O Levels and set up home in Keynes Tower, using the University facilities and even attending the odd lecture:

> *He said: "I am a bum. The life here suits me completely. I like living with students, even though I'm not one of them. I plan to stay here until I get bored".*
> *Danny admits he smokes pot when he can scrounge enough money to buy it.*[30]

An Osbert Lancaster cartoon in the same newspaper bore the caption: "And this is little Alison, our youngest, who's going up to Essex just as soon as she can get an O level – if not sooner!"[31]

182. *This cartoon by Sir Osbert Lancaster appeared in the* Daily Express *on 27th June, 1969.*

In March, 1969, four students were sent for trial on thirty-one drugs charges and in the summer there was a spate of drugs stories when a student was charged at Ipswich.[32]

Five M.P.s from The Commons Select Committee on Education and Science conducted an inquiry at the University into the disorders, but it was broken up by students, among them David Triesman. The Speaker of The House of Commons was asked if this was a breach of Parliamentary privilege. He ruled that it was, but The Committee of Privileges recommended that the House should not exercise the power of penal jurisdiction and so handed the matter back to the University authorities. When the Select Committee presented its report it commented adversely on the tower blocks. At that time the fifth and sixth tower blocks, and certainly the last, were rising. They are slightly more spacious than the other four.[33]

In October, 1969, the number of undergraduates rose by three hundred, to 1,700. Almost a quarter of them began the new academic year by demanding that Pam Thompson, a coloured student who had failed her examinations, and three others, should be reinstated. The Senate met to discuss her future and was barricaded in for several hours. Disciplinary action was taken against fourteen students.[34]

In February, 1970, two hundred confidential files were taken from The School of Social Studies. In a demonstration against Barclays Bank, for supporting South Africa, three students tried to set the branch on campus alight. They were banned from the University and sent for trial. This prompted fifty other students to occupy the vice-chancellor's office; one was expelled, a second suspended and eighteen given suspended sentences. The three would-be arsonists continued their training at Borstal. They might have subsequently returned to Essex, but chose not to do so. In sentencing them, Mr. Justice Milmo remarked: "Discipline and the ordinary standards of civilised behaviour are not in the curriculum at Essex University". Before the academic year was over, seven students were fined for possessing drugs; an archdeacon's daughter was named as the leader of the group.[35]

Let us remember that this was a time of sit-ins, which also occurred at the Universities of East Anglia, Oxford, Manchester, Kent and Bristol, and The London School of Economics.

The University was learning how to contain and control its troubles. It administered justice through a Disciplinary Committee comprising three members of the staff and two students, and an Appeals Committee also comprising staff and students. Two more staff and student bodies were set up to deal with the suspension of students: the Membership Committee and the Membership Review Committee. This, surely, would have satisfied those students who wanted to take part in the running of the University? On the contrary, they argued, to be sentenced by a court of law and then by the University, as several of them had been, was to be tried twice for the same offence. A bonfire was lit on Square Four in protest and there was a tussle with the firemen who put it out; had the fire reached the gas main that lies directly beneath, Square Four and everyone on it would have been blown sky high.[36]

Two days later, *The Daily Telegraph* published a long article by R. Barry O'Brien, which began:

> *An attempt to create a new type of university in Essex by housing students in restriction-free blocks of flats instead of supervised halls of residence is collapsing in a wave of student vandalism and drug-taking.*[37]

The article may have been unfairly slanted, but the principal target, the tower blocks, was a perfectly fair one and though there was talk of reporting the author to the Press Council this was never done, which implies that his facts were not seriously in dispute. We shall never know how many students smoked pot at that time, but the allegation by one of them that about half did so seems an exaggeration. Vandalism there certainly was, with lifts wrecked, the long hosepipes in the tower blocks used to hose down other tower blocks, and graffiti everywhere. Rightly, Mr. O'Brien had a good deal to say about the unhappiness which people suffered from living in the towers.

The students themselves had already tried to cope with this problem by instituting a sevice called Nightline. Anyone who felt depressed could ring a certain number and receive comfort and advice. It is still an integral part of campus life. I have already cited one unhappy student. At about this time I met others. One man, who had previously worked in London, welcomed the lack of restrictions as regards formal dress and behaviour. Yet almost in the same breath he said, "It's like purgatory. It's like going into retreat". Another, who had managed to obtain his release from the R.A.F. to come here, said, "There's some element missing. I can't quite put my finger on it . . ."[38]

The Daily Telegraph had a leader which backed up Mr. O'Brien's article:

> *. . . Today we present an account of what life at this place is ordinarily like. It is hard to see how any parent or responsible person, believing it to be true, as we do, could read it without profound disgust and alarm . . .*
>
> *Who is to blame for the result? Not surely the students, though many misfits must be drawn to Essex by its unenviable reputation. For the most part they can feel bitterly resentful of the fact that they have been deprived of the guidance, discipline, peace and loving concern which is their due. To the system itself much blame must attach, as also to those who preside over it with such complacency and who, if they knowingly and without interference allow their premises to be used for drug-taking, are neglecting their own responsibilities as citizens. An inquiry is overdue . . .*[39]

The experiment was not collapsing. Even during its worst years it was held firmly together by the work ethic, a belief shared by staff and students alike that it was a good thing for facts to be put into heads. Although the University sets and marks its own papers, its academic standards are generally respected.

The University turned a very bad side to the world, but even in the dark years it had a good side as well. The students played a fair amount of sport and founded a University Sailing Club. It was not long before the arts were well served. The Gabrieli String Quartet, supported by a grant from the Gulbenkian Trust, came to Essex in 1971 and has remained. In the early seventies many of the world's most distinguished musicians performed at the University, including Vladimir Ashkenazy, John Williams and Ravi Shankar, and many of the top names in the world of folk and pop music. In May, 1971, the University Theatre opened, built in some haste when a suitable hole in the ground was offering. It is reasonably well-equipped, especially in the matter of dressing-room space, though it has neither wings nor a fly-tower and the entrance resembles a public lavatory. The student-run Film Society is an excellent organisation. In February, 1970, a domestic radio station was opened.

The Daily Telegraph was not the only paper to censure the University. James Wentworth Day wrote a vitriolic article for the *Essex Chronicle*, which listed everything that had gone wrong, then continued:

> ... Dr. Sloman is incapable of the realisation of his own inadequacy in a situation created by his own folly ... It can be truthfully argued that a new Vice Chancellor must precede any attempt to establish the university on a normal basis ...

The writer called for the removal of Sociology and Government from the curriculum, also that his readers should urge the County Council to cut the grants: "It's your money they waste in riots, arson and anarchy. Put a stop to it".[40]

The right-wing Essex Monday Club called for Dr. Sloman's resignation, whereupon the University Students' Council issued a statement urging critics of the vice-chancellor "to get off Albert's back or else". Or else ... ? What would they, or could they, have done?[41]

It seemed to many that Dr. Sloman was running a higher educational Dartington Hall, but to say so publicly took a good deal of courage because the University was still very new and still very much in the spirit of the swinging times, so that the man who attacked it was by that token a reactionary. The local press was somewhat divided. The leaders of the two nearest weeklies, the *Essex County Standard* and the *Colchester Express*, tended to be tongue-clucking and conciliatory, but the *Evening Gazette* felt its role called for a more trenchant approach, as did the *East Anglian Daily Times*.[42]

1971 was a quiet year; in 1972 things took off again.

The miners' strike of January brought two hundred miners to Wivenhoe House, who defied both a University action for trespass and their union leaders.

Students and miners clashed with police at Rowhedge. However, by 26th January they were gone. Then an edition of *Wyvern*, extolling the I.R.A., was shown by an M.P. to the Attorney General.

On 30th May, 1972, eight youngsters, aged twenty-one to twenty-five, were charged at the Old Bailey with conspiring to cause explosions. Three of them were University of Essex alumni.[43]

3 The Angry Brigade.

Among the freshmen in the Autumn Term of 1967 were two girls called Anna Mendelson and Hilary Creek. Miss Mendelson's father, Maurice, was a Jewish market trader and an alderman of the Stockport Borough Council, who had fought against Franco and Hitler. Her mother worked with refugee children from concentration camps after the War. Anna was head girl at Stockport High School; at Essex she read English Literature and American History. Hilary Creek's father, Kenneth, was a city businessman. She attended a private school at Bristol where she was a Sea Ranger and a prefect; at Essex she read History. The girls became friends and were soon involved in the various protests current at the time.

Meanwhile, France was having trouble with its students. There were 30,000 more of them than the Sorbonne could decently hold, so offshoot universities were built at Nanterre and Orsay, the former, like Essex, composed of tower blocks, without facilities and isolated. There already existed an international student organisation called The Situationists, which unlike other student groups, favoured revolution rather than reform. French students now formed an organisation of their own, modelled on this, called Les Enragés. In May, 1968, there was rioting at the Sorbonne followed by dialectical debates, just as Essex was having debates of its own. Anna Mendelson visited the Sorbonne at this time, as did Christopher Bott, a graduate of Strathclyde University, who went on to Essex for a postgraduate course in Government and Politics. So did John Barker, a journalist's son who had won a scholarship to Clare Colege, Cambridge.

Anna Mendelson, Hilary Creek and Christopher Bott all left Essex prematurely, sent down, according to the authorities, for lack of academic progress, but continued to haunt the area, visiting and staying at 7-9, Queens Road, Wivenhoe, the former *Anglesey Arms*. Meanwhile, at Cambridge, John Barker tore up his examination papers and left for London where he was joined by James Greenfield, a contemporary at Trinity College who had arrived with five A Levels to read Medicine, then changed to Economics. They ran a secondhand bookshop in Camden and joined up with Mendelson, Creek and Bott. Together, the five took part in political activities and helped minority

183. *The Angry Brigade at the Old Bailey. Top: (left to right), John Barker, Christopher Bott, Angela Weir and Stuart Christie. Bottom: (left to right), Catherine McLean, Anna Mendelson, Hilary Creek and James Greenfield. This drawing appeared in the magazine Oz which offered the defendants genuine, if insubstantial, sympathy.*

Drawing by Roy Knipe

groups they felt were oppressed, in particular squatters and those on the dole. For the latter they formed the Claimants Union, an organisation that soon had eighty branches.

These youngsters and their friends were filled with hatred and resentment. Somewhere, they believed, a malevolent establishment was exploiting them. The best form of defence is attack, so they hit back, by planting bombs on enemy territory. Their victims were important people, such as the Attorney General and the Home Secretary, commercial organisations, such as the Ford Motor Company and Iberia Airlines, and other objects of particular hatred and scorn, such as the site of the new Paddington Police Station and B.B.C. vans transmitting a Miss World contest from the Royal Albert Hall. In all, twenty-five bombs were planted and nineteen exploded.

The incidents, financed by a wholesale theft of chequebooks and credit cards, fifty-five alone from the Universities of Oxford, Cambridge and Essex, were extremely well-planned and executed. They were also effective. There was extensive damage to property and though nobody was killed there was the constant fear that somebody might be. The public was most concerned and Scotland Yard mounted an elaborate operation to find the Brigade.

Early in 1971, some members of the group were stopped by the police. Drugs and a chequebook stolen from the University of Essex were found on them, so they were bailed to Colchester Police Station, though under false names. From then on, the University of Essex was important to the team from Scotland Yard, who discovered that Greenfield had appeared in a local court after stealing two turkeys at Wivenhoe; they also found a University typewriter at the Manchester address. Greenfield and Mendelson skipped bail, but even as fugitives continued the bombings. Eventually, on 20th August, 1971, Greenfield, Barker, Mendelson and Creek were all arrested in London and the next day Christopher Bott as well.

Up to this moment the Angry Brigade had been enterprising, elusive and well-organised. It now did considerably better. The police had eight youngsters in custody, the five just mentioned, together with Catherine McLean, Angela Weir and James Christie. They were in prison for nine months and during that time one or more might have confessed and so brought down the whole group, especially since the police, whom they had made up their minds to hate, could hardly have treated them kindly. Yet they stayed silent and united, and in court became the attackers rather than the defendants.

Moreover, they succeeded. The old adage about the man who conducts his own case having a fool for a client was gloriously disproved. This was the longest trial of the century. It was probably the most hotly defended; it was certainly very well defended.

Anna Mendelson asked for the trial to be postponed for two years, to allay prejudice. The jurors were challenged. The judge allowed certain questions to be put to them and as a result fifty-four potential jurors were ruled out; of the twelve empanelled five were living on social security. The Angry Brigade wanted a working class jury and it obtained one; it was an excellent move.

The defendants had explanations for all the evidence brought against them, the general defence being that it had been manufactured and planted by the police. Their closing speeches lasted for eight days; Anna Mendelson alone spoke for a day-and-a-half.

The jury considered its verdict for fifty-two hours. It later appeared that seven members had wanted to convict all the defendants on every charge, but two had declined to convict any of them on any, and in order to accommodate both sides and the other three jurors, a deal had been struck: four convictions in return for four acquittals. Moreover, there was a strong recommendation for mercy, which the judge accepted, taking into account that the bombings had not been carried out for vengeance or gain and that the group had tried to help people. Instead of fifteen years apiece, Mendelson, Creek, Barker and Greenfield received only ten.

Why had these youngsters behaved in this way? It is not absolutely certain they had, for they have not confessed and some of the crimes with which they were charged may have been committed by others. However, I shall assume their guilt.

They were not the only dangerous people about at that time. America, for instance, had its Symbionese Liberation Army and the fanatical devotees of Charles Manson, and Germany the murderous Baader-Meinhof gang. The Angry Brigade, which never intended to kill people, was not as unpleasant as these, but must be seen in conjunction with them. The Permissive Society, the age was called; it seemed to tolerate, even encourage, outrageous and bloody-minded behaviour.

These people, and many others like them, felt they were being exploited. On the face of it, this was a curious phenomenon, for the age was neither oppressive nor authoritarian. National Service had recently ended and there was no war in sight; patriotism was laughed to scorn and the media were beginning to satirise and ridicule public figures with a vengeance.

It may be that this very freedom contained the heart of the problem. People like to know where they stand. Remove the guidelines and the result can be an institutional neurosis, especially in the isolated, Orwellian surroundings which Kenneth Capon created.

These people hated authority. Again, I believe there is a good reason for this. At heart, we are all revolutionaries. As we grow up, so there comes a time when the authority from which we have learned the ways of this world is replaced by our own. The father, headmaster, commanding officer and so on in our lives is deposed, mentally, and we take his place. What is one to do if such a figure does not exist, or is perceived merely as a phantom?

Ponder this curious fact. In the whole torrent of vilification that Dr. Sloman endured from his pupils, nobody, as I have yet discovered, ever accused him of living in comfort while everybody else at the University was obliged to live in slum tenements. A gross unfairness, and palpable, for the lodge stands at the head of the largest lake, visible to all, though trees have since been planted to hide it. Were they not Marxist-Leninists, Worker Revolutionaries and the like? Or thought they were? Yet they passed no comment on this glaring inequality. For the lodge served a useful purpose: it formally identified the vice-chancellor as the enemy. Had Dr. Sloman been content with a flat in the Rebow mansion he might have been ousted altogether.

Yet for all that, three of his former students and five others managed to flush out the foe. After nineteen loud bangs he showed himself. At long last, satisfyingly, comfortingly, robed and wigged, there was Authority, the

184. *The Vice-Chancellor's Lodge.*

Essex County Newspapers

challenger, ready to be fought and overcome. For in this affair of the Angry Brigade I believe it is the trial that was important, not the bombings.

Authority heard these youngsters out, listened to them for 111 days, and when he had done so, told them that there were rules and that they had broken these rules. At last, at long last, in the shifting, impalpable world of the sixties and early seventies, they had the blessed relief of knowing where they stood.

Both sides emerged from the trial with credit. The law displayed tolerance, patience and, at the end, mercy; the defendants, courage, loyalty and panache.

After the trial the students at the University of Essex held a one-day strike and were addressed by two of the acquittees, Christopher Bott and one of the girls, probably Catherine McLean. The national press had a good deal to say about the case, but offered the public no coherent account of what had happened or why. *The Sun* produced an imaginative piece, written for it by a Colchester news agency, called Sex Orgies at the Cottage of Blood:

The University of Essex

The tiny cottage, (7-9, Queen Street), had become a country-style "crash-pad".
A place where men and girls would mass for drugs, conspiracies, and sex.
Most revolting of all their activities was the ritual slaughter. Turkeys stolen from a local farmer were torn and slashed to pieces.[44]

Their landlord, Mr. Ken Ardley, told the *Essex County Standard* of men and women dressed in white sheets taking part in strange rituals.[45]

Give a dog a bad name. No, these boys and girls were at odds with the world, but not devilish, nor even revolutionaries. They may have thought they wanted to destroy the established order, but their deeds and words do not bear this out. The bombings, though well executed, were not part of coherent pattern, and the communiqués they sent to the police display merely a hatred and envy of a world they were incapable of enjoying.

The two girls were released from prison prematurely because their health had deteriorated, Mendelson in February, 1977, Creek two months later. Naturally, neither could admit to any crime, but Anna Mendelson told her M.P. that what she had done had been "stupid and nonsensical", and Hilary Creek, it was reported, had abandoned her political beliefs.[46] In order to get out of prison there had, of course, to be some sort of climbing down, but in truth there may have been a change of heart. After all, these girls had got what they wanted. They had gone out into the world and crudely – but youth *is* crude – fought their way, with their companions, to maturity. The skills and knowledge they acquired might be put to very good use. Let us hope they are, for the investigation and trial of the Angry Brigade cost £1,000,000, which is an expensive way of educating people.

4 1973-1974.

Early in 1973 the University launched a campaign to rid itself of its permissive image, but this was soon offset by a 25-year-old research student who tried to commit suicide after smoking cannabis. "I convinced myself I was on the verge of a spiritual and religious conversion", he said. "I felt I was being tested to see how far I would go". So he crashed a car into a ditch.[47] It was also offset by the next wave of student unrest.

Hitherto, the troubles at Essex had arisen out of its character and administration, also politics, national and international. Insofar as they concerned ugly buildings and squalid accommodation they were justified, insofar as they concerned unacceptable prime ministers they were a luxury; but the Sixties was the age of the Student and the Student knew it. The Seventies, however, was not, and as the grants failed to keep pace with inflation fresh conflicts were provoked, far more bitter than any which had gone before.

In the academic year 1962-63, the highest grant paid to a student was £320. Ten years later it was £445, a rise of 39 per cent, but retail prices had meanwhile risen by 66 per cent. So the students felt justified in asking for a 20 per cent rise. They were also rightly concerned about the way in which the money was given.[48]

Some grants were mandatory, that is, could be claimed as a legal right. Others were discretionary; it was for the local education authority to decide if a student should have one or not. All degree courses carried mandatory grants, but not those at the Colchester Institute, whose students made common cause with the University. Moreover the size, even of a mandatory grant, was determined by the parental income. The richer the parents, the smaller the grant, the intention being that they would make up the difference.

This presented several difficulties. First of all, there was the breach of privacy; from the size of his grant the student could estimate his parents' income. Secondly, it put the student in the position of a child who had to ask for pocket money, which might, and often was, withheld. The parents might say, "We don't charge you when you come home . . . ", or, "Well, we did give you a pullover for Christmas . . . " Encounters between parents and their offspring were often painful. In 1973, the University thought that about a third of the parents declined to make up the grants.

There was also the case of the married female student. Her grant was not £445, but only £275. She had therefore a standing temptation to live in sin, and her parents and groom a temptation to encourage her in this, for the size of her grant was based, not on her husband's, but on her parents' income.

Some students at this time told me what trying to live on a grant was like.

There was nineteen-year-old Colin Oxley, a first year Comparative Studies student. His father was dead and his mother worked at a London play-centre. Accordingly, he received the full grant of £445, which was incidentally paid, not to him, but the University, which deducted rent before passing the remainder to his bank account. What the University did not deduct, from him or anyone else, was the tuition fees, which were taken care of by endowments and the local education authority. He paid £160 rent for a thirty-nine week year in a University tower block which included the Christmas and Easter holidays. This rent procured him a personal cell, heating, lighting, running water, kitchen facilities and a common area which he shared with fifteen others. He had already paid £20 for a library of fifty books and expected to pay more. Cigarettes cost him £1.75 a week and he went into the bar five nights out of seven to spend 30p to 50p. Six single tickets between Colchester and London cost £9 and he spent about 75p a week on such things as soap, washing powder, paper and pens. He played squash with a racket he had bought with cigarette coupons. He had not bought any clothes, but looked quite tidy.

Here is a rough estimate of his outgoings for a year:

Rent	*39 weeks*	*£160.00*
Cigarettes	*52 weeks @ £1.75*	*£91.00*
Food	*30 weeks @ £3.00*	*£90.00*
Bar	*52 weeks @ £1.50*	*£78.00*
Extras	*52 weeks @ 75p*	*£39.00*
Books		*£28.00*
Travel		*£9.00*
		£495.00

So it looked as if he would end the academic year at least £50 in debt. He had had no job over Christmas and to keep going had borrowed money. On one occasion his mother had sent him £1.

Mark Bond, eighteen years old and reading English, received only £243. Since there was insufficient accommodation at the University he was spending his first year at Clacton where he paid £4.20 a week for bed and breakfast. He owned an Austin Mini van which cost him £220 a year to run and his extras, which included new strings for a guitar, came to £52. He spent £30 on clothes. Otherwise, his outgoings were much the same and he expected to be over £400 out of pocket at the end of the year.

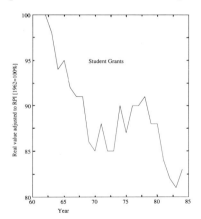

185. *Graph showing the decline in real value of the student grant.*

Compiled by Dr. David Bebbington

A third student, Annalena McAfee, unable to make ends meet, was working, ironically as a University waitress, until she could earn enough money to resume her studies.

Such was the background to the national one-day strike called by the National Union of Students on 14th March, 1973. Five hundred students from the University and two hundred from the Colchester Institute marched round Colchester; during the demonstration a policeman was knocked unconscious.[49]

In October, 1973, the University's tenth academic year began. There were now 2,100 students, a far cry from the original forecasts. 1973-74 was the year of the greatest disruptions, the one that has lingered in the public memory. Let it therefore be remembered that these disruptions had nothing whatever to do wth politics, either national or domestic. They were about grants, that and that alone.[50]

The trouble started on 15th November, 1973, with another one-day strike called by the N.U.S. At the end of it, Ronaldo Munck, a Latin-American postgraduate, and William Rich, a second year sociologist, were charged with several offences by the University. Four days later a forcible occupation of certain rooms, mostly in Square Four, was begun, in order to make the authorities reduce rents and the price of food. The occupiers, who defied a summons brought by the University, were joined by sympathisers from the Universities of Leeds, Southampton and East Anglia, and to show support for Essex students at East Anglia began an occupation of their own Arts Block. On 29th November about four thousand protesters marched round Colchester and the occupation was extended to the Hexagon Restaurant. A student spokesman estimated that 270 were involved.

Meanwhile, the N.U.S. conference at Margate gave strong backing to the opinion of *The Times Higher Education Supplement*, that:

> *The student case for more money is just, reasonable and urgent. Rent strikes are perhaps the only way they can press home the strength of their arguments, and strikes were used with some success on 44 campuses last year...* [51]

The students took files from Wivenhoe House and gave them to a chartered accountant so that a better case for the reduction of rent and the price of food might be established. The occupation lasted for twenty-four days, though students left the area to attend lectures, but support for it dwindled as the authorities switched off the heating and the end of term approached. When the occupiers left they were told that charges would be brought against them and on these terms everyone broke up for the Christmas holidays.

Thirty-four students were charged with offences arising out of the occupation and five more when members of the University Grants Committee were besieged in the Hexagon Restaurant by angry students. When the first student to come before the Disciplinary Committee was found guilty, there was a sit-in which included the vice-chancellor's office and barriers were erected at the lower entrance to the University so that no supplies should reach it. On 28th

February it was reported that the disciplinary hearings had been halted after the student members of the five-man committee had walked out on the instructions of the Students Union.

The police asked the students to take down barriers at the picket line because they were illegal and the students voted to do so. However, a minority thought that this was giving in and it seems the £6,000 worth of damage done during the night of 7th to 8th March was a direct result of this. The vice-chancellor, it appears, knew who the culprits were but asked the police not to charge them.

On 15th March, Ronaldo Munck and William Rich were found guilty of disrupting a class and a lecture, by the Disciplinary Committee, the University's court of first instance; it recommended expulsion until their case could be heard by the Appeals Committee. Munck and Rich defied an order to leave and that same night took part in a demonstration outside the vice-chancellor's lodge. The students banged dustbin lids and shouted for his resignation; one of his windows was broken. The next day the ballroom was taken over as a base for picketing and the barriers were up again. The police

186. *A scene in Square Four during the troubled years.*

Photograph by Des Blake

187. *The barricade at the lower entrance to the University in 1974.*

Photograph by Des Blake

arrested fifteen students at the barriers on 18th March and the next day issued a final warning that they must be removed. The students were due to vote on the matter the next day, but were forestalled by the police, who arrived at 10 a.m., in eighteen vans. The student leaders met immediately and soon two hundred students were facing the police. Seventy-eight males and twelve females were arrested and removed to custody in Colchester and Chelmsford, but were bailed the next day on condition they took part in no more picketing.

On 21st March, six hundred students arrived from all over the country and joined those at Essex in a protest march through Colchester. An effigy of the vice-chancellor, carried in the procession, was later burnt. Some students burst into his office and threw a copy of his Reith Lectures at him. That same day the academic staff passed a vote of No Confidence in the administration's handling of the affair, by fifty-six votes to ten.

Meanwhile, a High Court judge had ruled that the expulsion of Munck and Rich was just. On this note the University broke up for Easter, but not before the *Evening Gazette* had produced a front page story about a small group of anarchists who claimed responsibility for the damage of 7th March, hinted they had also burnt down Woolworth's in Colchester High Street, which had recently been gutted, declared they could make explosives from chemicals they had taken from the University laboratory and vowed they would be satisfied with nothing less than the removal of the vice-chancellor.[52]

Picketing continued throughout the Easter holidays and the Summer Term began with a mammoth teach-in, on the lines of the earlier dialectical debates. 24th April was a day of Student Protest, but only about a quarter of the expected two thousand turned up. Two days or so later a student, but it is believed he was not at Essex, told Dr. Sloman during a confrontation in his office, "Albert, you're a bloody boring little academic".[53]

On 30th April, Messrs. Munck and Rich returned to the campus, for the High Court judge's order had been varied by another judge. Early in May the University Appeals Committee reduced their expulsion to a suspended expulsion, which to many seemed weakness. On 14th May, it was announced that student grants were to be raised; three days later the picketing ended. Towards the end of June, 103 of the 105 demonstrators arrested in March had their cases heard at Colchester. Eighty-two of them were discharged but ordered to pay £10 costs, sixteen pleaded not guilty, three were remanded on bail and two failed to turn up.

By this time the national press had adopted the University of Essex as a symbol for disruption. The cartoonists of the right wing newspapers, in particular, were scathing. Cummings of the *Daily Express* showed Mr. Anthony Wedgwood Benn saying, "What a lovely day! Let's go and smash something!", and underneath was a caption – Lord Whitelaw is talking to Mr. Edward Heath – "Apparently Mr. Benn took a Correspondence Degree in Disruption from Essex University". Jak of the *Evening Standard* drew a professor showing a gallery of group photographs to visitors. The party arrives at a hole in the wall: "... and this was a class of '74". *The Daily Telegraph* had a leader: "Should Essex be Closed."[54]

The University had worked hard to achieve this reputation, yet in a sense the reputation was unfair. The violence was for the most part a myth. True, the students sometimes grappled with the police and even their own staff; three alumni had recently been tried for bomb outrages; there was a good deal of vandalism. Yet the only overtly destructive incident at the University was the damage of 7th to 8th March, 1974. Of this, £5,500 was caused by smashing plate glass, which is both vulnerable and expensive; the other £500 was damage to computers. If, say, the Bullingdon, flown with insolence and wine, were let loose on the campus it would achieve, with little effort, damage many times worse than this.

As the heart of the Angry Brigade episode was the trial, not the bombings, so the struggle of those years, and of that year in particular, was a war of attrition, conducted with words, not blows. It was a litigious business, sometimes literally so. Two barristers, one representing the University, the other the Students Union, would spend hours closeted together, arguing over the exact intepretation of the rules the University had made for itself. Undergraduates, after all, are intellectuals and, despite appearances, it was the intellectual mode they used to fight the management.

Disruption there was, but it never seriously disrupted the working life of the University. Throughout the years of the sit-ins, strikes and picketing, lectures and examinations continued with minimal interruption. Even while there were barricades at the University's lower entrance The Gabrieli Quartet played regularly in the Lecture Theatre Block above, and during this academic year an undergraduate called Ian Granville Bell achieved some lovely productions on the stage of the University Theatre.

In the wake of 1973-74 came a series of ten discussions to try and discover what was wrong with the University. One of them, The Quality of Life, concluded that:

> *Essex University is not a place to recommend to your friends, whether staff or students, for its social life or atmosphere. The most frequently quoted reason for the poor environment was the inadequacy of the unified university concept to provide people with a sense of belonging . . . and the present application of university policy resulted, as one participant said, in everybody having an equal share of nothing.*

It therefore called for a purpose-built union building. I had an interview with Dr. Sloman at this time and put this request to him. He said, "I would be in favour of any financial provision which the Grants Committee might make to improve the amenities of the University. It is entirely unlikely that additional moneys for this purpose will be available in the near future". In other words, "No". I also met the president-elect of the Students' Union, Colin Beardon, who made it plain that the students wanted somewhere of their own.[55]

In December of that year, this was achieved. The ballroom, a largish, gloomy, asymmetrical, subterranean place, together with several committee rooms, was handed over to the students in lieu of a proper union building which to this day has not been erected.

There was also the Annan Report. At Lord Butler's request, Lord Annan produced an analysis of the unrest. He decided that, "The immediate cause of the disturbances at the University in 1973-74 was the action of a small number of militant students, well organised, unscrupulous in their methods, and determined to cause a confrontation with the University authorities", and that the University was therefore justified in the actions it took against them. His report was naturally berated by the students, but *The Times Higher Education Supplement* was equally hostile: "The content of the analysis is clear, crude and wrong".[56] However, it was used by the University as the basis for a working party set up to make changes.

Another result of 1973-74 was that applications for places at the University rose by 5 or 6 per cent. The authorities must have wondered, with a shiver, what sort of people this 5 or 6 per cent comprised.

Thus ended the first, inglorious decade of the University of Essex, which made social history by creating an archetype, one that lingers in the public mind to this day. The Student – a bookish young ragamuffin with a grievance.

5 The Survival Game.

The fortunes of the University were now at their nadir. Five or six years of constant disruptions had produced national publicity of the worst possible kind and there was not the slightest reason to suppose that things would improve. Up, in the autumn of 1974, came students still pressing for the vice-chancellor's removal; evidently, more sit-ins, strikes and picketings were on the way. Instead, it was from this moment that the conflict began to die down.

The new year brought a rent increase of 40 per cent, though with the top grant at £605, £6.30 a week was not too unreasonable. However, there was a rent strike, which the University countered by stopping students from taking examinations. Six students retaliated by trying to stop the examinations. The University banned four of them and withheld examination results from those who had not paid their rents by the end of the academic year.[57]

In October, 1975, there were 2,275 students, far more than the campus could hold, so some slept on floors, others commuted from as far away as London and there were hour-long queues for meals. The Union had a personal showdown over this with the vice-chancellor, but it was announced that the University would take 275 more students in 1976.[58]

So it continued. A rise in rent or tuition fees, or a lack of proper accommodation, would provoke a sit-in. Then the University would try to discipline the occupiers or, if they were not too numerous, bring in the police to remove them, which would provoke a further sit-in.

Visiting speakers were still roughly received. When Sir Keith Joseph attempted to address the students on "the moral and material case for capitalism", he was pelted with eggs and flour. That a Conservative cabinet minister should choose to speak on such a subject, at such a time, at such a place, must surely prove that politicians will do anything to attract attention. When the Prime Minister, Mr. James Callaghan, visited the Colchester Lathe Factory in 1977, he sported a white raincoat. "When I know I am coming near the University", he said, "I always wear my anti-demonstration gear".[59]

As the years passed, so the rumblings died down. The provision of union accommodation was evidently an important turning point. Hitherto, the University had thought of itself as a unit. Seemingly, this was what everyone wanted under the charter of militant left-wingery which many of the staff and students extolled with the utmost vigour. Seemingly, but in fact the old saw that age and youth cannot live together had been amply proved. Besides, the University was in fact administered by the management. Evidently, it is as much the nature of a university as, say, a factory, that there should be two sides. I guess that part of the virulent hatred that attached itself to the vice-chancellor was that he intruded, physically and mentally, on his pupils' living space. There was nowhere they could get away from him. For from this moment their hatred of him diminished.

Now the students had a place of their own. The underground ballroom was not much of an asset, but the new, union-run, bar certainly was and in the seventies a custom-built sports complex was opened. These facilities are not generous, but give the students a little more to do and somewhere to go. The walls of the goldfish bowl are more opaque than they used to be. Moreover, the students acquired their own staff, including men and women who could fight their battles better than they, so that the need for informal confrontations of the kind that make headlines disappeared.

Further, the times were changing. Ironically, even as the students and management formally parted company, so they were united by the knowledge that the academic world was no longer expanding, that if the University could not give a good account of itself it might be abandoned by the University Grants Committee and its charter withdrawn. The University had survived internal dissension; now it began to work at public relations, to talk of degree ratings and of links with industry. There had in fact been a public relations officer at the University almost from the very beginning. Walter Evans had taken the brunt of the earliest disruptions; he was succeeded by a lively young intellectual, Graham Greene, who weathered the storm of 1973-74 and became a don elsewhere. Michael Ripley, a down-to-earth North countryman, founded a magazine called *Wivenhoe* which appears weekly during term time. It is the management's organ of propaganda. Students and staff shake hands as cheques for good causes are handed over, sportsmen are congratulated, degree ratings extolled and everybody is wreathed in smiles. The undergraduate view, understandably less roseate, is contained in a magazine called *Vulture*.

Little can be done to ameliorate the ugliness of the existing architecture or add on even reasonably attractive buildings. However, early in 1979 all plans for further high-rise blocks were formally abandoned and beside one of the towers was erected the Wolfson Building, hideous but more spacious. It would be pleasant to record that the University has had a change of heart in this matter, but it seems it was built with the holiday tourist trade in mind. Meanwhile, Wivenhoe Park House has been turned into a conference centre and suitably expanded.

One or two subjects have been added to the curriculum, including law; lawyers tend to be less trouble than, say, sociologists. One or two dons who mistook the University for a place of complete *laissez-faire* have, as *Wivenhoe* puts it, "relinquished their appointments".

The miners strike of 1984-85 was an interesting indication of how things have changed. How the class of 1973-74 would have revelled in it! There would have been more miners at the University than students. As it was, some miners were indeed accommodated on campus, and some students did indeed assist the picketing at the Wivenhoe and Rowhedge wharves where cargoes of coal were unloaded, and some were indeed arrested, but the incident was a wraith of what it would have been twelve or fifteen years earlier.

When H.M. The Queen toured Colchester, on 28th May, 1985, she paid a brief visit to the University. How earlier generations would have sabotaged

188. *The visit of H.M. The Queen to the University of Essex in 1985. On Her Majesty's left is Dr., (now Sir), Albert Sloman.*

Essex County Newspapers

The Story of Wivenhoe

that visit! Courageously, the University ventured on an acid test – which passed off successfully.

At the end of the academic year 1986-87, the Old Survivor slipped quietly away. Dr. Sloman was by this time the longest-serving vice-chancellor in the country. He had eluded Hitler and his pupils; he was given a knighthood.

People have short memories these days, but the reputation of the University of Essex survives and in the media and places where they satirise it is still a jest. In the television series, *Yes, Minister*, there is a scene where the Minister for Administrative Affairs, James Hacker, carpets his Permanent Under-Secretary, Sir Humphrey Appleby, for the loss of £40,000,000, a mistake the latter made some years previously. Sir Humphrey defends himself:

"Minister, aren't we making too much of this? Possibly blighting a brilliant career because of a tiny slip thirty years ago. It's not such a lot of money wasted".

The Minister is incredulous. "Forty Million?"

"Well", parries Sir Humphrey, "that's not such a lot compared with Blue Streak, the TSR2, Trident, Concorde, high-rise council flats, British Steel, British Rail, British Leyland, Upper Clyde Ship Builders, the atomic power station programme, comprehensive schools, or the University of Essex".[60]

189. *Lord Butler of Saffron Walden confers degrees.*

Photograph by Des Blake

The University of Essex

6 Interim Report.

Because the University of Essex is partly within Wivenhoe's parish boundary, it has had a chapter to itself. In truth, it deserves a book, for not only was the bizarrerie of its first decade a very noticeable part of the sixties and early seventies, but the origin and nature of behaviour as extraordinary as this should be understood, as it was certainly not understood at the time. Let me, therefore, offer some conclusions from the facts I have presented.

As I have said, the phenomenon was worldwide; nor, so far as this country was concerned, was it a new one. Between the Wars, many upper and middle class children behaved badly and strangely; from 1945 onwards the number of educated youngsters who were unable to enjoy life multiplied. I believe that John Osborne shed a significant ray of light on the subject when he caused the anti-hero of his play, *Look Back in Anger,* Jimmy Porter, to mourn the lack of "brave causes". Jimmy would never admit it, but I guess he misses the satisfyingly formal pattern which John Gurdon Rebow and his contemporaries imposed on life, or hoped they had. My researches through the local columns of a provincial newspaper for information regarding one small town suggest to me that it was in order to preserve this formality that Man invoked his most favourite and formal game. If so, vainly; the Battle of the Somme proved that the game was now too horrible to play and every succeeding generation has had to live with that knowledge.

No brave causes. Youth wins its way to maturity by engaging in a healthy dialectic with life. When, in the late forties and fifties, a host of restraints with regard to speech, dress, appearance and morals were lifted, it seemed as if this dialectic had vanished. As television brought the world into people's drawing rooms, so it banished their illusions about it. It showed, for instance, the Vietnam War. At the same time there occurred a mighty upsurge in learning and the arts as has not been known since the Renaissance. The choices laid out before the rising generation were multitudinous and bewildering. If society as a whole was obliged to find new bearings at this time, small wonder that the adolescents were more than usually difficult. Some, shy of the world, dropped out, did their own thing or didn't want to know, took to drugs or declared a tacit war on their fellows by embracing left-wing political creeds, but in forms so grotesque as to preclude any serious intention. Others, assuming that morality was a dead letter, treated life as an orgy. People behaved oddly at this time; to reach one's majority, especially to attend a university, was to be a part of that oddness.

Such was the social background to the unrest at the University of Essex and so far as the general public was concerned it was the cause of that unrest; the students rebelled because they were those sort of people. This was not so, but I believe that the background was an essential factor.

University! The word comes down the centuries charged with a mystique, an idea of learning not for gain, nor even for its own sake, but for its ethical value:

> *He knoweth nothing as he ought to know, who thinks he knoweth anything without seeing its place and the manner how it relateth to God, angels and men, and to all the creatures in earth, heaven and hell, time and eternity.*[61]

This is how Thomas Traherne formulated the ideal and most of us believe, albeit obscurely, that education is a spiritual activity. So when it was known that a university was coming to Wivenhoe Park there was an upsurge of joy. The first subscription lists contained several small, even nominal sums, given by men and women who symbolically paid tribute to this ideal.

Then came the Reith Lectures:

> *The fundamental aims of a university are not in dispute . . . That is why in this series of lectures I have said so little about the function of a university and so much about the methods by which that function may be discharged.*[62]

What should we think of a clergyman who ascended to the pulpit, told his flock that the fundamental aims of Christianity were not in dispute and then gave a lecture on the design, construction and administration of his parish church? The province of a man who runs a university is metaphysics; its buildings and the organisation of its social and scholastic life are merely the shell which contains his efforts to promote his pupils' ethical training. I find it odd that David Triesman and others imagined that these lectures contain a vision of Utopia; they contain no vision whatever. I also find it odd that the lectures attracted so little adverse comment; considering the tremendous importance of the subject the first six essays to be written at the University of Essex scarcely deserve a modest gamma apiece. Apart from the odd piece of spit and polish, these lectures are a description of how specialist training would be provided at a boarding establishment for young men and women whose skills were needed in large numbers by industry.

For Dr. Sloman and his masters, the Academic Planning Board, the name university evidently indicated little more than legal status. Armed with a charter, this organisation might confer its own degrees, which in turn would attract mandatory grants, and generally order its own affairs. The title also had a mystique which would impress the public and make money-raising comparatively easy. Morally speaking, the place was to be an institution.

The architecture was of a piece with the lectures. Kenneth Capon produced functional buildings and by their very functionalism these buildings contained an implied sneer at their occupants: that students were second-rate citizens, that to be young, inexperienced and penurious, was to be foolish, even culpable.

As we have seen, the first phase of the unrest was a revolt against this shallow mental and physical conception. Moreover, it achieved some success. So long as the students and staff debated the function of a university, then indeed it *was* a university. Eventually, the management reluctantly disgorged a substitute for the union accommodation which, through parsimony, it had failed to provide earlier. The second phase, starting with the year of the barricades, 1973-74, was the campaign for better grants. Though a national issue, it was Essex that fought with the greatest vigour and, in the event, successfully.

It is unfortunate, but quite understandable, that the excellent reasons for the unrest were obscured by the accompanying anger, hatred, lethargy, dirtiness and eccentricity, also by politics, the reddest of red herrings, dragged firmly across the trail. The students of those days were disliked. Rightly so; they went to great lengths to make themselves disliked. Not for what they did, but for how they did it, an odium was produced which lingers in the public nostril to this day.

Let me reiterate two truths about the protests at the University of Essex: they were justified and they were effective.

Let me also emphasise that these justified and effective protests were made, not by well-organised and disciplined young men and women, but by ill-organised, amorphous groups of boys and girls who scarcely knew what they were doing or why. The undergraduate is the vaguest animal on the face of the earth; these generations were vaguer than any. Desperately shy of the formal world, they turned their backs firmly on the methods by which things are actually achieved in the world. Indeed, they turned their backs on the world itself. They were *against* the establishment, *against* the ruling prime minister, *against* the vice-chancellor. There was a tremendously negative, joyless, life-eclipsing element in the life of the university at this time. Yet, for all that, these protests were effective.

But let us suppose there had never been a single strike, sit-in, procession, demonstration or expression of discontent? Suppose the students, like the obedient little termites it was assumed they would be, moved into their brand new slum tenements uncomplainingly, so that all twenty-eight were built, and quietly embraced an undergraduate life based on inadequate facilities and an inadequate grant? What, then, should we think of the University?

We should be disappointed. We had thought that a university implied a form of training that extended beyond the mere putting of facts into heads, that the youngsters who attended would receive a moral leadership, one that might happily influence the world outside. Instead, there appeared a technical college where the pupils boarded and some of the terms used, such as "faculty", "readership" and "don", and some dressing up once a year, hinted obscurely at a possible ideal.

How much does this matter? If the boys and girls at the Colchester Institute who train to be shorthand typists, cooks, restaurateurs, mechanics, electricians, teachers of English as a foreign language, graphic artists and musicians, never bother about the nature and purpose of education, why should the boys and girls at Wivenhoe Park who train to be computing engineers, electrical engineers, physicists, historians, sociologists and lawyers, do so? Indeed, would it not be a form of intellectual snobbery if they did? Consider, too, the grotesque blunders made down the centuries by applying carefully considered formulae of education. And what, formula, pray, could possibly be devised for the needs of several thousand emancipated youngsters of many different backgrounds, nations and creeds? Far better, far safer, to put facts into heads and let education take care of itself.

Besides, since the youngsters are living away from home, most for the first time, they are also learning a good deal more than can be discovered in textbooks. Since its inception the University has taught its sons and daughters such ancient truths as that the weakest go to the wall and that beggars cannot be choosers. Everybody ought to rough it somewhere along the road to maturity. So let studenthood be a time of penury and humiliation. All the better to keep young noses to the grindstone. Three years pass quickly enough and then the man who was diligent will discover that the skills taught at Essex are often well rewarded in the world outside. Very soon he may enjoy the good things of life, may own, perhaps, a house like the one at the head of the lake, with six bedrooms and three bathrooms.

Such, unspoken but implied, is the University's attitude towards its pupils. Against all this, I believe there are excellent reasons why it should undertake their education.

At the beginning of this century life was formal. Men were divided by the barriers of social class, with accompanying speech, dress and behaviour, and even different professions had their own vocabulary and lifestyles. There were rigid divisions between age groups; childhood, adolescence, early manhood, middle-age and old age all had their uniforms and behaviour patterns. Today, we live informally, and a youngster in search of a profession, ideals and ethical code has no pattern to copy or rebel against. I suggest that this has made life harder, just as it is harder to paint an abstract picture than a representational one or write free verse rather than a sonnet. I also suggest that this has made life truer and fairer. The world is every man's oyster and so it ought to be. When the adult world first beheld the shaggy-haired young man of the Sixties it supposed he was Siegfried with his sword already forged. It proved not so; much of that seeming self-assurance was a bluff. If the world was his oyster then he lacked the courage or the means to open it. Mature in some ways, he was immature in others and often prone to frustration, anger and despair. The youngster of today has the world laid out in front of him; before he chooses his profession he ought to live widely, fulfil himself in as many ways as possible. The previous century discovered the value of training; the present has discovered that training never ends, that what has been begun in the home, continues at primary school, secondary school, university and ever after. What a challenge to the educationalist!

> *Apart from its formal teaching the university ought to have allowed him, (the graduate), a the chance to think and argue . . . to stand on his own feet . . . have given him a respect for learning and for people, and developed his character . . .* [63]

But in the days when Albert Sloman went up to Oxford it was still a finishing school and his sports-jacketed, grey-flannelled contemporaries arrived with their prejudices and opinions largely formed. Today, young men of the same age travel lighter and stay younger longer. They must not merely be given a chance to think, argue, stand on their own feet and respect learning and people, but be shown how to do so.

How ought the University to set about its task? It is not my purpose to provide the campus up the road with a social blueprint, but I have some practical suggestions.

When the freshmen arrive at the beginning of the academic year, many of them are seeing the University for the first time, which proves conclusively that the management is not the slightest bit interested in the students as human beings. It also helps to ensure that the quality of social life at the University is as low as possible. Before any boy or girl, other than an overseas student, is accepted as an undergraduate he or she should spend a night on campus and be interviewed there. The University is far too preoccupied with degree ratings. Given that a student's academic showing is reasonable, it ought to be to his credit that he has, say, worked with spastics, built a sailing dinghy or written a musical.

In this context, let me remark on the dismal fact that from three thousand undergraduates and graduate students the University can produce neither an orchestra nor a choir. True, there has been a University Choir for many years, and latterly Nigel Hildreth, who runs the Music Department at the Colchester Sixth Form College, has been coaching a somewhat exiguous chamber orchestra, but both are heavily complemented with outsiders. For most of its history, the University has hosted four of the most distinguished musicians in the country. The Gabrieli Quartet provides the backbone of the subscription concerts, but is not felt by the students to be an integral part of the University. Let the management seek out talented violinists, violists and 'cellists, who can be coached by the Gabrieli, for it is well-nigh immoral that this golden opportunity has been neglected.

Let the University be a place where people are encouraged to do things, indeed expected to do things, for undergraduates in general, and the troubled generations at this university in particular, are singularly unable to tell the difference between illusion and reality in this matter.

One evening, a student, high on drugs, was observed capering about stark naked at the lower entrance to the University, to the considerable annoyance of the traffic, bellowing, "I am the Resurrection and the Life!"[64] At that moment, that young man mistook his gesture for reality. Had Mary Martin Rebow beheld him she would have been reminded of her visits to Bedlam. To my mind, he typified his generation. Not the least value of a good education is that it teaches us to distinguish between doing things and pretending to do them.

If every potential British student were interviewed at the University, a large proportion would turn it down. Aesthetics are ultimately a matter of opinion, but it is the general opinion that Essex is ugly and now the concrete is starting to weather inelegantly, it looks dirty and tatty as well. Thirty years ago, Oxford and Cambridge were the two leading universities in the country. So they are today. They may no longer be the two cleverest places, but they are far and away the most beautiful. All other things being equal, this is where the brightest minds head for. In fact, other things are unequal; some faculties at Essex stand high in public estimation and some provide the right sort of specialist training for certain individuals, and therefore some students are prepared to put up with the physical shortcomings.

Essex is in need, in urgent need, of a facelift. Thanks to the work of the gardening staff, the grounds are in good condition and the hardness of the architecture has been ameliorated to a certain extent; the view from the west side of the Hexagon Restaurant towards the tower blocks has been considerably improved by a large bed of flowering shrubs; Square Four, with its fountains, hanging baskets and other greenery is, in the summer months, not altogether unattractive. More, much more, needs to be done. The centrepieces in Squares Three and Two are quite ridiculous; indeed the whole central area should receive the attentions of a professional designer. The tower blocks are, of course, the great difficulty and this leads us on to the next consideration, accommodation.

I hope I have made it clear that the University's record in this matter has, from its inception, been unspeakable. Apart from the ugliness and inconvenience of the tower blocks there is the plain fact that a large proportion of the students have only one year out of three on campus, another conclusive proof that the management is totally uninterested in them. Accommodation outside the University varies a good deal. The University-owned premises are generally tolerable and some privately-let diggings are pleasant, but many is the tale I have heard of high rents and wretched facilities. A university is nothing if not an exercise in living together. Moreover, today's students are often living away from home for the first time. It therefore behoves the University to pay considerable attention to this problem.

Two principles should be established. First, every student should have two years on campus. Numbers are not going to rise so new accommodation should be built. The most obvious place for it is Square One which at present exists merely as a shelf on pillars. At a stroke, the bleakest part of the University might become the pleasantest. This would also relieve the strain on the search for diggings outside the campus. Here, the University must strive to improve standards under the terms of a second principle: that students should report on off-campus diggings.

This needs a word of explanation. A student who lives off-campus in his second year finds himself diggings. Perhaps he thinks himself fortunate, until it dawns on him that the rent is extortionate, the plumbing faulty, the heating inadequate, the lights dim, the furniture shoddy and the cooking facilities entirely lacking. He realises he is being exploited, but since he has paid a year's rent in advance out of his grant, what can he do? Nothing, except put up with a bad job and hope for a final year in towers. When his year is up he leaves, thankfully, but takes no further action beyond telling his friends how bad these diggings are. No matter, it is now over. The landlord, for his part, has no need to worry. Diggings are a seller's market and he knows it; next year another greenhorn will put up with what he has to offer.

What can be done? Suppose that after each letting a student goes to the management's Accommodation Office and fills in a form about his diggings. The information could be stored on a computer and perhaps a letter written to the landlord suggesting how things might be improved. At the very least the student would feel he had done something about his bad year and that the management was on his side. I myself believe that such a scheme, if it were carefully organised, would yield results, not at first but over two or three years. The rackrenters could be eliminated, the bad diggings improved, the better landlords commended and all of them given a standard by which to measure themselves. True, it is a seller's market and there are many others, besides University undergraduates, in and around Colchester, who want diggings. Nevertheless, I believe it could be made to work.

Here, in brief, are some pointers in what I think is the right direction, which in the name of charity the University ought to consider.

Yet these things are mere details beside the vital need to redefine and proclaim the ideal of education, the task that was adroitly side-stepped in 1963.

When Lord Butler was Master of Trinity College, Cambridge, he enjoyed the reputation of a great host and a great character. So far as is known he ran the college perfectly well, and for its part the college believed it had made a great catch in having him as Master. Yet what in the world was he to do with education, he, who had never taught or tutored in his life, nor ever written or spoken wisely and profoundly about this subject? No matter. The fundamental aims of a university were not in dispute and if a retired politician looked well in academic dress then he ought to wear it, and if any student were to spend three years in the company of such an imposing figure against a background of Cotswold stone and emerald lawn, how could he possibly say that he had not been educated? Yet not everybody was willing to take form for content; as we have seen, two undergraduates slipped quietly off to London and made their way towards maturity by painful trial and error.

And what was good enough for Cambridge was more than good enough for Essex. If a scarlet-and-gold panjandrum, by courtesy of Hardy Amies, was placed, like a wedding cake, in the middle of a degree-giving ceremony once a year, and if we were all agreed that the fundamental aims of a university were not in dispute, then what more could anyone possibly want? As we have seen, not a few of the first pupils wanted a great deal more.

In 1963, the first chancellor, not the vice-chancellor, should have reminded the world that education is not learning but ethics, and then set out the way in which the first generation of informal youngsters, so obviously bewildered by the world about them, could achieve moral growth while putting facts into their heads. It is still not too late to do so.

Has the institution up the road been, as Sir Humphrey Appleby suggests, a waste of money? Pending some radical improvements I reserve judgement. However, I would suggest that it has done Wivenhoe much good and very little harm.

First and foremost, it has maintained a green belt between Wivenhoe and Colchester, for had it not been founded the two towns would by now have run into each other. Moreover, the Park has been properly maintained with many new trees planted. The public can always wander around, local schools hold sports days there and, for a nominal charge, the University's own facilities can be used by the public.

The public is also welcomed to the artistic scene, both as spectator and performer. The University Library, which holds a fair amount of local material, is used by students other than natives; let me repeat my thanks for the facilities afforded me to research this book, also to the Department of Sociology, which lent me transcripts of conversations with Wivenhovians now dead.

As the *Standard* foretold, the University has brought money to the area. Wivenhoe's shops and public houses have benefited, of course, and many Wivenhovians make money letting their homes, or bits of them, to students. Beech Avenue and Woodland Way, where the houses are considerably larger than any built since the War, were created with dons in mind. The University's

The University of Essex

190. *The University of Essex, with Wivenhoe and the Colne Estuary in the background.*

Photograph by Des Blake

two most southerly tower blocks, Eddington and Bertrand Russell, were originally within the parish boundary and earned us a good deal in rates.

Long before the University opened, the Academic Planning Board thought that two hundred acres would be insufficient and urged that options should be obtained on more land.[65] If the University was merely double its present size it might well have extended southwards, overrunning Wivenhoe Lodge Farm, demolishing farm buildings as it did so. Thanks to its ugliness it is one of the smallest universities in the country. It has not swamped the town; after the stagnant, inter-War years it has socially enhanced it.

The students, considered generally, have changed a good deal over the years. In the sixties and early seventies they were often sullen and arrogant; it seemed that the grants went on for ever and they knew it. Their costume was often bizarre and some of them were incredibly dirty. With the climax of the unrest came Mr. Edward Heath's three-day week and thereafter things gradually changed. The students realised that the world did not owe them a living and are now far pleasanter. Wivenhoe would be a dull place without them.

The senior common room has enriched local societies and organisations to a certain extent, though the dons keep a fairly low profile. They have assisted the Labour Party, of course, one or two are active in The Wivenhoe Society and one at least has acted with The Wivenhoe Players. A University sub-librarian, Mr. Austin Baines, has been a town councillor for many years. I am sure that without academics in the vicinity The Wivenhoe Bookshop would not have opened.

The big yachts boosted not only the town's finances, but its reputation. The Unversity has done the same. Between 1961 and 1980 Wivenhoe was very near a place where social history was being made, albeit sadly and painfully. To be marginally involved in this was to be involved in the social history of the age. Though it never gave us a new identity or purpose, we always had something to talk about.

CHAPTER 10

Who Are These People?

1 Expansion.

"Who are these people, who haven't been in the town five minutes, trying to tell us what to do?"

The question is perennial, and if the town is indigenous and clannish then five minutes represents many years. In the days when the Barrs, Hams, Turners, Saintys, Harveys, Martins and the rest of them all intermarried and everyone knew everyone else's business, it took a long, long time to be accepted and until the end of the Second World War Wivenhoe retained its social integrity. Yet, when the late William Sparrow voiced his concern at the intrusion of the newly-formed Wivenhoe Society it was almost too late to ask the question.

For the crude, hard, vivid, emotional, gossipy, neighbourly way of life that had obtained since Wivenhoe began was disappearing, as it was everywhere else. The New Wivenhovian is cosmopolitan; the idea that he might not belong to the community never crosses his mind. In the sense intended by William Sparrow none of the post-War newcomers, nor indeed their children who were born here, have been in the town longer than five minutes.

Between 1961 and 1970, Essex was the fastest growing county in England and Wales, and Wivenhoe the fastest growing town in Essex. The population shot up by 94.8 per cent, to 5,136, far ahead of the projected figures for 1981 and continued to expand vigorously during the next decade. The post-War years up to 1980 have produced the most radical changes Wivenhoe has known since it was founded.

The town swept northwards. Early in the sixties, The Nook was pulled down and on its site rose The Dale, Bobbitts Way and a close called The Nook. The eastern side of Park Road was built up and Valley Road appeared. The gaps in Manor Road, Ernest Road and Stanley Road were filled in. To the west, Woodland Way and Beech Way stretched up to Wivenhoe Wood; these houses, designed for lecturers and executives, are reasonably large, with decent gardens; Parkwood Avenue, also abutting the wood, comprises small bungalows jammed together. Vine Farm lost its outbuildings and was encircled by the Vine Farm Estate; beside the water tower Heath Road and its ancillaries appeared.

Thus the town expanded, and the Wivenhoe Urban District Council encouraged it to expand, without minding very much how it did so. The house designs, taken from the pattern books of the day, produced genteel, characterless dwellings that could belong to any town in the kingdom. Such are the homes of people who have not been in the town five minutes.

The area between Britannia Crescent and Heath Road was filled in, and too hastily. For in the summer of 1978 large cracks appeared in some of the houses in the Spring Chase Estate, particularly in Vanessa Drive, and the inhabitants feared that their five-year-old properties might collapse altogether. An engineer's report disclosed that the houses had been built on land containing an unpiped stream and household refuse. To those involved, such as Mr. Mick Glozier, who moved to Alresford, it was a harrowing time. Suddenly, the chattel which represented a large part of his personal savings was uninsurable and unsaleable. It seems that Mr. Leslie Kemble was given permission to build before the household refuse had had time to settle. The insurers' action against him was finally heard early in 1986; it was settled out of court for a "not inconsiderable" sum.[1]

Beyond the parish boundary the Dene Park Estate swept over the old gravel pits, up to Farmer Bowes' acres. Linsbrook Developments extended the Heath Road area westwards, but not before it had been challenged by a Broomfield Residents Association. At a public inquiry, in November, 1972, Linsbrook promised that the Lower Lodge Estate should have play areas and the houses be screened from the river. There are one or two open spaces on the estate; the rest have vanished, mockingly, into limbo. On the land below are some diminutive evergreens which I have heard described as "protected weeds".

The Vine Farm Estate moved towards the Elmstead Road; an addition, Broadfields, was built. This, and the houses on the outskirts of Lower Lodge, are in accordance with the Essex Design Guide and far more attractive.

There, for the moment, development halts, with a couple of full stops at either end of the town to keep it in place. At the north, the Broomgrove Infants School opened in September, 1966, and the Broomgrove Junior School in July, 1972. At the east, Millfields School opened in April, 1981.

Land is at a premium in the South of England and Wivenhoe may expand further; meanwhile, it is contained by local government policy and infilling is the order of the day.

The number of houses in Wivenhoe has at least trebled since the late fifties;

Who Are These People?

191. *The Quay, August, 1988.*

Photograph by Terry Weeden

192. *Millfields County Primary School, June, 1988.*

Photograph by Sue Murray, L.R.P.S.

the value of property has soared. Houses on The Quay are worth over fifty times their value thirty years ago. Detached houses in the former slum area of Wivenhoe, now the conservation area, are selling at over six figures. It is pleasant to record that Wivenhovians who once went barefoot, cadged sprats and stood in the dole queue, have retired to homes that are warm, comfortable and valuable, but not that newly-weds cannot afford to live here.

In the year this chapter begins, 1965, the *Colchester Express* recorded the regret of the old folk who no longer knew everyone they met in the stret and the *Essex County Standard* noticed that Wivenhoe was becoming a dormitory town.[2]

These were fair comments. The town needed to recover a sense of community. Not a few Wivenhovians have tried to do something about this over the past twenty-five years with, as we shall see, varying success. First, however, let us look at the threat from industry to our peace and integrity.

Who Are These People?

2 Big Lorries into Small Roads.

A century ago The Avenue was an avenue, a country lane along which there rattled the occasional gig, brewer's dray or carrier's cart. Today, this spinal route contains more cars than it can decently hold and is quite insufficient because it contains many lorries as well.

When the Urban District Council received an application from Forrestt's to build a wharf at the upstream shipyard in 1888, it was delighted.[3] Rightly so; Wivenhoe depended on the new firm. Access was no problem in those days; steel sheeting was brought into the yard by rail and the finished products left by rail or river. The Council was castigated for failing to consider access with regard to the Gliksten's application of 1965, yet excuses can be made. The lorries in those days were smaller and fewer than they are now, and indeed were already bringing steel to the downstream shipyard. Most of the councillors could recall the desperate inter-War years. The shipyard was empty; here was a nice, clean industry that would employ locals. What an opportunity!

Others perceived a danger. Long before the Council had made up its mind, Mrs. Margery Dean invited a number of people to the Old Rectory on Friday, 14th January, 1966, and The Wivenhoe Society was formed.[4]

Mrs. Dean was the moving spirit behind the Society and Mr. George Gale, the national journalist, who had come to Ballast Quay House the previous year with his wife and four young sons, the first chairman. J. Gliksten & Son Ltd., (later absorbed into the large Merediths consortium), wanted to use not only the former shipyard, a ten acre site, but the adjoining twenty-five acres of saltings. The Wivenhoe Society protested and, perhaps because of this, the firm was allowed to use only the shipyard, but might store its timber on the "hard standings" as they were called, the area of concrete let into the saltings upon which the Mulberry Harbour pontoons had been built.[5]

Permission was given in July, 1966; in September work was begun on clearing up the shipyard and adapting it. The White City, crumbling and derelict, was demolished. The thirteen pillars of the huge gantry were brought down with gelignite and oxy-acetylene burners. The *Cap Pilar,* a mere wraith of a vessel, still lay in the dry dock where the big yachts had come to be overhauled and the *Valfreyia* sojourned for the best part of a decade and Naval vessels had been repaired, the very last occupant of Forrestt's dry dock and a sad symbol of the town's former maritime glory. Nor, indeed, did she ever leave it. For Gliksten's had no use for the dock and filled it in. They broke up the *Cap Pilar,* using explosives which on more than one occasion brought out the fire brigade. Not a little of her timber was used in local bread ovens, but her keel, lower frames and garboard planking proved intransigent and were decently entombed in liquid concrete.[6]

193. *The bottleneck at the junction of High Street and Station Road, a daily commonplace.*

Essex County Newspapers

So Gliksten's put their lorries on to the spinal route, which was never built for that purpose; worse, permission for warehousing, once given, remained with the site – the lorries were here for good.

In 1968 Gliksten's sought permission to close the Rowhedge Ferry Road, which passed through the shipyard, on the grounds of public safety, though the real reason was increased efficiency, and tried to close the road before permission had been given. Feelings ran high and the new Wivenhoe Society faced its first big battle when it opposed this closure at two public inquiries.[7]

In October, 1970, it was decided that the road should be closed, but there remained a pedestrian right of way along the route. The firm, foolishly, tried to bar this also. Eventually, the footpath was rerouted behind the new warehouse.[8]

Throughout this affair the Urban District Council did nothing. It is not hard to see why. To people such as Percy Chaney the ironmonger, Betsy Grasby the schoolteacher and William Sparrow who kept *The Rose and Crown*, Gliksten's was the management class. It was not for the the likes of them to question the decisions of a firm whose annual turnover ran into millions of pounds.

Counterpointed with the Rowhedge Ferry Road incident was that of the

Who Are These People?

194. *The gantry and dry dock at the upstream shipyard shortly before they both disappeared.*

Essex County Newspapers

Wivenhoe Wood, whose owner, Mr. Leslie Kemble, wanted to make it into a housing estate. Twenty years earlier the town would have hardly troubled itself about the wood, but the New Wivenhovians recognised it as an amenity and wanted it preserved. Again, the Council sat on the fence. There was a public inquiry early in 1970 and it was decreed that the wood should not be built on; three years later, to its credit, the Urban District Council bought twenty-and-a-half acres of it. All that remained in private ownership was some four-and-a-half acres, (the Eastern Spur), most of which Mr. Kemble's son was allowed to use for building fifteen years later.[9]

It was the same story with *The Falcon*, which, as we have seen, was for centuries an important social venue. It was now running downhill; custom was nominal, the clientele extremely raffish. In May, 1971, the Urban District Council decided to allow the owners, Messrs. Truman, Hanbury, Buxton & Co. Ltd., to replace it with a shop, three cottages, two flats and a maisonette. Calmly, almost absent-mindedly, these men and women who called themselves Wivenhovians voted their most prestigious building into oblivion. Who were these people who *had* been in the town longer than five minutes *not* to look after it more carefully and plan its future more intelligently? The answer is contained in the question. They were inadequate because they were indigenous, unable to see the town in perspective because they were intrinsically part of it. It was the strangers and newcomers who reversed this decision, got up a petition to save the building, had it listed, squashed a further application to rebuild but keep the facade, and finally, after the landlord left in 1975, turned it into three maisonettes.[10]

The Local Government Act of 1974 eliminated the Wivenhoe Urban District Council and the town benefited greatly. As we have seen, its history was chequered and its members hardly able to cope with their responsibilities. They were also too elderly and complacent; one councillor thought it perfectly proper to doze fitfully through meetings and most of their deliberations took place behind closed doors.

Its successor, the Wivenhoe Town Council has, nominally, much less power but I believe that it is nevertheless more effective. What we have is a body which thinks of itself as a pressure group pitted against a remote and hostile Colchester Borough Council. The weapon in the hands of the nine councillors is smaller, but by that token more wieldy. From 1974 onwards the councillors have changed to New Wivenhovians who are better able to perceive and deal with the town's problems.

195. *The entrance to Wivenhoe Wood at the foot of Rosabelle Avenue, December, 1986.*

Photograph by Terry Weeden

Who Are These People?

On the whole, whether a man is Conservative or Labour is not important in the Council Chamber. Yet the parties are vital, for it is they that provide the machinery by which people are induced to stand at all. As it happens, some, such as Mr. Austin Baines, who scored the second highest vote in 1987, are independent.

However, at borough and county level independence is impossible and with only two effective choices before it, the electorate votes for the party rather than the individual. I say "effective" because the Alliance Party, though a force at Colchester, has so far produced only nonsensical candidates for Wivenhoe. This is a pity. With three candidates, the ancient temperamental battle between left and right must surely disappear and the electorate vote not for red, yellow or blue councillors, but for good councillors.

In the summer of 1981, Gliksten's was succeeded by Wivenhoe Port Ltd., created as a subsidiary of Property Associates Ltd., a firm of developers with headquarters in Colchester. Its managing director, Mr. Danny Watts, put his brother, David, in charge of the Wivenhoe operation. Goods other than timber were now imported, and dusty cargoes, such as coal and tapioca, produced a further problem, while the size and number of ships using the wharf increased dramatically, as did those of the lorries. At the same time Whitehead

196. *The coal tips at the upstream shipyard, December, 1986.*

Photograph by Terry Weeden

Harbourmaster, a firm of marine engineers, was succeeded on the same site by Chelmer Cargo Services (Shipping) Ltd., a firm of forwarding agents. Regrettably, the Borough Council gave the newcomer permission for warehousing, so that even more lorries appeared.

The town was now fully aware that these juggernauts, as they scraped round the corner at the top of Station Road, or came to a standstill as they tried to pass each other on the railway bridge, or damaged listed buildings as they fumbled their way down on to Anchor Hill, or drowned conversation and scattered coal or grain dust as they roared slowly up the High Street, were a menace. The former shipyard was the wrong venue for wholesale importing and if this activity could not be moved it had to be contained.

So when Wivenhoe Port Ltd. applied, as it almost immediately did, for permission to build a new warehouse, The Wivenhoe Society was able to make common cause with The Wivenhoe Sailing Club, the newly-formed Wivenhoe Port Action Group and, which would have been unthinkable a decade earlier, the Wivenhoe Town Council. The Port Co-Ordinating Committee was formed; chaired by the reigning mayor, it comprised representatives from these four bodies.[11]

A public inquiry was held in July, 1983, when the Inspector had to consider two appeals by Wivenhoe Port Ltd.: a warehouse next to West Street and a bulk grain storage building on the saltings. Wivenhoe prepared its brief with exemplary thoroughness, but the appellants' barrister, Mr. Michael Barnes, Q.C., undismayed by rows of statistics, staked his client's case on a single throw. A new warehouse, he asserted, would produce no more traffic. To everybody's surprise the Inspector accepted this and allowed one of the two applications, the bulk grain storage building. However, he attached certain conditions. The building must be painted and a tree-planting scheme prepared. It was duly erected; to this day it is innocent of paint and there is not a single tree near it.[12]

In February, 1984, representatives of various Wivenhoe organisations were invited to the Borough Council's Planning Department to discuss "the amelioration of conditions at the Wivenhoe Wharf". A blind; they were invited to see how they would react to the idea of a haul road along the north bank of the Colne. If the haul road were built it is certain that, despite promises to the contrary, lorries would enter Wivenhoe by one route and leave by another, and that industry would follow the road down from The Hythe, factory after factory, and each one the final one, until Wivenhoe and Colchester ran into each other. Wivenhoe was dubious about the idea, but I think we have not heard the last of it.[13]

The next public inquiry was held in January, 1985. Mr. Barnes was again briefed by the appellants, but this time he was faced by another barrister. For The Wivenhoe Preservation Trust, begotten by The Wivenhoe Society, had knocked on every door and raised the necessary £5,000 or so. There were three applications before the Inspector, two pieces of window dressing and the real one: was Wivenhoe Port Ltd. to store coal on the Mulberry Harbour hard standings or not? To everybody's surprise, it was not.[14]

The town was defending itself with increasing vigour; it was also learning how to attack. On 30th November 1984, after numerous local complaints, Wivenhoe Port Ltd. was prosecuted for causing a nuisance with its dusty cargoes and fined £4,000. A second prosecution, on 2nd December, 1987, cost the firm £13,000 and it was threatened with closure if things did not improve. Mr. Glyn Davies, who served Wivenhoe admirably as a town and borough councillor before he left in October, 1986, saw to it that discontinuance, the option of paying Wivenhoe Port Ltd. to go away, was included in the Colne Estuary Study, a policy document compiled by a large group of councillors and civil servants. It was he, too, who successfully agitated for a restriction on lorry movements at night.[15]

The value of discontinuance is that it openly acknowledges the mistake of 1966; the upstream shipyard is the wrong place for an industry that produces lorries. It will never be implemented, for besides the gargantuan expense of compensation the problem is solving itself; the cargo boats are getting too big for the Colne and before the century is out they may well disappear. Property Associates Ltd. knows this; on 29th January, 1988, it submitted a planning application for 375 houses on the upstream site.[16]

3 Making the Party Go.

I now consider the social life of Wivenhoe over the past twenty-three years and in particular the quest for a social base to serve a community that is not only much larger but split wide apart.

For Broadfields and Lower Lodge in the north know little of The Quay and the High Street, and the spinal route, a danger at every hour of the day and night, sunders east from west. Not even the tribalism of Upstreet and Downstreet remains to bind this amorphous wilderness of undigested housing into a whole.

Nevertheless, the town's social life, though scattered, is substantial. Most of the visible amenities are in the lower part of Wivenhoe where life is relatively villagey. The shops that once fringed East Street and West Street have almost all disappeared. Now the High Street has to compete with the transformed Co-operative Stores at the top, the supermarket at The Cross, and Colchester. It does so with reasonable success; only in the past few years have any shops in the High Street, whose proprietors worked properly, succumbed. Moreover, the number of shop premises has hardly diminished. The only notable casualty is 1, Anchor Hill, which was converted into a private house in 1987-88.

197. *The Quay, 1984.*

Photograph by Doug White

Four public houses have closed during the past thirty-five years: *The Shipwright's Arms*(1954), *The Grosvenor Hotel*(1968), *The Falcon*(1975) and *The Brewery Tavern*(1986). Now we have seven, exactly a third of the number a century ago, yet the facts are deceptive, for not only do four of the town's sporting clubs possess licensed bars but the surviving public houses are better patronised. In 1982-83, *The Black Buoy* united three small rooms and practically doubled its floorspace, and its clientele, mostly youngsters, immediately expanded to fill the space available for its reception.

It is impossible to list or number the sporting, recreational, educational, political, conservational, charitable and social societies in the town because they are always changing and some are too exiguous to mention, but there are at least sixty.

The sporting scene is dominated by the dramatic rise of the Wivenhoe Rangers, who in 1974 readopted their former title, The Wivenhoe Town Football Club. In 1965 they were using the unsatisfactory slope of the King

George V Playing Fields. An enterprising urban district council would have secured a pitch-sized section of Spion Kop before it disappeared. An unenterprising council merely added a drab changing room to the Playing Fields. However, in 1977 an enterprising club bought a carrot field at Broad Lane, off the Elmstead Road, for £2,500 and with grants built itself a clubhouse. In the following season it moved up to the Essex Senior League. To these premises were later added floodlights, a grandstand and a barrier round the pitch with a turnstile.[17]

Meanwhile, the club has scaled the amateur ladder, league by league, and attracted players from all over the Colchester area. The glories of the 1987-88 season, the best in its history, included 105 goals and competing for the Football Association Cup. Though still an amateur club, professional status, in Football League Division Four, is now only two rungs away and the players already think in professional terms, and off the field wear a club tie and blazer. There is talk of Colchester United, deprived of its Layer Road pitch, coming to play at Wivenhoe; there is talk of The Wivenhoe Town Football Club playing Colchester United. This tremendous achievement slightly divorces the club from the town. For of the sixteen players from which the First Team is drawn, only three or four are Wivenhovians; the same goes for the Reserve Team. However, there is also a Sunday team composed mostly of locals.

The Cricket, Sailing and Bowls Clubs all remain fully integrated. The first-named, with fifty to sixty players out of a membership of about three hundred, fields three teams, besides a Wednesday night team that plays friendly matches. The original clubhouse was recently refurbished and extended at a cost of £20,000. The 250 or so members of the Sailing Club own sixty to seventy boats, ranging from sailing dinghies to thirty foot sailing cruisers. The premises, in a sail loft on The Quay, are homely and pleasant, but the Club would like to build new ones, preferably on the downstream shipyard site. As I write this, The Bowls Club is extending its premises for the third time since the present clubhouse was built in about 1978. Some 130 people play on six rinks from May to September.[18]

At the beginning of the century church parade was a well-nigh compulsory social ritual with a religious flavour; today, four denominations attract congregations they cannot compel, but are also social nuclei.

When the Rev. Douglas Gaye, rector of St. Mary's from 1960 to 1976, left Wivenhoe the Elizabethan Settlement came to an end. His successor, the Rev. Stephen Hardie, knew that changes had to be made. Accordingly, he and his parochial church council decided to hold the principal Sunday morning services an hour earlier, and conduct christenings during church services.[19]

In 1987, there were some physical changes. John Gurdon Rebow's pitch pine compartments, which stretched to the walls of the interior, were shortened and made free-standing; the nave was levelled and carpeted; a kitchen unit and lavatories were added on at the west end. Some people have found these changes distasteful, the last two almost blasphemous. I suggest they are for the best. We have noticed earlier reorganisations of the church interior, both imposed on the congregation and both, if the cruel truth be told, social rather than religious exercises. This one is for the benefit of people who go to church because they are members of it.

The services have also changed. Series II, in fact, made its appearance during the interregnum between the two rectors; in September, 1981, the new prayer book was formally adopted. The church music was also revivified and the loudest singing voice is invariably the rector's own trained baritone which is also heard in The Gilbert and Sullivan Society. His Sunday morning service attracts up to 150, which he thinks is not particularly good, and a traditional evensong about forty.

Around this church cluster the usual groups: the Choir, the Bellringers, about half of whom worship at St. Mary's, Toddlers, Infants, Junior Church, a Youth Group which meets once a fortnight and a Wives Group shared with the other denominations.

In the middle fifties, the Congregational minister, the Rev. E. J. E. Briggs, decided that the chapel in Quay Street was no longer adequate. A parcel of land off the High Street was bought for the site of a new one and a summerhouse which had belonged to Wivenhoe Hall became the new manse. In 1960, Mr. Briggs was succeeded by a vigorous feminist with degrees in science and theology, who rode to hounds and had served in the Israeli Army. Miss Clementina Gordon sailed into Wivenhoe on a trimaran, realised a long-standing ambition by being ordained and, with her usual energy, saw to it that a new chapel was built. It was dedicated on 14th July, 1962. Next to it is a church hall used by scouts, guides, brownies, a Junior Church and Youth Club. The present pastor, the Rev. Christopher J. Damp, attracts congregations of about seventy to his Sunday morning services.[20]

While this new chapel was a-building, the Congregationalists worshipped for a short while at the Methodist Church, which in 1959 had almost closed for lack of support. However, it was now beginning to revive and in 1966 plans were drawn up for a thorough reorganisation of the building, with the altar moved from the east to the west end, and meeting rooms, kitchens and lavatories added on. This work was begun in 1970. Now the church is one of six served by the Rev. J. W. R. Robinson, and has its own Luncheon Club, playgroup, Sunday School and Badminton Club. About fifty to sixty people attend a monthly family service.[21]

In 1908 the first mass since the Reformation was celebrated in Brightlingsea and at some time after the Second World War a priest from that parish began to

Who Are These People?

visit Wivenhoe regularly. The first venue was the Old School in the High Street, but on 20th April, 1967, the small Roman Catholic Church of St. Monica was opened off De Vere Lane. About a hundred people attend Mass there every Sunday, celebrated by a priest from Brightlingsea. The Co-Workers of Mother Teresa, though ecumenical, are attached to this church.[22]

Thus, in the course of two decades, our churches have become places where people worship in contemporary English, talk in normal tones, laugh, eat and excrete. And no fire falls from Heaven. A century ago they were at loggerheads; since 1973 they have been united by an ecumenical service. Here, if ever there was one, is the subject for a sociology thesis.

There was also, in the post-War years, a lone voice that cried in the wilderness. If you bought groceries at the Alma Stores in the mid-fifties the conversation went something like this:

"Good afternoon. May I have half a pound of butter, please?"

"Half a pound of butter. Praise the Lord".

"... and two packets of tea ..."

"Two packets of tea. Hallelujah".

"... and a dozen eggs".

"A dozen eggs. Jesus saves".

So people stopped going to the Alma Stores and its proprietor was free to wander round Wivenhoe and Colchester, playing hymns on a piano accordion and handing out tracts to a faintly embarrassed but totally uninterested public.

198. *Black Buoy Hill. In the foreground is the Gables Cafe, the first home of The Nottage Institute, with Mr. Terence Endean's butcher's shop beyond it and in the background the Alma Stores, once The Live And Let Live public house. All these shops have now closed.*

Essex County Newspapers

Hyman Goldstein, the son of a Polish-Jewish enamel dealer, grew up in the East End of London and was, initially, a barrow boy. He enlisted as a soldier in the Second World War and was then converted to Christianity. After the War he changed his name to Paul St. John Johnstone, married the daughter of a Welsh clergyman, who eventually left him, joined the Plymouth Brethren, broke with them, and came to Essex where he failed as a shopkeeper at Braintree, St. Osyth and Wivenhoe. He had several nicknames, including "Wonk" and, particularly, "Holy Joe". For the last ten years of his life he was joined by Alexander McLeod, a Tynesider, and they lived and worked together.[23]

Besides the sporting and religious giants, a range of other groups exist for particular ages and interests.

Youth is well served by a network of Scout and Guide groups; the elderly, who easily feel lost in the transformed Wivenhoe, are cared for by The Over 60's Club, Senior Citizens, Meals on Wheels and others. Hardy perennials, such as the British Legion, formed soon after the First World War, and the Women's Institute, flourish. In 1975 the latter held a competition for a Wivenhoe sign, which was won by Dr. Walter Radcliffe. It incorporates his Wivenhoe One Design, a wyvern bird, (which has actually no connection with the town), and an oyster; it stands at the entrance to the King George V Playing Fields.

These activities and others not yet mentioned, are the outward signs of a thriving community; we now examine the efforts which have been made to bind this community together.

After the demise of the Foresters' Hall, (which was finally converted into housing in 1987-88), the town was thrown back on the disused Boys' School, but in 1963 the Urban District Council, using the profits from the sale of the waterworks and urged on by Councillor William Loveless, built the present public hall, while the School was demolished to make way for a public library. The Council could hardly have done less; it should have done a great deal more, for the hall is drab, unimaginatively designed, without parking space, badly sited and, above all, too small. Would that the Council had bought a slice of Spion Kop and built a hall for three thousand Wivenhovians, but with room to extend that hall and its facilities when the population doubled, as it was obvious it would. As it is, we have a bleak main hall and a couple of committee rooms that the University of Essex wouldn't throw to a student. Moreover, this inadequate building stands in the way of providing something that is adequate. Nevertheless, the William Loveless Hall is a focal point in our social lives. The October Civic Service is followed by a reception at which ladies wear hats and visiting nabobs chains of office; the front of the stage is decorated with potted plants and brownies pour out glasses of wine; the mayor makes a speech in which he publicly thanks the people who have made the party go. The Annual

Who Are These People?

Town Council meeting in May, to which everybody is invited, used to be dull, but in 1988, Councillor Peter Hill, as mayor, turned it into a pleasant social occasion at which the societies put up stalls.

There was a Badminton Club at the William Loveless Hall almost as soon as it opened, in September, 1963, but it has never fulfilled its potential because there is only room for a single pitch in the main hall and hardly enough height for that. So the best players in the town go elsewhere.[24]

Drama is also restricted, as the Wivenhoe Players discovered in 1968. For the stage is a long, narrow shelf which is difficult to light, and the acoustics are poor, and when an extension is added the hall seats only 130.

In 1981, the centenary of the year in which the *Chloris* was launched, a Gilbert and Sullivan Society was formed. It added more rostra to the sides of the stage and set itself a high standard of design, even making its own costumes. A third group which started life at the William Loveless Hall is Brian Critchley's Palace of Varieties, a music hall that covers a wide range of styles and periods.[25]

The William Loveless Hall is inadequate, but it is in constant use. People go there to vote, dance, give blood, play bridge, ice cakes, perform aerobics and drink the bride's health.

199. *The Wivenhoe Players take their curtain call at the William Loveless Hall after Strike Happy, a comedy they performed in April, 1985. Left to right: Sue Smith, Val Murray, Shirley Taussig, John Rayner, Paddy Bane, Lionel Bryant, Stevie Belcher, Nigel Walford and Debbie Allcock.*

Photograph by Sue Murray, L.R.P.S

Three years after it opened, another social centre was created, primarily for the town's artistic colony.

The first artists to settle here, in 1945, were Denis Wirth-Miller and Richard Chopping, who bought The Storehouse on The Quay. Denis Wirth-Miller's forte is studies of marshland, vast, menacing landscapes in which the impersonal cruelty of nature is very apparent. He is the first living artist to sell a picture to H.M. The Queen. Richard Chopping uses tempera to create delicately detailed trompe d'oeils; his oeuvre includes dust-covers for Ian Fleming's James Bond novels. He has taught at the Colchester Institute, the Central School of Art and The Royal College of Art.

In 1959, Roy Cross, who once taught art to John Lennon and Paul McCartney, moved to Wivenhoe and in that year married a fellow-artist, Gail Mills. He painted semi-abstract landscapes and nude lovers, with primary reds and blues predominating; she, local scenes and portraits.

In 1962, John and Pamela Dan came to live at 56, High Street, a small, timber-framed cottage set back from the road. He, the son of a Wivenhovian,

200. *A group of Wivenhoe artists outside The Black Buoy public house at some time in the sixties. Standing: (left to right), Michael Heard, Pamela Dan, John ---, Gail Cross and Tony Young. Sitting: (left to right), Alan Taylor, Roy Cross and John Dan.*

Loaned by Mrs. Pamela Dan

was a potter and taught at the Braintree College of Further Education. He produced plates with naked, nubile girls tucked up on them, also vast phallic pots. John Dan died in 1983. Pamela Dan paints intricate studies of gorse and bracken, also cows.

Michael Heard, who arrived in 1964, sells his watercolours of the Colne in local shops, and Tony Young, who came the following year, draws portrait heads and paints austerely coloured studies of emaciated nudes. Ted Atkinson, a sculptor who lives in De Vere Close, has won kudos at various times and places; in 1988 he was chosen to represent British art in Australia.

From 1970 to 1974, John Doubleday, an alumnus of Stowe and Goldsmith's College, who sculpts, mostly in bronze, and also draws and paints, lived at 10, Alma Street. Here he created heads of archaic warriors, strangely mutilated, also heads on poles, "mace figures" as he calls them, while building up a national and international reputation as a portraitist. His commissions included busts of Sir Maurice Bowra, Archbishop Ramsay, Lord Louis Mountbatten and Prince Philip. In 1972, he organised the Wivenhoe Festival, the first and last of its kind, with exhibitions at a number of private houses, one of which honoured a mythical Victorian poet, Gabriel Winthrope.

Ernie Turner, the brother of John Turner, the *Britannia* mastheadman, retired from his job, as a shipwright at Cook's, in 1964, and started painting in oils on hardboard. His pictures, of local boats and riverside scenes, executed in cheerful colours and innocent of perspective, are a good-humoured and very personal evocation of an environment.

These were the best known of the Wivenhoe artists. They exhibited locally, especially at *The Brewery Tavern*, which was run for some years by Roy Cross's elder brother, Jack.

It was only logical that sooner or later all this talent would be brought together under one roof. The impetus came from Ballast Quay, for even as George Gale was helping to found The Wivenhoe Society, he was also planning to create an arts club in the former stables and coach-house of his new home, where Wivenhoe could meet the dons from the new University and he could entertain his friends.[26]

These outbuildings form three sides of a square. Two of these wings became an L-shaped club, with a bar and exhibition gallery in one of them, and a kitchen, lavatories and snooker table in the other. The third was converted into a bungalow for Mr. Gale's mother. On 15th October, 1966, the Rt. Hon. Edward Heath, M.P. opened the Wivenhoe Arts Club.[27]

John and Pamela Dan, Jack, Roy and Gail Cross, Tony Young and Michael Heard were all long-serving members of this club. It also attracted people from the larger new houses in the town, a convivial don or two, and some locals, including Mr. David Clarke, the curator of the Castle Museum, and Dr. and

201. *The Wivenhoe Arts Club, September, 1971. One of the very few existing photographs of this organisation. I am unable to identify the two artists or members.*

East Anglian Daily Times

Mrs. William Dean. George Gale was the first chairman of the club, Jack Cross the first secretary.

The visual arts came foremost, but there were dances, quizzes, jumble sales, and entertainments of various kinds. The annual *Gallery Gaities*, a home talent night, usually included specially written verses by David Clarke and a skit, written and directed by Jack Cross, which sent up, yet deferred to, the management.

The opening years were rowdy and some undesirable elements had to be ejected; then the enterprise settled down as an arts and social club for two hundred people and as such it remained. As far as this went it was pleasant enough, but for its own sake and that of the town it should have gone much further. The courtyard within the outbuildings should have been given a roof and turned into an assembly hall, while Farmer Bowes next door would have surely sold some of his own outbuildings for squash courts and the like.

The ostensible reason for this lack of progress was that George Gale would never give the club a lease of more than one year. The members knew this perfectly well; they should have pressed for expansion or gone elsewhere. They never did. The lethargy of the sixties hung heavily over this establishment.

Yet the club held a many a good exhibition. I remember one of cartoons, organised by George Gale himself; almost every national newspaper, and many local ones, were represented, while at one end there loomed Gerald Scarfe's Chairman Mao in the likeness of a club armchair.

Towards the end of the seventies the club went into a decline. The funds were eroded by amateur barmen who consumed the alcohol on the premises into the small hours without paying for it. The members were vaguely aware of this but seemed not to mind and things drifted gently on until Mr. Gale, who now wanted to leave Wivenhoe, decided to close. The relationship between landlord and tenants, always slightly uneasy, now flared into open rebellion as the peasants refused to dance to the squire's tune. Mr. Gale moved to Tattingstone, but his club remained for a while until his successor as landlord managed to oust it on the pretext of turning the buildings into a health resort.

Deprived of premises, the club might have expanded into new ones. Instead, it toyed vaguely with the idea of moving into the basement of the Co-operative Supermarket and finally expired with a party and exhibition at the Old Rectory on Saturday, 24th March, 1984. Thus ended the Wivehoe Arts Club, as vague and amiable as anything that ever came out of the sixties.

Meanwhile, four months after the schoolchildren had left Phillip Road, in July, 1971, the former school became, under the aegis of the County Council, a centre for sport and education. A thousand people go there every week for typing, knitting, art, dressmaking, pottery, calligraphy, popmobility, keep fit, yoga, creative writing and French, to name a few of its multitudinous activities. Children play tennis, pool, snooker, darts and five-a-side football, and 280 learn dancing.

An attempt was soon made to fill the gap left by the Wivenhoe Arts Club. A Wivenhoe Community Association Steering Committee was formed, which met for the first time on 21st June, 1984, under the aegis of the Town Council. Before it, was a report drawn up by a Wivenhoe Community Centre Exploratory Working Committee which had discovered three suitable sites: the Elmstead Road, the William Loveless Hall and the King George V Playing Fields, The committee was torn almost equally between the three. Eventually, the Wivenhoe Community Association was formed, chaired by Councillor Peter Hill, on 30th January, 1985. A young architect called Terry Vanner produced plans for extending the William Loveless Hall, taking in the two policemen's cottages nearby and building another large hall behind them, a sensible idea, yet as I write this the trail, once again, has gone cold. In three years the association that was formed to bind the town together, has done no more than produce a newsletter, organise some public activities and add carpets and curtains to the William Loveless Hall. So the ball has been thrown back to the Town Council and the former exploratory working party has been resurrected and, who knows, it might do something . . . ?

4 The End of an Aeon.

It was probably the water that attracted the first settlers to Wivenhoe. By Elizabethan times the town was a thriving port and with the big yachts came a century of prestige. Then there was a gradual decline and the story of the present century is that of the Wivenhovian turning, year by year, from a water animal into a land animal. Indeed, it has been the story of the Colne generally, as one by one the shipyards have closed down.

On 19th September, 1986, the town lost Cook's. Up to the end of the sixties this firm had produced a stream of tugs, motor launches, dumb lighters and pontoons, with here and there something more esoteric, such as a sand hopper or grab dredger. In the seventies the orders were fewer but larger, with dredgers and coasters predominating, and thus it continued into the eighties, save that now there were gaps in the orders and a constant fear they would run out. There were rumours of closure, but then an order would come along, such as for the *Buffalo Express* and *Zebu Express*, which loomed up over the shipyard, their vast interiors stuffed with steel cattle pens for the transportation

202. *Cook's largest shed, empty and derelict after the closure of the shipyard.*

Photograph by Des Blake, 4th December, 1986

Who Are These People?

203. *One of the downstream shipyard's final commissions.*

Essex County Newspapers

of unfortunate livestock somewhere on the other side of the equator. It was a happy day when the Jubilee Trust commissioned the 140 ton *Lord Nelson*, a square-rigged schooner specially designed for physically handicapped sailors and indeed the largest sailing boat to be built in this country for seventy-five years. She was launched in October, 1985; early in the new year the Duke of York, as patron of the Trust, paid her a visit while she was fitting out. Here was something to recall the great old days and once again reflect honour on the town. Here, also, was a fitting note on which to end the long history of large-scale professional boatbuilding at Wivenhoe, for it was now but a few months away. The blow fell in May, 1986. Just before the *Lord Nelson* set off for Southampton, Cook's went into voluntary liquidation.[28]

And nothing very unusual in that, you will think, for if this polyglot history has any theme at all it is the unreliability of the boatbuilding industry. Yet this occasion was different. No grandee installed a new manager; no tug-building enterprise from the Thames bought the place up and started again, for boats can now be built much more profitably at places such as Taiwan and Korea where there are no trade unions.

343

Over half the eighty or ninety jobs were lost in May; the firm, with a little work in hand, struggled on. At the end of August six men were engaged in finishing off the very last ship to be launched at Cook's, the dredger *Kilbourne*, destined for the Southern Iceland fisheries; in September the yard finally closed.[29]

Friday, 19th September, 1986. The date should be remembered, not because

204. *The Quay, opposite Wilkin's warehouse.*

Essex County Newspapers

it marked the end of a boatbuilding firm, but because it marked the end of Wivenhoe's large-scale professional engagement with the water. It was the end of an aeon.

The end of an aeon – and Wivenhoe hardly noticed, so thoroughly had it forgotten its maritime past.

Yet the land animal still trails a toe in the water. If you want a boat designed, go to David Cannell, whose drawing-board is situated on the ground floor of the old Congregational Church. If you want a boat built go to Guy Harding, who is waiting in the middle of The Quay to assemble his team of craftsmen for the man who wants a wooden yacht, or to Colin Scattergood whose premises are but a stone's throw away from the old upstream shipyard. Wood still has the edge on fibreglass in the racing world, so Malcolm Goodwin, who operates from custom-built premises in St. John's Street, has built 220 sailing dinghies in the past ten years. He used to make *Hornets*, but now the demand is for *Fireballs*, which he exports all over the world. Some, in the Forrestt's tradition, go in the form of do-it-yourself kits in crates; others are towed away on trailers.[30] The fresh fish sold at Ken Green's shop in West Street, and at the fish-and-chip shop run by his cousin, Brian Green, in East Street, are caught by the four fishing boats that still ply full-time from The Quay. Cargo vessels, as large as the Colne can decently hold, glide majestically up and down at high tide, and at night the throb of machinery at the Wivenhoe and Rowhedge ports, and the brilliant lights, indicate that we are still linked with Belgium, Holland and Scandinavia.

One day in late May, 1982, I went for a trip on the 22 ton *CK 399*, a fishing vessel moored at The Quay, to see for myself how, and indeed if, the contemporary Wivenhovian makes a living from the sea.

I joined the boat at 10 a.m. on an overcast, slightly chilly day, as she was being refuelled by a lorry. A day's trip uses about forty-five gallons of oil. On this particular one the owner, Richard Jacobs, intended to fish specifically for Dover soles and he carried three trawling nets. Two of them could be lowered simultaneously from metal booms on either side of the mast; the third, not used on this occasion, was in the stern.

It took the boat two-and-a-half hours to motor down the Colne to the East Swin, a point some seven or eight miles off the Clacton to Felixstowe coast. Here, the trawling began. The two nets were raised up to the booms and then the booms themselves gently descended until they jutted out at right angles from the boat, and the nets disappeared.

All this was done by pressing a button. Externally, apart from the absence of sails, the *CK 399* is not unlike the smacks Wivenhovians were using a century ago, but in fact she is a sophisticated box of tricks worth the best part of £100,000. Continuous chart readings were provided by Decca equipment, while radar told Mr. Jacobs his exact distance from the seabed and if there were any fish about. There is still plenty of manual work aboard a fishing smack, but the ancient backbreaking toil has gone. Only a crew of two are needed. Richard Jacobs had an assistant called Terry. Their conversation was minimal; the two men knew what to do and got on with it.

After ninety minutes the booms were raised and the nets hauled in. The ends were untied and a shower of shells, starfish, crabs and debris was released on to the deck, with soles and other fish. It was a small catch. Soles above a certain size were retained, others thrown overboard.

In all, six hauls were made. Apart from the soles, some bass and dabs appeared, also large crabs. The last haul produced the iron stock of an old anchor, quite a common find in this area.

At about 9.25 p.m. the fishing smack made for home. By now the wind had freshened and the vessel buffeted its way through waves that broke over her. Just before midnight we reached The Quay. The fish were landed and packed with ice at Ken Green's factory in East Street. My host generously gave me a plastic carrier bag full of fish.

The seas are grossly overfished and a fishing smack is hard put to compete with the giant fishing vessels. Mr. Jacobs thought that this particular trip had just about broken even, because he had £50 worth of bass aboard. He had been fishing for twenty years, ever since he had left school and he loved the independence. It was all he had done; it was all he wanted to do.

On 16th December, 1986, there was an auction at Cook's Shipyard. Soon afterwards, the cranes fell from their plinths and every piece of metal that might be sold for scrap had disappeared. All that remained was a rubble-strewn wilderness.

Who would buy it? Throughout 1987 rumour was rife and in the spring of 1988 it was disclosed that the property had been bought by Bumble International, a company based in the Channel Islands, and resold to the Zurich Group. Bumble sent in its asset strippers to tear down the metal sheds put up by Vospers', but after a pitched battle with Zurich retired, and Zurich submitted an application to demolish the old sheds, together with an outline application for a housing estate.[31]

Then in January, 1989, Anglian Water announced that it wanted to build a surge barrier across the Colne at the Cook's site in order to prevent the lower part of the town from floods. When we know whether it will actually do so, Zurich will surely submit its planning application.

Meanwhile, at the upper end of The Quay, Danny Watts had made his opening bid for securing the maximum profit from the former shipyard and adjacent saltings.[32]

His planning application was a scheme for 375 houses and a marina for very small craft. This estate would have created mammoth traffic jams in the High

Street. To the marina, a few inches of fetid water, would have come amateur yachtsmen, content to bob up and down at weekends on fibreglass bottoms among a litter of plastic bottles and crisp packets. However, the Wivenhoe Town Council and The Wivenhoe Society considered the application with straight faces and listed its innumerable failings. Before it reached the Planning Committee in Colchester it was withdrawn.

The next bid comprised two, mutually incompatible, applications, one for residential development on the former shipyard and hard standings, the other to extend the port. Which one of these was a blind and which the real one is still a matter of controversy. My own theory is that Mr. Watts was simply asking Wivenhoe to tell him which of the two it preferred. After the Borough had failed to determine either application within the statutory period, Mr. Watts took both of them to appeal, and accordingly a public inquiry was held in December, 1988. On this occasion the one voice able to cope with the acoustics of the William Loveless Hall was that of the solicitor who appeared as a barrister for The Wivenhoe Society, The Wivenhoe Preservation Trust, The Wivenhoe Sailing Club and The Wivenhoe Town Council, Mr. A. Peel, and he certainly presented his case extremely well. In the event the Minister decided that . . .

And what the Minister decided may be known to you who read this history, but not to me, for as I write this the Minister has not yet made up his mind and it is time to take this final chapter to the printers.

However, I do know that several Wivenhovians will fight hard and effectively for the very best development upstream and downstream. I must name two of them. Whatever finally appears will owe a great deal to the professional expertise of Mrs. Margaret Dunne, a former town councillor who used to work in the Borough Council's Planning Department, and the unflagging and single-minded zeal of Mrs. Lalla Hughes.

A compromise it will be, can only be. Two and three centuries ago men built by instinct, putting up houses and warehouses whenever and wherever it was convenient so to do. The idea that Wivenhoe was beautiful never crossed their minds. Now The Quay is to be topped and tailed by men who, however carefully they mimic what has gone before, must, with drawing-boards in front of them, build self-consciously. Downstream, with a panorama of the river restored to us and the river wall reinstated on the river bank, we may like what comes better than what has been there since 1940. Upstream, the haggling for something reasonably acceptable will be long and loud; we must prepare for a long war of attrition.

Are we, as a community, capable of fighting it?

We have seen that a century ago the town was run by the male grandees and leading tradesmen, for everyone else was tacitly excluded by ignorance,

205. and 206. *Two identical views of West Street, ancient and modern, the former indicating how it ought to be sympathetically restored.*

Left: Essex County Newspapers   Right: Photograph by G. Martin

poverty, sex or social status. The man in the shipyard, the man aboard the big yacht, would have blushed to think of taking an effective part in local government; it was not his place to do so.

Yet we have seen that even then local government, that sophisticated system of councils with all their ramifications, at parish, borough and county level, was quietly, organically, growing and already the man up at the Big House counting for less and less with each passing year. Now the man up at the Big House has gone, indeed so has the house, with only a few yards of boundary wall to mark the spot where he lived and reigned.

We can get along very well without him, for are we not, most of us, rich, healthy, literate, leisured, enfranchised and, above all, properly informed, (or capable of being properly informed)?

Yet the plain fact is that no greater proportion of the community takes an effective and unselfish interest in the future of the town than did so in the days when the big yachts lay at the river wall.

Wivenhoe will soon, most likely, possess two more housing estates, which will stand where Wivenhovians for centuries built boats. To ensure that these are of the highest possible standard we must invoke local government, by lobbying councillors, writing letters to councils, inspecting plans, calling public meetings. And if a large enough number of us are involved, of the highest possible standard those estates will surely be.

How many people *are* involved?

As far as local government is concerned, the average citizen is agnostic. All he knows is that a certain power, outside himself, which he calls "They", digs holes in the road, paints yellow lines along the road and puts up traffic signs beside the road. The power is probably benevolent; but it is inscrutable. Nothing is known about it; nothing can be known. It is "They" who will build those two estates.

Most of those who claim to understand local government are fatalists. They are aware of a power wielded by creatures not unlike themselves, but creatures inimical to the comfort and security of the community. Even a little pub-going will acquaint you with elected officials so idle and foolish, and paid officials so stewed in corruption, and both so hand in glove with the developers, that opposition is futile. A holocaust is surely on the way and we may as well have another round of drinks before it arrives.

Such are the general attitudes to the machine which man has created with his own hands for his own use but with this machine comes an implied obligation to understand and use it. Yet for the most part the machine is unknown, unused or unloved. It is over fifty years since loyal retainers bore Charles Gooch the Elder to his grave and still we have not learned the necessary art of living without the grandees. What percentage of the electorate ever bothers to vote in a local election?

The developers want to develop. Of course they do. It is as much their nature to develop, as it is the nature of fish to swim. It is also the nature of people to need houses.

And these developers are one half of what ought to be a healthy dialectic. The other half is composed of Wivenhovians. The technical owners of the two old shipyards are confronted by the moral owners who, acknowledging the need for houses, not just here, but in the country as a whole, must press for the best possible houses.

Yet how many of us are doing so? One in a hundred? Developers may be greedy men, but their Greed is never, never, never worse than our Sloth.

Finally, what about the phantom community centre that has hovered benignly over the town for a hundred years? As it happens, we now have plenty of social and sporting facilities. Do we really need it?

As we have seen, most of the improvements made in Wivenhoe down the centuries occurred for one of four reasons: the self-interested whim of a grandee, such as the workhouse and the restoration of St. Mary's Church in 1860; a desire to score off opponents, such as the National School and the first Methodist Chapel; money-making, such as street lighting and the railway; and dire and long-standing necessity, such as made-up roads and proper sewerage. As I write this, Wivenhoe needs, for its nine thousand inhabitants, a sports and social centre. There is a need for this, but not a crying, desperate need. If we have it, it will provide a focal point for the town and promote its physical and social well-being; if we don't have it . . . we will, in truth, hardly miss it. All the better reason for building it. For if a grandee reached into his pocket and gave us The John Gurdon Rebow Recreation and Pleasure Hall; or if it were built only because a sizeable faction in the town was determined that it should not be built, or if it were built because a hundred moderately rich men wanted to become excessively rich; or it were built to fend off open insurrection; then, morally speaking, it would not so much fulfil a need as beg a question.

Let us, for once, do better than previous generations and not be prodded into action. The Terry Vanner plan for the High Street would do, but better still would be a skilful adaptation of a single bay of the Gliksten's warehouse or the warehouse built after the 1983 public inquiry, buildings likely to become redundant before very long. Here, within smelling distance of river mud, let us create a complex with squash courts, committee rooms and a bar, and one huge indoor space which will serve for several games of badminton, spectacular theatricals and, on one glorious and never-to-be-forgotten night, the venue where several thousand Wivenhovians will welcome in the new century.

Let us, who live in these years of plenty, with their riches, leisure and opportunities, be aware of their goodness, not wait for our grandchildren to name them as such. Who are these people? Why, New Wivenhovians who, freed from the dirt, misery and poverty of every preceding age, were as happy as the Old Wivenhovians who struck their happiness out of the dirt, misery and poverty around them, New Wivenhovians who, when offered a simple opportunity to improve their town seized it and in so doing created more happiness for themselves and bequeathed it to their successors.

APPENDIX A

Witchcraft

There was a general belief in magic up until recent times. The *Calendar of Assize Records* informs us that in the reign of the first Queen Elizabeth, Edmund Morell of Fingringhoe was indicted at Witham on 27th July, 1584, for practising magic, by which means it was alleged he had burnt a barn, a stable, a cartload of hay, a waggon and horses, and several domestic utensils, all belonging to the rector, Edmund Burgess, and further had made the rector ill for six months. He was found guilty on the first count.

Such cases were fairly common at this time, but not until the following century was there a wholesale witch hunt in this country. In fact, England has a good record in this respect compared to, say, Germany or Scotland, but in the years at the end of the Civil War there was a brief spate of witch-hunting, mostly in Essex and Suffolk, and mostly under the supervision of a self-styled Witchfinder-General from Manningtree called Matthew Hopkins, who flourished from 1644 to 1647.

For a substantial fee of twenty shillings this worthy nosed out witches just as the Colchester Borough Council finds vermin, and as successfully. At the Chelmsford Assizes of 1645, thirty-six women were charged with witchcraft. Of these, nineteen were hanged, nine died of gaol fever, six were still in prison three years later, one was released after turning king's evidence and one acquitted altogether. All but one of the thirty-six came from villages within a fifteen mile radius of Manningtree.

Wivenhoe supplied two of the victims, Alice Dixon, a widow who was accused of killing Thomas Mumford, which accusation was endorsed by Margaret Mumford, presumably his widow and therefore biased, and Mary Johnson, a spinster, who was accused by no fewer than four ladies of entertaining three evil spirits, two in the likeness of rats and the other in the likeness of a mouse. Alice Dixon was hanged at Chelmsford, Mary Johnson imprisoned there for at least three years. (See *Witch Hunting and Witch Trials, collected and edited by V. L'Estrange Ewen, (1929), Kegan, Paul, Trubner & Co. Ltd.,* page 226 and Appendix 1.)

As a tailpiece to this subject I refer you to Jane Barr, who died on 2nd September, 1893, from opium. "Though it would appear incredible in the present age", said the *Essex County Standard*, on 9:ix:1893, "it is a fact that the deceased bore in Wyvenhoe, the reputation of a witch and many persons solemnly and sincerely declare that their health has been much better since her evil eye has been off them".

APPENDIX B

The Australian Connection

1 Wivenhoe, Queensland.

The New South Wales Government Gazette of 20th June, 1849, records an application by John Ferriter and Edmund Uhr, to graze cattle on a 30,000 acre estate beside the River Brisbane, at Wivenhoe, Queensland. The property soon passed into other hands, but the name survives and has recently been enhanced by the building of the prestigious Wivenhoe Dam.[1]

For in the fifties and sixties of the present century the city of Brisbane was afraid it might run out of water and it was eventually decided to dam the Brisbane River ninety miles from its mouth. Work was begun in 1975 and the dam opened on 18th October, 1985. It is well over a mile long and holds 252,964 million gallons of water. Besides supplying Brisbane and its suburbs, it helps to prevent flooding at Brisbane and Ipswich, and the artificial lake created is ideal for water sports.[2]

Before the work was put in hand, the National Trust of Queensland rescued a timber house which had been built by Uhr and Ferriter's successors at some time before 1867 and resited it four-and-a-half miles away. The handout for Bellevue Homestead says that Wivenhoe was "named after the Uhrs' hometown near Colchester in England", but I cannot find the name Uhr in the Parish Register.

2 Wivenhoe, Tasmania.

In 1853, Captain Henry Butler Stoney explored Van Diemen's Land, recording his impressions in a book, *A Residence in Tasmania*, which he published the following year. He describes the town of Burnie at Emu Bay on the north coast and, to the east of the Emu River, "the newly-formed township of Wyvenhoe; which, we trust, will one day rival many a town as yet more esteemed than this very pretty, if but little known, locality. It was in contemplation to form a military settlement there . . ."[3]

This contemplation was the author's. His regiment, the 99th, was to be discharged and he hoped that he and they might settle down together at Wivenhoe, (as it was eventually spelt), and he could be their employer. He chose this spot because he thought that the soil was rich and therefore potentially valuable. The Australian authorities were interested and invited the British Government to assist the scheme. However, the Crimean War intervened and neither the 99th nor Captain Stoney returned.[4]

It seems that Stoney either bought, or acquired the right to buy, some three thousand acres of land and it was evidently he who named the township and the roads. Pearl, Anglesea, (mispelt as at Wivenhoe), and Ormsby, all suggest an acquaintance with yachts, and Corcellis (sic), together with Brummell, a knowledge of the town as perhaps seen from the river, rather than a personal knowledge of the individuals named. If he had known the grandees of the town he would surely, as a military man, have produced a Rebow Street.[5]

Colchester Street, together with projected streets called St. Osyth, Chelmsford, Raleigh, Rochford, Manningtree and Witham, suggest, too, a general affinity with this part of the country. Clarke, Hull, Ready and Smith were, apparently, all contemporary settlers and landowners.[6]

Wivenhoe was formerly residential; now, a suburb of Burnie, it is devoted to light industry.

As the connection between Edmund Uhr and our Wivenhoe is a conundrum, so is that of Captain Stoney.

APPENDIX C

The Place-Names of Wivenhoe

A century or so ago, they called the lane which ran down past the Manor Hall into Wivenhoe, Wivenhoe Street or, simply, The Street. A Colchester Borough court roll of 1509 refers to "Chirchstrete"; perhaps this was the same road.[1]

In the days when a butcher's shop, once Isaac Blyth's, stood at the corner of Blyth's Lane, no self-respecting young Wivenhovian would have called that lane anything other than Blood Alley, or Blood-and-Guts Alley. Similarly, no Wivenhovian ever called St. John's Road anything other than Gas Road so long as it boasted two gasometers. Phillip Road, the Dan family claims, is named after Philip Chamberlain, albeit mispelt, the shoemaker whose shop was at 52, High Street. The children called it School Lane. Almost opposite is an archway behind which Joliffe the coal-merchant kept his stock; as I write this it is pleasant to record that his name will be preserved in the shopping development to be made there. Rectory Hill was once called Joliffe's Hill.

Bethany Street, I think, pays tribute to nineteenth century evangelism. The Hamilton of Hamilton Road was, Mr. Leslie Kemble thinks, a relation of the Rebows; doubtless it was John Gurdon Rebow who inspired Rebow Road, which was named at about the time of his death.

By oral tradition, Anglesea and Paget Roads were built by the Marquis and his son, Lord Alfred. However, a sale catalogue for 24th April, 1857, tells us that among plots of land offering is one in Paget Road and another "upon the intended new road to be called Anglesea Road".[2] By this time the Marquis had long ceased his association with the town; perhaps his son built Paget Road and put up the money for Captain's Row, (1 to 11, Anglesea Road), as well, hence the courteous title. If the Marquis *had* paid for his road, nearer the time of *Pearl*, then it would have probably been spelt correctly. The Wivenhoe correspondent of the *Essex County Standard* in 1957 tells us, on three separate occasions, that the bridge in Anglesea Road is called Garling's Bridge; the derivation eludes me.[3]

Park Road recalls the park of Wivenhoe House. A house built in a bend of the road was called The Nook for this reason. Towards the end of the last century people used to picnic on the rough ground now covered by Valley Road and particularly near a spot called Bobbitts Hole, land owned by William Bartlett. I am told that Bobbitt is how one young member of the Bartlett family tried to say the name "Robert". It is recorded that W. E. Denton played cricket at Wivenhoe in the sixties and that "W. E. Denton & Co. of Wyvenhoe" lost the schooner *Foxhound* in 1877, which was the subject of a Board of Trade enquiry. Very likely it was he who put up the money for Denton's Terrace.[4]

Until the arrival of the railway, Wivenhoe stumbled on its place-names and the names it stumbled on were sensible and pleasant. Thereafter, the overwhelming majority of the titles chosen by the local council, the borough or the developers, have been grandiose, inane or egotistical, and without any consistent pattern or policy.

The short row of houses from Park Road to the Park Hotel were originally known as Belleville Place. No doubt this was when the equally vulgar Belle Vue Road was created, the sort of titles that perhaps sell property. Hence, I also presume, the Grosvenor Hotel, which would remind commercial travellers of London, and Clifton Terrace, which would remind househunters of a fashionable Bristol suburb. The speculator, Ernest Stanley Beard, named two of the roads over Spion Kop after himself and a third after the manor he had bought. Harvey Road refers to Sir John Martin-Harvey, not his father or grandfather. The little lane which runs from a bus stop in The Avenue to Ernest Road is, by oral tradition, Smith's Lane, because the photographer and solicitor, "One-Arm" Smith, used to live there.

De Vere Close and Lane, near the site of the manor hall, recall the Earls of Oxford; nearby are the meaningless but genteel Woodland Way, Beech Avenue, Elm Grove and Parkwood Avenue.

Rosabelle Avenue reminds us of the last big yacht that lay at the river wall and Britannia Crescent of the prestige that accrued from the King's yacht, but if it is fitting to commemorate the *Vanessa* and *Victoria*, which also lay at the river wall, then other heavyweights, such as the *Sunbeam* should not be left out. Nobody today would kow-tow to the bounty that was tossed ambiguously from the *Valfreyia*; it was foolish to remember that yacht, still more so to misspell it Valfreda.

Spring Lane reminds us that there is a brook here. Heath Road is pedestrian, though this area, once covered with rough gorse and broom, was a heathland known as "The Broomy".

It so happened that at the very last meeting of the Wivenhoe Urban District Council, on Monday, 25th March, 1974, names had to be found for four little cul-de-sacs on the Lower Lodge Estate. Somebody suggested Lodge Close, a reasonable reminder of the farm which disappeared so obligingly and discreetly when the new estate was mooted. As a tribute to the two longest-serving members of the Council, Grasby and Cracknell Closes were created. Then Councillor Terence Endean pointed to the photograph of the late Councillor Percy Chaney and he was given a close. It seemed a pity to leave the late Councillor William Loveless, whose photograph hung beside it, out in the cold, so Lodge Close became Loveless Close. A few moments later everybody present linked arms and sang *Auld Lang Syne* and that was the end of the W.U.D.C.

This incident had an amusing sequel. The first inhabitants of the brand new Loveless Close knew nothing whatever of the great "W.G."; all the name suggested was a want of charity. Accordingly, they rose in rebellion and took their case to the local magistrates, who supported them and allowed them to call their road Cap Pilar Close. The erstwhile W.U.D.C., now the Wivenhoe Town Council, was furious and might have appealed to the Crown Court. However, Councillor Grasby had a better idea, that of naming the public hall the William Loveless Hall. So it was, on the spot, and by a fluke the title is not unreasonable for, "W.G" had quite a hand in building it.[6]

At about the same time Jack Hatch Way, Endean Court and Westlake Crescent were named after other living members of the W.U.D.C. Other names on the estate comprise flowers, Buddleia, Rosetta and Lilac; Tolliday, after Mr. G. E. Tolliday who built the estate, Dixon, after the managing director of Linsbrook, and two girls' names and two surnames which defeat me: Frances, Saran, Wilson and Sonell.

The Vine Farm Estate gave us Vine Farm Road and Drive, and the drivelling imbecility of Mede Way and half-a-dozen others like it. The second phase of the development, Broadfields, included Feedham's Close, a reminder of an ancient bounty, and a clutch of kings and queens.

In or near the Dene Park Estate, Captain Albert Turner, Hector Barr the sailmaker, and Elizabeth Sandford the benefactress, are commemorated, also Farmer Bowes over whose land the relevant road was built. The other place-names are those of historic houses, castles and gardens of Great Britain and Ireland.

Thus Wivenhoe acquired its polyglot jumble of place-names. Those up to about 1860 are reasonable; the rest of the town is patently waiting to be rechristened. What names shall we choose?

It is ironic that although one or two of the vessels that were laid up here have been commemorated, no boat that was ever built here has been. What about the glorious oeuvre of John Harvey: *Audax, Dagmar, Shearwater, Chloris* and the rest of them? Another source would be the names of families indigenous at the turn of the century: Munson, Chamberlain, Ellis, Madder, Worsp, some already commemorated through individuals.

It will, of course, never happen. However, there remain two more housing estates at the foot of the town and here intelligence and imagination must take precedence over egotism and silliness.

The first four towers of the University of Essex are named after Lord Rayleigh, a Nobel prize winner for physics who was Chancellor of Cambridge University, William Morris, the poet, artist and socialist, Professor Richard Henry Tawney, an economist, and John Maynard Keynes, another economist, who was ennobled. The two southernmost towers commemorate Sir Arthur Stanley Eddington, the astronomer, and Lord Bertrand Russell, the philosopher. It is believed that all these names have local connections.

I opened this history by giving what I think is the correct derivation of Wivenhoe; I close by referring to the funny little matter of the spelling variation which occurred towards the end of the nineteenth century.

The first time that I can find Wivenhoe, up till then spelt with an "i", spelt with a "y", is in the *Essex County Standard* for 1st March, 1867. Thus it remained for over half a century. Moreover, the railway adopted this spelling and so did the directories. Yet it was never universal and it seems that the Post Office favoured "i".

The double spelling endured for a while after and it would seem that the town was rather proud of it. However in 1911, the Postmaster-General asked the railway to change to "i", which it evidently did, and at about the same time the press followed suit.[7] (It was in 1912, incidentally, that *The Black Boy* was changed to *The Black Buoy*).

How did this curious variation occur? I have not the slightest idea.

FOOTNOTES

ABBREVIATIONS

A.F.J.B.	Notes lent to me by Mr. A. F. J. Brown.
Annals	Annals of Evangelical Nonconformity in the County of Essex, by T. W. Davids, (1863), Jackson, Walford & Hodder. E.R.O. R1.
Beaver	The Nonsuch Ketch, article by Phil Day in the magazine Beaver, Winter 1968, a copy of which is at The Nottage Institute.
Brochure	An illustrated brochure brought out by Forrestt's in about 1905, a photostatted copy of which is at the Castle Museum.
Brown	Essex at Work 1700-1815, by A. F. J. Brown, (1969), E.R.O.
C.A.R.	Calendar of Assize Records.
C.E.	Colchester Express.
C.G.	Colchester Gazette.
C.P.R.	Calendar of Patent Rolls.
C.St.P.Dom.	Calendar of State Papers Domestic.
Chamber's	Chamber's Biography.
D.N.B.	Dictionary of National Biography.
Defoe	Tour Through the Eastern Counties, by Daniel Defoe, (1724-6).
Douglas	Yachting on the Colne: Some Preliminary Observations, a thesis for the University of Essex by Gavin Douglas. Ms. at the University of Essex.
Dunn	A thirty page ms. history of Wivenhoe by Mr. C. J. M. Dunn, also his notes on boats owned by Wivenhovians.
E.A.D.T.	East Anglian Daily Times.
E.A.M.	East Anglian Magazine.
E.A.S.	Essex Archaeological Society.
E.A.S. N.S.	Essex Archaeological Society, New Series.
E.A.T. N.S.	Essex Archaeological Transactions, New Series.
E.C.	Essex Countryside.
E.C.S.	Essex County Standard, or Essex Standard as this newspaper was called before 23rd July, 1892.
E.G.	Evening Gazette.
E.R.	Essex Review.
E.R.O.	Essex Record Office.
Emmison	Elizabethan Life, by F. G. Emmison, (1970-1980), Essex County Council.
Essex Militia	Essex Units in the War 1914-1919, Volume IV: The Essex Militia, by John William Burrows, F.S.A., (1929).
Feesey	Wivenhoe Park, a monograph by Rosemary Feesey, (1962).
Gordon	Wivenhoe Congregational Church, by Rev. Clementina M. Gordon, B.D., (1965-1966).
Graveson	Notes supplied to me by Professor R. H. Graveson, Q.C.
Haining	The Great English Earthquake, by Peter Haining, (1976), Robert Hale.
Hodgkinson	They Went . . . And Then They Came Back, a thesis for the University of Essex by Jonathan Hodgkinson. Ms. at the University of Essex.
I.J.	Ipswich Journal.
King	A History of Wivenhoe Methodist Church, by Geoffrey King, (1988).
Leather	The Northseamen, by John Leather, (1971), Terence Dalton Ltd.
Leslie	Memoirs of the Life of John Constable, by C. R. Leslie, (1843).
Letters	Letters to I. M. Rebow 1767-1779, photostats of 117 ms. letters. E.R.O. Accession No. 47.
Manning	The Mary Martin Rebow Letters, an essay by Josephine Asaro Manning. Ms. at the Colchester Public Library.

Martin-Harvey	The Autobiography of Sir John Martin-Harvey, (1932), Sampson Low.
Ministry List	Buildings of Special Architectural or Historic Interest, compiled by the Department of the Environment.
Morant	The History and Antiquities of Essex, by Philip Morant, (1763).
One Design	The Wivenhoe One Design Jubilee Year Book, (1985), booklet by The Wivenhoe Sailing Club.
Pearce-Higgins	The Rebows of Colchester and Wivenhoe, by W. M. Pearce-Higgins, (1966). Ms. at the Colchester Public Library.
Pedigree	Pedigree of The Family of Corsellis, by G. Milner-Gibson Cullum, F.S.A., (1914), Mitchell Hughes & Clarke.
Penfold	Notes supplied to me by Dr. J. B. Penfold from the archives of the Colchester Medical Society.
Peters	An untitled essay written by Mavis Peters for the University of Essex, (1975). Ms. at the Univerity of Essex.
Reaney	English Place-Name Society Vol. XII: The Place-Names of Essex, by P. H. Reaney, (1955), Cambridge.
Recognizances	The Register of Ale-House Recognizances, E.R.O. Q/RLv 24-82.
Rent Book	Rent Book 1722-1768. E.R.O. D/P 277/11/1.
Rush	Seats in Essex, by J. A. Rush.
School Logs	Eleven leather-bound ledgers dating from 1868 to the present day, kept at the Broomgrove Junior School.
Slaughter	The Growth of Popular Education in Wivenhoe, a monograph by Basil Slaughter, (1954), Workers Educational Association. Ms. in Colchester Public Library.
Sloman	The Making of a University, six lectures by Albert Sloman, (1963), B.B.C.
U of E – Mrs. Etta Dan	An interview with Mrs. Etta Dan, made by an anonymous research student at the University of Essex. Ms. at the University of Essex.
V.H.E.	Victoria History of Essex.

To this list of abbreviations I must add some further explanations:

1. A number in brackets after a footnote indicates the number of paragraphs covered by that footnote. For example, Footnote No. 66 in Chapter 8 gives three references from the *Essex County Standard*. As you might guess, the one for May, 1926, refers to the race for sailing-boats at the beginning of the paragraph, the one for October, 1926 to the prize-giving at the club, and the one for 1932 to the death and burial of Dr. Kevern. But Dr. Walter Radcliffe is given the figure (2) after his name, which means that he gave me the rest of the information in that and the succeeding paragraph, or pretty well all of it for I have not ascribed every single fact in this history to an individual or written source.

2. Inverted commas indicate the title of a newspaper story, as opposed to a feature article.

3. "Etc." indicates that there are other references to this item, which are too numerous, repetitive or nominal to mention.

4. Some Essex County Standard references have "W.U.D.C." and "W.W." after them. The former refers to meetings of the Wivenhoe Urban District Council, which were often reported separately, the latter to the Week in Wivenhoe column.

5. In Chapter 9 I have tried to cite local newspapers as far as possible, with enough national titles to indicate that these events were of national interest. "National Press" means that the event was reported in all the national newspapers and it would be pedantic to name any one of them.

In addition to the sources mentioned above I must acknowledge three other books which have helped me:

Wivenhoe, its Attractions, Pleasures and Eccentric Natives, by Dick Barton, (1975), Dick Barton Enterprises.

The Angry Brigade, by Gordon Carr, (1975), Gollancz. (This book provided most of the facts recorded in Section 3 of Chapter 9.)

The Day Before Yesterday, by Olive Whaley, (1980).

Footnotes

CHAPTER 1 – SAXON, MEDIAEVAL, TUDOR

1. Letters 14:viii:1778.
2. Bottle: E.C.S. 16:iv:1932; Pottery: *Archaeology in Essex to A.D. 1500*, (*Council for British Archaeology Research Report 34*), (*1980*), ed. D. G. Buckley, p. 42.
3. E.A.S. III, 136.
4. Reaney.
5. V.H.E. I, 517, citing Domesday Book.
6. Morant II, 187-9, (my principal source for the history of the manor).
7. C.P.R. Ed. III, 1327-1330, 276.
8. E.A.S. X, 320, citing the court rolls.
9. C.P.R. H. V 1413-1416, 151.
10. Morant II, 188.
11. C.St.P.Dom. H. VIII 1530, 2849.
12. C.St.P.Dom. H. VIII 1538, I, 255 & II, 39.
13. V.H.E. II, 22 & 29.
14. Reaney.
15. Emmison, V, 124-5.
16. Ministry List.
17. E.R. XXXVII, 156-69. (3)
18. North and west galleries: E.C.S. 8:vi:1860.
19. Emmison, II, 63.
20. E.R.O. D/ACA (1599) 24. fol. 250.
21. E.R.O. D/ACA (7:ix:1582) fol. 70v.
22. E.R.O. D/ACA (March 1589-90) 17 fol. 308.
23. E.R.O. D/ACA (1596) 24 fol. 23.
24. C.A.R. Witham Assizes 27:vii:1586.
25. Presentation by churchwardens: Emmison, II, 222; Beckes: E.R.O. D/ACA (March, 1589-1590) 17 fol. 307v; "whoremasterly knave": Emmison, II, 222.
26. "Pickthankly knaves": Emmison, II, 222; "the harlott in John Browne's house: E.R.O. D/ACA (1595) 24 fol. 21; morris dancing: E.R.O. D/ACA (1598) f. 143.
27. E.R. XXXVII, 162.
28. *Wills of the County of Essex, F. G. Emmison,* (*1985*), II, pp.. 179, 297, 253 & 179.
29. Wife of Giles: E.R.O. D/ACA (1593) 21 fol. 198v; Gurnell: Emmison, II, 66.
30. Emmison, III, Part 2.
31. Conveying away pales: Emmison, III, 2557-8.
32. John Quixle: Douglas; Richard Quykesley: Manorial Court Rolls 23 H. VIII (1507) T/B 122; "lading places": E.A.T. XIVII, 153.
33. List of 1528: V.H.E. II, 276; return for 1564-5: V.H.E. II, 276; 1582 list: C.St.P.Dom. H. VIII (1528) Item 5101.
34. *Defeat of the Spanish Armada, State Papers ed. Loughton,* (*1894*), Vol. I, pp. 14 & 24, citing C.St.P.Dom.
35. Ibid, Vol. II, p. 96, citing C.St.P.Dom.
36. D.N.B.

CHAPTER 2 – SEVENTEENTH CENTURY

1 Religion and Politics.

1. E.R.O. D/ACA 29 fol. 206v, 243v & 264v.
2. E.A.S. XIV, 186-8.
3. D.N.B., Chamber's, Annals, 315-6 and *The Life and Death of that Holy Man of God Mr. Thomas Cawton, by Thomas Cawton the Younger,* (*1662*). (4)
4. Defoe.

5. C.St.P.Dom. Car. I: XIX, 159-60.
6. *Historical Manuscripts Commission, Fourteenth Report, (1895), Appendix Part IX,* p. 284.
7. D.N.B., Chamber's, and Annals, 587-8.

2 Admiralty Contracts.

8. C.St.P.Dom. Commonwealth: I, 317.
9. *The Rates, Kinds, Names, Origins, Dimensions, Burthens and Force in Men and Guns of every Ship and Vessel of the Royal Navy of England, from May, 1660 to 25th March, 1686, a book compiled by Samuel Pepys for King James II,* is kept at the Pepys Library, Magdalene College, Cambridge.
10. Beaver. (4)
11. C.St.P.Dom. Commonwealth: VII, 465, 466, 162 & 189.
12. C.St.P.Dom. Commonwealth: VII, 493, 503, 513 & 547.
13. C.St.P.Dom. Commonwealth: IX, 453, 514 & 519.
14. *Pepys' Diary,* 23rd January, 1665.
15. C.St.P.Dom. Car. II XI, 398.
16. C.St.P.Dom. Commonwealth: IX, 357, 444, 466, 467 & 472.
17. C.St.P.Dom. Commonwealth: IX, 480, 498, 503 & 511.
18. C.St.P.Dom. Commonwealth: X, 398 & 400.
19. C.St.P.Dom. Commonwealth: XI, 245.
20. C.St.P.Dom. Commonwealth: XIII, 237.
21. *Pepys' Record of Naval Vessels.*
22. C.St.P.Dom. Car. II: III, 444, IV, 174, V, 75, X, 307 & XI, 457.
23. Beaver.
24. C.St.P.Dom. Car. II: VII, 472.
25. C.St.P.Dom. Car. II: XXV, 343.

3 The Corsellis Family and the Town.

26. Pedigree, Notes on the Corsellis Family from Mr. E. H. C. Squire, also E.A.S. N.S. XIV, 185, where the entire transaction is recorded as £10,000.
27. Deaths: Parish Registers, (E.R.O. D/P 277); Hewers: *English History from Essex Sources, by A. C. Edwards, Essex County Council,* pp. 97-8, citing Q/SR 406/104.
28. Pedigree.
29. E.R. XVIII, 137. (3)
30. C.St.P.Dom. Car. II VII, 243 & 324.
31. Gordon, 4.
32. V.H.E. II, 69 (note) & Gordon, 5.
33. Annals, 355-356, citing *Palmer's Nonconformist Memorials* II, 188.
34. E.A.T. N.S. XXII, 298, citing Bramston MSS.
35. Buildings: Ministry List; token coinage: E.A.T. N.S. XIV, 146 & XVII, 242; Maiden's Head etc.: Mr. Richard Chopping and Mr. Denis Wirth-Miller.
36. E.R. LVI, 92, citing Mich. Q/SBa 2/44 of 1641.
37. E.R.O. D/DA M4, & E.A.S. XIX, 288.
38. Pargetting: E.A.S. V, 73; wall-paintings: E.A.T. N.S. XXIV, 132.

CHAPTER 3 – THE REBOWS AND WIVENHOE PARK

1. Pearce-Higgins.
2. E.R. XI, 158. (2)
3. *History of Parliament: The House of Commons 1754-1790, by Namier and Brooke, (1964),* p. 350.
4. Feesey, 10-14 and Rush, 185.
5. Essex Militia, 127-41.
6. Feesey, 15-18 and Manning.
7. Letters to I. M. Rebow 1767-1779.

Footnotes

8. Letters: 24th August, 1770, (No. 16).
9. Essex Militia, 133-5.
10. Letters: 3rd July, 1778, (No. 73).
11. Letters: 17th July, 1778, (No. 77).
12. Letters: 19th July, 1778, (No. 78).
13. Letters: 7th August, 1778, (No. 87).
14. Letters: 14th August, 1778, (No. 90).
15. Letters: 5th August, 1778, (No. 85).
16. Letters: 26th July, 1778, (No. 81).
17. Letters: 23rd August, 1778, (No. 94).
18. Essex Militia, 133-5.
19. Letters: 17th August, 1779, (No. 99).

CHAPTER 4 – EIGHTEENTH CENTURY

1 The Grandees and the Clergy.

1. Pedigree; "Barmaid": Mr. E. H. C. Squire.
2. South Sea Bubble: Mr. E. H. C. Squire.
3. Pedigree.
4. I.J. 10:ix:1763.
5. Letters: 14th August, 1778, (No. 90).
6. I.J. 4:viii:1789.
7. Pedigree.
8. Gates at Chapel Street: Mr. L. H. Martin.
9. D.N.B.
10. Gordon, 8-9.

2 Dr. Flack, Dr. Tunmer and the Baths.

11. A.F.J.B.
12. Mary King: A.F.J.B.; treated soldiers: A.F.J.B.; possessions: I.J. 2:x:1756.
13. Rented stable: Rent Book; Mary Whitley: I.J. 1790.
14. Indenture owned by Mr. John Stewart.
15. Letter to Dr. Walter Radcliffe from Mr. Rowland G. Smith of Hove, citing the Parish Register.
16. I.J. 17:v:1755.
17. *A Treatise on Sea-Bathing etc.* A copy is in the Colchester Public Library.
18. *Brown, 126, also I.J. 20:iii:1762, 14:v:1763 and 18:vi:1763.*
19. *I.J. 6:viii:1763.*
20. *Penfold.*
21. *A.F.J.B.*
22. *D.N.B.*

4 Commerce, Fishing and Boatbuilding.

23. Defoe.
24. I.J. 17:vii:1790.
25. Rent Book.
26. A.F.J.B.
27. Cardinal: I.J. 1:xii:1759; Bawtree's marriage: A.F.J.B.; brick-fronted: I.J. 1:viii:1772.
28. *Mayflower & Providence*: Dunn.
29. I.J. 26:ii:1760, 9:ii:1760, 15:v:1762 & 11:iv:1789, and an article by L. C. Cockrell in E.C.S. 16:iii:1945.
30. Dunn.

363

5 The Inspector and the Comet.

31. I.J. 7:ii:1778, 30:x:1779 & 13:v:1780.
32. *The Captain's Log of the Inspector,* P.R.O. Kew ADM 51 472.
33. *The Captains' Logs of the Inspector and the Comet,* P.R.O. Kew ADM 51 1191 & 1185. (10)
34. V.H.E, II, 310.

6 Smuggling.

35. Edward: Dunn; I.J. 19:vi:1784 & 23:x:1784; *Liberty:* Dunn.
36. *English History from Essex Sources, by A. F. J. Brown,* p. 89, citing Q/SBb 58 for Michaelmas 1713.
37. Dunn.
38. I.J. 18:vi:1743.
39. Letters: 2nd August, 1778, (No. 84).
40. *The Smuggler's Century, by Hervey Benham,* pp. 36-43. (2).

7 Education.

41. Charity School: A.F.J.B.; Wenham: I.J. 9:i:1773.
42. Tunmer: I.J. 1:i:1763; Alefounder: I.J. 10:iii:1764; Field: I.J. 4:vi:1768; Powell: I.J. 29:vi:1782.

8 Sporting and Social.

43. Ledger. (4)
44. Sales: I.J. 17:vi:1758 & 28:xi:1766.
45. Rent Book.
46. Recognizances. (2)
47. Renaming of *The Woolpack*: Mortgage dated 30th May, 1828, in respect of "a tenement used as a public house formerly called the Woolpack and now known by the name of the Ship at Launch..." owned by Mr. John Stewart.
48. Bowling Green: I.J. 14:vi:1766; Cockfighting: I.J. 14:iv:1781; Cricket: I.J. 20:vii:1771, 18:vii:1772 & 22:vi:1765; Corder: A.F.J.B.
49. Wayland: I.J. 18:v:1771; Wivenhoe Association: I.J. 1:i:1785, 5:iii:1785, 20:vi:1789, 19:xii:1789, etc.
50. Chelmsford Chronicle 6:vii:1798.
51. I.J. 23:viii:1783 & 30:viii:1783.
52. I.J. 23:vi:1792, 27:vii:1793 & 10:viii:1793, also *The First Yachtsmen,* article by *John Leather* in E.C.S. 6:xii:1963.
53. I.J. 28:vii:1753.
54. Essex Militia, 137-9.
55. Essex Militia, 137-9.
56. *In Essex, by Phoebe Fenwick Gaye,* (*1949*), p. 28, alludes to the rumour that soldiers were installed in Garrison House at the time of the Napoleonic Wars.
57. I.J. 21:ii:1789.
58. 1726: E.R.O. D/P 277/25/20; 1750: E.R.O. D/DEl L8.
59. E.R.O. D/El L8.
60. *Report of Essex Charities 1819-1837.* E.R.O. T5.
61. A.F.J.B.

Footnotes

CHAPTER 5 – FRANCIS SLATER AND JOHN GURDON

1. E.R. LIII, 87-91.
2. Leslie, ch. 4.
3. Correspondence: Vol. VI, 6:ix:1812.
4. *The Story of the Household Cavalry, by Captain Sir George Arthur, Bart.*, II, p. 569 footnote.
5. Correspondence VI, 21:viii:1816. (7)
6. Correspondence VI, 30:viii:1816. (4)
7. Correspondence VI, 19:ix:1816.
8. Correspondence VI, 13:viii:1819.
9. Correspondence VI, 28:viii:1819. (8)
10. *Essex People 1750-1900, by A. F. J. Brown*, p. 101, citing *John Hanson of Great Bromley Hall's Diary*.
11. Railway: E.C.S. 15:ii:1839; Town Hall: E.C.S. 21:v:1841.
12. E.C.S. 14:vii:1837.
13. E.C.S. 29:vii:1836.
14. E.C.S. 20:i:1837.
15. E.C.S. 23:x:1840. (2)
16. E.C.S. 23:x:1840.
17. *History of Congregation in Wivenhoe, by Rev. W. Franklin Tyler*, (*1896*), a copy of which is kept at the present Congregational Church, and Gordon, 21.
18. Pearce-Higgins, 44.
19. E.C.S. 17:viii:1833.
20. Application to change name: Rebow Papers V, where the date of the application is given as 19:viii:1935.
21. Rebow Papers II.
22. Father: E.C.S. 22:ii:1839.
23. E.C.S. 6:ix:1844. (3)
24. E.C.S. 20:iii:1840.
25. E.C.S. 29:ii:1856.
26. E.C.S. 14:vii:1837, 19:vi:1840 & 10:vi:1842.
27. E.C.S. 22:ii:1839. (2)
28. E.C.S. 5:xii:1845.
29. E.C.S. 3:xi:1848, 19:ix:1851 & 3:ix:1852.
30. *Dictionary of Architectural Biography.*
31. Feesey. (2)
32. Rush, 185.
33. Feesey.
34. E.C.S. 11:vi:1847.
35. E.C.S. 17:x:1851.
36. E.C.S. 4:vi:1847.
37. Ibid.
38. E.C.S. 20:viii:1847 & 27:viii:1847.
39. E.C.S. 8:viii:1851.
40. E.C.S. 3:ix:1852 & 24:vi:1853.
41. E.C.S. 25:v:1856.
42. E.C.S. 6:ii:1857.
43. E.C.S. 6:v:1859 & 2:xii:1859.
44. Rebow Papers V. (2)
45. E.C.S. 20:xi:1868.
46. E.C.S. 6:xii:1861. (11)
47. Sermon preached on Sunday, 23rd October, 1870, E.R.O. Parish File.
48. E.C.S. 4:vi:1847.
49. E.C.S. 20:xi:1868.
50. Expenses: Pearce-Higgins 50, 55, 59, also E.C.S. 20:ii:1857 & 27:ii:1857.

The Story of Wivenhoe

CHAPTER 6 – THE BIG YACHTS 1801-1881

1 The Dawn of an Era: Philip Sainty and Pearl.

1. *Trafalgar Diary*, a photostat copy of which was deposited at the E.R.O. by the author's great-great-grandson, Mr. L. H. Martin. E.R.O. T/B 135.
2. Mr. L. H. Martin.
3. E.C.S. 1:iii:1879, reprinting an article from *The Field*. (2)
4. Leather, 90-95.
5. Leather and Dunn.
6. *Two Essex Sea Pearls*, article by Eric Rayner in E.C.S. 19:vii:1968.
7. V.H.E. II, 305.
8. Dunn.
9. Bankruptcy: E.C.S. 28:vi:1834; Philip Mosely Sainty: Leather, 264-5.
10. E.C.S. 2:xii:1836.
11. Dunn.
12. Dunn.
13. *Wivenhoe's Century of Splendour*, article by Hervey Benham in E.C.S. 9:vii:1943.

2 Grandees and Tradesmen.

14. Pedigree.
15. Mr. E. H. C. Squire.
16. Savill: E.C.S. 8:vii:1831; Capel: E.C.S. 11:ix:1840; Brown: letter from Stephen Brown to J. T. Hedge of 2:ix:1845 E.R.O. D/DB C4.
17. E.C.S. 11:i:1861.
18. E.C.S. 27:ii:1886.
19. *Sea Belle*: E.C.S. 3:vii:1874; Locomotive: E.C.S. 24:xii:1875; telephone: E.C.S. 3:v:1878; knighthood: E.C.S. 17:viii:1877.
20. *History and Topography of the County of Essex*, by Thomas Wright, (*1836*).
21. *Gentleman's Magazine 1853*, I, 658 and Vestry Minutes 1847-1925 E.R.O. D/P 277/8/1-4.
22. *The Life of George Brummell, Esq.*, by Captain William Jesse, (*1840*), Chapter 4.
23. *Pages of the Past*, by Gerald Rickword, in E.C.S. 15:v:1953.
24. Martin-Harvey, 9. (2)
25. E.C.S. 18:ii:1848.
26. 1848 lease: E.R.O. D/DU 1140; 1882 fire: E.C.S. 18:xi:1882; also E.C.S. 25:viii:1876.
27. E.R.O. D/DU 1140; see also Leather, in which the oyster journal is given a chapter to itself.
28. *Wivenhoe Overseers's Acts* E.R.O. D/P 277/12/2; cholera: E.C.S. 28:ix:1849.
29. This ledger, formerly in the possession of Dr. William Dean, was presented by him to the Essex Record Office in 1988. E.R.O. Accession No. 227.

3 Education and Religion.

30. Gordon, 15, citing the Minute Book of the Wivenhoe Congregational Church.
31. Anniversary: C.G. 20:vii:1816; report: A.F.J.B.
32. London Diocesan Board of Education E.R.O. D/P 30/28/19.
33. Slaughter.
34. Archdeanery Return of 1841, E.R.O. D/A CM12.
35. Ecclesiastical Census of 1851: E.R.O. T/A 470/3.
36. *The Intellectual Repository and New Jerusalem Magazine* 1:iv:1864, p. 194
37. *The Revival*, (a Methodist magazine), No. 404, 18:iv:1867, pp. 216-7 & No. 338, 11:i:1867, p. 24.
38. *The Revival*, No. 404, 18:iv:1867, pp. 216-217 and Martin-Harvey, 12; reading room: obituary of Edgar Chapman in E.C.S. 28:iv:1934.
39. *The Revival*, No. 404, 18:iv:1867, pp. 217-8.
40. *The Revival*, No. 421, 15:viii:1867 & No. 444, 23:i:1868.
41. King. (3)

Footnotes

42. Gordon, 28-31.
43. Slaughter, quoting the letters of Rev. E. T. Waters.
44. Slaughter.
45. Reading room: E.C.S. 14:iii:1862; volunteers & gas company: E.C.S. 24:viii:1860.
46. "Barn-like arrangement": E.C.S. 14:i:1867; Taylor and Chapman: E.C.S. 6:xii:1839.
47. E.C.S. 8:vi:1860.
48. Slaughter.
49. School Logs. (11)
50. *Return to the London Diocesan Board of Education*, E.R.O. D/P 30/28/19.
51. Slaughter.
52. Ibid.

4 Thomas and John Harvey.

53. Leather, 277 and Dunn. (2)
54. E.C.S. 8:i:1841.
55. Strike: Gordon, 26; Small Debts Court: E.C.S. 21:i:1848.
56. E.C.S. 20:vi:1845.
57. E.C.S. 14:ix:1860.
58. *Gentle Recluse and Eastern Sage*, article by Noel McCourt in *The Lady* 31:iii:1983.
59. E.C.S. 19:ix:1855 & 11:iv:1856.
60. E.C.S. 30:viii:1872. (2) ; Sculpture: Martin-Harvey, 5.
61. Tools: E.C.S. 30:viii:1872; insurance policies: E.C.S. 29:i:1873.
62. E.C.S. 29:i:1873.
63. E.C.S. 2:v:1873.
64. Martin-Harvey, 5.
65. Reprinted in E.C.S. 28:iv:1873. (4)
66. *A Voyage in the Sunbeam, by the Baroness Brassey, (1878), Longman's.*
67. Mr. Don Mason.
68. Leather, 274 and Dunn; Fire: E.C.S. 16:xi:1878; *Silver Spray*: Leather, 271.
69. Dunn.
70. E.C.S. 23:ii:1855. (2)
71. *Memories of a Wivenhoe ropewalk*, article in E.C.S. 16:iii:1945.
72. Joy rides; E.C.S. 18:vi:1954; machinery: E.C.S. 20:i:1865 & 19:v:1865.
73. E.C.S. 9:viii:1872.

5 Sporting and Social.

74. 1869 incident: E.C.S. 20:viii:1869.
75. E.C.S. 22:vii:1870.
76. E.C.S. 1:x:1873.
77. E.C.S. 27:viii:1858.
78. E.C.S. 22:vii:1859.
79. E.C.S. 31:viii:1883.
80. Martin-Harvey, 7-9. (6)
81. Ibid, 7.
82. *The Smuggling Century, by Hervey Benham, (1986)*, E.R.O., pp. 85-6.
83. Village Delicatessen: letter to me from Mr. W. G. Harlow 5:x:1974; The Storehouse & different smuggled spirits: Mr. Richard Chopping & Mr. Denis Wirth-Miller; Smith: C.G. 16:v:1835.
84. The Cage: E.A.T. VII, 37: "through The Cage": Mr. L. W. Kemble.
85. E.C.S. 9:viii:1872, where the A.G.M. is described as the seventeenth, etc.
86. E.C.S. 22:xi:1874 & 30:x:1874.
87. E.C.S. 7:x:1882.
88. E.C.S. (W.W.) 24:iv:1953.

6 The Railway.

89. *Report on the Navigation of the River Colne with a Proposal for Constructing a Ship Canal from Wivenhoe to Colchester, by Peter Bruff, (1842).* Colchester Public Library.
90. Meeting of the Paving and Channel Commissioners to study Mr. Bruff's Report: E.C.S. 7:x:1842; two letters about the proposed channel up to the Hythe, one from Bruff: E.C.S. 14:x:1842; Meeting of The Channel and Paving Commissioners to consider the report and cross-examine Mr. Bruff: E.C.S. 11:xi:1842; two more letters: E.C.S. 2:xii:1842 & 23:xii:1842.
91. E.C.S. 2:i:1863 & 8:v:1863.
92. E.C.S. 15:v:1863 & 2:x:1863.
93. E.C.S. 21:xii:1860.
94. E.C.S. 25:ix:1863.
95. £40,000: *Wivenhoe and Brightlingsea Railway, by Paul Brown, (1985), Ian Henry,* p. 20; inspection: E.C.S. 8:xii:1865.
96. E.C.S.20:iv:1866.
97. Leather, 28-29.
98. E.C.S. 31:iii:1865.

7 Mid-Victorian Expansion.

99. E.C.S. 23:vi:1854, 25:vii:1856, 3:iv:1857, 5:vii:1857, etc.
100. E.C.S. 9:i:1863.
101. E.C.S. 30:vii:1873; rules: E.C.S. (W.W.) 8:ii:1974.
102. E.C.S. (W.W.) 23:ii:1973 & (W.W.) 16:iii:1973.
103. E.C.S. 25:i:1861, 20:ix:1861 & 3:i:1862.

8 The End of an Era: John Harvey and Chloris.

104. E.C.S. 1:iii:1879, quoting The Field.
105. Papers of W. S. Gilbert: British Library, Vo. 47, MS. 49335. (2)
106. Martin-Harvey, Chapter 3.
107. Ibid, p. 5.

CHAPTER 7 – LATE VICTORIAN AND EDWARDIAN
1881- 1914

1 The Earthquake.

1. E.C.S. 26:iv:1884. (4)
2. School Logs.
3. Betts: Haining, 112; Squire: Haining, 40; repairs: Haining, 155.
4. E.C.S. 24:v:1884.
5. E.C.S. 10:v:1884 & 2:viii:1884.
6. E.C.S. 12:xii:1884.

2 Wivenhoe Park: Hector Gurdon-Rebow and Charles Gooch.

7. Gurney Benham writing Colchester and County Notes in E.C.S. 29:xi:1930.
8. County Council: E.C.S. 9:viii:1890; School Board: E.C.S. 18:iv:1891; wedding: E.C.S. 25:iv:1896.
9. Purchase of Wivenhoe Park: Mrs. Marguerite Cole.
10. E.C.S. 21:ix:1901 & 28:ix:1901.
11. E.C.S. 25:iv:1908 & 25:vii:1908.
12. Most of the details in these two paragraphs were supplied by Mrs. Marguerite Cole. (2)
13. "The true sort": Mr. Albert Scales.

Footnotes

3 Wivenhoe Hall: James Jackson, Claude Egerton-Green Alexander Barlow.

14. Cricket: E.C.S. 18:iii:1882; regatta: E.C.S. 8:ix:1883; bazaar: E.C.S. 25:viii:1883.
15. Wedding: E.C.S. 30:vii:1887; death: E.C.S. 17:ix:1904.
16. Mrs. Marguerite Cole is my principal informant.
17. Purchase of Wivenhoe Hall: E.C.S. 27:x:1906.
18. Ibid.
19. Marriage: E.C.S. 25:iv:1896; sale of manor: Graveson.
20. Graveson.

4 John Sinclair Carolin.

21. Mrs. P. L. J. Le Poer Power.
22. Ham: E.C.S. 11:ii:1893; Letter: E.C.S. 18:xi:1893.
23. Letter: E.C.S. 21:xi:1896.
24. E.C.S. 28:ix:1912.
25. E.C.S.(letter) 26:x:1901.
26. E.C.S. 17:iv:1909.
27. E.C.S. 8:v:1909.
28. E.C.S. 14:xi:1903.
29. Gladstone: E.C.S. 28:v:1898; Victoria: E.C.S. 2:ii:1901.
30. E.C.S. 30:v:1903.

5 Edwin Wilkins and Forrestt's.

31. E.C.S. 2:i:1892.
32. Nile boats: E.C.S. 13:ix:1884; *Kara*: E.C.S. 12:iv:1884 & 27:ix:1884.
33. E.C.S. 10:vii:1886.
34. Mr. R. J. McEune.
35. E.C.S. 31:iii:1888.
36. E.C.S. 30:v:1891.
37. Ibid.
38. *Manola*: E.C.S. 13:ix:1930; *Elfin*: Westmoreland Gazette 25:viii:1894; *Otto: The Great Age of Steam on Windermere*, by George H. Pattinson, (1981), The Windermere Nautical Trust, p. 71; *Pearl*: Mr. D. R. Matthews of the Windermere Nautical Trust; *Gunilda*: E.C.S. 27:xi:1897.
39. E.C.S. 30:v:1891.
40. Dock: E.C.S. 27:x:1888 & 9:iii:1889; galvanising plant: E.C.S. 14:v:1898; electricity: E.C.S. 1:xii:1900.
41. *Advance*: Brochure & *In Darkest Africa*, by H. M. Stanley, (1890), Sampson, Low, Marston, Searle & Rivington, Vol. I, passim; *Lady Hermione*: Wivenhoe's Century of Splendour, article by Hervey Benham in E.C.S. 6:viii:1943.
42. Brochure. (4)
43. E.C.S. 25:xi:1899. (2)
44. Wreck: E.C.S. 13:ii:1904.
45. Bankruptcy and history: E.C.S. 22:viii:1903; cottages: E.C.S. 26:xi:1904.
46. E.C.S. 10:vi:1905, Interview with Albert E. Simons in E.C.S. (W.W.) 22:x:1954, *The Wivenhoe Submarine*, article by R. J. Bradley in E.C.S. 12:x:1962 & *The Wivenhoe Submarine*, article by Les Stockdale in E.C. X, 40-41. (9)
47. E.C.S. 14:viii:1909 & *A Salvage Tube on the Colne*, article by G. W. Martin in E.C. IX, 344.
48. Boats: Brochure; Bankruptcy: E.C.S. 16:iii:1912.
49. E.C.S. 10:ii:1912.
50. *Exmouth II*: E.C.S. 15:iii:1913; *Mansa Kila Ba*: E.C.S. 4:x:1913; *Beacon*: E.C.S. 20:xii:1913.
51. *Ala*: Dunn; *King Coel*: E.C.S. 12:iii:1898 & 7:v:1898.
52. E.C.S. 7:ii:1896 & 29:vii:1899.

6 The River or the Shipyard?

53. Jezebel: Hodgkinson; nude bathing: Douglas.
54. Mrs. K. G. Everitt.
55. Mr. Don Mason.
56. Douglas, talking to Bill Woodward.
57. Peters.
58. Peters.
59. E.C.S. 22:viii:1896, 4:vi:1910 & 11:vi:1910.
60. Peters.

7 The Social Scene.

61. Round: E.C.S. 12:i:1889; Boxing Day: E.C.S. 29:xii:1906.
62. Round etc.: E.C.S. 31:xii:1881; Poor and Aged: E.C.S. 4:i:1913 records this dinner as the eighth.
63. E.C.S. 21:i:1893.
64. Tea: E.C.S. 26:xi:1881, 13:i:1883, 26:i:1884, 31:i:1885, etc.; Property: E.C.S. 6:viii:1881, 12:x:1889, etc.
65. E.C.S. 9:iii:1889.
66. E.C.S. 18:vi:1892, 8:xii:1900, 15:xii:1900, 15:ii:1902, 1:iii:1902 & 18:x:1902.
67. E.C.S. 8:ix:1883, 6:ix:1884, 12:ix:1891, 11:ix:1897, 13:ix:1902, 9:ix:1911, etc.
68. E.C.S. 8:xi:1884, 9:xi:1889, 8:xi:1890, etc.
69. E.C.S. 15:xi:1884, 16:xi:1889, 15:xi:1890, 15:xi:1902, etc.
70. E.C.S. 10:xi:1906 & 11:xi:1905.
71. Mr. Don Mason.
72. Mrs. Etta Dan. (3)
73. E.C.S. 1:ix:1894 & 26:v:1894.

8 Bayard Brown and the Sporting Scene.

74. E.C.S. 20:vii:1889.
75. *Stories of the Colne*, by L. W. Southern, (1949), p. 35; *A Floating Gold-Mine*, article by F. R. Temple in *World Wide Magazine*, May, 1907, p. 184 & Mr. Paul Brown.
76. Mr. and Mrs. Robert Skilton, and Miss Dorothy Skilton.
77. E.C.S. 6:i:1894 etc.
78. E.C.S. 5:x:1889, 14:xii:1889, 19:iv:1890, 28:vi:1890, 9:viii:1890 & 11:x:1890.
79. Tennis: E.C.S. 30:v:1891, 17:iv:1897; Tom Tit: E.C.S. 10:vii:1897; quoits: E.C.S. 11:viii:1888; billiards: E.C.S. 29:ix:1900 & 6:iv:1901.
80. E.C.S. 13:ii:1886.
81. E.C.S. 8:xii:1888 & 1:xi:1890.
82. E.C.S. 14:ii:1891, 21:ii:1891, 7:iii:1891, 15:ix:1900, 2:ix:1905 & 27:iv:1907.
83. Mr. Don Mason.
84. E.C.S. 9:vii:1904, 29:xii:1906, 6:vi:1908, 29:v:1909 & 15:ii:1913.

9 Education.

85. E.C.S. 4:xii:1886 (letter), 27:xi:1886, citing the I.J., & 14:v:1887.
86. Poll: E.C.S. 28:iv:1888.
87. E.C.S. 9:vi:1888, 24:i:1891 & 7:iii:1891.
88. E.C.S. 23:xi:1889, 14:xii:1889, 3:v:1890, 17:v:1890, 23:v:1891 & 19:ix:1891.
89. E.C.S. 8:viii:1891, 12:ix:1891 & 9:i:1892.
90. School Logs. (2)
91. Mr. Don Mason. (8)
92. Accidents: School Logs; Fights: Mr. Ernest Hatch.
93. Mr. Don Mason, (5), save for orchard and chestnuts: Mr. Ernest Hatch.

Footnotes

94. U of E – Mrs. Etta Dan. (3)
95. School Logs.
96. U of E – Mrs. Etta Dan. (2)
97. School Logs.
98. U of E – Mrs. Etta Dan.
99. Mrs. Millie Mason.
100. School Logs.
101. Slaughter.
102. Nottage, *A Viking Influence on Wivenhoe Quay, monograph by Bill Ellis, (1984).* (3); bequests: E.C.S. 2:v:1896.
103. Ibid.

10 Politics and Amenities.

104. E.C.S. 8:xii:1894 & 22:xii:1894.
105. E.C.S. 9:iv:1898. (2)
106. E.C.S. 16:iv:1898. (3)
107. E.C.S. 30:iv:1898. (2)
108. Sanitation: E.C.S. 1:x:1892; Barlow: E.C.S. 30:iv:1898.
109. Mrs. Millie Mason.
110. E.C.S. 5:i:1901.
111. E.C.S. 5:vii:1902.
112. Mr. Don Mason.
113. Mr. L. H. Martin & Mr. Don Mason.
114. Mr. Dan Chapman.
115. Mr. E. G. Barnes.
116. Mr. Don Mason.
117. E.C.S. 28:xii:1889.
118. Mr. Don Mason & Mr. Philip Dan in E.C.S. (W.W.) 22:xi:1974.
119. E.C.S. 28:ix:1901 & 7:vi:1902.
120. E.C.S. 12:vii:1902.
121. E.C.S. 5:iii:1904, 9:iv:1904, 11:vi:1904, (letter), & 9:vii:1904.
122. E.C.S. 16:vii:1904.
123. E.C.S. 21:iii:1908, 20:iv:1912 & 10:v:1913.
124. E.C.S. 29:i:1910.

11 The Wivenhoe Flier.

125. E.C.S. 3:iv:1909 & 10:iv:1909.
126. E.C.S. 17:iv:1909 & 24:iv:1909.
127. E.C.S. 22:v:1909.
128. E.C.S. 16:x:1909 & 23:x:1909.
129. E.C.S. 23:iv:1910 & *The Wivenhoe Flyer, article by Les Stockdale* in E.A.M., June, 1985, 8.
130. E.C.S. 8:v:1909, 22:v:1909 & 5:vi:1909.

12 Spoiling for a Fight.

131. E.C.S. 3:iii:1900.
132. E.C.S. 10:iii:1900, 11:viii:1900, 20:x:1900 & 29:xii:1900.
133. Smoker: E.C.S. 26:v:1900.
134. E.C.S. 14:vii:1900.
135. E.C.S. 26:v:1900.
136. E.C.S. 16:vi:1900 & 16:x:1900.
137. E.C.S. 5:i:1901 & 19:1:1901.
138. E.C.S. 14:ii:1903.

139. E.C.S. 2:v:1903, 13:v:1911, 9:vii:1904 & 29:xii:1906.
140. E.C.S. 3:x:1903, 25:xi:1905 & 28:x:1905.
141. E.C.S. 26:v:1906.
142. E.C.S. 30:v:1908.
143. Scouts founded: E.C.S. 7:viii:1909; taken seriously: Mrs. Maud Prior; everything else: School Logs.
144. More Scouts: E.C.S. 15:x:1910; National Service League: E.C.S. 7:v:1910 & 24:ix:1910; Red Cross: E.C.S. 12:xi:1910.
145. E.C.S. 24:vi:1911 & 28:x:1911.
146. E.C.S. 4:v:1912, 19:vii:1913 & 1:xi:1913.
147. E.C.S. 21:ii:1914 & 23:v:1914.
148. E.C.S. 27:vi:1914.
149. E.C.S. 4:vii:1914.
150. E.C.S. 1:viii:1914.

CHAPTER 8 – INTO THE SLUMP AND OUT OF IT 1914-1965

1 1914-1918.

1. E.C.T. 8:viii:1914.
2. Territorials: E.C.S. 15:viii:1914; R.A.M.C.: E.C.S. 5:vi:1915; hose: E.C.S. 19:ix:1914; blankets: 26:ix:1914.
3. Mrs. K. G. Everitt.
4. Mill Field & Spion Kop: Mr. P. J. Edwards; concert party: E.C.S. 28:xi:1914; Congregational Chapel: 24:x:1914; recreation area: E.C.S. 14:xi:1914; ad hoc urinal: School Logs.
5. Proper urinal: E.C.S. (W.U.D.C.) 25:xi:1916; baths: Mr. Dan Chapman.
6. E.C.S. 7:xi:1914.
7. *Vanessa's* crew: E.C.S. 31:x:1914; *Venetia, Vanessa, Rosabelle & Miranda: British Warships 1914-19,* by F. J. Dittmar & J. J. Colledge, (1972), Ian Allen; *Lady Blanche:* E.C.S. 8:iii:1919.
8. Dittmar & Colledge.
9. R.A.M.C.: E.C.S. 5:vi:1915; Suffolks: 30:i:1915; Dinner: E.C.S. 1:i:1916.
10. E.C.S. 18:iii:1916, 8:iv:1916, 15:iv:1916, 29:iv:1916, 3:vi:1916 & 13:i:1917.
11. King George V: School Logs; summonses: E.C.S. 1:vii:1916.
12. E.C.S. 6:ii:1937 & 11:i:1985, & *Future Viability of Colchester Port, a report for the Colchester Borough Council by Peter Fraenkel & Partners,* (1986).
13. E.C.S. 1:vii:1916.
14. E.C.S. 19:v:1917.
15. Lawton: E.C.S. 28:x:1916; Hawkins: E.C.S. 2:ix:1916; Barlow: E.C.S. 6:v:1917.
16. Volunteers: E.C.S. 15:vii:1916; Agricultural Committee: E.C.S. 13:i:1917 & (W.U.D.C.) 17:iii:1917; pigs: E.C.S. 17:iii:1917, 24:iii:1917 & 24:xi:1917; War Savings: E.C.S. 2:vi:1917; food: 16:vi:1917 & (W.U.D.C.) 18:viii:1917; vermin: E.C.S. (W.U.D.C.) 14:iv:1917; collections: E.C.S. 1:vi:1918.
17. E.C.S. 21:iv:1917. (2)
18. Graveyard: E.C.S. (W.U.D.C.) 16:ii:1918; Ballast Quay: E.C.S. 30:iii:1918; War Weapons Week: E.C.S. 6:vii:1918 & 22:vii:1918; Mrs. Gooch: E.C.S. 8:vi:1918.
19. E.C.S. 16:xi:1918.
20. Football and yachts: E.C.S. 8:iii:1919.
21. E.C.S. 29:iii:1919.

2 Unemployment.

22. Dinner: E.C.S. 28:vi:1919; procession: E.C.S. 26:vii:1919; bell-ringers: E.C.S. 12:vii:1919.
23. *Maindy Transport:* E.C.S. 27:iii:1920.
24. E.C.S. 15:v:1920.
25. E.C.S. 29:v:1920.

Footnotes

26. Fair: E.C.S. 11:ix:1920; Armistice Day: E.C.S. 13:xi:1920; regatta: 9:x:1920; Social Club: E.C.S. 9:x:1920; Swedenborgian demise: *Annual Yearbook of the General Conference of the New Church for 1933*; Salvation Army: Mr. L. W. Kemble; Council houses: E.C.S. (W.U.D.C.) 19:vi:1920; *Tower:* E.C.S. 15:v:1920; *Keep:* E.C.S. 13:xi:1920.
27. Mr. Don Mason.
28. E.C.S. (W.U.D.C.) 15:i:1921, 12:ii:1921 & 8:x:1921.
29. E.C.S. 18:ii:1922; E.C.S. 4:iii:1922. (2)
30. E.C.S. 3:vi:1922.
31. E.C.S. 8:vii:1922.
32. Dinners: E.C.S. 4:xi:1922; Ratepayers: E.C.S. 18:xi:1922 & 2:xii:1922.
33. E.C.S. 24:iii:1923.
34. E.C.S. 31:iii:1923.
35. E.C.S. (W.U.D.C.) 17:xi:1923, 16:viii:1924 & 13:ix:1924.
36. E.C.S. 7:iii:1925 & E.C.S. 9:vii:1927.
37. E.C.S. 10:iv:1926, 26:iv:1926, 31:vii:1926, 11:xii:1926 & 19:xi:1927.
38. Rice: E.C.S. 9:iv:1927; Pollock Anderson: E.C.S. 5:iii:1932; rumour: E.C.S. 22:iv:1933; *Rodney:* E.C.S. 9:vi:1934; towing boat: Mr. V. E. Annis.
39. Burke: E.C.S. 24:iii:1923; receiving order: E.C.S. 11:viii:1934.
40. *A Range of Dinghies*, article in Yachting World 13:ii:1931, *A 60-ft Motor Yacht*, article in The Motor Boat 21:ii:1930; Edwards: E.C.S. 22:vi:1935; liquidation: E.C.S. 19:vii:1937.

3 The Changing Scene.

41. E.C.S. 28x1922.
42. R. v. Crooks: E.C.S. 9:xii:1922 & 10:ii:1923; fires: E.C.S. 15:viii:1925 & 16:i:1926; sale: 21:iii:1927.
43. Mr. Cecil Riches. (7)
44. E.C.S. 1:xi:1930 & 29:xi:1930.
45. Mrs. M. Marshall.
46. Mr. L. W. Kemble.
47. Funeral: E.C.S. 28:ix:1929 & 12:x:1929; the rest: Mr. James Harvey.
48. Visit: E.C.S. 17:x:1928; the rest: Martin-Harvey.
49. Mr. James Harvey.
50. Mrs. May Potter.
51. Mr. & Mrs. E. J. Knappett, Mrs. Ruth Munson & Mr. L. W. Kemble.
52. E.C.S. 4:vi:1932 & (W.U.D.C.) 15:x:1932.
53. E.C.S. (W.U.D.C.) 15:x:1932 & 12:xi:1932, & Mr. Lewis Worsp. (2)
54. Mrs. R. J. McEune.
55. Mrs. Violet Page.
56. Mr. Walter Wix.
57. E.C.S. 24:xii:1932.
58. E.C.S. 26:iv:1930.
59. E.C.S. (letter) 23:iii:1935.
60. *Round the World with Wivenhoe's Man in the Iron Mask*, article by Dick Barton in E.C.S. 22:x:1971.
61. E.C.S. 9:x:1931, 6:xi:1931 & 19:xii:1931, & Mr. L. H. Martin.
62. School Logs.
63. Ibid. (4)
64. E.C.S. (W.U.D.C.) 13:xii:1930, 17:xii:1932, 25:ii:1933, (W.U.D.C.) 16:v:1936, 22:viii:1936 & 6:ii:1937.
65. E.C.S. 30:vii:1938.
66. E.C.S. 22:v:1926, 23:x:1926 & 9:iv:1932, & Dr. Walter Radcliffe. (2)
67. One Design.
68. E.C.S. 5:viii:1933 & 12:viii:1933.
69. Clubhouse: E.C.S. 11:i:1936 & 28:iii:1936, & One Design.

70. E.C.S. i:viii:1936, 15:vii:1939, 26:viii:1939, etc.
71. Rice: E.C.S. 8:ii:1936; *Shipbuilders' Security: Is Wivenhoe to be Murdered Again?*, article by Hervey Benham in E.C.S. 22:ix:1944.

4 Charles Gooch the Younger.

72. E.C.S. 13:iii:1937 & 20:iii:1937.
73. Mrs. Marguerite Cole & Mrs. P. L. J. Le Poer Power. (3)

5 1939-1945.

74. Ballot: E.C.S. 2:ii:1935; End War & Red Cross: E.C.S. 10:iv:1937; Munro: E.C.S. 2:iv:1938.
75. A.R.P.: E.C.S. 2:iv:1938; gas-masks: E.C.S. 8:x:1938; demonstrations; E.C.S. 15:x:1938 & 29:x:1938; firemen: E.C.S. (W.U.D.C.) 17:xii:1938.
76. National Service: E.C.S. 21:i:1939; evacuees: E.C.S. (W.U.D.C.) 18:ii:1939.
77. Films: E.C.S. 4:iii:1939, etc.; Nurse: E.C.S. 12:iii:1938; Doctor: E.C.S. 11:iii:1939.
78. Evacuees: E.C.S. 9:ix:1939 & (W.U.D.C.) 21:x:1939; weddings: E.C.S. 9:ix:1939 & 16:ix:1939; Dutton: E.C.S. 23:ix:1939; Shaw: E.C.S. 30:ix:1939.
79. Wivenhoe Shipyard: E.C.S. 17:ii:1940; Work: *Essex at War*, by Hervey Benham, (1939), *Essex County Standard*, p. 151; Lieutenant-Commander: Dr. Walter Radcliffe.
80. Essex at Work, p. 152.
81. E.C.S. 2:iii:1945.
82. Mrs. P. L. J. Le Poer Power.
83. Mr. & Mrs. P. L. J. Le Poer Power.
84. E.C.S. (W.U.D.C.) 13:iv:1940.
85. Shelters: E.C.S. (W.U.D.C.) 13:vii:1940, School Logs & E.C.S. (W.U.D.C.) 14:ix:1940; German aeroplanes: Mr. E. J. Knappett.
86. Fire Station: Mr. R. J. McEune.
87. War Working Party: E.C.S. 22:vi:1940, etc.; War Weapons Week: E.C.S. 12:vii:1941, etc.; fruit centre: E.C.S. 6:vi:1942.
88. E.C.S. 13:vi:1942.
89. E.C.S. 9:vii:1943; see also letters from Mrs. Marjorie Dean in E.C.S. 6:ii:1943 & 20:iii:1943.
90. E.C.S. 15:viii:1942.
91. School Logs.
92. Savings Committee: E.C.S. 22:viii:1942, etc.; Wings for Victory: E.C.S. 28:v:1943, etc.; grand scrounge: *Programme for "Wivenhoe's Week"*.
93. Mr. Glendower Jackson. (11)
94. E.C.S. (letter) 21:vii:1944 & (letter) 16:vi:1944.
95. *Essex at War*, by Hervey Benham, p. 151 & *Wivenhoe's D-Day Secret*, article by Andrew Phillips in E.C.S. 1:vi:1984.
96. E.C.S. 29:ix:1944 & 13:x:1944.
97. E.C.S. 23:ii:1945 & 20:vii:1945.

6 Brave New World.

98. E.C.S. 5:iv:1946.
99. E.C.S. 11:vii:1947.
100. The voyage of the Cap Pilar is chronicled in two books: *Voyage in a Barquentine*, by Peter Roach, (1952), Hart-Davis, & *The Voyage of the Cap Pilar*, by Adrian Seligman, (1939), Hodder & Stoughton; Cadets: E.C.S. 29:vii:1939. See also E.C.S. 25:xi:1949.
101. E.C.S. 1:xii:1950 & 9:iii:1951.
102. Mr. Guy Harding. (2)
103. E.C.S. 8:ii:1952, 26:ix:1952 & 3:x:1952.
104. E.C.S. 13:ii:1953 & (W.W.) 13:ii:1953, 13:xi:1953, 18:xii:1953, 8:i:1954 & 5:ii:1954.
105. E.C.S. 25:iii:1955 & 1:iv:1955.

106. E.C.S. 6:ii:1953 & (W.W.) 6:ii:1953.
107. E.C.S. 2:iv:1953.
108. E.C.S. 12:vi:1953, 19:vi:1953, 10:vii:1953, 31:vii:1953 & 16:x:1953.
109. E.C.S. 17:xii:1965.

CHAPTER 9 – THE UNIVERSITY OF ESSEX

1 The Making of a Troublespot.

1. *Building the New Universities,* by Tony Birks, *(1972)*, pub. *David & Charles,* Chapter 1.
2. Ibid. 21:vi:1960.
3. "Little Chance of University at Colchester" C.G. 21:vi:1960.
4. "Town is Delighted Over University" E.C.S. 26:v:961.
5. E.C.S. 25:i:1946 & 8:ii:1946.
6. "University Site to cost County Council £175,000" E.C.S. 22:xii:1961.
7. University Press Statement of 4:vii:1962.
8. "University – A New Town" E.C.S. 25:x:1963.
9. *The Making of a University,* by Albert Sloman, *(1964)*, *B.B.C.*
10. *The Builder* 1:xi:1963, citing a University brochure.
11. *The Architects Journal Information Library* 20:ix:1972, in particular pp. 669-670 & 646-647.
12. Sloman, 50.
13. Sloman, 59.
14. Sloman, 12.
15. *An Academic Success or Social Failure?,* article by *Nicholas Butler* in C.E. 10:xii:1970.
16. £127,800: "Planning Board for University" E.C.S. 15:ix:1961; £1,100,000: University Press Release 13:iii:1964.
17. C.G. 6:viii:1964.

2 The Troubles Begin.

18. E.C.S. 9:x:1964.
19. Wyvern & Theatre Arts Society: E.C.S. 27:xi:1964; blood sports: E.C.S. 20xi1964; "Police angry at rag hat trick" E.C.S. 16:iii:1965.
20. "University Faces a Serious Student Lodging Problem" E.C.S. 1:x:1965; Wyvern: C.E. 28:x:1965; Lodge: *The house John Constable never dreamed of,* article by *Wyn Jones* in E.C.S. 24:vi:1966; Lecture Block: E.C.S. 6:v:1966.
21. *An Academic Success or Social Failure?,* article by *Nicholas Butler* in C.E. 10:xii:1970. 10:xii:1970.
22. Ibid.
23. "Slow Handclaps and Boos for Mr. Crosland" *Sunday Telegraph* 12:ii:1967; "Students Protest Over Fee-Raising" E.A.D.T. 23:ii:1967; "Students angry at university 'drug' raid by police" E.A.D.T. 28:ii:1967.
24. *An Academic Success etc.* C.E. 10:xii:1970.
25. *Evening News* 20:v:1967.
26. C.G. 1:iii:1968; *Leicester Mercury* 6:iii:1968.
27. National Press.
28. Ibid.
29. Ibid.
30. *Daily Express* 21:ii:1969. (3)
31. *Daily Express* 20:ii:1969.
32. National Press.
33. Ibid.
34. Ibid.
35. Ibid.
36. Ibid.

37. *Campus Freedom Plan Crashes In Wave Of Violence*, article by R. Barry O'Brien in *The Daily Telegraph* 26:xi:1970.
38. *An Academic Success etc.* C.E. 10:xii:1970.
39. *Anarchy at Essex*, leader in *The Daily Telegraph* 26:xi:1970. (3)
40. *A damning record of riot, arson, anarchy and insulting behaviour at this Academy of Marx*, article by James Wentworth Day in *Essex Chronicle* 28:i:1972. (3)
41. National Press.
42. Ibid.
43. Ibid.

3 The Angry Brigade.

44. *The Sun* 7:xii:1972.
45. E.C.S. 8:xii:1972.
46. Mendelson: *The Times* 15:ii:1977; Creek: *Daily Express* 22:iv:1977.

4 1973-1974.

47. E.A.D.T. 20:ii:1973.
48. *Their Daily Bread*, article by Nicholas Butler in C.E. 29:iii:1973. (10)
49. National Press.
50. National Press.
51. *The Times Higher Education Supplement* 30:xi:1973.
52. E.G. 25:iii:1974.
53. "Academic": *Sunday Times* 28:iv:1974.
54. *Daily Express* 2:viii:1974; *Evening Standard* 1:viii:1974; *The Daily Telegraph* 1:viii:1974.
55. *University of Essex: The First Ten Years*, article by Nicholas Butler in C.E. 11:vii:1974.
56. *The Times Higher Education Supplement* 16:viii:1974.

5 The Survival Game.

57. National Press.
58. Accommodation: C.E. 22:x:1975; more students: National Press.
59. Daily Express 3:iii:1977.
60. *Yes Minister*, by Jonathan Lynn & Antony Jay, *(1983)*, B.B.C., Vol. III, p. 173.

6 Interim Report.

61. Centuries, by Thomas Traherne. (2)
62. Sloman, 89.
63. Sloman, 50.
64. Phenomenon observed by Mr. L. R. James.
65. University Press Statement of 4:vi:1962.

CHAPTER 10 – WHO ARE THESE PEOPLE?

1 Expansion.

1. A solicitor's letter which was read to me.
2. *The Changing Face of Wivenhoe*, article by Ray McSweeney in C.E. 21:i:1965 and *Wivenhoe's Future?*, article by Wyn Jones in E.C.S. 3:xii:1965.

2 Big Lorries into Small Roads.

3. E.C.S. (W.U.D.C.) 5:v:1888.
4. E.C.S. (W.W.) 21:i:1966.

Footnotes

5. E.C.S. (W.U.D.C.) 18:ii:1966, letters from The Wivenhoe Society in 18:ii:1966 & 8:vii:1966, and 15:vii:1966.
6. E.C.S. 15:vii:1966, 2:ix:1966, 9:ix:1966 & an article by Wyn Jones on the *Cap Pilar* in 23:ix:1966.
7. "Townsfolk fight for Wivenhoe's ferry road" C.G. 4:xi:1969, "Ferry Road – Fire Risk or Necessity?" E.C.S. 7:xi:1970, "A village fights back at big business" C.E. 16:iv:1970, "Ferry Road: first round goes to the residents" E.C.S. 17:iv:1970, "Danger to public stressed in second path inquiry" C.E. 2:vii:1970, etc.
8. "Ferry Road Must Be Shut Rules Minister" E.G. 26:x:1970, "Timber firm's gates are forced open" E.C.S. 13:xi:1970, etc.
9. "Stop The Rape Of Wivenhoe Wood", letters in E.C.S. 13:vi:69, "Wivenhoe Fights To Save Wood" E.C.S. 23:i:1970, "Victory for the 'Save our wood' campaigners" C.G. 12:v:1970, "Minister bans Wivenhoe wood housing scheme" E.C.S. 15:v:1970, "Building tries again for homes in wood" C.G. 26:i:1970, "'Buy Woods' Plea To Council In Fight To Save Beauty Spot" E.G. 9:viii:1970, "Wivenhoe inquiry protest" C.E. 19:viii:1971, "Wivenhoe Woods can't be developed" E.C.S. 7:i:1972, etc.
10. "Wivenhoe's oldest pub to be pulled down" E.C.S. 18:ii:1972, "Fight To Save Pub" C.E. 11:v:1972, "'Save the Falcon' movement spreads" C.E. 25:v:1970, "Historic pub is saved" C.E. 15:iii:1973, etc.
11. Planning Application COL/960/81 WIV.
12. Inspector's Report on the Public Inquiry to determine Planning Applications COL/960/81 WIV & COL/953/82 WIV.
13. "Fears of siphon road 'sucking in industry'" E.C.S. 16:iii:1984; "Wivenhoe Port's deal rejected" E.C.S. 25:v:1984.
14. Wivenhoe Preservation Trust: "Fund launched to fight port plans" E.C.S. 23:xi:1984; letter from The Department of the Environment 18:vi:1985 giving the decision on Planning Application COL/442/84 WIV.
15. "Port company is fined for dusty scenes" E.C.S. 7:xii:1984 & "Dusty port is fined again" E.C.S. 4:xii:1984.
16. "£20m housing plan for port" & "How the Colneside face of Wivenhoe may change" E.C.S. 29:i:1988.

3 Making the Party Go.

17. Wivenhoe Town F.C. Football Yearbook 1986-87 and a letter to me from Mr. John Button, the club's programme editor.
18. Sailing: Mr. Alan Tyne; Bowls: Mr. David Collins.
19. Changes: Rev. Stephen Hardie.
20. Gordon, 50-55 and Pastor Victor Cameron.
21. King, pp. 44-49 and Rev. J. W. R. Robinson.
22. Father Michael Butler.
23. *Spreading the word of the Lord*, article by Dick Barton in E.C.S. 27:viii:1971.
24. Mrs. P. J. Excell.
25. Gilbert-and-Sullivan: Mr. Ian Hunter & Mrs. Janet Turner.
26. "Wivenhoe may have the first arts centre in N. Essex" E.C.S. 14:i:1966.
27. E.C.S. 21:x:1966.

4 The End of an Aeon.

28. "James Cook goes into voluntary liquidation – Threat to 80 jobs at shipbuilding yard" E.C.S. 22:v:1986.
29. "Who is shipyard buyer?" E.C.S. 5:xii:1986 and "Shipyard liquidators face £1m legal claim" E.C.S. 22:i:1987.
30. Mr. Malcolm Goodwin.
31. "Nearly £1m for shipyard" E.C.S. 10:vii:1987 and "Housing planned by new shipyard owner" E.C.S. 18:iii:1988.
32. Planning Application COL/170/88 WIV.

General Index

Bold type indicates a principal or substantial reference; *italics* indicate an illustration. (U of E) refers to the University of Essex.

Abell, William, 10
Academic Planning Board, The, 277, 312, 319
Admiralty Warehouse, The Cinque Port, 116
Agriculture, (see Farming)
Air Raid Shelters 256, 258
Albert, Prince, of Saxe-Coburg, 70, *75,* 75-76, 101
Aldridge, George, 116
Alefounder, Mrs. ---, 53
Allcock, Miss Debbie, *337*
Allen, Mr. Derrick, 267
Allen's Farm 255
Alliance Party, The, 329
Allies Concert Party, The, 211
Allotments 215-216, 217, 245
Alma Stores, The, *335,* 335
Alma Street 96, *97,* 97, 125, 167, 187, 190, 207, 208, 210, 213, 220, 234, 236, 259, 339
Almshouses, (see also The Workhouse), 10, 125, 163, 218
Alport, Lord, 289
Alresford 3, 31, 95, 102, 178, 182, 198, 236, 322
Alresford Creek 2, 122, *121,* 198, 245, 258, 261, 262-263
Alresford Grange 230
Alresford Hall 31, 37, 38, 63, 83, 91, 109, 141
Alresford Sand and Ballast Co. Ltd., The, 261

Ambulance No. 1 Brigade *257*
Anchor Hill 11, 46, 54, 115, 116, 125, 167, *231,* 252, 330, 331
Anchor House 29
Andersen, Otto, (see also Otto Andersen & Co. (London) Ltd.), 224, 227
Anglesea Road 3, 93, 125, 159, 190, 238, 355
Anglesey, The Marquis of, 83, *84,* 85, 87, 88, 106, 247, 355
Anglia Water Authority 346
Angry Brigade, The, **294-299**, *295,* 306
Annan, Lord, 277, 306
Annan Report, The, 306
Apprentices and Apprenticeship 10, 59, **161-162**, 184, 221
Archard, Peter, 288
Archidiaconal Court, The, 8-9, 10, 11, 15
Ardley, Mr. Ken, 299
Argor, John, 28
Armada, The Spanish, 13
Armistice, The, and Armistice Day 218, 220, 242
Art and Artists *338,* **338-341**
Arthur R. Brown & Co. 227
Atkinson, Brian, 10
Atkinson, Mr. Ted, 339
Auctions and Sales 52, 55, 88, 116-117, 123, 135, 141
Audley, Thomas Lord, 6
Auxiliary Fire Service, The, *257,* 258
Avenue, The, 6, 111, *112,* 139, 165, *173, 193,* 202, *208,* 210, 271, 325, 356

Baillie, Rev. John, 76, 80, 129, 132, 133, 141
Baines, Mr. Austin, 320, 329
Baker, Gustavus, 240
Ballast and Ballast Quay 56, 89, 210, 211
Ballast Quay Farm and House 93, 139, 141, 217, 263, 325, 339
Bands, Brass, 97, 113, **117,** 122, 138, 141, 143, **167,** *168,* 202, 203, 207, *209,* 209, 210, 211, 218, 220, 248
Bane, Mrs. Paddy, *337*
Barker, Elizabeth, 143
Barker, John, 294, *295,* 296, 297
Barker, Jonathan, 54
Barlow, Alexander Kay, **139,** 156, *165,* 172, 173, 187, 188, 194, 195, 198, 200, 213, 215, 227
Barlow, Mrs. Alexander Kay, 139, 198
Barlow, John, (son of the two above) 215
Barnes, Mr. Michael, Q.C. 330
Barr, Hector, 245, 357
Barr, Mrs. Hector, *246*
Barr, James, 110-111, 126
Barr, Jane, 352
Barrell Brothers, The, Ben and Martin, 222, 228
Barrell's Timber Yard *222,* 222 , 228
Bartlett, William, 354
Batayle Family, The, 3
Bath Street 43, 88, *157*
Baths (c. 1750-1800 and 1914) 1, **43-44,** 47, 213
Bawtree, John, 47
Bawtree, Samuel, 94
Beard, Ernest Stanley, also Beard & Co. 139, 152, 190, 356
Beardon, Colin, 306
Beaumont, George Frederick, 141
Beaumont, William Viscount *5,* 5, 6
Beaumont, Viscountess Elizabeth, later The Countess of Oxford, neé Scrope, *5,* 5, 6
Beckes, Thomas, 10
Beech Avenue 318, 321, 356
Belcher, Mrs. Stevie, *337*
Bell, Arthur, 267, *272*
Bell, Ian Granville, 306
Bell, Mr. James, *246*

Belle Vue Road 6, 29, 139, 159, 164, 167-168, 188, 202, 210, *251,* 262, 356
Belleville Place 356
Bellmann-Taylor, Miss ---, 210
Benefit Societies, (see Friendly Societies)
Bensley, Harry, 239, *240,* 240
Bentall, E. H., 108
Bertrand Russell Tower Block, (U of E), 319, 358
Bethany Street 96, 355
Betts, Emily, 132
Bevan, ---, 38
Bicknell, Maria, (see Constable, Maria)
Bigges, Jeremiah 15
Bigges, Jeremy, 15
Bishop, Deecee, 229
Black Buoy Hill, *335*
Blagrave, William, 28
"Blood Alley," (see Blyth's Lane)
Blyth, (or Bligh), Isaac, **93-94,** 129, 355
Blyth, (or Bligh), Mrs. Isaac, ("Aunt Bligh") 93-94
Blyth, Captain Joseph, 104
Blyth's Lane, (Blood Alley) 194, 230, 353
Boatbuilding and Shipbuilding 11, **18-20,** 22, **25-26,** 30, 46, **47, 48,** *49,* **50-51,** 53, **83, 85-88, 104, 106-111, 126, 127, 144-146,** *145,* 145-146, *147, 148,* **148-149,** *150, 151,* **151-154,** *153, 155,* **156,** *159, 160,* **161-162,** *185,* 186, *213,* **213-214, 218,** *219,* **221,** 222, **224,** *225,* **226, 227, 245,** *246,* 247, 248, *253, 254,* **254- 255,** 261, *263,* 264, **265, 266,** *267,* **268- 269,** 325, *342,* **342-345,** *343*
Bobbitts Hole 356
Bobbitts Way 321
Boer War, The, **202-204,** *203,* 252
Boilermakers, Iron and Steel Shipbuilders, The Amalgamated Society of, 161, 207
Bond, Mark, 301
Boothroyd, Rev. G. W., *244*
Bott, Christopher, 294, *295,* 296, 298
Bourne, Major Nehemiah, 20
Bow, Henry, *165*
Bowen, Colonel ---, 130
Bowes, Farmer A. E., 263, 322, 340, 357
Bradley, George, 119, 122
Branch, John, 27

General Index

Bransby, H. N., 103
Brassey, Thomas Lord, 110, 160
Brassey, Lady, 110
Brewers, Brewing and Breweries 47, 94, 116, 133
Bridge, Samuel, 28
Briggs, Rev. E. J. E., 334
Brightlingsea, (see also Wivenhoe and Brightlingsea Railway) 10, 11, 32, 52, 56, 85, 97, 107, 114, 119, 122, 123, 125, 154, 169, 172, 173, 178, 186, 227, 230, 238, 242, 265, 270, 271, 334
Britannia Crescent 265, 322, 356
British Aeroplanes Syndicate Ltd. 197, 199
British Legion, The Royal, and The British Legion Hall 29, 239, 336
Broad Lane 333
Broadfields Estate, The, 322, 331, 357
Bronze Age, The, 2
Brook Street 4, 7, 54, 122, 188, 234, 258
Brooks, George, 234
Broom Field, The, 167
Broomfield Residents Association, The, 322
Broomgrove Schools, (see Schools)
"Broomy, The," 356
Brotherhood, The, 210
Brown, Fred, *165*
Brown, John, 15
Brown, McEvers Bayard, **169, 172,** 174, *177,* 224, 227
Brown, Stephen, 90
Browne Family, The, 47, 93, 111, 112, 113, 132, 156
Browne, John, 10
Browne, William, (eighteenth century) 47
Browne, William, (nineteenth century) 93, 112, 113
Bruff, Peter, 117, 122
Brummell, George Bryan, *92,* 92-93
Brummell, William, 92, 93, 94, 123
Bryant, Mr. Lionel, *337*
Buck, Sir Antony, Q.C., M.P. 289
Buddleia Close 357
Buffaloes, The Ancient Order of, 163, 220
Bumble International 346
Burgess, Edmund, 9-10, 351
Burnham, Mr. Jack, *271*

Burnie, Australia 353-354
Bus service 230
Butler of Saffron Walden, Lord, *278,* 279, 288, 306, *310,* 317-318
Byles, Frank, 214, 239-240

Cage, The, 11, 115-116
Callaghan, The Rt. Hon. James, M.P. 307-308
Camulodunum 2
Canham, John, 172
Cannell, David, 345
Cap Pilar Close 357
Capel, The Hon. A., 90
Capon, Kenneth, *280,* 281, 282, 283, 284, 297, 312
Captains of the Big Yachts, The, (see also Yachts, The Big,) 85, 95, **158-159,** 161, 163, 164, 178, 187, 197, 220, *223,* 230, 232, 245, *247,* 247
"Captains Row", (1-11, Anglesea Road) 159, 355
Captains' Tea, The, 163-164
Cardinal, Clarkson, 47
Cargo Boats, (see Merchant Vessels)
Carolin, Elizabeth, 143, 197, 202, 204, 214
Carolin, Rev. John Sinclair, (1856-1922) **141-144,** *142,* 163, 164, 173, 174, 186, 187, 188, 197, 202
Carrington, George, 116
Carroll, Mr. D., 267
Caston, Edward, 103
Cawton, Elizabeth, neé Jenkin, 17
Cawton, Thomas, the Elder **15,** *16,* **17, 18,** 28
Cawton, Thomas, the Younger 17
Cedric's Garage *193,* 228, *229,* 262
Chamberlain, George, 68, 113
Chamberlain, John Green, 93, 101, 129
Chamberlain, Philip, *162, 165,* 204, 355
Chaney, Grace, 228
Chaney, Percy, *257,* 326, 357
Chapel Street 42
Chapman, Daniel, 208
Chapman, William, 101
Charity and Charities 7, 10, 60, 70, 74, 80, 81, 133, 163, 172, 332
Chartism 73

381

Chelmer Cargo Services (Shipping) Ltd. 330
Chelmsford, including Chelmsford Gaol 70, 71, 85, 91, 132, 256, 271, 275, 304, 351
Child, Sir Caesar, Bart. 41
"Chirchstrete" 355
Chopping, Mr. Richard, 338
Christie, James, *295*, 296
Church of England Religion, The, **7-10, 15, 17,** 43, 68, 74, 95, 99, 103, 167, 178, 179, **333-334**
Church, The Parish, of St. Mary the Virgin:
Roman foundations: 2; chantry chapel: 4, 6; acquisition of a tower and clock: 6; life and appearance in Elizabethan times: **7-10;** acquisition of a gallery in 1566-1588: 8; Elizabethan rectors: **9-10;** patronage by John Gurdon Rebow: 76; alterations of 1859-1860: 101; new bells in 1903- 4: 204; church parade: *205,* 207, 210, 220, 333; alterations in 1987: 333-334; also 4, *5,* 5-6, 37, 38, 41, 42, 68, 70, 71, 76, 93-94, 115, 125, 129-130, 135, 137, 141, 142, 143-144, *170,* 204, 207, 210, 218, 220, 227, 230, 249, 350
Churchill, Sir W. S., *255,* 255, 263
Churchwardens **8, 9, 10,** 29, 68, 70, **93,** 101, 141, 143, 144
Cinema and cinematography 151, **228-230**
Civic Service, The, 336
Civil War, The, (1642-1649) 17-18, 28, 56, 351
Clarke, Mrs. Coralie, *272*
Clarke, Mr. David, 339, 340
Clarke, Thomas, 27
Clifton Terrace 124, 125, 261, 356
Clothmaking 18, 27, 47
Coal, Coalyards and Colliers 25, 46, **89,** 94, 123, 218, 266, *329*
Cobbe, Sir John, 4
Cobbold, J. C., 118
Cock, Richard, 11
Cockaynes 3
Cockrell, W. F., 156
Coker's Field 165, 167

Colchester 2, 18, 27, 31, 46, 70, 85, 97, 115, 119, 123, 129, 130, 132, 214, 230, 271, 272, 275, 288, 289, 302, 304, 305, 317, 318, 330, 331, 333, 335
Colchester Borough Council 328, 330, 347, 351
Colchester Express 293, 324
Colchester Institute of Higher Education, (formerly The Albert School of Science and Art, The Colchester Polytechnic and the Technical College) 134, 183, 184, 221, 300, 302, 303, 314, 338
Colchester Manufacturing Co. Ltd., The, 236, 238
Colchester Mechanics' Institute, The, 70, 75
Colchester Medical Society, The, 44
Colchester Polytechnic, (see Colchester Institute of Higher Education)
Colchester Road 44, 57, *58*
Colchester Royal Grammar School 7, 70, 114, 181
Colchester Sixth Form College 315
Colchester Town Council 133-134, 135, 139, 194, 195, 267
Colchester United Football Club 174, 333
Cole, Billy, 115, 194
Cole, Daniel, 88
Cole, Henry, 249
Cole, Hannah, (see Tunmer, Hannah)
Cole, Joseph, 88
Cole, Mrs. Marguerite, neé Gooch, 137, *249,* 249
Cole, William, 56
Collin, Thomas, 27
Collins, Mr. ---, 130
Colne Boating Club, The, 113
Colne Estuary Study, 331
Colne Fishery Company, The, 149
Colne, The River:
Peter Bruff's scheme: 117; changed by the railways: 123; proposed bridge: **194-195,** *195,* **214,** *215,* 223; proposed haul road along the north bank: 330; proposed surge barrier: 346; also 2, 37, 46, 83, 116, 123, 146, 154, 172, 262, 263, *319,* 331, 342, 345
Colne Terrace 125

General Index

Colne Marine and Yacht Company, The, 236, 266, 267
Colne Social Bowls Club, The, 245
Colne Social Club, The, 245
Colne Yacht (and Boat) Club, The, 144, 169, 172, 173
Common Wealth Party, The, 259
Community Centre, The proposed, 331, **336-341,** 349-350
Congregationalists, The Congregational Chapels and Schoolroom **28, 43, 68, 95,** *98,* **99,** 125, 130, 167, 179, 211, 236, **334,** 345
Conservation and the Conservation Area, (see also The Wivenhoe Society), 234, 324, 332, *348*
Conservative Party, The, and Conservatives 68, 73, 74, 76, 133, 137, 141, 144, 187, **195,** *196,* **197,** 210, 218, 227, 289, 329
Constable, John, (1776-1837) **61-64,** *65, 66*
Constable, Maria, neé Bicknell 61-64
Cook, Samuel, 88
Cook's, (James W. Cook & Co. Ltd.) 264, 265-266, *267,* 339, *342,* **342-345,** *343,* 346
Co-operative Stores and, later, Supermarket, The, 139, 182, 331, 341
Copperas 112
Corder, Thomas, 55
Cornwall, John, 15
Coronation Celebrations *164, 165, 206, 208,* 208-209
Corsellis, Elizabeth, neé Taylor, (wife of Nicholas Corsellis IV), 41, *42*
Corsellis Family, The, **27-28,** 38, 39, **41-42,** 76, **89,** 93, 139
Corsellis, Frances, neé Child, (wife of Nicholas Corsellis IV) 41
Corsellis, Frederick, 27-28
Corsellis, Rev. John M., 89
Corsellis, Joseph Goodall, (1764-1835) 89
Corsellis, Mary, neé Bond, (wife of Nicholas Corsellis VI) 89
Corsellis, Mary, neé Goodall, (wife of Nicholas Corsellis V) 1, 39, 41
Corsellis, Nicholas I, (1600?-1665) 27
Corsellis, Nicholas II, (1634?-1674) 27

Corsellis, Nicholas III, (1661-1728) 41, *42,* 43, 57
Corsellis, Nicholas IV, (1697-1761) 41, 43, 46, 54
Corsellis, Nicholas V, (1744-1826) 39, **41-42,** 55, 67, 89, 94
Corsellis, Captain Nicholas Caesar VI, (1763-1833) 89, *90*
Corsellis, Nicholas Caesar VII, 89, 123, 125
Corsellis, Zegar, (d. 1625) 27
Council Houses 221, 263, *265,* 265
Council Offices, The, (see also Little Wick), 187, 190, 213, 230, 239-240, 260
Country, Captain Jeremy, 22, 25
Country, Captain Richard, 22, 25
Court, Archidiaconal, (see Archidiaconal Court)
Court, Manorial, see Manorial Court
Courtauld, J. M., 108
Cox & King, Messrs., later Cox & King Ltd. 146, 156, 218, *225,* 227
Cracknell Close 357
Cranfield, Captain ---, 186
Creek, Hilary, 294, *295,* 296, 297, 299
Crewing and Crewmen 85, 110, 111, 112, **156, 158-161,** 162, 167, 230, 248
Crickitt, C. A., 42
Crime, (see also Smuggling and Witchcraft) **9-11,** 15, 74, 115-116
Critchley, Mr. Brian, 337
Cross, Mrs. Gail, neé Mills, *338,* 338, 339
Cross, Mr. Jack 339, 340
Cross, Roy, *338,* 338, 339
Cross, The, 6, 29, 47, 102, 111, 167, 178, 182, 190, 195, 210, 222, 245, 252, 331
Cunyham, William, 28
Currell, William "Shreddy", 194
Customs House Lookout Tower 266
Cuttelee, John, 11

Daily Telegraph, The 292, 293, 305
Dale, The, 321
Damant, Philip, 132
Damp, Rev. Christopher J., 334
Dan, Etta, **183-184,** 262
Dan, John, *338,* 338-339

Dan, Mrs. Pamela, *338*, 338-339
Davies, Mr. Glyndwr "Glyn", 331
Davies, Rev. W., 221
Day, P.C. "Tolly", 261-262
de Champion Crespigny, Sir Claude, (son of the below) 91, 113
de Crespigny, Bart., Sir Claude, **90, 91,** 101, 113, 114, 118, 122, 125
de Crespigny, Lady, (wife of the above) 106
de Power, Marcus, 28
de Vere, (see Oxford, Earls of)
De Vere Close 339, 356
De Vere Lane 335, 356
Dean, Marjorie, 253, *260,* 260, 264, 265, 325, 340
Dean, Dr. William, 252, 253, 259, *260,* 339-340
Dean's Antiques 96, *97,* 265
Dedham 61
Defoe, Daniel, 17, 46
Dene Park Estate, The, 3, 89, 211, 322, 357
Dennis, H.A., 54
Denton, C. W., 188
Denton, W. E., 356
Denton's Terrace 125, 356
Digby, Aylmer W., 218
Disease 13, 17, **27, 44,** 60, 78, 94, 96, **102,** 103, **163,** 188, 191, **242,** 351, 352
Dissenters, (see also Nonconformists and Congregationalists) 17, 68, 69, 73, 74, 77, 96,
Dixon, Alice, 351
Dixon Close 357
Dolphine, Richard, 6
Domesday Book 2, 3
Dorman Long 263
Doubleday, Mr. John, 339
Dowser, or Douser, Edward, 54
Dry Dock, The, built by Forrestt's, 146, 149, 152, 153, 179, *232,* 254, 265, 325, *327*
Duncan, George, 223
Duncan, Captain Henry, 50
Dunn, Mr. C. M. J., 56-57
Dunne, Mrs. Margaret, 347
Durrell Family, The, 47, 111

Durrell, Joseph, 47
Durrell, Zena, 228
Dutch, The, fear of, Quarter, Wars, etc. 20, 22, 25, 26, 28, 29, 31
Dutton, Harold (farmer) 253, 259, 260
Dyer, Miss ---, 1, 38

Earthquake of 1884, The, **129-133,** *130, 131, 132*
East Anglian Daily Times 293
East Donyland, including the Hall 51, 52, 88, 173
East Street 7, 29, 94, 210, 234, 331, 345, 346
Easter Tea, The, 91, 163
Eddington Tower Block, (U of E) 319, 358
Education, (see also The University of Essex), **53,** 70, 71, 73, 76, 77, 78, 80, **95-96, 99, 101-103,** 117, **178-184, 186, 240,** *241,* **242,** 332, 341
Egerton-Green, Claude Egerton, **137-139,** *138,* 174, 186, 188
Elaine Cottage 93, 130
Elaine House 214
Elections, General and Local, **32-33, 76, 77,** 80, 81, 102, **186-187, 195,** *196,* **197,** 218, 223, 264, 329, 337
Electricity and Electric Lighting 149, 228, 230, 251
Elliott, Captain Thomas, 20, 22
Ellis, Captain Charles, 187
Elm Grove 356
Elmstead, including Elmstead Church 47, 95, 102, 137, 139, 142, 210, 217, 236
Elmstead Market 277
Elmstead Road 322, 333, 341
Empire Day *206,* 207, 220, 242
Endean Close 357
Endean, Mr. Terence, 357
Erith, Mr. Raymond, 276
Ernest Road 139, 207, 321, 356
Essex and Suffolk Hunt, The, 69-70, 133, 252
Essex Chronicle 293
Essex County Council 135, 137, 138, 141, 194, 195, 273, 293, 341

General Index

Essex County Standard 67, 68, 74, 81, 109, 113, 179, 210, 252, 275, 293, 299, 318, 324, 352, 355, 358
Essex Militia, The 33, 37, 39, 56-57, 59
Essex Standard, see (*Essex County Standard*)
Evans, Mr. Walter, 308
Evening Gazette 293, 305
Evening Standard 305
Everitt, Henry, 54
Everitt, Mrs. K. G., 211
Eves, Barry, *272*
Eves, Captain ---, *235*
Ewing, Philip, *165*

Fair, The Annual, (c. 1700?-1921) 56, 59, 102, **165, 167,** 220
Falcon Yard 199, 230
Farms, Farming, Farmers and Farmworkers 3, 33, 37, 38, 39, 47, 57, 60, 70-71, 77, 78, 79, 80, 93, 97, 102, 125, 133, 134, 135, 137, 210, 215-216, 217, 234, 251-252, 255, 263
Feedham, Jonathan, 44, 60
Feedham's Close 357
Felgate, John, *165,* 187, 195
Ferriter, John, 353
Ferry to Fingringhoe *231,* 245, **267, 270,** *272*
Ferry, to Rowhedge 186, 188, 194, 197, *270*
Field, Mrs. ---, 53
Field, The, 110, 126
Fillto or Philto, Samuel, 43
Fingringhoe 29, 56, 57, 95, 194, 234, 236, 245, 267, 270
Fire, The Fire Brigade and Fire Equipment 22, 29, 94, **108-109,** 111, 113, 190, 211, 220, 222, 228, 229, 252, *257,* 258, 290, 291, 292, 304, 305, 325
Fishing, Fishermen, Fishing Smacks and the Fishing Fleet 3, 11, 13, 26, 28, **46,** 51, 55-56, 57, 86, 88, 104, 106, 109, 110, 111, 112, 113, 118, 123, 131, **156,** 162, 172, 230, 232, 234, *235,* 236, **345-346**
Fitzgerald, Edward, 107
Flack, Horace, 43, 47

Flack, Mary, neé King, 43
Flack, Mary, (probably the same as above) 54
Flacke, Anna, (see Tunmer, Anna)
Flood, The Great, of 1953 *270,* **270-271**
Flooding 191, 234
Folley, The, 234
Foote, Henry, 7, 9
Fordham, William, 9
Foresters, The Ancient Order of, 163, 165, 207
Foresters' Hall, (see Public Halls)
Forrestt Row 152
Forrestt's, variously known as Messrs. Forrestt & Son, Messrs. Forrestt & Son Ltd., Forrestt & Co. Ltd., The Rennie Forrestt Shipbuilding, Engineering and Dry Dock Co. Ltd., and The Rennie, Ritchie and Newport Shipbuilding, Engineering and Drydocking Company, *145,* **146,** *147, 148,* 148-149, *150, 151,* **151-154,** *153,* **155,** *156, 159, 160,* 160, 169, 179, 188, 203, *213,* **213-214,** *216,* **218,** *219,* **221, 222,** 265, 325, 345
Fraenkel Report, The, 214
Frances Close 357
Freemasons, The Colne Lodge of, 138, 139
French, Captain ---, 186
Friendly Societies 60, 94-95, 161, 163
Friendly Society, The 142-143, 202
Frostick, John, 218

Gables Café, The, *335*
Gabrieli String Quartet, The, 293, 306, 315
Gainsboro Products Ltd. 264
Gale, George, 325, 339, 340, 341
Game, Moses, 48, 51
Games, (see Sports)
Gardiner, E. J., 144
Gardiner, Jack, 114
Garling's Bridge 355
Garrett, Abraham, 133
Garrett, Arthur, *165*
Garrison House 29-30, *30,* 57, 230
Gas and the Gas Works 101, 125, 129, 132, **190-191,** *191,* 230, 234, 348

385

"Gas Road", (see St. John's Road)
Gaye, Rev. Douglas, 333
George V, King, 214, *215, 223,* 245, 247
George V Playing Fields, King, 243, *244,* 245, 261, 262, 332-333, 336, 341
Gernon, Robert, 3
Gilbert, Sir W. S., *124,* 126, 127
Giles, William, wife of, (sixteenth century) 10
Giles, William, (sixteenth century) 11
Giles, William, (seventeenth century) 28
Girling, John, 93
Gliksten's, J. Gliksten & Son Ltd., later Meredith's 272, 325, 326, 329, 350
Glozier, Mr. Mick, 322
Gooch, Mrs. Annabel, neé Greene, 277
Gooch, Mr. Charles, (son of Charles Gooch the Younger), *250,* 252, 277
Gooch, Charles, the Younger 137, *244, 249,* **249,** *250,* 251, 251-252, 255, 275, 277, 279
Gooch, Charles Edmund, the Elder 135, *136,* **136-137,** 141, 143, 195, 200, 207, 208, 210, 213, 215, 236, 249, *251,* 349
Gooch, Eleanor, (wife of Charles Gooch the Elder) 135, *136,* 137, *206,* 207, 218, 249
Gooch, Joan, neé Spicer, later Mrs. P. L. J. Le Poer Power *244, 250,* 251, 255, 258, 276
Gooch, Marguerite, (see Cole, Mrs. Henry)
Gooch, Mrs. Patricia, neé Spicer, 276
Gooch, Robin, (son of Charles Gooch the Younger) *250,* 252
Goodwin, Arthur, 203, 204
Goodwin, Clifford, 203
Goodwin, "Circumference", 183
Goodwin, John, 203, 204
Goodwin, John, "Jack", (builder and town councillor) *165,* 179, 187, 204
Goodwin, Malcolm, 345
Goodwin, Millie, 184
Goodwin, Samuel, 111
Goodwin, Thomas C., 113, 179, 186, 203
Goodwin, The Rev. Thomas, 60

Gordon, Rev. Clementina, 334
Gore-Booth, Sir Henry, Bart. 144
Gothic House 125, 130, 195, *196,*
Goyder, Rev. David, 96, 97
Goyder, Margaret, (see Harvey, Margaret)
Goymer, Samuel, 67
Grasby, Betsy, 27, 240, 259, 262, 326, 357
Grasby Close 357
Graveson, Professor R. H., Q.C. 141
Gray, John, 8-9
Gray, Peter, 8-9
Green, Mr. Brian, 345
Green, James, 210
Green, Mr. Ken, 345, 346
Green, Orbell George, 116
Green, William, 210
Greene, Graham, 308
Greenfield, James, 294, *295,* 296, 297
Grimes, John, 98
Groves, John, 36
Groves, Mary, 36
Guides, (Girl), 220, 336
Guillam, Captain Zachariah, 19
Gunn, Arthur William, *235*
Gunn, Charles, *235*
Gurdon, John, (see Gurdon Rebow, John)
Gurdon, Brampton, 77
Gurdon, William, 72, 76
Gurdon Rebow, Georgiana, neé Toler, (second wife of John Gurdon Rebow), 71, *72,* 72, 73, 76-77, 81
Gurdon Rebow, John **69-81**, *79,* 101, 106, 114, 123, 133, 134, 286, 311, 333, 350, 355
Gurdon-Rebow, Georgiana, (daughter of John Gurdon Rebow) 71
Gurdon-Rebow, Hector John, 71, 81, 106, 114, **133-136,** *134,*137, 145, 174, 179, 275
Gurdon-Rebow, Judith, neé Gurdon, (wife of Hector Gurdon- Rebow) 133
Gurdon-Rebow, Martin, 133, 135
Gurdon-Rebow, Mary, (daughter of John Gurdon Rebow) 71
Gurnell, Miles, 10
Guy Fawkes Day and Night 102, **167**

Halberstadt, Raphael, 288, 290
Hall, George William, (son of John Hall) 45
Hall, John, **44-45,** *45*
Hall, Mary, neé Feedham, (mother of John Hall) 44
Hall, Mary, neé Gilles, (wife of John Hall) 45
Hall, William, 44-45
Ham, Dick, *165,* 187
Ham, Captain William, (of *Pearl*) 85
Ham, Captain William, (a founder of The Nottage Institute), 186
Hamilton, Charles, 112
Hamilton Road 125, 230, 355
Hanbury, Sampson, 135
Hardie, Rev. Stephen, 333, 334
Harding, Mr. Guy, 266, 345
Harlow, Captain Henry, 145
Harris, John, *272*
Harrison, Michael, 47
Harvey, Captain Abraham, 218, 220, 230
Harvey, Charles, 127
Harvey, Chris, 54
Harvey, Captain Daniel, 52-53, 57
Harvey, George, 130
Harvey, Goyder, 127
Harvey, Mr. James, 234
Harvey, John, (1830-1901) 91, 96, *105,* 106, 107, **108- 110**, 113, **126-127,** 144, 145, 357
Harvey, John Martin, (see Martin-Harvey, John)
Harvey, Mrs. Joseph, 108
Harvey, Margaret, neé Goyder, (wife of John Harvey) 96, *105,* 127
Harvey, May, 127, 169
Harvey, Nathaniel "Satan", 98
Harvey Road 111, 356
Harvey, Thomas, (1803-1885) 88, 96, **104,** *105,* **106- 108,** 109, 116
Harvey, Mrs. Thomas, (wife of above) *105*
Harvey, Mrs. Thomas, (mother of James) 234
Harvey, Thomas, (brother of John) 109
Harvey, Thomas, (father of James) 234
Harvey, Captain William, 159

Harwich 20, 22, 25, 26, 28, 44, 51, 67, 137, 141, 197, 236
Hatch, Mr. Ernest, 182, *271*
Hatch, Jack, 228
Haul Road, The proposed, 330
Havens, Dr. Philip, 94, 113, 230
Havens, Polly, 230
Havens, William Rawdon, 76, 94
Hawkins, John Bawtree, 141, 142, 178, 194, 195, 202, 204, 207, 208, 210, 215, 217, 220
Hawkins, Mrs. John, (wife of above), 204
Hawkins, William, 86, 88, 91, 109, 123, 141,
Heard, Mr. Michael, *338, 339*
Heath, Charles, 91
Heath, The Rt. Hon. Edward, M.P. 319, 339
Heath Road 322, 356
Heath, James, *165,* 187, 195, 197
Herd, Ralph, 209
Hewers, ---, 27
Hexagon Restaurant, The, (U of E) 284, 289, 302, 316
High Street 7, 30, 42, 54, 93, 94, 99, 101, 103, 122, 124, 125, 139, 159, *162, 164,* 165, 167, 168, 178, 181, 182, 187, 188, 190, *192, 193,* 194, 197, 200, 203, 204, 209, 210, 214, 227, 230, 232, 242, 254, *326,* 330, 331, 334, 335, 338, 346-347, 350, 355
Hildreth, Nigel, 315
Hill, Mr. Peter, 59, 337, 341
Hill, Mrs. Peter, 59
"Holy Joe", (see Johnstone, Paul St. John)
Holmes, Stanley, M.P. 248
Home Guard, The, *253, 258,* 258, 263
Hopkins, Matthew, 351
Hopper, Thomas, 71
Howard, Elizabeth, 4
Howard, John, 104
Howard, Sir John, 4
Howard of Effingham, The Lord High Admiral, 13
Howell, Abigail, 15
Howes, John, 54
Howse, Mrs. ---, 54

Hudson's Bay and The Hudson's Bay
   Company 18, 19, 20, 26
Hughes, Mrs. Lalla, 347
Humphreys, Jack, 197-199
Husk, James, 96, 110, 126, 148
Husk, James, (son of above) 156
Husk, Jim, 110
Husk, William, 217
Husk's Yard 110, 111, 126, 156, 160, 218,
   225-226, 227
Hyde, James, 95
Hyde, Miss Jane, 103
Hythe, The, 46, 261, 270, 330

Iffe or Jeffo, John, 47
Inch, Dr T. D., 288
Ind, Rev. James, 96, 101, 103
Ipswich 106, 107, 112
Ipswich Journal, The, 52, 56, 178
Iron Age, The, 2

Jack Hatch Way 357
Jack, Rev. R. H., 259
Jackson, Glendower, **261-263**
Jackson, James, 114, 130, 132, 133, **137**
Jackson, Mrs. James, 137
Jacobs, Mr. Richard, **345-346**
James W. Cook & Co. Ltd., (see Cook's)
Jenkin, Elizabeth, (see Cawton, Elizabeth)
Jenkins, John, 179
Johnson, Mr. Charles, 271
Johnson, Mary, 351
Johnson, William, 173, 202
Johnstone, Paul St. John, né Hyman
   Goldstein, known as "Holy Joe" and
   "Wonk" **335-336**
Joliffe, ---, 355
Joliffe's Garden 122
Joliffe's Hill 355
Jones, Eliza, 102, 130, 180
Jones, Emma, 180, 184
Jones, John, 114
Joyce, David, 203
Jubilee Trust, The, 343

Keelars 3
Keelars Lane 238
Kemble, Mr. David, 327
Kemble, Mr. L. W., 236, 322, 327, 355
Ken Green Ltd. 95
Kent, Polly, 114
Kent, Polly "Pi", 181
Kevern, Dr. Travers, 245
Keynes Tower Block, (U of E) *284,* 290,
   358
King, Ernest, 214
King, Francis, 26-27
King, Mary, (see Flack, Mary)
King, Mr. and Mrs. ---, 9

Labour Exchange, The, 234, 236
Labour Party, The, 218, 223, 236, 239,
   264-265, 279, 320, 329
Lamb, Thomas, 54
Langbridge, Canon Frederick, 232
Langley, John, 9, 15
Lardner, G. R., 111
Lawton, Nicholas Caesar Corsellis, the
   Elder 91, 114, 137
Lawton, Nicholas Caesar Corsellis, the
   Younger 139, 188, 215
Lax, Frederick J., 143
Lay, Philip, 55
Laying-Up, (of yachts) 85, 88, 106, 110,
   112, 152, **160-161,** 164, 167, 266, 356
Le Poer Power, Mr. P. L. J., 276
Lecture Theatres and Block, (U of E) 282,
   287, 288, 306
Lee, Mary, 43
Lee, Thomas Tunmer, 43
Lever, Sir Arthur Levy, M.P., *196,* 197
Lexden and Winstree Guardians for the
   Poor, The, 59, 221
Liberal Party, The, 68, 74, 76, 133, 141,
   187, 195, *196,* 197, 210, 218, 248
Library, The, 336
Lido, The, (see Public Halls)
Lilac Close 357
Lind, Rev. Charles, 43
Lind, John, (1737-1781) 43
Ling, Dr. Charles, 94
Ling, Dr. W. S., 94

General Index

Linsbrook Developments 322, 357
Little Wick, (see Council Offices)
Locke, Captain Charles, 48, 50
Lord Mayor's Day 167
Lorries on the spinal route *325,* 325, 326, 330, 331
Loveless, William G., 214, *238,* 238, 243, *244,* 336, 355
Loveless, Mrs. William G., *244,* 259
Lower Lodge Estate 322, 331, 356
Lower Lodge Farm 93, 200
Lupton, Thomas, 33

McAfee, Annalena, 301
McEune, Mrs. R. J., 236
McLean, Catherine, *295,* 296, 298
McLeod, Alexander, 336

Madder & Son 111, 156
Maindy Transport Company, The, and their cargo boats 218, *219,* 221, 224
Maior, John, 11
Making of a University, The, (The Reith Lectures for 1963) 281, **284-286,** 304, 315
Mallet, J., 236
Malting House 47, 232
Malting Yard 47
Maltings, The, 47
Malvern Group, The, 259
Manor House or Hall (see Wivenhoe Hall)
Manor, Lord of the Manor and The Lordship of the Manor 3, 7, 10, 27, 41, 54, 76, 90, 94, 116, 139, 141
Manor Road 321, 354
Manorial Court and Customs, The, 3, 4, 10-11, 116
Maple Cottage 29, *130, 132*
Marina, The proposed, (1987) 346-347
Martelmore, John, 10
Martin, James, 83
Martin, L. H., 239
Martin, Mary, (see Rebow, Mary Martin)
Martin, Captain Matthew, 31-32, *32,* 34, 36, 73, 83
Martin, Captain Robert, 43, 52
Martin, Sarah, (sister of Mary Martin Rebow) 34, 36

Martin, Thomas, (father of Mary Martin Rebow) 34, 83
Martin-Harvey, Sir John, 93, 97, 103, 110, 114-115, 126-127, **169,** *232, 233,* **234,** 253, 356
Mason, Don, 181-183, 184, 191, 221
Mason, Fred, *247*
Masonic Hall, The, (see also Freemasons) 139
Matthews, Danny, 290
May Day, May-Ladying and The May Queen 102, **168-169,** 184
Mayer, Edward, 29
Meals on Wheels 336
Mede Way 357
Medicine and Medical Facilities 10, **43, 44,** 60, **94-95,** 102, 163, 208, 242, 245, 260
Mendelson, Anna, 294, *295,* 296, 297, 299
Merchant Vessels 11-13, 17, 18, 19, 25, 26, 46, 47-48, 83, 88-89, 104, 106, 117, 126, 218, *219,* 221, 222, 224, 331, 342-343
Mersea and Mersea Island 3, 55, 103, 113, 194
Methodists, The, and Methodist Churches **98-99,** 139, 165, 167, *193,* 197, **334,** 350
Middle Ages, The, 3-5
Mill, The, 29, 94
Mill Field, The 113, 195, 202, 211, *212*
Miller, Taverner John, 76, 81
Millfields School 322, *324*
Mills, Bawtree & Co. Ltd. 133, 180
Minesweepers 214, *253, 254* 254, 265
Minstrels iii, 167
Mitchell, Mrs. ---, 191, 194
Montgomery, Sir Thomas, 5
Moore, James, *165,* 210
Morell, Edmund, 351
Morgan, Mr. and Mrs. Roland, 218, 227
Morant, Philip, 5, 6
Mulberry Harbour 263, 325, 331
Mumford, A. G., 146
Mumford, Margaret, 351
Mumford, Thomas, 351
Munck, Ronaldo, 302, 303, 304, 305
Munnings, Captain George, 53
Munnings, Thomas, 44
Munro, William, 122

Munson, Jimmy, 190
Munson, Mrs. Ruth, 234, 262
Murray, Mrs. Val, *337*
Music, other than brass bands, 103, 141, 142, 143, 182, 184, 202, 203, 209, 293, 301, 306, 315

National Shipbuilders' Security Ltd. 248
National Union of Students 273, 301, 302
Navy, The (Royal), also The Admiralty, (see also Royal Naval Reserve) 18-21, 25-26, 48, *49*, 50-51, 87, 89, 149, *213*, 213-214, 227, *253, 254*, 254-255, 264, 325
Needham, George Carter, 97, 98, 99
Nesfield, W., 72
Nettleinghame, Mr. and Mrs. Frederick, 227, 228
Newton, H. K., M.P. 197, 213, 218
Nicholson, Frederick, 46, 56
Nitro-Compounds Ltd. 200
Nonconformity, (see also Congregationalists) 28, 43, 101
Nonsuch House 7
Nook, The, (house) 93, 124, 130, 141, 167, 321, 356
Nook, The, (road) 321
Nore, The Mutiny at the, 48, 50-51, 89
North Essex Film Society, The, 253, 258
North Sea Canners (Great Britain) Ltd. 236, 270
Nottage, Captain Charles, 186
Nottage Institute, The, *185, 186, 259*

O'Brien, R. Barry, 292
Oddfellows, The, 163, 207, 220
Ormsby, Major Sir Thomas, (1797-1833) 69, 88
Ormsby Rebow, Lady, (see Gurdon Rebow, Mary Martin)
Otto Andersen & Co. (London) Ltd. 224, 227
Over 60's Club, The, 336
Oxford, Lady, (see Viscountess Beaumont)
Oxford, The Twelfth to Seventeenth Earls of, **4-6**, 356
Oxley, Colin, 300-301
Oysters **46**, 91, 94, 99, 112, 123, 156 , 336

Page, Robert, 18, 20, 22, 26, 28
Paget, Lord Alfred, 106, 129, 355
Paget, Lord Clarence, 88
Paget Road 116, 125, 355
Pargetting 8, 29-30
Parish Council, The, 141, 163, 186-187
Parish Tea, The, (see The Easter Tea)
Parish Vestry, The, 57, 59, 68, 92, 124, 143, 163
Park Road 91, 93, 123, 167, 234, *264*, 321, 356
Parkwood Avenue 322, 356
Pawsey, H. W., 217
Peasants Revolt, The, 3
Peck, Cedric, 228
Peck's Garage, (see Cedric's Garage)
Peel, Mr. A., 347
Pepys, Samuel, 18, 22, 26
Phillip Road 180-181, 242, 262, 341, 355
Phoenix Company, The, 55
Pike, Percy, 215
Pim, Theodore, 108, 145, 230
Pim, Mrs. Theodore 145
Pirates and Privateers 18, 22, 25
Plague, (see Disease)
Plampin, Sarah, 89
Plummer, Mr. ---, 262
Politics 31, 32-33, 40, 68, **73-74,** 76, 77, 80-81, 133-134, 137, 138-139, 141, **186-188, 195, 197,** 199, 210, 218, 264, 265, 273, 279, 328-329, 332
Polley, John, 112
Pollock Anderson Oil Engines 227
Popps, William, 47, 57
Population 7, 125, 321
Port, Wivenhoe as a, 11, 18, 46-47, 329-330, 342
Post Office, The, 186
Potter, Mrs. May, 234
Poverty and the Poor 7, 54, **57-60,** 94-95, 102, 139, 144, 163, 169, 172, 221, 222, 223-224, 234, 236, 260, 324
Powell, Rt. Hon. Enoch, M.P. 288
Powell, William, 53
Pratt, Francis, 227
Processions 95, 117, *164,* 167-168, 202, 203, 204, 207, 208- 209, 210, 218, 220, 289, 302, 303, 304, 313

General Index

Proctor, Miss Isabel, 103, 184
Property Associates Ltd. 329, 331
Pryer, George, 108, 109, 113, 126, 127
Public Halls, general, **164-165**
Public Halls, individual:
  National/Board/County School, used as such 101, 142, 165, 174, 186, 195, 197, 204, 211, 213, 335, 338
  Foresters' Hall, later a cinema, (see Cinema and Cinematography), later still The Lido 139, 165, *166,* 197, 209, 210, 211, 218, 228-230, 253, 258, 260, 264, 336
  Public Hall, (a shed near the Station) 165
  St. John's Ambulance Hall, The, 99
  William Loveless Hall **336-337,** *337,* 341, 347, 357
Public Houses, general 15, 29, **54-55,** 78, 80, 95, 115, **116-117,** 164, 174, 178, 318, 332
Public Houses, individual:
  Anchor, The (Blue), 44, 54, 55, 91, 116, 125, 128, 129, 145
  Anglesey Arms, The, 116, 294
  Backus, The, 55
  Baytree, The, 54
  Beehive, The, 128
  Black Buoy, The, (formerly *The Black Boy),* 7, 54, 95, 104, 112, 113, 115, 116, 128, 179, *185,* 186, 245, 332, *338,* 358
  Black Horse, The, 54
  Brewery Tavern, The, 116, 128, 174, 258, 332, 339
  Bucks Horns, The, Colchester 67
  Bull, The, 128
  Cross Keys (Tavern), The, 54
  Duke of Wellington, The, Brightlingsea 119
  Falcon, The, 7, 29, 41, 54, 55, 128, 174, *203* 327-328, 332
  Flag, The (Union), 54, 60, 128, *200*
  Grapes, The, 54
  Greyhound, The, 97, 110, 128, 161, 203
  Grosvenor Hotel, The, 91, 117, 123, 128, 163, 169, 236, 261, 332, 356
  Horse and Groom, The, 54-55, 128
  Kings Arms, The, 54, 55
  Kings Head, The, Colchester 67
  Lamb, The, 54
  Live and Let Live, The, 128, 335
  Maidenhead, The, and Maiden's Head, (see *The Swan*)
  Park Hotel, The, 117, 122, 123, 128, 139, 174, 178, 204, 210, 254, 356
  Pointer, The, Alresford, 178
  Red Lion, The, 128
  Rose and Crown, The, 54, 55, 56, 57, 71, 88, 114, 116-117, 128, 158-159, *170,* 174, 326
  Sailor's Return, The, 128, 266
  Ship at Launch, formerly *The Woolpack* 43, 54, 55, 95, 116, 117, 128, *157*
  Shipwright's Arms, The, 103, 108, 116, 128, 332
  Station, The, (formerly *The Station Hotel*) *120,* 123
  Sun, The, 54, 55, 128
  Swan, The (White), (formerly *The Maidenhead*) 29, 54, 128
  Woolpack, The, (see *The Ship at Launch*)
  Yachtsman's Arms, The, 128
  Yachter's Arms, The, 128
Pullen, Walter, *165,* 187
Purkins, Albert, 229

Quay, The, 2, 11, 27, 29, 43, 46, 47, 54, 88, 89, 91, 98, 104, 109, 110, 112, 113, 115, 116, 129, 131, 156, *157,* 158, 159, 160, 186, 194, 230, 234, 236, *237,* 245, 248, 263, 270, *323,* 324, 331, *332,* 333, 338, *344,* 345, 346, 347, *349*
Quay House 127
Quay Street *98,* 99, 230, 334
Quayside Cottage 27, *130, 132*
Queen, H.M. The, *309,* 309, 338
Queens Road 190, 228, 294, 299
Quixle, Quixley or Quykesley, Family, The, 11

Radcliffe, Dr. Walter, 245, 247, 248, 252, 261, 336
Railways 42, 67, 89, 91, 96-97, 99, **117-119,** *120-121,* **122-123, 180, 186, 194,** *220,* 255, 261, **270-271,** *271,* 325, 330, 350, 356

391

Railway Quay, or Railway Wharf, The, 118, 123
Rayleigh Tower Block, (U of E) *284*, 358
Rayner, Mr. John, *337*
Read, F., 103
Rebow Family, The, 31, 42, 73, 93, 104, 355
Rebow, Francis Slater, (see Slater-Rebow, Francis)
Rebow, Sir Isaac, (1655-1726) 31, 81
Rebow, Isaac Lemyng, (1705-1735) 31
Rebow, Isaac Martin, (1731-1781):
 youth: 32; politics: 32-33; Wivenhoe Park: 33; commands the East Essex militia: 33; farms: 33; marriage: 34-36; absence with the Militia: 37-40; death: 40; also and generally: 1, **31-40**, *34*, 77
Rebow, John, (1603-1679) 31
Rebow, John Gurdon, (see Gurdon Rebow, John)
Rebow, Mary Hester, (see Slater-Rebow, Mary Hester)
Rebow, Mary Martin, (wife of Isaac Martin Rebow – d. 1804):
 youth and education: 34-35; character: 35-36; courtship of Isaac Martin Rebow: 35-36; relations with her mother-in-law: 36; marriage: 36-37; children: 37-40; also and generally 1, **34-40**, 41, 52, 316
Rebow, Mary Martin, (mother of Isaac Martin Rebow), 31-32, 36, 37, 42, 58
Rebow Road 125, 355
Rebow, Sarah Emma, (d. 1798) 1, 37, 38, 39, 40
Rectory, The, 17, 93, 203, 325, 341
Rectory Close *265*, 265
Rectory Hill 355
Rectory Road 29, 94, 207, 210, 211, 221, 243, *265*, 271
Red Cross, The, 208, 209, 211
Redland Aggregates 238
Regattas, (see Sports)
Religion 15, 28, **95-99, 101**, 103, 220-221, *333-336*
Rennie & Co., Messrs. G., (see Forrestt's)
Rent Book of Nicholas Corsellis IV, The, 54, 58-59

Reynolds, Thomas, 33
Rhodes, Edith, 151
Rice, Sir Frederick, M.P. 227, 245
Rice, Henry, 141, *165*, 187, 190, 195, 202, 207, 215
Rice, John, *165*
Rich, Sir Richard, 6
Rich, William, (student) 302, 303, 304, 305
Rich, William, (citizen) 9
Richardson, Bessie, 239, 240
Richardson, J., 223, 239
Riches, Mr. Cecil, 228-229
Riggs, Charles, 68-69, 96
Ripley, Michael, 308
Roads 188, 223, 350
Robbins Report, The, 273, 279
Roberts, Miss ---, 38
Robins, Dr. John Andrew, 44
Robinson, Rev. J. W. R., 334
Rochester, Robert, 6
Roman Catholics 8, 74, 77, 334-335
Romans and Roman Remains, The, 2
Roots, Mr. Michael, 214
Ropemaking 47, 111-112, 156
Roperies and Ropery House:
 fatal accident of 19:ii:1855: 111; also 47, 57, **111- 112**, *112*, 132, 138, 156, 261
Rosabelle Avenue 145, 265, *328*, 356
Rose Lane 127
Rosetta Close 357
Ross, Bob, *165*
Round, Edmund, 93, 110, 113, 130, 132, 144, 163, 172, 174
Round, Edward, 110, 144
Round, James, M.P. (seventeenth century) 18
Round, James, M.P. (nineteenth century) 145, 197
Rowe, Percy, *165*
Rowhedge, 51, 85, 88, 95, 104, 123, 125, 129, 142, 144, 146, 173, 186, 188, 194, 195, 214, *215*, 223, 270, 294, 309, 345
Rowhedge Ferry Road, The, 214, 270, 326
Rowhedge Ironworks Ltd. 254
Royal Army Medical Corps 211, 214, 218
Royal Naval Reserve 202, 211, 213
Ruffell, Henry and Martha, 97
Rush, Hayward, 42, 47, 53

General Index

Sailmaking 47, 111, 156, 245
Sainty, Arthur, 115
Sainty, John, (son of Philip John) 85
Sainty, Mosely, brother of Philip John, 85, 87, 88
Sainty, Philip John, (c.1754-1844) **83, 85-88,** 104, 106
Sainty, Philip Mosely, (son of Philip John Sainty) 88
Sainty, Robert, (brother of Philip John Sainty) 85
Sales, Public, (see Auctions)
Salmon, Walter, 223
Saltings, The, 167, 194, 197, 199, 261, 263, *270,* 325, 330, 346
Salvaging 88, 154
Salvation Army, The, 167, *168,* 221, 234
Sandford, Benjamin, 46
Sandford, John, 99
Sandford, Mary Ann, 125, 357
Sandford, Thomas, 94, 99, 123
Sandford, William, (eighteenth century) 46
Sandford, William, (nineteenth century) 94
Saran Close 357
Savill, George, 89
Saxons, The, 2
Sayer's Grove 44
Scattergood, Mr. Colin, 345
Schneider, Frank, 146
School Board, The (Wivenhoe), 135, 142, 164
School Logs, The, **101-3, 180-181,** 183, 184, 240, 242
Schools, individual, (see also Education):
 Boys' School/Department of the National/Board/County School in the High Street 103, *179,* **181-183,** *206,* 207, 208, 240, *241,* 252
 British 95, 99, 103, 117, 178
 Broomgrove Infant 322
 Broomgrove Junior 322
 Charity **53**
 Colne High 242
 Colne House Academy 103
 Dame 102, 180, 184
 Girls Department of the National/Board/County School in the High Street and Phillip Road 103, *180,* 180, 181, **183-184,** 207, 208, 222, 240, *241*
 Infants Department of the National/Board/County School in the High Street and Phillip Road **102-103,** 130, *179,* 180, 181, 183, 207, 211
 National/Board/County, in the High Street and Phillip Road 70, 71, 95, **96, 99,** *100,* **101-103,** 111, 117, 130, 132, 138, **178-184,** *179, 180, 192,* 195, 207, 208, 211, 213, 240, 242, 256, 260, 262, 350
 Private **53, 103,** 184, 186, 221
Scofield, Charles, 174, 243, 245
Scouts, (Boy), 208, 209, 220, 336
Scrambler, ---, 54
Scrope, Elizabeth, (see Viscountess Beaumont)
Seale, Captain, 22
Senate, The, (U of E) 289, 291
Senior Citizens 336
Septaria 112
Sewerage 188, 222-223, 234, **238-239,** 350
Shaw, George Bernard, 253
Shipbuilding, (see Boatbuilding and Shipbuilding)
Shipwrights' Society, The, 161, 207
Shipyard, The, and Shipyards generally 11, 46, 102, 116, 117, 125, 131, 258, 261, 342, 348, 349
Shipyard, The Downstream, 88, 110-111, 126, 156, 160, 218, *225-226,* 227, 254-255, 263, 264, 265-266, *267,* 333, 339, *342,* 342-345, *343,* 346, 347
Shipyard, The Upstream, 11, 47-48, 51, 86-88, 96, **104, 106- 110,** 113, 126, 127, 129, **144-146, 148-149, 151-154, 156,** *159, 160,* **161-162,** 203, 218, 218, *219, 220,* 221-222, 224, 227, 230, 234, 248, *253, 254,* 254, 263, 264, 265, 272, 325-326, *327, 329,* 329-331, 345, 346-347
Shops and Shopkeepers 8, 112, 115, 141, *162,* 163, 230, 318, 320, 331, 355
Simons, Albert, 154
Sladen Brothers, The, Alfred and Mortimer, 148, 149

393

Slater, Francis, (see Slater-Rebow, Major-General)
Slater-Rebow, Major-General Francis, (1770-1845) 40, **61-64,** *62,***67-69,** 74, 77, 88, 94, 96, 99, 115
Slater-Rebow, Mary Emma, (daughter of Major-General Rebow – 1797-1804) 61
Slater-Rebow, Mary Hester, (wife of Major-General Slater-Rebow - d. 1804) 1, 37, 38, 39, 40, 61, 62, 63, 69
Slater-Rebow, Mary Martin, (1804?-1842) 61, 62, 63, 69, 71
Sloman, Sir Albert, **277,** 278, **279-280,** *280,* 281, 282, 283, 285, 286, 287, 288, 289, 293, 297, 303, 304, 305, 306, 307, 308, *309,* 310, 312, 313, 315
Sloman, Lady Marie-Bernadette, 277
Smallpox, (see Disease)
Smith, Dr. Benjamin, 44, 94
Smith, "Dimmy", 186, 221
Smith, Mr. Don, *185*
Smith, Ethel, 240, 242, 262
Smith, F. W. "Plumber", 213, 228
Smith, John, (woodranger employed by General Rebow) 115
Smith, "One-Arm", 176, 208, 356
Smith, Mrs. Sue, *337*
Smith's Lane 356
Smugglers Cottages 234
Smugglers and Smuggling 26-27, 43, **51-53,** 83, **115**
Smyth, Frances, 9
Social Club, The, (at the former Swedenborgian Chapel) 220
Sociology, (U of E) 278, 279, 287, 289, 293, 302, 309, 314, 318
Soldiers 56-57, 209, 211, *212,* 213, 214, 217, 255-256, **256,** 262, 263, 276
Sonell Close 357
Sparke, William, 9
Sparrow, William, 321, 326
Special Air Service, (1st and 2nd Battalion) 255-256, *256,* 262, 263, 276
Spicer, Joan, (see Mrs. Joan Gooch)
Spicer, Patricia, (see Mrs. Patricia Gooch)
Spion Kop 202, 211, 243, 333, 336, 356

Sport, general, 55-56, 75, **169,** *170-171,* 172-174, *173, 174, 175-176,* 178, 182, 184, 209, 211, *212,* 220, *242, 243,* **242-243, 245,** *246,* 247-248, 279, 282, 293, **332-333,** 341, 349, 350
Sports, individual:
  Archery 75
  Badminton 334, 337, 350
  Billiards 174
  Bowling (skittles) 11
  Bowls 55, 245, 333
  Bridge 337
  Cards, (see also Bridge and Whist) 11
  Cockfighting 55
  Coursing 91
  Cricket 55, 75, 78, 91, 113-114, 133, 137, 138, 144, 154, 173, *175,* 178, 195, 220, 242-243, 245, 262, 333, 356
  Cycling 142, *173,* 174, 178
  Darts 341
  Five-a-Side Football 341
  Football 11, 75, 78, 133, 144, **174,** *176,* **178,** 195, 210, 218, *242, 243,* 243, 245, 279, **332- 333**
  Gymnastics 75, *175,* 178, 207
  Hockey 178
  Hunting 69-70, 91, 133, 252
  Jacking and Towing the Line 182
  Pool 341
  Quoits 75, 174, 178
  Regattas **55-56,** 102, 113, 117, 137, 144, 165, 167, **169,** *170-171,* **172-173,** 204, 220, *248,* 248, 263
  Rifle Shooting 113, 165, **207**
  Rounders 184
  Sailing and Racing (amateur) 55-56, 113, 172, 173, **245, 247-248,** 263, 333, 345
  Shinty 262
  Shooting 90
  Shoveha'penny 11, 15
  Squash 300, 340, 350
  Snooker 341
  Swimming 113, 178, 261
  Tennis 133, 142, 173-174, *174,* 245, 279, 341
  Whist 209, 260
Sprats 112, 118, 149, 156, 172, **236,** *237,* 324

General Index

Spring Chase Estate, The, 322
Spring Lane 356
Squire, E. H. C., *201*, 227
Squire, Dr. Samuel, 94, 112, 132, 142, 195, *201*
St. Botolph's Station 122, 123, 229, 230
St. John's Road, ("Gas Road") 4, 125, *131, 191*, 191, 345, 355
St. Monica, The Roman Catholic Church of, 335
St. Valentine's Day 168-169
Stanley, (or Staples), Austin, 47
Stanley Road 139, 217, 321, 356
Starfish 112-113, 156, 346
Start, J. W., 178, 179
Station, Wivenhoe Railway, 118, *120*, 122, 124, 263, *271*
Station Road 124, 125, 330
Stebbing, "Pug", 230
Sterling, Dr. ---, 1, 38
Stoney, Captain Henry Butler, 353-354
Storehouse, The, 29, 115, 338
Stowboating 163, 172
Street, The, (see High Street)
Students Council and Union, (U of E) 287, 293, 303, 306, 308
Sun Yard 96, 234
Sunday Schools 137, 144, **167-168,** 209
Surge Barrier, The proposed, 346
Sutton Family, The, 3, 4
Sutton, Daniel, 115
Swan, H. D., 154
Swedenborgian Society, The, and the Swedenborgian Chapel **96,** *97*, 97, 99, 125, 167, 220-221, 265

T. Cadbury Brown 287
Talisman's Shop 230
Tapling, Alfred, 214, 232, 234, 245
Tarrey, Thomas, 28
Taussig, Mrs. Shirley, *337*
Tawney Tower Block, (U of E) *284*, 358
Taylor, Mr. Alan, *338*
Taylor, John, 101
Telephone **191, 194**
Tenacres 173, 195, 207, 209, 218, 245
Theatre Arts Society 287

Theatricals, Amateur, (see also The Wivenhoe Players and The Wivenhoe Gilbert and Sullivan Society) 127, 141, 142, 204, 253, 293, 306, 337, 350
Thompson, Pam, 291
Tills, Newton, 44
Todd, William, 104
Todd, Mrs. ---, 104
Toler, Lady Georgiana, (see Gurdon Rebow, Georgiana)
Toll House, The, *270*, 270
Tolliday Close 357
Tower Blocks, (U of E) *281*, 281, *282*, 282, **283,** *284,* 284, 285, 286, 287, 290, 291, 292, 300, 308-309, 313, 316, 317
Tower, Water, (see Water)
Towler, Billy, 165
Town Crier, The, 194
Townshend, Horatio, (later Viscount Townshend – 1630?-1687) 25
Townshend, Sir John, 13
Townshend, Sir Roger, (1543?-1590) 6, *12*, 13
Townshend, Sir Roger, (1588-1637) 13, 15, 17, 27
Townshend, Roger, (d. 1648) 27
Trade Unions 161, 207
Traherne, Thomas, 312
Triesman, David, 286, 288, 291, 312
Trinity House, (the property), 29, *130, 132*
Trotter, Alexander, 141, 146, 164, 169, 173, 174, 179
Tunmer, Anna, neé Flacke, 43
Tunmer, Hannah, neé Cole, 43, 53
Tunmer, Thomas, **43-44,** 53
Turner, Captain Albert, 222, *223*, **232,** 245, *247*, 247, 357
Turner, Albert, (son of the above) *223, 247*
Turner, Ernie, 339
Turner, John, 339
Tye Farm 277
Tyler, Sir Henry, M, 91
Tyler, John, 28
Tyler, Rev. William Franklin, 179, 197, 202

395

Uhr, Edmund, 353, 354
Unemployed Assistance Committee, The, 236
Unemployment 60, **221-224, 234, 236, 238-239,** 240, 264
University Disciplinary Committee, including the Appeals Committee, The, 288, 291, 302-303
University Grants Committee, The, 273, 275, 286, 302, 306, 308
University of Essex, The, iii, 183, 272, **273, 275-320,** *280, 281, 282, 284, 298, 303, 304, 309, 310, 319,* 336, 339, 358
University of Essex Association, The, 289
University of Essex Choir, The, 315
University of Essex Film Society, The, 293
University of Essex Library, The, 284, 287, 318
University Sailing Club, The, 293
University Theatre, The, 293, 306
"Upstreeters and Downstreeters" 139, 262, 331

Valfreda Way 356
Valley Road 211, 321, 356
Vanessa Drive 322
Vanner, Terry, 341, 350
Vestry, The Parish, (see Parish Vestry, The,)
Vice-Chancellor's Lodge, The, (U of E) 286, 287, 297, *298,* 303
Vice-Chancellor's Office, The, (U of E) 302, 304, 305
Village Delicatessen, The, 115
Vine Farm 322
Vine Farm Drive 357
Vine Farm Road 357
Vine Farm Estate, The, 322, 357
Vinson, Arthur, 214, 220, 245
Volunteer Soldiers 75, 91, 178, *202,* **202,** 203, 207
Vosper Ltd. 254-255, 264
Vulture 308

Wace, or Wast, Henry, 15
Wadley, William, (schoolmaster), *165,* 181, 182, 183, 208, 240
Wadley, William, (organist, perhaps the same as above) 143
Wadley, Captain William, *165,* 186, 187, 197, 239
Walford, Mr. Nigel, *337*
Walker, Captain Robert, 25
Wallis's Ironmongery 106
Walton Family, The, 4
War Agricultural Committee, The, 215, 263
War Memorial, The, *217,* 218
War Savings Association, The, 216
War Weapons Week 218, 258
Warren, Sir William, 19
Water Supply and the Water Tower **188,** *189,* **190,** 211, 216, 222, *237,* 322
Waters, Rev. E. T., 76, 99
Watsham, F., 178, 195
Watson, John, 186, 187
Watts, Mr. Danny, 329, 346, 347
Watts, Mr. David, 329
Wayland, George, 55
Weir, Angela, *295,* 296
Wenham, Richard, 53
Wenlock, Captain ---, 213
Wesleyans, (see Methodists)
West House 29
West Street 7, 29, 94, 95, 99, 103, 184, 188, 210, 234, 330, 331, 345, *348*
Westlake Crescent 357
Wheatley, George, 56
"White City, The", *220,* 221, 227, 325
White House, The, 103, *196*
White, Humphrey, 20, 22
Whitehead Harbourmaster 329-330
Whitley, Mary, 43
Widows 57, 60, 125, 132, 163, 351
Wiggoner, Giles, 17, 18, 20, 25
Wilkins, Edwin Joseph, 129, 144-145, 146
Wilkins' Store 236, *344*
William Morris Tower Block, (U of E) *284,* 358
Williamson, Thomas, *165,* 187
Wilson Close 357
Winch, Samuel, 47
Windermere, Lake, *147,* 148-149
Wings for Victory Week 260
Winthrope, Gabriel, 339

General Index

Wirth-Miller, Mr. Denis, 338
Witchcraft **351-352**
Wivenhoe (U of E management magazine, which from 11th January, 1989, is called *Wyvern*) 308, 309

Wivenhoe, Essex, England:
the name and its derivation: 2; appearance in Tudor times: 6-7; physical unhealthiness: 17; development as a port and a boatbuilding in the seventeenth century: 18, 20, 22, 25-27; appearance in Stuart times: 29; commerce, fishing and boatbuilding in the eighteenth century: 46-48; Victorian expansion: 121-123; expansion in the late twentieth century: 321-322, 324; spelling of the name in the late nineteenth century and early twentieth century: 356; also *29, 46, 60, 118, 119, 319, 323*

Wivenhoe, Queensland, Australia **353**
Wivenhoe, Tasmania, Australia **353-354**
Wivenhoe Allotment Holders' Association, The, 245
Wivenhoe and Brightlingsea Railway and Railway Company, The, **119-123**, *121*, **238, 270-271**
Wivenhoe and District Rifle Club, The, 207
Wivenhoe Arts Club, The, **338-341**, *340*
Wivenhoe Association, against thieves etc., (eighteenth and nineteenth centuries) 41, 55, 116, 164
Wivenhoe Athletic and Cycling Club, The, 178
Wivenhoe Athletics and Gymnastic Club, The, 178
Wivenhoe Badminton Club, The, 337
Wivenhoe Bookshop, The, 320
Wivenhoe Bowls Club, The, 245, 333
Wivenhoe Choral Society, The, 143
Wivenhoe Cinema Company, (see Cinema and Cinematography)
Wivenhoe Community Association, The, 341
Wivenhoe Community Association Steering Committee, The, 341
Wivenhoe Community Centre Exploratory Working Committee, The, 341
Wivenhoe Dam, The, 351
Wivenhoe Festival, The, (1972) 339
Wivenhoe Flier, The, and its successor, the monoplane, **197-200**, *198, 199*
Wivenhoe Gas Company Ltd, The, (see also Gas) 101, 125
Wivenhoe Gilbert-and-Sullivan Society, The, 334, 337
Wivenhoe Gymnasium Club, The, 178, 207
Wivenhoe Hall 5, 41, 55, 57, 76, 89-91, 93, 114, 125, 130, 137-139, *140*, 182, 188, *192*, 211, 218, 227, 228, 230, 243, 245, 334, 348, 355, 356
Wivenhoe Heath or Common 11, 44, 47, *60*, 60
Wivenhoe Holiday Week (1942) 260
Wivenhoe Horticultural Society, The, 245, 248
Wivenhoe House, (built by Captain Matthew Martin) 31, 36, 42
Wivenhoe House, (owned by William Brummell) 92, 107, 123, 356
Wivenhoe House, (the name given to the Rebow mansion after the opening of the University of Essex) 287, 293, 297, 302, 309
Wivenhoe Lawn Tennis Club, The, 142, 173, 174
Wivenhoe Lodge Farm 319
Wivenhoe Minstrels, The, 167
Wivenhoe New Park *276*, 276
Wivenhoe One Design, The, 245, *246*, 247, 336
Wivenhoe Palace of Varieties, The, 337
Wivenhoe Park:
purchase of estate in 1734: 32; house built and park laid out: 33; reconstruction in 1847-1860: 71-73; site for the University of Essex: 275-277; also and generally: 1-2, **33**, 36, 37, 40, 41, 57, 62, 63, 64, *66*, 67, 69, 70, **71-73**, *75*, 75, 76, 77, 80, 81, 93, 130, 133, 134, 135, *136*, 136, 137, 211, 236, 249, *250*, 251, 252, *255*, 255, 256, 262, 272, *274*, 286, 312, 314, 318

Wivenhoe Players, The, 320, *337,* 337
Wivenhoe Port Action Group, The, 330
Wivenhoe Port Coordinating Committee, The, 330
Wivenhoe Port Ltd. 329, 330, 331
Wivenhoe Preservation Trust, The, 330, 347
Wivenhoe Property Owners and Ratepayers Assciation, The, 222-223
Wivenhoe Rangers, The, 332
Wivenhoe Red Cross Voluntary Aid Detachment, The, 209
Wivenhoe Rifle Club, The, 207
Wivenhoe Sailing Club, The, 245, 247, 248, 330, 333, 347
Wivenhoe Sand, Stone and Gravel Company, The, *238,* 238
Wivenhoe Savings Committee, The, 260
Wivenhoe Shipyard Ltd. 254
Wivenhoe Sign, The, 336
Wivenhoe Society, The, 320, 325, 326, 330, 339, 347
Wivenhoe Town Council, The, 328, 329, 330, 336-337, 341, 347, 357
Wivenhoe Town Cricket Club, The, 91, 114, 137, 138, 173, *175,* 178, 195, 220, 242-243, 333
Wivenhoe Town Football Club, The, 178, 195, 210, 218, *242, 243,* 243, 245, **332-333**
Wivenhoe United Football Club 178
Wivenhoe Urban District Council, The, 139, 164, **187-188, 190,** 195, 209, 214, 216, 217, 218, 220, 221, 222-223, 230, 234, 236, **239-240,** 243, 252, 256, 258, 263, 264- 265, 322, 325, 326, 327, 328, 332, 333, 336, 356-357
Wivenhoe Volunteers Football Club, The, 178
Wivenhoe Wafflers, The, 253
Wivenhoe War Working Party, The, 258

Wivenhoe Wood, The, 182, 254, 261, 321, 327, *328*
Wivenhoe Youth and Adult Education Centre, The, 165, 341
Wix, Mr. Walter, 238
Wolfson Building, The, (U of E) 309
Women's Institute, The, 220, 260, 336
Wood, Stacey, *165*
Woodland Way, 318, 321, 356
Woodruffe, William, 10, 27
Workhouse, The, or Poorhouse, 10, **57-60,** *58*
World War I 210, **211, 213-218,** 224, 227, 245, 252, 264
World War II 154, 236, **252-256,** *253, 254, 255, 256, 257,* **258-264,** *258, 259, 264,* 265, 336
Worsp, Mr. John, *185*
Worsp, Mr. Lewis, 158, *185,* 236, 245, 261
Wrawby House, (see also Elaine House) 214, 232, 234
Wright, Eliza, **183-184,** 208, 240
Wright, H. L., (husband of above) 183, 208
Wright, Herbert, 217
Wright, Mabel, 183
Wyatt, George, 47, 48
Wyatt, Robert, *201,* 234
Wyvern (mythical heraldic bird) 336
Wyvern (U of E student magazine) 287, 294

Yachts, The Big, racing and cruising, 56, **83, 85-88,** 106- 111, 112, 123, **156, 158-161,** 167, 211, 213, 218, 234, 240, 247, 255, 325, 342, 348, 356
York, H.R.H. The Duke of, 343
Young, Mr. Tony, *338,* 339

Zurich Group, The, 346

Index of Boats and Ships

Adela (cutter) 110
Advance (rowing boat) 149, *150*
Ala (sloop) 156
Alarm (cutter) 86
Alexandra (steam yacht) 108, *160*
America (racing schooner) 106
Arrow (cutter) 85
Arundel (cutter) 85
Atlanta (cutter) 85
Audax (cutter) 357

Beacon (steam ship) 154
Beta (fire float) *155*
Blonde (cutter) 245
Boarhound (cruising schooner) 186
Britannia (passenger steamer) 148
Britannia (cutter) 222, *223*, 245, *247*, 247, 339, 354
Buffalo Express (cattle boat) 342

C.K. 399 (fishing boat) **345-346**
H.M.S. Calton (minesweeper) 265
Cap Pilar (barquentine) **265,** *266,* 325
Cecil Rhodes (twin screw steam ship) **151-152**
Centipede (sternwheel steamer) 154
Chloris (yawl) *124,* **126,** 337, 357
Comet (fireship) **48, 50-51,** 55
Cornelius ("Ostender") 22
Creole (cutter) 151
Crusoe (yawl) 110
Cupid (snow) 88
Curlew (yawl) 111
Cygnet (passenger steamer) 148

Dagmar (cutter) 108, 357
Daisy (smack) 236
Deerhound (cutter) 186
Dreadnought (tug) 197
Druid (yawl) 108
Druidess (yawl) 124

Eaglet (ketch, square-rigged) 19, 26
Edward (coaster) 51
Elaine (cutter 93, 113, 144
Elfin (launch) 148
Elfreda (yawl) 145, 146, 151
Elizabeth Jonas (man-of-war) 13
Emerald (cutter) 83, 85
Esperance (passenger steamer) 148
Exmouth II (auxiliary schooner) 154, *155*

Fagons (frigate) **20, 22**
Fancy Lass (brigantine) 88
First Fruits (smack) 110
Fox (lugger) 115
Foxhound (cutter) 356
H.M.S. Furious (gun brig) 89

General Rebow (cargo boat) 104
Gloucester (man-of-war) 29
Grebe, (see Otto)
Gunilda (steam yacht) 149, 151
Gurdon Rebow (cargo boat) 104

Herald (sloop) *268, 269*
Hind (ketch, square-rigged) **22, 25-26**
Hussar (schooner) 85

Industry (man-of-war) 29
Inspector (man-of-war) **48,** *49,* **50-51,** 55
Ione (yacht) 104
Island Home (yawl) 151

Jersey (man-of-war) 20
Jesse Annandale (brigantine) 89
Jullanar (yawl) 108, 124

Kapelli (sternwheel steamer) 154
Kara (ketch) 144
Kilbourne (dredger) 344
King (man-of-war) 27
King Coel (cutter) 156
King Salamon (man-of-war) 22
Kitten (cutter) 106
Kittiwake (cutter) 111

Lady Blanche (steam yacht) 160, 211, 213, 218
Lady Hermione (sloop) 149
Lady of the Lake, The, (ketch) 152
Lady Rebow (cargo boat) 104
Leading Star (barque) 88
Liberty (smack – eighteenth century) 51
Liberty (smack – nineteenth century) 104
Liberty (yacht) 83
Lord Nelson (square-rigged schooner) 343
Lutine (frigate) 154

Maindy Cottage (cargo boat) 221
Maindy Keep (cargo boat) 221
Maindy Tower (cargo boat) *219,* 221
Maindy Transport (cargo boat) 218
Manola (yacht) 148
Mansa Kila Ba (motor yacht) 154
Maria (smack) 236
Marlborough (cargo boat) 31
Mayflower (coaster) 47
Mayflower (smack) 56
Medora (schooner) 129
Milford, (see Fagons)
Milliped (sternwheel steamer) 154
Miranda (schooner) 213
Morning Star (cutter smack) 86

Naseby (man-of-war) 20
Ndoni (sternwheel steamer) *151*

H.M.S. Neptune (man-of-war) 83
Nonsuch (ketch) **18-20,** *21, 23*

Otto (launch) *148,* 148

Pearl (cutter) 83, **85,** *86,* 87, 115, 355
H.M.S. Pearl (sloop-of-war) *87,* **87-88**
Pearl (launch) 149
Phoenix (smack) 56
Pirouette (minesweeper) 214
Pleione (schooner) 124
Polypode (sternwheel steamer) 154
Prima Donna (cutter) 106
Prince (man-of-war) 29
Prince Rupert (ketch, square-rigged) 26
Princess Mary (revenue cutter) 52
Prospero (cargo boat) 104
Providence (coaster) 47
Pyefleet (paddle dredger) 149, *150*

Rannoch (steam yacht) 158, 160
Raven (passenger steamer) 148
Repulse (six revenue cutters with the same name) 52-53
Resolute (cutter) 106
Rodney (tug) 227
Roe (ketch, square-rigged) 19, **22, 25-26**
Roe Kitchin (ketch, square-rigged) 19, **26**
H.M.S. Roebuck (man-of-war) 89
Rosabelle (five vessels, all owner by Theodore Pim, all with the same name. No. 1 was a yawl, No. 2 an auxiliary steam yacht and the other three steam yachts) 108, 145, 151, 158, 211, 213, 218, 230, *231,* 236, 255, 266, 356
Rose of Devon (yawl) 108

Santa Cecilia (steam yacht) 129, *132*
Scandal (schooner) 107
Sea Belle (schooner) 91
Shearwater (yawl) 357
Silver Spray (yawl) 111
Slater Rebow (cargo boat) 104
Snowdrop (cutter) 106
Snowflake (schooner) 111
Softwing (yacht) 108
Southern Cross (auxiliary schooner) 146, 147

Index of Boats and Ships

St. Kilda (steam yacht) 151
Star of Asia, The, (see Valfreyia)
Success (pink) 26
Sudan (sternwheel steamer) 154, *155*
Sunbeam (auxiliary steam topsail
    schooner) 110, 160, 356
Sunflower (cargo boat) 17
Surge (cutter) 110
Swallow (cutter) 85
Syren (cutter) 108

Tartar (smack) 108
Teal (passenger steamer) 148
Tern (passenger steamer) 146, *147*, 148
H.M.S. Triumph (man-of-war) 89
Tugrador (motor yacht) 266
Two Sisters, The, (smack) 56

Union (smack) 86

Valfreyia (steam yacht) 151, 169, 172,
    194, 217, *224*, 224, 227, 325, 356
Valonia (pilot house vessel) 265
Vanadis (steam ship) 149
Vanessa (steam yacht) 158, 213, 355
Varuna (steam yacht) 159

Venetia (steam yacht) 158, 213
Venus (brigantine) 86
Venus (smack) 86
Victory (man-of-war) 29
Volante (cutter) 106
Volta (submarine) **152-154,** *153*

Walrus (steam ship) 151
Warspitt (man-of-war) 29
Water Witch (cutter) 88
Waterlily (yawl) 106, *107*
H.M.S. Wave (special service vessel) 214
Whydash (cutter) 111
William and Ann (smack) 56
William and Mary (three-masted barque)
    88
William Fall (trawler of the Strath class)
    213
Wivenhoe (ketch) **26,** 28
Wivenhoe (smack) 43
Wyvern III (yacht) *226*
Xantha (yawl) 106
Xanthe (smack) 236

Zebu Express (cattle boat) 342

401